Understanding Families

Understanding Families

Supportive Approaches to Diversity, Disability, and Risk

Second Edition

by

Marci J. Hanson, Ph.D.
Department of Special Education
San Francisco State University

and

Eleanor W. Lynch, Ph.D.
Department of Special Education, Emerita
San Diego State University

·P A U L·H·
BROOKES
PUBLISHING Cº ®

Baltimore • London • Sydney

Paul H. Brookes Publishing Co.
Post Office Box 10624
Baltimore, Maryland 21285-0624
USA

www.brookespublishing.com

Typeset by Scribe, Inc., Philadelphia, Pennsylvania.
Manufactured in the United States of America by
Sheridan Books, Inc., Chelsea, Michigan.

The individuals described in this book are composites or real people whose situations are masked and are based on the authors' experiences. In all instances, names and identifying details have been changed to protect confidentiality.

Cover photo and photos on pages 27 and 162 ©iStockphoto.com. Photograph on page 179 by Terry Joseph Sam.

Library of Congress Cataloging-in-Publication Data

Hanson, Marci J.
Understanding families : supportive approaches to diversity, disability, and risk / by Marci J. Hanson, and Eleanor W. Lynch with Mary Kanne Poulsen.—2nd ed.
     p.   cm.
  Includes bibliographical references and index.
  ISBN-13: 978-1-59857-215-5 (pbk.)
  ISBN-10: 1-59857-215-6 (pbk.)
  1.   Family social work. 2.   Family services. 3.   Dysfunctional families—Services for.
4.   Families—United States. I.   Lynch, Eleanor W. II.   Poulsen, Mary Kanne. III.   Title.
  HV697.H35 2013
  362.82—dc23   2012037588

British Library Cataloguing in Publication data are available from the British Library.

2017   2016   2015   2014   2013

10   9   8   7   6   5   4   3   2   1

Contents

About the Authors

Marci J. Hanson, Ph.D., Department of Special Education, San Francisco State University, 1600 Holloway Avenue, San Francisco, California 94132

As Professor at San Francisco State University (SFSU), Dr. Hanson is actively engaged in teaching, research, and service related to young children and their families. In addition to these responsibilities, she directs the SFSU joint doctoral program in special education with the University of California, Berkeley, and codirects the early childhood special education graduate program. She is a consultant with the child and adolescent development faculty of the Marian Wright Edelman Institute for the Study of Children, Youth, and Families at SFSU.

Dr. Hanson received her doctorate in special education with a minor in developmental psychology from the University of Oregon. Prior to joining the faculty at SFSU, she worked as a research scientist in charge of the Early Intervention Unit of the Institute for the Study of Exceptional Children, Educational Testing Service, in Princeton, New Jersey. For many years, Dr. Hanson has been actively involved in research and community service related to young children who are at risk for or have disabilities and their families. She was one of the principal investigators of a national research institute, the Early Childhood Research Institute on Inclusion.

She also has directed a number of federally funded personnel preparation and research grants in early childhood and has directed two model demonstration early intervention programs. The graduate training programs and the early intervention programs reflect the cultural diversity of the San Francisco Bay Area. Dr. Hanson has presented and consulted widely in the United States and internationally.

Dr. Hanson has contributed actively to the peer-reviewed professional literature, and she has authored, coauthored, or edited several books including *Teaching the Infant with Down Syndrome: A Guide for Parents and Professionals, Second Edition* (PRO-ED, 1987); *Teaching the Young Child with Motor Delays: A Guide for Parents and Professionals* (PRO-ED, 1986), with Dr. Susan Harris; *Homecoming for Babies After the Intensive Care Nursery: A Guide for Parents and Professionals in Supporting Families and Their Infants' Early Development* (PRO-ED, 1993), with Kathleen VandenBerg; *Atypical Infant Development, Second Edition* (PRO-ED, 1996); the *Me, Too!* series, with Dr. Paula J. Beckman (Paul H. Brookes Publishing Co., 2001); *Early Intervention Practices Around the World* (Paul H. Brookes Publishing Co., 2003), with Dr. Samuel L. Odom, Dr. James A. Blackman, and Dr. Sudha Kaul; and *Coming Home from the NICU: A Guide for Supporting Families in Early Infant Care and Development* (Paul H. Brookes Publishing Co., 2013) with Kathleen

VandenBerg. Dr. Hanson and Dr. Lynch have also collaborated on *Early Intervention: Implementing Child and Family Services for Infants and Toddlers Who Are At-Risk or Disabled, Second Edition* (PRO-ED, 1995); and *Developing Cross-Cultural Competence: A Guide for Working with Children and Their Families, Fourth Edition* (Paul H. Brookes Publishing Co., 2011).

Eleanor W. Lynch, Ph.D., Professor Emerita, Department of Special Education, San Diego State University, San Diego, California 92182

For nearly 35 years, Dr. Lynch was involved in teaching, research, and community and family services that focused on improving the lives of young children who had, or were at risk for, disabilities. Prior to joining the faculty at San Diego State University (SDSU), Dr. Lynch received her doctorate in teaching exceptional children from The Ohio State University and joined the faculty of Miami University. She subsequently joined the faculty of the University of Michigan working in both academic and clinical positions.

She is Professor Emerita at SDSU, after chairing the Department of Special Education, directing the Early Childhood Special Education graduate program, and serving on the faculty of the SDSU–Claremont Graduate University joint doctoral program. Over the course of her career, Dr. Lynch directed a model demonstration project and personnel preparation grants in early intervention and early childhood special education as well as a series of research grants on topics such as parental perspectives on special education, the status of educational services for children with ongoing medical conditions, individualized family service plan development, and the use of behavioral data and reflective practice to improve novice teachers' skills.

Dr. Lynch has served on numerous local and statewide committees and was one of the national collaborators on the Culturally and Linguistically Appropriate Services Early Childhood Research Institute. Before her retirement, she served as one of the Regional Coordinators of the federally funded Early Intervention Distance Learning Program, a collaborative project involving five California state universities and state partners. In 2003, she was honored by SDSU as one of the Top 25 on the campus and as the Outstanding Faculty Member from the College of Education. Dr. Lynch has lived in and taught special education to college instructors in Indonesia, taught human services professionals in American Samoa, given invited presentations in Australia and Taiwan, and lived in India while her husband served on a U.S. Agency for International Development project. She is the author or coauthor of numerous books, articles, and chapters and has been a frequent presenter and workshop leader in the area of cultural competence.

As an emerita faculty member, Dr. Lynch continues to write in the area of early intervention and cultural competence. Her commitment to family support and social justice continues through her volunteer work within the San Diego community.

About the Contributor

Marie Kanne Poulsen, Ph.D., Department of Pediatrics, Keck School of Medicine, University of Southern California, 4650 Sunset Boulevard, Los Angeles, California 90027

Dr. Poulsen is Professor of Clinical Pediatrics at the Keck School of Medicine at the University of Southern California (USC). Her work in policy, research, and program development focuses on building resilience in infants and young children at risk due to biological and psychosocial circumstances. She specializes in infant/family and early childhood mental health issues related to maternal depression, child welfare, trauma, prematurity, substance exposure, and autism. Recently, Dr. Poulsen was Coprincipal Investigator of a Substance Abuse Mental Health Services Administration cooperative agreement to develop an integrative service system of care for infants, preschoolers, and their families.

Dr. Poulsen has worked extensively with state departments of developmental services, mental health, social services, and education; with drug and alcohol abuse prevention programs; and with Head Start and other child care programs. She has received gubernatorial appointments to the California Child Development Policy Committee and the California Interagency Coordinating Council on Early Intervention. On the national level, Dr. Poulsen has participated in the White House Conference on Mental Health, the Surgeon General's Workshop on Violence and Public Health, the National Infant and Early Childhood Mental Health Systems Summit, and the National Head Start Strategic Plan. She has presented internationally in Amsterdam, the Netherlands; Kyoto, Japan; and Ra'anana, Israel. Dr. Poulsen is Chief Psychologist at the USC Center for Excellence in Developmental Disabilities at Children's Hospital Los Angeles, where she works directly with infants, young children, and their families.

Acknowledgments

We are grateful, once again, for the opportunity to work with the staff of Paul H. Brookes Publishing Co. We would especially like to acknowledge the many years of help and support provided by Executive Vice President Melissa Behm and Editorial Director Heather Shrestha. Acquisitions Editor Johanna Cantler, too, has been a source of inspiration and support on this edition. Throughout the editorial process, Cathy Jewell and Susan Hills have been competent, kind, and enjoyable. We would also like to thank the design, marketing, and other members of the Brookes family for their many contributions.

This edition of the book includes a new chapter on infant–family mental health, and we would like to express our sincere appreciation to its author, Marie Poulsen. Dr. Poulsen is a leader in California and throughout the nation on issues related to young children, families, and mental health issues. We are delighted that she contributed her time and expertise to this volume.

Most of all, we would like to acknowledge our own families: our parents who taught us about love and values and gave us a safe "nest" from which we flew, and the families we have entered and created who give us the bonds of love, support, and understanding.

We are fortunate to work in occupations that bring us into close contact with many families who come from a variety of diverse backgrounds. From our experiences with those families, we have continued to grow and learn; and we thank them for the contributions that they have made to our thinking and this volume. Last, we would like to thank the families whose photographs are featured in this book; most of them are close family and friends and it is a special pleasure to have their participation.

To the families into which we were born:
Max and Maxine Hanson, Laurene, and Brett
Leo and Virginia Whiteside

To the families we

have created   *belong to*
Laura   *Patrick Harrison*
and Jillian   *and Erin*

and

To the families with whom we have worked

Introduction

For many, the word *family* conjures up love, smells of cooking wafting from the kitchen, comfortable relationships, special moments, and joy. Others may be reminded of hard times, sadness, anger, and loss. *Family* connotes one of the narrowest and one of the broadest concepts in the world. It may include only two people, a kinship network of biologically related or unrelated people, or the human race. But whatever it is and wherever it is found, family is central to the fabric of life and the social structure of cultures around the world. This book is about families in their many forms, their strengths and challenges, and the ways in which human service professionals can extend their effectiveness by working in partnership with families.

Family-centered services, whether in early intervention, health care, or social services, have become one of the benchmarks of quality programs and services. Emphasis on working within the family context is a part of service delivery at all age levels—from infants and toddlers to the oldest members of the community. The value placed on creating and maintaining family–professional partnerships has changed services and the way in which they are delivered. It is an approach that acknowledges family strengths; respects and is aligned with family culture, language, and beliefs; and helps create interventions that are acceptable and realistic for families and individual family members.

PHILOSOPHY

This book is based on the authors' beliefs about families and the essential role that family members play in intervention. These beliefs have been gained by working with families of children with disabilities; conducting research with and about families; teaching graduate classes on working with families in early intervention; listening to our students as they attempt to reconcile recommended practice and reality; and seeking, coordinating, and experiencing services for our aging or ill family members. Our thinking has evolved over time. Although these beliefs will continue to be elaborated and evaluated as research, interactions, and changes in practice create new possibilities and new visions, several basic beliefs are foundational. These beliefs are emphasized throughout the book and can be summarized as follows:

1. Family–professional partnerships require that professionals acknowledge and respect each family's strengths, culture, language, and ability to make decisions that are right for that family. Family decisions may differ from those that professionals would prefer, but they are to be respected as the family's decisions.

2. All families have strengths. At times, those strengths are overshadowed by difficulties that the family or an individual family member is confronting, but these strengths may be marshaled at another time in the family's life cycle.

3. When working with family members, it is essential to listen, follow their lead, and make their agenda a priority. Although professionals bring extensive knowledge, expertise, and experience to bear in their work with families, in general, each family knows what is best for them.

4. When working with a child with disabilities or another family member with special needs, professional support and recommendations must be consistent with the well-being of the entire family.

5. Families' lives are influenced by the sociocultural, economic, and political environment in which they live. Families are often forced to cope with external forces that may include nonsupportive and destructive factors. Professionals have the responsibility to help families understand and negotiate these influences in ways that give families more control and understanding of their life circumstances.

Before beginning Chapter 1, readers may want to examine their own and their organization's beliefs about families. Are your beliefs consistent with those that underpin this text, or do they differ?

ORGANIZATION

This book is organized into 11 chapters, including three chapters new to this edition, and a concluding section. Each chapter links theory, recommended practices, and research to daily practice, but some focus more on knowledge and theory than practice. Others provide multiple suggestions and recommendations for improving family services.

Chapter 1 introduces readers to contemporary families, with emphasis on their diversity in structure, composition, and ways of living. Chapter 2 focuses on cultural and linguistic diversity among families and the importance of professionals' cultural understanding and competence in their interactions with families and colleagues. Chapter 3 describes several major conceptual models and frameworks that provide the underpinnings for family-centered approaches and for understanding and describing human development. These theories and frameworks underscore the service approaches advocated in this text. Chapter 4 focuses on family systems frameworks and family functions—the roles and responsibilities that families in this society are expected to fulfill. Chapter 5 discusses families and disability and the ways in which disability may affect the family system. Chapter 6 provides an in-depth discussion of risk and resilience, with special emphasis on the effects of poverty on families.

A discussion of risk factors and their impact on families continues in Chapter 7, which focuses on the effects of addiction, violence, abuse, trauma, and loss on children and families. Chapter 8 considers early childhood mental health and infant/family mental health, as well as the ways in which professionals can promote healthy, responsive, nurturing relationships within the context of the family. Chapter 9 discusses the importance of building family–professional alliances and partnerships, and Chapter 10 suggests strategies for working collaboratively with families and developing effective communication between parents and professionals. Chapter 11 revisits some of the work that is foundational to working with families and their children, as well as strategies for achieving family outcomes. The conclusion provides some final thoughts on working with families. Each chapter includes several activities to extend the discussion and apply the concepts discussed in the chapter to one's own community.

SUMMARY

Families are the building blocks of society. When programs and services designed for families and individual family members respect the centrality of families in intervention, the quality of programs will change and their outcomes will improve. It is the authors' hope that this book will stimulate thought, alter policy, and change practice to reflect a truly family-centered approach.

Families in the 21st Century

Eleanor W. Lynch

"Families . . . At their best they make a profound contribution to the health of society and its individuals; preserving culture, values, ethics, and wealth; defending the weak; carrying out the great unpaid work of the world. At their worst, they resist change, restrict individual freedom, and indulge in prejudices that can lead to conflict. Their power to form and reshape human minds is forever being rediscovered. Good or ill, we cannot do without them, they are the building blocks of our world."

—Jo Boyden (1993, p. 20)

"Insight, I believe, refers to that depth of understanding that comes by setting experiences, yours and mine, familiar and exotic, new and old, side by side, learning by letting them speak to one another."

—Mary Catherine Bateson (1994, p. 14)

A hallmark of the American family is diversity. Families are not unitary, nor can they be narrowly defined. Across the nation, in every community–and within the heart, mind, and experience of each individual–family is personal. Our families help to define who we are and who we are not, how we view the world, how we live, and how we share our lives with others. Like the individuals within them, families change over time. In the United States and elsewhere throughout the world, families share many characteristics but differ dramatically in others. This chapter provides an overview of the dimensions of family diversity and the implications of that diversity for individuals who work with children and families.

DEFINING FAMILY

What is a family? Each reader of this chapter has his or her own definition, and those definitions likely differ from individual to individual. The word *family* is typically associated with specific mental pictures or images. The first picture that comes to mind is often one's own family–perhaps a mother, father, and little girl in a small Midwestern town; a grandmother and grandson living together in a city apartment; or a bustling houseful of brothers, sisters, grandparents, aunts, uncles, cousins, and other kin. Many people will see only themselves and their partners, whereas others may see a series of foster parents or a father, stepmother, and stepbrothers and stepsisters from previous marriages. A few images may resemble the classically depicted nuclear family with a mother, father, and two children; some people may see the faces of men and women in their military unit. Personal images of family may come from the family with whom an individual grew up or the family one has created. For more than 10% of people, their families will include at least one person with a disability; increasingly, families will include parents and siblings of different racial and ethnic backgrounds. The image may look more like a kaleidoscope that changes, blends, and is redefined as parents, partners, brothers, sisters, and other relatives change through marriage, divorce, remarriage, or death. With this ever-expanding album of different family pictures, it is no wonder that defining families is not an easy task.

A review of the historical and contemporary definitions of family suggests that the definition—like families themselves—has changed over time. The definition also differs between various systems and societal institutions. For example, the legal definition of family may not be the same as the definition used in the local school, hospital, or social service agency. From studies of families, it is evident that researchers and theoreticians often disagree when they describe families. According to Gelles (1995, p. 2), "No other social institution is as poorly understood as the family."

How, then, have families been viewed and described in the past? In 1926, Burgess defined family as "a unity of interacting personalities each with its own history" (as cited by Gelles, 1995, p. 10). A much more restrictive definition was used by Christensen (1964), who defined family as married couples with children. A series of studies conducted between 2003 and 2006 found that Americans' views on what constitutes a family are broadening. Although the predominant view of family was still a married heterosexual couple with children (99.8%), other configurations were also considered to be a family, including a husband and wife with no children (92%), unmarried couples living together with children (83%), and same-sex couples with children (64%; Powell, Bolzendahl, Geist, & Steelman, 2010). In these studies, the presence of children was critical to many of the respondents' views of family. The same relationships without children were far less likely to be viewed as families. For example, when there were no children, only 39.6% of respondents viewed a cohabiting unmarried couple as a family and only 33% thought that a cohabiting same-sex couple constituted a family. However, 60% of respondents indicated that if a group of individuals considers themselves to be a family, then they are a family.

There are many other ways to define families, such as extended families and broad kinship networks that include multiple generations often scattered around the world. A family may also be a group of individuals who live together to share companionship, care, and common interests. Each definition creates a different lens through which to view families, and the picture that emerges shapes both policy and practice. For services to be optimal, society must recognize the remarkable diversity of families and the many variations that exist across and within families. The definition of family used throughout this book has been developed as part of our work. In an earlier publication, we defined family as "any unit that defines itself as a family, including individuals who are related by blood or marriage as well as those who have made a commitment to share their lives" (Hanson & Lynch, 1992, p. 285). Inclusivity is the most important aspect of this definition. It allows for a wide range of family configurations, from nuclear families to extended kinship networks to same-sex partners to a group of older adults who have chosen to live together. Gender is not part of the definition, nor is the presence or absence of children. Instead, "the key elements are that the members of the unit see themselves as a family, are affiliated with one another, and are committed to caring for one another" (Hanson & Lynch, 1992, p. 285).

FAMILY STRUCTURE, MEMBERSHIP, AND DIVERSITY

Families are multidimensional and differ in almost every imaginable way, including size; membership; sociocultural and socioeconomic status; language; cultural, racial, and ethnic identification; and beliefs, values, and traditions. Families also differ in the way in which they organize to accomplish the day-to-day routines and requirements of life. In recent years, the diversity of families within the United States has increased, and this diversity is being acknowledged by all and celebrated by many. This section highlights some of the changes that have broadened the understanding of families.

Smaller Families, Longer Lives

Large families with extensive kinship networks were common in the United States for centuries, but they typically received less attention than the smaller nuclear families that were glorified in the 1950s and 1960s. Although much has been written about changes in family composition, it is difficult to precisely determine the numbers and size of families because of the differences in definitions and ways of counting. For example, the U.S. Census Bureau (2009b) estimated that the average household size for the period from 2005 to 2009 was 2.6 people, but their estimate for average family size during the same period was 3.19. The difference in numbers is based on the difference in definitions: The U.S. Census Bureau (2009a) defined a family as "a group of two or more people who reside together and who are related by birth, marriage, or adoption," whereas "a household includes all the people who occupy a housing unit as their usual place of residence" without regard to relationship. Even though the numbers differ, they confirm that families now are smaller (Fischer, 2011).

Although families are smaller, family members are living longer. More than 40 million people in the United States are 65 years of age or older, and those numbers are projected to rise rapidly in the coming decades (Jacobsen, Mather, Lee, & Kent, 2011). With the growing number of older adults, more studies have focused on family gerontology, with an emphasis on the aging family and aging family systems (Price & Humble, 2010). As a result of increased life expectancy, the amount of time spent child rearing has changed. In the early part of the 20th century, child rearing was a task that continued through most of an individual's adult life. People—especially women—tended to marry younger, start a family sooner, continue to have children over many years, and die younger than they typically do today. As a result, direct parenting continued for many years. For most adults, this is no longer true. Americans spend an average of 35% of the years between the ages of 20 and 70 in direct parenting roles (Riche, 2000), although this figure varies considerably based on sex, race, and socioeconomic status. Because women are more likely to retain custody of children after divorce or separation, slightly more of their years are devoted to parenting when compared with men. Men, however, are more likely than women to remarry, with many of these remarriages including responsibilities related to the new spouse's children. As a result, men may spend twice as much time parenting nonbiological children; these parenting years are often concurrent with the parenting that they continue to provide for children from a previous marriage (King, 1999; Riche, 2000).

Increased life expectancy also has contributed to changes in family composition. Because people are living longer but having fewer children, families span more generations but have smaller numbers in each generation. According to Riche (2000, p. 22), "Today's living family tree is taller than it used to be but its branches are shorter." These

taller family trees give rise to more opportunities for intergenerational contact and involvement in everything from recreation and education to various types of support. Many grandparents provide daily care for grandchildren, and some provide financial support for adult children, grandchildren, and even great-grandchildren. These opportunities are made increasingly possible as Americans experience more active, healthy years before the end of life.

Under Whose Roof?

As families have changed, so have living arrangements. In 2010, there were 74.2 million children (birth through 17 years) in the United States, making up 24% of the population. Of those, 66% of children lived with two married parents (compared with 77% in 1980), 3% lived with their own unmarried but cohabiting parents, 23% lived with only their mothers, 3% lived with only their fathers, and 4% lived with neither parent. Of the 3 million children who did not live with a parent, 54% lived with grandparents, 21% lived with other relatives, and 24% lived with nonrelatives (Federal Interagency Forum on Child and Family Statistics, 2011). These numbers, however, do not tell the whole story. Many children and teens spend evenings, weekends, or time during school breaks and holidays shuttling between homes. Some children live with their mother during the week but spend weekends with their father. School vacations may be spent with grandparents, a noncustodial parent, or other relatives; holidays may be split between two homes. For these children and families, there are multiple residences—each with neighbors, friends, and rules associated with it.

Not all children are born into their family. Every year, between 118,000 and 127,000 children join U.S. families through adoption (U.S. Department of Health and Human Services [DHHS], 2004). In 2000 and 2001, 40% of adoptions were through publicly funded adoption agencies, 15% were adoptions that brought orphaned children from other countries into U.S. families, and another 20% were kinship or tribal adoptions made through private adoption agencies. Some of these children have lived with one or a series of foster families prior to adoption, in orphanages outside the United States before adoption, or with a family member prior to their formal adoption by that family member. Some adopted children maintain contact with their birth parents and their country of birth, whereas others do not. Whatever the circumstances of adoption, adopted children become a part of the adoptive family.

In 2009, there were approximately 423,773 children living in foster families in the United States (DHHS, 2010). The length of stay in foster care varies from less than 1 year to 20 years, averaging just over 2 years. For nearly half of the children residing with foster families, the goal is reunification with their parents or principal caretaker. Some children in foster families are being fostered by a relative or a preadoptive family, but far more of these children reside in the homes of nonrelatives, group homes, or institutions.

Your family may be the one you are born into, one that you have joined through adoption, or one that serves as family through the foster care system. The next section describes the range of parental possibilities that are part of 21st-century families.

Divorce, Blended Families, and Single Parenting

The commonly cited divorce rate for the United States is approximately 50% (Copen, Daniels, Vespa, & Mosher, 2012; Gelles, 1995). This marriage-to-divorce ratio suggests that nearly half of all marriages end in divorce. Such a ratio, however, is both inaccurate and invalid because it compares the number of divorces among all married people to the number of marriages in just a single year. The crude divorce rate is the number of divorced individuals per 1,000 people in the population. In 2008, the crude divorce rate was estimated to be 3.5 (Hughes, 2010). Although this statistical approach improves the marriage-to-divorce ratio, it is also inaccurate because children are included in the number of unmarried people. The refined divorce rate calculates the annual number of divorces per 1,000 people, using only married individuals older than 15 years as members of the population (Gelles, 1995). The refined divorce rate is estimated to be 20.9, much lower than the 50% often cited (Hughes, 2010). A further complication in determining the actual rate of divorce is the lack of data. A number of states, including California, Indiana, and Louisiana, ceased collecting divorce data in the 1980s; the U.S. National Center for Health Statistics stopped collecting data on divorce in 1996. States that still gather data on divorce often use different methods of data collection, which makes comparisons across states complex to impossible. Although a precise number is elusive, all divorces affect those involved—the couple dissolving their marriage, children, other family members, and friends.

Many divorces are followed by remarriage. It is estimated, however, that 67% of second marriages and 73% of third marriages also end in divorce (Averbach, 2012). Remarriages often result in blended families that may include stepparents, stepchildren, stepbrothers, and stepsisters. Approximately 20% of children younger than 18 years live in households with a stepparent (Portrie & Hill, 2005) and 25%–33% of U.S. children will spend some part of their lives in blended families (Ahrons & Rodgers, as cited in Seibert & Willets, 2000). The complexities of blended families are not difficult to imagine: threats to emotional security imposed by new siblings and parents, changes in family rules and power structure, changes in available resources, multiple sets of relatives with whom to interact, moves back and forth from one home to another, and the residual issues related to the divorce. Although many families demonstrate on a daily basis that these complexities can be managed effectively, blended families face an array of potential obstacles.

Single parenting often occurs for at least some period of time following a divorce, primarily for parents who do not remarry, cohabit, or rely on members of an extended family or kinship network for coparenting. Census data from 2008 indicated that single parents maintained 29.5% of family households with children younger than 18 years (U.S. Census Bureau, 2011). Using this data, the Annie E. Casey Foundation estimated that 34% of U.S. children lived in single-parent families in 2009 (National Kids Count Program, 2010). Although there have been increases in the number of single-father families in recent years, relatively little research on these families has been conducted. However, demographic data suggest that single fathers have less education and considerably fewer financial resources than their married counterparts (Brown, 2010). Most single-parent families are headed by single mothers (Mather, 2010). It is estimated that 23% of children live only with a mother compared with 3% who live only with a father (Federal Interagency Forum on Child and Family Statistics, 2011). This disproportion between heads-of-household single fathers and single mothers may be partially attributed to custody laws, which tend to favor women in some states; in addition, fewer women than men remarry after a divorce (Teachman, Tedrow, & Crowder, 2000). Single motherhood varies considerably across ethnic and racial groups, with approximately 16% of white children, 27% of Latino children, and 52% of African American children living in single-mother families (Mather, 2010).

Single parenting has been blamed for a wide range of societal ills, but studies do not support such a simplistic cause-and-effect perspective: "Most indicators of declining well-being for children—low test scores, drug use, teen pregnancy, and growing crime rates—began to rise at the same time, or even shortly *before,* divorce and non-marital childbearing rates began to rise" (Furstenberg, as cited in Coontz, 1995, p. K10). Many of the challenges to a child's well-being may be attributable to the family's socioeconomic status, which is likely to be lower in a single-mother home (Mather, 2010; Shore & Shore, 2009). Although the risks for poor outcomes are greater in single-mother homes, it is difficult to tease out the actual causes because of the multiple variables at play, such as income, mother's education, child's age, and involvement of the noncustodial parent. Despite the reports citing negative outcomes for children in single-mother homes, many single mothers and their children have proven their resilience.

Many single mothers have never been married. The rate of childbearing among unmarried women has increased considerably in the past 25 years, from 22% in 1985 to 41% in 2009 (Federal Interagency Forum on Child and Family Statistics, 2011; Shore & Shore, 2009). The increase in births to unmarried women has occurred for women in all age groups studied. In each age group, the increase in birth rates between 1980 and 2009 is striking: from 62% to 94% for ages 15–17 years, from 40% to 84% for ages 18–19 years, from 19% to 62% for ages 20–24 years, from 9% to 34% for ages 25–29 years, and from 8% to 20% for ages 30–39 years (Federal Interagency Forum on Child and Family Statistics, 2011). However, the designation of "unmarried" does not necessarily mean that there is no one else in the home or in the family. Unmarried mothers may be cohabiting with a man or same-sex partner; living with their parents, grandparents, or other relatives; or residing with friends or roommates. Regardless of the living situation, the dramatic increase in the number of unmarried mothers alters the way in which many people think of families, as well as the most effective ways to provide programs and services.

Same-Sex Parents and Families

The gender makeup in families is also changing. An increasing number of gay and lesbian adults are establishing families that include children. The number of gay and lesbian families is difficult to determine, so estimates vary (Sileo & Prater, 2012). Based on data from the 2007 American Community Survey, it was estimated that 741,000 households include same-sex partners (Shore & Shore, 2009). Of those, 21% of the male-partnered unmarried couples and 31% of the female-partnered unmarried couples had children living with them. The Family Equality Council data indicates that there are approximately 1 million families with same-sex couples raising 2 million children in the United States (Onderko, 2011). Although the largest numbers of gay and lesbian families in the United States live on the coasts or in major urban centers, same-sex families reside throughout the country. Utah, Hawaii, Wyoming, and Nevada are among the top 10 states with the largest number of same-sex couples for every 1,000 households (Onderko).

Children typically become part of a gay or lesbian family through second-parent adoption or coparent adoption (Gates, 2011). Second-parent adoption most often occurs when a child from a previous marriage is adopted by the new same-sex partner, just as one partner may adopt the other partner's child in a heterosexual marriage. In a number of states, it is legal for gay or lesbian couples to adopt a child who is not biologically related to either partner (i.e., coparent adoption). The right to coadopt is important because it provides both parents and child with the same rights as those afforded to children and parents in a heterosexual partnership (Crawford, 1999). In addition to adoptions of children from previous heterosexual relationships as well as traditional adoptions by same-sex couples, an increasing number of lesbian women are choosing to have children via donor insemination (Patterson, 2000). As the number of gay and lesbian families with children increases, so does the research on their children's outcomes. Research comparing children of gay men or lesbian women with those of heterosexual couples has found no significant differences in psychosocial development, gender identity, separation individuation, locus of control, intelligence, self-concept, personality, or moral judgment (Ahmann, 1999; Patterson, 2000, 2006; Rimalower & Caty, 2009). Across children's age levels, a parent's gender does not have a significant impact on a child's outcomes. The quality of the relationship between parents and children in both heterosexual and gay and lesbian families is a much more salient variable. Thus, the greatest concern about the well-being of children in gay and lesbian families is not about how the children will be raised but about negative societal perceptions and persecution.

Teenage Parents

The number of births to teenagers decreased substantially between 1991 and 2005, with a slight increase in 2006 (Edelman, 2008). But even with those decreases, nearly 2,000 babies were born each day in 2008 to teenagers between 15 and 19 years of age—a total of 434,758 infants (Annie E. Casey Foundation, 2011). The teenage birth rate in the United States is nearly twice that of the rate in the United Kingdom (which has the highest rate in Europe) and nearly three times the rate in Canada (Annie E. Casey Foundation). The rate of births varies across racial and ethnic groups, with the highest rate among teens of Latino origin, followed by teenagers who are African American, American Indian, and Alaskan Natives.

Any discussion of teenage pregnancy and teenage parenting includes a catalogue of risk factors. These factors are not simply moral platitudes. They are real issues that stem from research that describes the challenges of child rearing by those who are just leaving childhood themselves. Teenagers who give birth prior to high school graduation are more likely to have academic difficulties or mental health problems than their peers who graduate (White, Graham, & Bradford, 2005). Teenage parents face numerous challenges, including limited education and reduced educational opportunities, economic insecurity, social isolation, and emotional immaturity (Korfmacher, 2005). Discussion of teenage parenting is typically focused on teenage mothers. In the vast majority of teenage pregnancies, the father is an older man; only one in seven teenage pregnancies involves a teenage boy. When the father is also a teenager, the issues increase in complexity because of the personal characteristics of adolescent boys that predict teen fatherhood: sexual intercourse from an early age, gang membership, high levels of antisocial behavior, and chronic drug use. Coupled with low self-esteem, poor education, large families, and limited financial resources, these characteristics of teenage fathers paint a picture of extremely high risk (Fitzgerald & McKelvey, 2005). The stories of teenage parents, as with any individual or family, cannot be told with statistics. Each story differs because of the resources, resilience, and support systems that are available and actively engaged. As a result, a number of children of teenage parents develop without difficulties and become stable, productive adults. Others, however, are not so fortunate. The challenges faced by their parents become their own, increasing the number of risks they face throughout their lives.

Grandparents as Parents

As a result of improved health, increased life expectancy, the high divorce rate among adults with children, and the increases in teenage pregnancies, the number of adults raising their children's children also has increased. In many families, grandparents are responsible for raising their grandchildren (or even great-grandchildren) because of the biological parents' lack of competence or their incapacity due to imprisonment, abuse, drug addiction, psychiatric disorders, economic conditions, or extended military deployments (Bengston, 2001; Letiecq, Bailey, & Dahlen, 2008). Data from the U.S. Census Bureau indicate that 4.9 million children (7%) younger than 18 years live in homes headed by grandparents (Goyer, 2010). Nearly 1 million (20%) of these children live with their grandparent(s) with neither parent present in the home. In 2000, the percentage of children living with grandparents without their parents present was even greater (33%). The increased presence of parents in 2010 may have been a result of the serious economic downturn, causing unemployment and home foreclosures in the late 2000s. In that austere economy, many families moved in together and created multigenerational families (Goyer, 2010).

The state of New York has recognized the number and value of grandparent-headed families. A state law requires that grandparents be informed whenever a child is placed in foster care so that they can step forward to take care of the child if possible. In 2005, New York City also acknowledged the needs of grandparents raising their grandchildren. The city developed the first public housing complex specifically for grandparent-headed households. Grandparent Family Apartments in the South Bronx is a six-story, 51-unit apartment building with a range of in-house services for children as well as their grandparents (Gordon, 2006).

Grandparents provide a range of support to their children and their children's children, not the least of which is financial (Bengston, 2001). This phenomenon has been increasingly evident, with grandparents spending an unprecedented amount of money on diapers, toys, private-school tuition, car insurance, and college (MetLife & Francese, 2011). Of course, not every grandparent has the resources to provide financial support to their children and grandchildren. Grandparents who raise their grandchildren are more likely to have lower socioeconomic status than grandparents who do not raise their grandchildren (Gordon, 2006). Even in situations in which grandparents are not immediately involved in supporting their children and raising their grandchildren, they play a role that Hagestad (as cited in Bengston, 2001, p. 7) has titled the "Family National Guard." When their children, grandchildren, and great-grandchildren experience crises, many grandparents who would otherwise have stayed in the background marshal their resources to try to ensure the younger generation's well-being.

Families in the Military

In 2011, the U.S. military included over 1.4 million men and women—many with spouses, partners, and children (U.S. Department of Defense, 2011). In 2002, slightly over half of all service members were married and 71% had children (Segal & Segal, 2004). The volunteer army of today differs considerably from the military of the mid-20th century. As Segal and Segal (p. 3) pointed out, today's "all-volunteer military is more educated, more married, more female, and less white than the draft-era military." Military personnel are racially, culturally, ethnically, and economically diverse. In fact, serving in the U.S. military has been viewed as an opportunity for many citizens with limited resources to be assured of employment and further their education through government-sponsored programs. Some documented immigrants who are not yet U.S. citizens serve in the military and use their service as a more rapid path to citizenship. For many, military service has paved the way to a new and better life. Others, however, gave their lives before they could reach their personal goals.

During the wars in Afghanistan and Iraq, the extent and frequency of deployments increased substantially, which separated, stressed, and generally disrupted family life for those serving their country (Chandra et al., 2011). Active military personnel have been joined by those in the National Guard and Reserve forces for months and even years at a time, thus forcing families to accommodate rapidly and unexpectedly to separation, reduced income, loss of day-to-day companionship, help with child rearing, and overall support. In 2009, approximately 700,000 children had at least one parent deployed overseas; more than 500,000 children younger than 5 years were waiting for a parent on active duty in the Reserves or National Guard to return home (Turner, 2009).

Even when not engaged in war or disaster relief, military families face the stressors of frequent relocation. It is not unusual for a military family to move every 3 years, and their moves are much more likely to take them greater distances than civilians who move or are relocated by their employer (Segal & Segal). Within the Armed Forces, there are dramatic differences in pay and perks. As in any organization, those in the lowest ranks are at the lowest pay grade. Young enlisted personnel are more likely to be married than their civilian counterparts, and many have children. Because military pay at the lowest pay grades is not sufficient to support a family, many young military families are eligible for civilian welfare benefits (Segal & Segal).

Another significant change in military families is the number of women and women with children who are active duty personnel. Coupled with the increasing number of families in which both husband and wife serve in the military, changes in family functioning occur, especially when the couple has children. Dual-military couples with children and single parents are required to have a written plan specifying who will take care of their children in case of deployment (Segal & Segal).

As previously mentioned, the wars in Afghanistan and Iraq have taken a toll on military families. Not only have there been long and frequent deployments, but the wars themselves have been fought on hostile ground with enemies that are not always easy to recognize. New technologies have proven to be invaluable and battlefield medicine has accomplished things that were unheard of in previous wars, but the loss of life and limb has been great. Each of those losses has affected the men and women on the battlefront as well as their families back home. For those who return home, the battles are not always left behind. There may be months or years of hospitalization, therapy, and adjustment to lifelong physical disabilities. There may also be years of anxiety, depression, and medication management for those who continue to wage a battle against posttraumatic stress disorder. Even for those who return physically and mentally healthy, the complex tasks of reestablishing expectations and renegotiating roles within the family system still remain (Turner, 2009).

Parents with Disabilities

In more than 10 million families with children, at least one parent has a disability (Kirshbaum & Olkin, 2002). Information about these families is sparse, but it is safe to say that there are no generalizations that apply. Each family is unique, and the challenges and needs differ based on the disability as well as the family's support system. Intellectual, sensory, physical, and psychiatric disabilities or a combination present different capacities as well as limitations. Too often, research has been conducted on the broad category of parents with disabilities without regard to the type or extent of their disability or their functional levels.

The progressive philosophy of normalization with its emphasis on the rights of individuals with disabilities has been an important and expanding social and political movement since the 1970s. Mainstreaming, inclusion, community-based services, and individual rights and responsibilities for individuals with disabilities have evolved from the normalization movement. Although it has taken nearly a half century, the number of individuals with learning and intellectual disabilities electing to exercise those rights—including the right to establish their own families through marriage, partnerships, and children—has increased (Lightfoot, Hill, & La Liberte, 2010; Young & Hawkins, 2006). For those with learning disabilities, parenting may present no more challenges than it does for others. Their learning problems are primarily related to academic skills and do not affect their decision making, judgment, or interpersonal interactions. For others, disabilities may make parenting more challenging. Organizing, managing, remembering, disciplining, and assisting with schoolwork may be problematic; however, even if this is the case, there are strategies to compensate for the majority of these issues. When strategies are not available, studies suggest that partners may assume responsibility for providing the necessary knowledge and skills (Young & Hawkins).

The tasks of parenting may be more difficult for individuals with deficits in areas of functioning and performance that are associated with more severe intellectual disabilities. Research in the United Kingdom has established that an individual's potential to parent and the types of support received are key for families in which a parent has learning or intellectual disabilities (Young & Hawkins, 2006). Parents with intellectual disabilities typically need training in critical areas of parenting such as child care, decision making, effective communication, providing appropriate activities for children, behavior management, stress management, home safety, health care, food preparation, and cleanliness (Wade, Llewellyn, & Mathews, 2008). In a federally sponsored project in Southern California focusing on parents with mild and moderate intellectual disabilities, weekly home visits were used to teach skills, model appropriate behavior, provide opportunities to practice these skills and behaviors, and review family needs (Lynch & Bakley, 1989). Challenging aspects of the intervention included helping clients to generalize or reduce overgeneralization. For example, one child disliked eating, so her mother asked the home visitor to teach her to make pancakes—a food that she thought her daughter would enjoy. The mother quickly learned how to follow the recipe. During a visit several weeks later, the home visitor asked the mother how her daughter was eating. The mother happily reported that her daughter was eating very well. The daughter loved the pancakes so much that the mother made them every day for breakfast, lunch, and dinner.

Parents with significant intellectual disabilities require considerably more external support to successfully manage the routines and responsibilities of daily life than parents without intellectual disabilities. However, data indicate that children of parents with intellectual disabilities can have successful outcomes (Lightfoot et al., 2010).

Studies that focus specifically on parents with sensory and physical disabilities are sparse in the professional literature. Although it is often assumed that individuals with physical disabilities and their families experience many stressful events with ensuing adjustment problems, it has been argued that these families are more similar to than dissimilar from families in which neither parent has a disability (Mazur, 2007). In fact, in a study of 19 parents with a range of acquired disabilities (multiple sclerosis, rheumatoid arthritis, fibromyalgia, degenerative disk disease, and lupus), parents and their adolescent children reported many more positive than negative events related to the disability (Mazur). Although physical disabilities can certainly make many of the responsibilities of parenting more difficult, they do not necessarily reduce its quality.

Individuals with psychiatric problems or mental health issues present a range of complex and challenging concerns. Individuals may be limited in the range of responses that they have in their interactions with others. They may misperceive others' actions and intentions, lack flexibility, and have difficulty trusting and relating to others (Tomlin, 2002). Many lack insight into their own behavior and engage in behaviors that are not understood by others. Individuals may be frustrated by interactions with professionals and systems that are unaware of their needs and the daily challenges that they experience. These characteristics make effective, consistent parenting and attachment difficult; however, treatment methods can be used successfully with many individuals who experience these challenges.

The Sandwich Generation

Although many adults play a supportive role in the lives of their children and grandchildren, not every older family member is able to help. Instead, adult children must provide care and support for their aging parents as well as their own children. The population of people engaged in such double duties has been described in the popular press as the "sandwich generation" (Pierret, 2006). For these families, juggling jobs, dependent children, and the needs of older family members is challenging. An estimated 9 million adults find themselves in this situation. Although both men and women are

affected by their parents' aging, women are more often squeezed in this multigenerational sandwich: 70% of the caregivers are women, and 60% of these women work full time (McCombs, 2001). Longer life expectancy, later childbearing, smaller families, and greater physical distance between family members all contribute to the plight of the sandwich generation (Pierret).

The day-to-day needs associated with the care of older parents include monitoring medication, making doctor's appointments, providing or arranging transportation, handling financial affairs, maintaining a social support system for homebound older adults, ensuring physical and psychological safety, and advocating for required care; these tasks can be demanding and exhausting (McCombs, 2001). In some respects, the role reversal may be even more difficult than these daily demands.

SOCIOECONOMIC DIFFERENCES: THE DOLLAR DIVIDE

One of the most potent differences between families may be their socioeconomic statuses. Although money cannot buy happiness or love, it can buy access to education, health care, enriching life experiences, and numerous opportunities that are not available to those with limited resources. Socioeconomic status can dramatically affect families and every aspect of family life.

During the late 1990s, the United States had a strong economy in which the overall wealth of the nation grew; unemployment was low and there was little inflation.

Newspaper headlines and stock market reports were rosy. However, in many instances, the words of an old adage were accurate: The rich got richer and the poor got poorer. During that time, the gap between the wealthiest 5% of American families and the poorest 20% of families reached a 52-year high (Children's Defense Fund, 2000). For many families, things have only gotten worse since then. In 2008, despite the recession and some loss of income, the richest 1% of U.S. households received 21% of the nation's total income, and the top 10% of households received 48.2% of the country's income (Children's Defense Fund, 2011).

For those households that control nearly half of the country's income, life is good. Adler (1995) described these families as the "over-class." Difficult to define through statistical measures, members of this group have both incomes and attitudes that set them apart from the middle class. These individuals are not necessarily the beneficiaries of family fortunes and wealth that has been accumulated over generations; rather, they likely have created the wealth that has catapulted them into this group. These individuals tend to be achievement oriented. They are in the top 20% of the nation on income, have degrees from prestigious universities, and are clustered primarily on the East and West Coasts but are transnational in perspective. These families have emerged as a new elite class (Adler), although *elite* may not be the word that they would choose. It may be difficult for many in the overclass to recognize that they live a life of privilege. Some may have a conviction that success flows from merit, which makes it difficult for them to understand that failure is often based on societal, rather than personal, shortcomings.

With the increase in affluence for these households, two issues that are especially relevant to this book emerge: the lack of involvement in child rearing in some affluent families and the income inequality in the United States. Just as economic strain can prevent parents from giving full attention to parenting (White & Rogers, 2000), so can the strain to earn more, do more, and get ahead faster. The drive to become ever wealthier and more successful can take parents' attention away from children. As stated by Mack (2000, p. 11), "Where once maternal engagement was hampered only by the burdens of critical subsistence tasks, today the principal thief of time is a fast-moving market economy offering a cafeteria of ever-changing, often senseless temptations." For many families on the fast track, the temptations become realities as they watch out for the next best thing that will replace today's toys, smart phones, sport utility vehicles, and exercise gurus. Although the advantages and opportunities associated with growing up in a wealthy family cannot be ignored, money does not guarantee success for children in affluent families. Shootings and other violence in schools have occurred in suburban areas with average and above-average material resources. Material advantages do not outweigh the importance of spending time with children, including instruction and modeling of values such as compassion and social justice.

Concern is mounting over the widening income gap within the United States. As the gulf widens, attitudes may become more rigid and policies related to families with low socioeconomic status may shift. The shift could take many directions, from paternalistic forms of support to punitive approaches; however, it is important for service providers to be aware of the dangers that exist for families who live in the margins. Endorsement of a meritocracy in which rewards are believed to flow fairly to those who work hardest does not take into account the systemic societal biases in many policies, programs, and services that favor individuals who are already on top. Service providers are in a position to consider the context of each family's life, as well as the opportunities that have been unavailable to families because of their socioeconomic status, race, educational level, or primary language. In addition, it is important for service providers to consider how they can help families overcome those barriers.

In 2008, when the top 10% were getting richer, the bottom 90% of households had the largest single-year drop in income since 1938 and their lowest incomes in a decade. Almost all of the gains that these families had made during the 1990s were lost during the recession (Children's Defense Fund, 2011). Many families lost more than income; they lost their savings, homes, and jobs. In 2010, 46.2 million men, women, and children were living in poverty—a 50-year high (Lee, Levey, & Lazo, 2011). As families faced crises in income, employment, and shelter, 3.4 million children received assistance through Temporary Assistance for Needy Families in 2010—a decrease of 59% compared to the number receiving assistance in 1996. Chapter 6 provides a comprehensive discussion of these issues in the United States.

Poverty affects both families and children; it can impair children's emotional, intellectual, and physical development (Children's Defense Fund, 2011). In 2009, 20% of children (15.5 million) in the United States lived in poverty. Almost half of those children lived in extreme poverty, which is defined as an annual income of half the poverty level (amounting to $11,025 per year for a family of four). In 2010, the number of children living in low-income U.S. households reached its highest level since 1962 (Lee et al., 2011). For children in families with such limited incomes, almost nothing is certain. A place to sleep, food, clothes, toilets, sinks, medicine, and an education are not assured. The energy that goes into healthy development must often be used for survival.

Poverty is not evenly distributed across types of families. Nearly 60% of children living in poverty in 2009 lived in single-parent households, with the majority of those being single mothers (Children's Defense Fund, 2011). More than one in three African American children and one in three Hispanic children lived in poverty in 2009, compared with one in ten white, non-Hispanic children. However, wide variations exist within each racial and ethnic group. For example, the poverty rate in 2009 was 3.5% for childless, married African American families with a householder who held a bachelor's degree or higher. For married African American couples with children in the home and a householder without a high school diploma, the poverty rate was nearly 50%. For families with African American single mothers without a high school diploma or equivalent, the poverty rate was nearly 75% (Children's Defense Fund, 2011).

Poverty is frequently associated with developmental risk because it promotes an accumulation of risk factors that compound its hardships (Hanson & Carta, 1996). Insufficient food, inadequate housing, lack of health care, nonexistent transportation, homelessness, and neighborhoods plagued by violence interact to reduce resilience. Although many parents and families struggle mightily against the factors that surround poverty, they face many obstacles. Inadequate nutrition, substance abuse, maternal depression, exposure to environmental toxins, trauma, and physical abuse are often part of the everyday experience. Children are particularly vulnerable to these frequently co-occurring circumstances. The first years of life contribute significantly to emotional and cognitive development, so the risk factors faced by millions of children living in poverty or extreme poverty place them at considerable risk for negative outcomes, including less-than-optimal brain development (Brooks-Gunn, Klebanov, Liaw, & Duncan, 1995; National Center for Children in Poverty, 1997). In a complex statistical analysis of data gathered between 1983 and 1996 from the National Health Interview Survey, poverty emerged as a significant predictor of disability (Fujiura & Yamaki, 2000). In 1983, poverty did not statistically predict disability; however, by 1996, the odds of having a disability were 86% higher for a child living in poverty than for a child living above the poverty threshold. On reflection, this finding is not surprising given that children living in poverty are more likely to be exposed to conditions that are predictive of disability, such as low birth weight, chronic health problems, limited access to health care, inadequate nutrition, and trauma.

RACIAL, CULTURAL, AND ETHNIC DIVERSITY

Cultural diversity has received increasing attention lately. When considering cultural diversity, it is typical to think in terms of race, culture, ethnicity, and primary language. Because of the long-standing power structures in the United States, it has been common to assume that those with Anglo-European roots are the norm and everyone else is diverse. This is the first myth that needs to be dispelled. With the transformation of the United States into a country in which no single group will hold the majority, there is no norm. We are all diverse.

The Demographics of Diversity

Data from the decennial census indicate that 308.7 million people lived in the United States in 2010 (Mather et al., 2011). White, non-Hispanic Americans accounted for 63.7% of the population, with 16.2% Hispanics/Latinos, 12.2% African Americans/Blacks, and 4.7% Asians. American Indian and Alaskan Natives were approximately 1% of the U.S. population, with Native Hawaiian and other Pacific Islanders at less than 1%. For the first time, the 2010 census allowed individuals to indicate that they belonged to more than one race. Nearly 2% of the population checked that they were from more than one race (Pew Hispanic Center, 2011). Although Hispanic/Latino Americans made up only 16% of the population, they were the fastest growing group in the years between 2000 and 2010, with a 43% increase. The number of Latino children increased 39% during the same decade, making them 17.1% of all children in the United States younger than age 18 (Pew Hispanic Center). The considerable growth in the number of young Latinos, as well as the youthful composition of other groups, suggests that the 2020 census will confirm the changing demographics within the United States. Chapter 2 provides a comprehensive discussion of cultural, ethnic, racial, and linguistic diversity in the United States.

The Effect of Diversity

Many people seldom think about the role that culture, ethnicity, race, and language play in their lives; they may assume that others' perspectives and worldviews are the same as their own. White Americans in particular tend to see themselves as being without a culture (Lynch, 2011). However, culture is reflected in all that individuals think and all that they do. Interactions with others, food, views on childrearing, the kind of medical care used, religious and spiritual beliefs, and ceremonies and rituals of celebration and mourning are all reflections of culture, ethnicity, and race. These practices and beliefs are not monolithic, and cultures are not static. They evolve over time and even location, but they provide a framework for living one's life. These deep-seated, if unrecognized, roots affect daily life in myriad ways. For example, it is typical in the United States for a couple expecting a child to visit the doctor together, take childbirth classes together, and have the father present during the delivery. In some other cultures, such as Middle Eastern, pregnancy and childbirth are viewed as women's affairs. Fathers are not as involved in the pregnancy and are seldom present during the delivery (Sharifzadeh, 2011).

Beliefs about child rearing also differ from culture to culture. In many U.S. homes, children are expected to become independent as soon as possible. Sleeping alone, toilet training, dressing, and feeding oneself are valued goals. This is not the case in every culture. In many families with roots in countries throughout the world, infants sleep with parents for an extended period of time. Toilet training is not taught or scheduled and occurs when the child seems to be ready. Mothers, grandmothers, and older siblings may follow a toddler around with their meal, spooning food into the child's mouth as they play. The milestones that are viewed as so important in mainstream American culture do not have the same power for many families with Chinese, Southeast Asian, and South American roots. Expectations related to independence and self-care for children in those cultures, however, increase after the age of 5 or 6 years, becoming far greater than expectations for the majority of children in the United States.

The ways in which families and communities view death and dying and honor the dead also differ from culture to culture. For some, burial or cremation must take place within 24 hours. For others, the deceased may be prepared for burial but remain in the home for several days while family members and friends keep a vigil or celebrate the life of the deceased. In many cultures, such as Mexican and Chinese, there are annual rituals of remembrance of ancestors, cleaning of the graves, and eating traditional foods (Chan & Chen, 2011; Zuniga, 2011). Throughout much of the world outside North America and Great Britain, it is not uncommon to see women walking down the street holding hands or men walking arm in arm. Same-sex greetings may include kissing. However, in the United States, the same displays of affection typically suggest a more intimate relationship.

Even when people are unaware, they are often thinking and behaving in ways that reflect their cultural, ethnic, or racial heritage. These ways of being in the world give meaning and structure to each individual and each family. In many ways, the practices are sustained because they bring people together. Sometimes, however, beliefs and practices limit tolerance of others and cause conflict with those who do not share the same traditions.

The roles that culture, color, ethnicity, and language play in each individual's life are as unique as that person. Generalizing about the impact of diversity is difficult. However, when diversity (culture, color, race, ethnicity, or language) deprives an individual or family of equal access and opportunity or puts them in danger, the well-being of the family and its members is in jeopardy. For most individuals and families in the United States, the impact of their culture, ethnicity, and home language appears to be minimal. They go about the tasks of everyday living without thinking about these characteristics or the ways in which they are touched by each of them. For others, these characteristics define who they are and profoundly affect daily interactions with others. They may be viewed with curiosity, suspicion, dislike, disdain, or indifference, and each day may bring challenges that other people do not face.

IMPLICATIONS OF NEW FAMILY
PARADIGMS FOR SERVICE PROVIDERS

Families in the United States were never as monolithic as some nostalgic politicians and screenwriters would have the public believe. Diversity in family size, membership, and intergenerational involvement has always existed, but the diversity of family structures that is publicly acknowledged and celebrated by many has increased dramatically since the middle of the 20th century. The challenges, failures, and successes that have emerged as family structures evolved have provided new ways of defining, studying, and working with families. These new paradigms have, in turn, taught everyone that there is no "right way" to be a family.

What are the implications for service providers? How can those who work with families and children improve their practice to ensure that the wide range of family structures, life circumstances, racial and cultural identifications, and needs are addressed and met? Two characteristics of service providers and the systems in which they work are essential to effective practice: The first characteristic is an openness to listen, learn, and change, whereas the second characteristic is a commitment to engage in reflective practice. Listening, learning, and changing sounds simple, yet it is one of the most difficult skills required of professionals. On the surface, it is easier, faster, and less stressful to find a way of doing things and to follow that routine over and over again. However, if you rely on a routine approach, you may lose the ability to listen. Instead of hearing what the family is saying, you will hear what you expect to hear. When this occurs, you can miss what the family is saying about their needs, resources, and preferences. When you follow the same routines that you have used in the past, there is no guarantee that you will be meeting the family's current or future needs. It is more likely that you are simply meeting your own needs to complete the paperwork. As a result, putting one's practice on automatic pilot is not, in reality, easier, faster, or less stressful for the professional or the family because it greatly reduces the likelihood that the intervention and support will be effective.

Reflective practice is a hallmark of the effective professional (Schön, 1987). It requires professionals to continuously review their actions, consider the results of those actions, and when necessary alter their approach to improve outcomes. Committing to reflective practice means that professionals must continuously analyze their experiences in order to learn from them. The constant process of experience, analysis, and application to practice results in lifelong learning—another hallmark of an effective professional.

Professionals who work with families come from a broad array of disciplines, including education, special education, and early intervention; psychology; social work; child development; nursing, medicine, occupational, physical, and speech therapy; and law. Working with families is one of the most challenging as well as one of the most rewarding career choices. It is also a career with many responsibilities—the first of which is to support families in their own growth and development.

SUMMARY

Family diversity is increasing in many ways. Families vary in membership, socioeconomic status, culture, race, ethnicity, and language. Many families have a single parent who is responsible for providing for children's financial and emotional well-being. Other families may appear to have a single parent responsible for all aspects of family life, but in reality they have a wide range of family and kinship support available. Divorce is no longer unusual; many children will live in homes with stepparents, stepbrothers, and stepsisters. More often than one would hope, children of divorced parents will experience a second divorce. Grandparents often become primary caregivers when children live in homes without either biological parent. Other children may live in foster homes until they are adopted.

It can no longer be assumed that two-parent families are composed of male and female parents. Gay men and lesbian women are forming strong family units, as well as adopting and having their own children. Families who serve the nation as members of the military service face special challenges because of frequent and extended deployments, low pay for those at the bottom of the chain of command, and frequent relocations. Parents with disabilities are another group with unique needs that require understanding and adaptation of strategies and services provided by practitioners.

Families' financial circumstances vary dramatically, with a growing gap between those with resources and those without. At the same time that the top 10% of Americans are becoming wealthier, many others struggle daily just to feed, clothe, and house their families. The differences in sociocultural experience of the majority of providers and many of the families that they serve provide additional challenges to effective policy and practice.

In addition to the diversity of family membership, the cultural, ethnic, racial, and linguistic diversity among families is on the increase. The nation's demographics paint a colorful picture. Challenges related to the way in which families are organized; their values, beliefs, and behaviors; and what they find meaningful in their lives demand attention and new skills from professionals.

If families are to benefit from professional skills and knowledge, it is incumbent on professionals to understand each family's context and to develop interventions that fit those contexts. One size does not fit all when working with families. Instead, both programs and services need to be tailored to fit. When the match between family needs, perspectives, and resources can be made by a service provider, outcomes for children and families will be improved—the ultimate goal of intervention.

ACTIVITIES TO EXTEND THE DISCUSSION

1. **Join a group within your class and discuss the questions that follow.** When you have answered the questions, compare the responses of group members to develop a profile of the similarities and differences of the families that are represented within the group.

    -   How many members are part of your family?

    -   How is each one related to you (e.g., biological father, stepmother, maternal aunt, half-brother)?

    -   How many families have you lived in since your birth?

2. **Investigate the family structure and diversity within your own community.** Find statistics from the U.S. Census Bureau or other sources on families within your state, community, or neighborhood. Develop a profile to share with other class participants describing the percentage of different family structures, racial/cultural diversity, educational levels, income levels, individuals without health insurance, and any other statistic that you find interesting.

3. **From this week's newspapers and/or magazines, clip at least one article that addresses some issue that affects families.** Prepare a synopsis of the article and be prepared to discuss which families may be most affected.

TO LEARN MORE: SUGGESTED WEB SITES

The Annie E. Casey Foundation
http://www.aecf.org

Children's Defense Fund
http://www.childrensdefense.org/child-research-data-publications

Military Homefront Supporting Troops and Their Families
http://www.militaryhomefront.dod.mil

National Center for Children in Poverty
http://www.nccp.org

Population Reference Bureau
http://www.prb.org

U.S. Census Bureau
http://www.census.gov

U.S. Department of Health and Human Services, Administration for Children and Families: Child Welfare Information Gateway
http://www.childwelfare.gov/systemwide/statistics/adoption.cfm

REFERENCES

Adler, J. (1995, July 31). The rise of the overclass. *Newsweek, 126*(5), 32–46.

Ahmann, E. (1999). Working with families having parents who are gay or lesbian. *Pediatric Nursing, 25,* 531–536.

Annie E. Casey Foundation. (2011). *Kids count data book.* Retrieved August 25, 2011, from http://datacenter.kidscount.org/databook/2011/OnlineBooks/2011KCDB_FINAL.pdf

Averbach, L. (2012). Second and third marriages are failing at an alarming rate. *Huffington Post.* Retrieved August 2, 2012, from http://www.huffingtonpost.com/leo-averbach/second-and-third-marriage_b_1326785.html

Bateson, M.C. (1994). *Peripheral visions: Learning along the way.* New York, NY: HarperCollins.

Bengston, V.L. (2001). Beyond the nuclear family: The increasing importance of multigenerational bonds. *Journal of Marriage and the Family, 63,* 1–16.

Boyden, J. (1993). *Families: Celebration and hope in a world of change.* London, UK: Gaia Books.

Brooks-Gunn, J., Klebanov, P., Liaw, F., & Duncan, G. (1995). Toward an understanding of the effects of poverty upon children. In H.E. Fitzgerald, B.M. Lester, & B. Zuckerman (Eds.), *Children of poverty: Research, health, and policy issues* (pp. 3–37). New York, NY: Garland Science Publishing.

Brown, B.V. (2010). The single-father family: Demographic, economic, and public transfer use characteristics. In A.D. Yarber & P.M. Sharp (Eds.), *Focus on single-parent families: Past, present, and future* (pp. 38–41). Santa Barbara, CA: Praeger.

Chan, S., & Chen, D. (2011). Families with Asian roots. In E.W. Lynch & M.J. Hanson (Eds.), *Developing cross-cultural competence: A guide for working with children and their families* (4th ed., pp. 234–318). Baltimore, MD: Paul H. Brookes Publishing Co.

Chandra, A., Lara-Cinisomo, S., Jaycox, L.H., Tanielian, T., Han, B., Burns, R.M., et al. (2011). *Views from the home front: The experiences of youth and spouses from military families.* Santa Monica, CA: RAND Corporation.

Children's Defense Fund. (2000). *The state of America's children: Yearbook 2000.* Washington, DC: Author.

Children's Defense Fund. (2011). *The state of America's children: Yearbook 2011.* Washington, DC: Author.

Christensen, H.T. (1964). *Handbook of marriage and the family.* Chicago, IL: Rand McNally.

Coontz, S. (1995). The American family and the nostalgia trap. *Kappan Special Report, 76,* K1–K20.

Copen, C.E., Daniels, K., Vespa, J., & Mosher, W.D. (2012). First marriages in the United States: Data from the 2006-2010 national survey of family growth, *National Health Statistics Reports.* Retrieved August 1, 2012, from http://www.cdc.gov/nchs/data/nhsr/nhsr049.pdf

Crawford, J. (1999). Co-parent adoptions by same-sex couples: From loophole to law. *Families in Society, 80,* 271–278.

Edelman, M.R. (2008). *Teen pregnancy in America today.* Retrieved March 26, 2012, from http://www.childrensdefense.org/newsroom/child-watch-columns/child-watch-documents/teen-pregnancy-in-america-today.html

Federal Interagency Forum on Child and Family Statistics. (2011). *America's children: Key national indicators of well-being, 2011.* Washington, DC: Government Printing Office.

Fischer, C.S. (2011). *Still connected: Family and friends in America since 1970.* New York, NY: Russell Sage Foundation.

Fitzgerald, H.E., & McKelvey, L. (2005). Low-income adolescent fathers: Risk for parenthood and risky parenting. *Zero to Three, 25*(4), 35–41.

Fujiura, G.T., & Yamaki, K. (2000). Trends in demography of childhood poverty and disability. *Exceptional Children, 66,* 187–199.

Gates, G.J. (2011). Family formation and raising children among same-sex couples. Retrieved March 26, 2012, from http://williamsinstitute.law.ucla.edu/wp-content/uploads/Gates-Badgett-NCFR-LGBT-Families-December-2011.pdf

Gelles, R.J. (1995). *Contemporary families: A sociological view.* Thousand Oaks, CA: Sage Publications.

Gordon, P. (2006). *Grandparents raising grandchildren.* Retrieved August 30, 2011, from http://www.gothamgazette.com/print/1816

Goyer, A. (2010). *More grandparents raising grandkids: New census data shows an increase in children being raised by extended family.* Retrieved August 29, 2011, from http://www.aarp.org/relationships/grandparenting/info-12-2010/more_grandparents_raising_grandchildren.print.html

Hanson, M.J., & Carta, J.J. (1996). Addressing the challenges of families with multiple risks. *Exceptional Children, 62,* 201–212.

Hanson, M.J., & Lynch, E.W. (1992). Family diversity: Implications for policy and practice. *Topics in Early Childhood Special Education, 12,* 283–306.

Hughes, R. (2010). What is the actual divorce rate in the US? *Huffington Post.* Retrieved August 1, 2012, from http://www.huffingtonpost.com/robert-hughes/what-is-the-real-divorce-_b_785045.html

Jacobsen, L.A., Mather, M., Lee, M., & Kent, M. (2011). America's aging population. *Population Bulletin, 66,* 1–16.

King, R.K. (1999). Time spent in parenthood status among adults in the United States. *Demography, 3,* 377–385.

Kirshbaum, M., & Olkin, R. (2002). Parents with physical, systemic, or visual disabilities. *Sexuality and Disability, 20,* 65–80.

Korfmacher, J. (2005). Teen parents in early childhood interventions. *Zero to Three, 25*(4), 7–13.

Lee, D., Levey, N., & Lazo, A. (2011, September 14). U.S. poverty totals hit a 50-year high. *The Los Angeles Times,* pp. A1, A15.

Letiecq, B.L., Bailey, S.J., & Dahlen, P. (2008). Ambivalence and coping among custodial grandparents. In B. Hayslip, Jr., & P.L. Kaminski (Eds.), *Parenting the custodial grandchild: Implications for clinical practice* (pp. 3–16). New York, NY: Springer.

Lightfoot, E., Hill, K., & LaLiberte, T. (2010). The inclusion of disability as a condition of termination of parental rights. *Child Abuse and Neglect, 34,* 927–934.

Lynch, E.W. (2011). Developing cross-cultural competence. In E.W. Lynch & M.J. Hanson (Eds.), *Developing cross-cultural competence: A guide for working with children and their families* (4th ed., pp. 41–78). Baltimore, MD: Paul H. Brookes Publishing Co.

Lynch, E.W., & Bakley, S. (1989). Serving young children whose parents are mentally retarded. *Infants and Young Children, 1*(3), 26–38.

Mack, D. (2000, June 12). Valuing family time over wealth. *Christian Science Monitor,* 11.

Mather, M. (2010). U.S. children in single-mother families. Retrieved August 17, 2011, from http://www.prb.org/Publications/PolicyBriefs/singlemotherfamilies.aspx

Mather, M., Pollard, K., & Jacobsen, L.A. (2011, July). *PRB reports on America: First results from the 2010 census.* Retrieved September 9, 2011, from http://www.prb.org/Articles/2010/2010-unitedstates-census.aspx

Mazur. E. (2007). Negative and positive disability-related events and adjustment of parents with acquired physical disabilities and their adolescent children. *Journal of Child and Family Studies, 17,* 517–537.

McCombs, B. (2001, January 8). Demands on boomer bloom: Need of kids, and parents squeeze sandwich generation. *The Denver Post,* p. B1.

MetLife & Francese, P. (2011). *The MetLife report on American grandparents: New insights for a new generation of grandparents.* Retrieved August 29, 2011, from http://www.metlife

.com/assets/cao/mmi/publications/studies/2011/mmi-american-grandparents.pdf

National Center for Children in Poverty. (1997). *Poverty and brain development in early childhood*. Retrieved May 7, 2001, http://www.nccp.org/

National Kids Count Program. (2010). Data across states: Children in single-parent families. Retrieved August 17, 2011, from http://datacenter.kidscount.org/data/acrossstates/Rankings.aspx?ind=106

Onderko, P. (2011). The (same-sex) family next door. *Parenting: Early Years, 25*(2), 74–77.

Patterson, C.J. (2000). Family relationships of lesbians and gay men. *Journal of Marriage and the Family, 62*, 1052–1069.

Patterson, C.J. (2006). Children of lesbian and gay parents. *Current Directions in Psychological Science, 15*, 241–244.

Pew Hispanic Center. (2011, March). *Census 2010: 50 million Latinos, Hispanics account for more than half of nation's growth in past decade*. Retrieved September 10, 2011, from http://pewhispanic.org/files/reports/140.pdf

Pierret, C.R. (2006). The "sandwich generation": Women caring for parents and children. Retrieved August 31, 2011, from http://www.bls.gov/opub/mlr/2006/09/art1full.pdf

Portrie, T., & Hill, N.R. (2005). Blended families: A critical review of the current research. *The Family Journal, 13*, 445–451.

Powell, B., Bolzendahl, C., Geist, C., & Steelman, L.C. (2010). *Counted out: Same-sex relations and Americans' definitions of family*. New York, NY: Russell Sage Foundation.

Price, C.A., & Humble, A.M. (2010). Stress and coping in later life. In S.J. Price, C.A. Price, & P.C. McKenry (Eds.), *Families and change: Coping with stressful events and transitions* (4th ed., pp. 51–71). Thousand Oaks, CA: Sage Publications.

Riche, M.F. (2000). *America's diversity and growth: Signposts for the 21st century*. Washington, DC: Population Reference Bureau.

Rimalower, L., & Caty, C. (2009). The mamas and the papas: The invisible diversity of families with same-sex parents in the United States. *Sex Education, 9*(1), 17–32.

Schön, D.A. (1987). *Educating the reflective practitioner: Toward a new design for teaching and learning in the professions*. San Francisco, CA: Jossey-Bass.

Segal, D.R., & Segal, M.W. (2004). America's military population. *Population Bulletin, 59*(4), 1–40.

Seibert, M.T., & Willets, M.T. (2000). Changing family forms. *Social Education, 64*, 42–47.

Sharifzadeh, V.-S. (2011). Families with Middle Eastern roots. In E.W. Lynch & M.J. Hanson (Eds.), *Developing cross-cultural competence: A guide for working with children and their families* (4th ed., pp. 392–436). Baltimore: Paul H. Brookes Publishing Co.

Shore, R., & Shore, B. (2009). *KIDS COUNT Indicator Brief: Increasing the percentage of children living in two-parent families*. Retrieved August 17, 2011, from http://www.aecf.org/~/media/Pubs/Initiatives/KIDS%20COUNT/K/KIDSCOUNTIndicatorBriefIncreasingthePercentag/Two%20Parent%20Families.pdf

Sileo, N.M., & Prater, M.A. (2012). Overview of diversity among families and professionals. In N.M. Sileo & M.A. Prater (Eds.), *Working with families of children with special needs: Family and professional partnerships and roles* (pp. 91–106). Boston, MA: Pearson.

Teachman, J.D., Tedrow, L.M., & Crowder, K.D. (2000). The changing demography of America's families. *Journal of Marriage and the Family, 62*, 1234–1247.

Tomlin, A. (2002). Partnering with parents with personality disorders: Effective strategies for early intervention providers. *Infants & Young Children, 14*(4), 68–75.

Turner, J.S. (2009). *American families in crisis*. Santa Barbara, CA: ABC-CLIO.

U.S. Census Bureau. (2009a). *American FactFinder, Help glossary*. Retrieved August 2, 2012, from http://factfinder2.census.gov/help/en/american_factfinder_help.htm#glossary/glossary.htm

U.S. Census Bureau. (2009b). *American FactFinder, United States 2005–2009 American community survey 5-year estimates data profile highlights*. Retrieved August 2, 2012, from http://www.census.gov/acs/www/

U.S. Census Bureau. (2011). *Statistical abstract of the United States: 2011, Table 1136. Single-parent households: 1980 to 2009*. Retrieved August 17, 2011, from http://www.census.gov/compendia/statab/2011tables/11s1336.pdf

U.S. Department of Defense. (2011). *Military personnel strength figures*. Retrieved August 30, 2011, from https://kb.defense.gov/app/answers/detail/a_id/253

U.S. Department of Health and Human Services. (2004). *How many children were adopted in 2000 and 2001?* Retrieved August 13, 2011, from http://www.childwelfare.gov/pubs/s_adopted/s_adopted.pdf

U.S. Department of Health and Human Services, Administration for Children & Families. (2010). The AFCARS report. Retrieved August 14, 2011, from http://www.acf.hhs.gov/programs/cb/stats_research/afcars/tar/report17.htm

Wade, C., Llewellyn, G., & Mathews, J. (2008). Review of parent training interventions for parents with intellectual disability. *Journal of Applied Research in Intellectual Disabilities, 21*, 351–366.

White, B.A., Graham, M., & Bradford, S. K. (2005). Children of teen parents: Challenges and hope. *Zero to Three, 25*(4), 4–6.

White, L., & Rogers, S.J. (2000). Economic circumstances and family outcomes: A review of the 1990s. *Journal of Marriage and the Family, 62*, 1035–1052.

Young, S., & Hawkins, T. (2006), Special parenting and the combined skills model. *Journal of Applied Research in Intellectual Disabilities, 19*, 346–355.

Zuniga, M.E. (2011). Families with Latino roots. In E.W. Lynch & M.J. Hanson (Eds.), *Developing cross-cultural competence: A guide for working with children and their families* (4th ed., pp. 190–233). Baltimore, MD: Paul H. Brookes Publishing Co.

Cultural, Ethnic, and Linguistic Diversity

Eleanor W. Lynch

"There never were, in the world, two opinions alike, no more than two hairs, or two grains; the most universal quality is diversity."

—Michel de Montaigne (*Les Essais*,1580)

"Every tale can be told in a different way."

—Greek proverb

People may be more alike than different, but much can be learned from their differences. Differences in beliefs, behaviors, languages, viewpoints, and ways of thinking, interacting, and worshiping create both texture and tension in the world. In the early periods of immigration to the United States, many of the new Americans tried to shed the customs of the "old country." They sought a new beginning and worked ceaselessly to fit in, be recognized, and find a place for themselves and their families. In some families, the children of new immigrants moved even further away from their roots, causing breaks with parents and grandparents who felt that their children had lost their cultural anchor. In other families, the children of new immigrants sought to preserve the culture and the language that their parents wanted them to give up. Since the 1600s, immigrants have entered the country now known as the United States bringing new languages, skills, customs, and beliefs. Each group made a unique impact on the emerging nation, including the original people of the nation, the American Indians. The displacement and death suffered by American Indians and the forced immigration during the slave trade are the horror stories of immigration. With those exceptions, immigration has been a hallmark of the United States, making it stronger because of its diversity. Just as woven cloth is stronger than a single thread, so is a nation that has blended the skills, wisdom, and ingenuity of many people to create a whole that is greater than the sum of its parts. Each new immigrant brings something that was not here before—something from which everyone can learn.

No aspects of diversity have received more attention in the past decade than cross-cultural diversity—that is, differences in race, culture, ethnicity, and primary language. With the transformation of the United States from a country with a majority group to a country in which there will soon be no majority, the emphasis on cross-cultural issues is critical. For the wide range of professionals who serve families, this transformation demands new skills that lead toward cultural competence.

THE PATH TOWARD CULTURAL COMPETENCE

Cultural competence is a journey, not a destination. It has been defined in a variety of ways, but the definition used in this book is from Lynch and Hanson (1993, p. 50): "The ability to think, feel, and act in ways that acknowledge, respect, and build on ethnic, [socio]cultural, and linguistic diversity." In this definition, it is assumed that all groups and individuals are diverse, with no group viewed as normative. The definition also acknowledges that sociocultural factors such as education and socioeconomic status are equally (or even more) important than an individual's culture, ethnicity, or race.

So, how do professionals become more culturally competent? Three overlapping and lifelong ways can increase one's ability to be cross-culturally effective: increasing self-awareness; examining the values, beliefs, and behaviors associated with one's own background and cultural heritage; and learning about and understanding others' cultural perspectives (Lynch, 2011). Many individuals in the United States do not consider culture and ethnicity to be critical aspects of their identity. This may be especially true for Anglo-Americans who never struggled with negative treatment based on the color of their skin, their accent, or their place of origin. Therefore, the first step in increasing self-awareness is to explore one's own cultural, ethnic, racial, and religious heritage. The second step is to examine the beliefs, biases, behaviors, customs, and stereotypes associated with that heritage: How do these fit with your own beliefs? Are they familiar or unfamiliar? How do they manifest in your life? This deeper understanding of one's own heritage leads to the next step: learning more about the beliefs, values, behaviors, spiritual practices, and languages associated with other cultures. Finding a cultural guide from another culture who is willing to share his or her life and experiences is perhaps the best way to begin to learn about other cultures and traditions. Participating in events that involve cultural, ethnic, or racial groups other than one's own, such as celebrations, religious services, concerts, or dance, can also provide insight into other ways of being in the world. Reading, film, and theater can also open doors to understanding, as can web sites designed to promote cross-cultural understanding. Engaging in each of these steps with an open heart, an open mind, and a willingness to put aside prejudice is an ideal starting point on a lifelong journey toward greater knowledge, understanding, and the ability to work effectively across cultures.

DEFINING RACIAL, ETHNIC, CULTURAL, AND LINGUISTIC DIVERSITY

A first step in understanding families is to understand the racial, cultural, ethnic, and linguistic underpinnings of their lives. We begin with terms often used to describe these dimensions of diversity. For the past 200 years, physical anthropologists have used race as a way to describe people by their physical characteristics (Bulbeck, Raghaven, & Rayner, 2006; Gollnick & Chinn, 1997, 2009). Early racial categories included the Caucasoid, Mongoloid, and Negroid. When there was little interaction or commerce among people of the world, these racial distinctions may have had some descriptive functions. However, because the classification system was developed by people in the Caucasoid group, the descriptions typically involved comparisons among the races that favored the lighter-skinned people. With intermixing and intermarrying across all geographic boundaries, the original racial groups have blended. In addition, as the Human Genome Project has confirmed, race is not biologically meaningful (U.S. Department of Energy Genome Programs, 2012). No significant difference exists in the genetic makeup of the world's races (Olson, 2001; Royal & Dunston, 2004; Smith & Sapp, 1996). Why is race still important to many people in today's world? The undeniable scientific evidence of our similarities does not erase the centuries of racial stereotyping that attributed beliefs and behaviors to skin color and physical features, nor does it eradicate the centuries of privilege that have enabled some individuals at the expense of others (McIntosh, 1990). The construct of race affects people every day—whether they are aware of it or not—because personal identity and racial identity are inextricably linked. Even though race is not scientifically relevant, it is very socially relevant. Ladson-Billings (1996) argued that grappling with race, racism, and one's own racial identity is central to reducing oppression. Likewise, understanding race, racial identity, and racism are essential to working successfully with families.

Ethnicity has traditionally been defined to include a person's national origin, religion, and race (Gordon, 1964). Racial groups include many ethnic groups. For example, families with Asian heritage may have distant or recent origins in India, Indonesia, China, Japan, Korea, the Philippines, and many other Asian countries. People from each of these countries often speak a different language or dialect, participate in one of many different religions, and observe different traditions for birth, child rearing, death, and healing (Klein & Chen, 2001). Likewise, ethnic groups include members of different races. For example, Latinos as an ethnic group are composed of native peoples, as well as individuals with African, European, and Asian heritage.

Many families can trace their ancestry, and they think of themselves as Cuban, Mexican, African American, Lebanese, American Indian, Australian, Kenyan, Irish, Italian, Chinese, or as having roots in one of the many other countries in the world. Some individuals and families identify with multiple ethnic groups, whereas others may describe themselves as "just American." For some people, ethnic identity may be less relevant than other aspects of their background. They may identify more closely with their gender, sexual orientation, or some other aspect of their life. For example, some individuals within the Deaf community focus on deafness as the most salient characteristic of individual and group identity. For some families, religion is the most potent force in ethnic identity. For example, Orthodox Jews from Israel, Brazil, Russia, and the United States may have more in common with each other than they have with compatriots in their countries of origin. The search for an integrated theory of racial and ethnic identity development and its measurement is an area of interest for many researchers and advocates. As research in this area continues, the understanding of ethnicity and identity will increase.

Culture, often used interchangeably with ethnicity, has been defined in various ways. Benedict spoke of culture as customs, institutions, and ways of thinking:

> No man ever looks at the world with pristine eyes. He sees it edited by a definite set of customs and institutions and ways of thinking. Even in his philosophical probings he cannot go behind these stereotypes; his very concepts of the true and the false will still have reference to particular traditional customs. (1934, p. 2)

Hall put forth one of the most inclusive and most compelling definitions of culture:

> Culture is man's medium; there is not one aspect of human life that is not touched and altered by culture. This means personality, how people express themselves (including shows

of emotion), the way they think, how they move, how problems are solved, how their cities are planned and laid out, how transportation systems function and are organized, as well as how economic and government systems are put together and function. (1976, pp. 16–17)

Some definitions focus on what is known and shared by a group; others emphasize customs or what a group of people finds important and meaningful (Green, 1982). Regardless of the definition that one chooses to use, those who work with families should keep several important points in mind:

1. *Culture is not static; it is dynamic and ever changing.* The cultural practices that individuals remember and practice from their country or place of origin are often different from the practices that are occurring in that same place [today].

2. *Culture, language, ethnicity, and race are not the only determinants of one's values, beliefs, and behaviors.* Socioeconomic status, education level, occupation, personal experience, personality, ability or disability, religious affiliation, and the larger social and political contexts of the time combine to create sociocultural factors that exert a powerful influence over the way individuals view themselves and how families function. . . .

3. *In describing any culture or cultural practice, within-group differences are as great as across-group differences—sometimes greater.* In other words, no cultural, ethnic, linguistic, or racial group is monolithic. Wide variations exist in attitudes, beliefs, and behaviors; for all individuals, beliefs and behaviors change over time. To assume that people who share a common culture or language are alike is to make a dangerous mistake.

4. *Discussions of culture and ethnicity are typically framed in terms of differences in relation to another group.* In the United States, *diversity* all too often is used to refer to individuals who are not Anglo-European Americans. Diversity is relative (Barrera & Corso, 2003). To Anglo-European Americans, Latinos, African Americans, Cambodians, Guatemalans, and Tahitians may be considered diverse; however, to each of these groups, Anglo-Europeans would be diverse. . . .

5. *Everyone is the product of one or more cultures, and everyone has a culture.* Culture is neither something exotic nor something that only others have. One or more cultures help to define each person in the world. Just because one may not be able to articulate his or her culture does not mean that it does not exist. (Lynch, 2011, p. 24)

To begin to understand and serve families effectively, determining, acknowledging, and understanding their cultural identities and practices are important first steps.

DIVERSITY AND DEMOGRAPHICS

If one considers the United States a vast canvas on which we can paint a picture of diversity, statistics from the U.S. Census Bureau would be the broadest brush. Knowing the percentages of people from different cultural, ethnic, racial, and language groups in the United States provides one view of our national diversity. As reported in Chapter 1, data from the 2010 decennial census show that in April 2010, 308.7 million people lived in the United States (Mather, Pollard, & Jacobsen, 2011). White, non-Hispanic Americans accounted for 63.7% of the population, Hispanics/Latinos accounted for 16.2%, African Americans/Blacks accounted for 12.2%, and Asian accounted for 4.7%. American Indian and Alaskan Natives made up approximately 1% of the population and

Native Hawaiian and other Pacific Islanders were less than 1%. Nearly 2% of the population indicated that they were from more than one race (Pew Hispanic Center, 2011).

The United States continues to be a country of immigrants. Since the 1970s, the number of foreign-born Americans has increased, along with an increase in their percentage of the total population. A person who is foreign born is defined as someone who was not a U.S. citizen at birth, although many foreign-born people have become citizens through naturalization. In 1970, 4.7% of the U.S. population was foreign born. By 2009, that percentage had increased to 12.5% (Grieco & Trevelyan, 2010). The largest number of foreign-born Americans (53%) came from countries in Latin America, with Mexico being the most common country of birth. Nearly 28% were born in Asia, with China being the most common country of birth. Almost 13% were from Europe, 4% from Africa, and 3% from other regions, such as Oceania and North America. Although every state includes residents who were not born in the United States, more than half of the foreign-born population lives in just four states: California (9.9 million), New York (4.2 million), Texas (4.0 million), and Florida (3.5 million; Grieco & Trevelyan).

Between 1990 and 2000, the U.S. population grew by 13.2%—the largest increase in history (Perry & Mackun, 2001). Regionally, the West and South had the highest growth rates, but all states grew for the first time in a century (Perry & Mackun). In the decade that followed (2000–2010), growth slowed to 9.7%; this resulted in the slowest growth rate since the Great Depression, which began late in 1929 and lasted through the mid-1940s (El Nasser & Overberg, 2011). The growth that did occur in the first decade of the 21st century was uneven across racial and cultural groups. Based on the current population and these varying rates of growth, the U.S. Census Bureau estimates that the nation's population in 2015 will be 62% white non-Hispanic, 18% Hispanic, 13% African American, 5% Asian, 1% American Indian or Alaska Native, and less than 1% Native Hawaiian and other Pacific Islander (U.S. Census Bureau, 2011). If these projections are correct, the number of individuals with Hispanic heritage will exceed the number of African Americans for the first time in the United States.

Although four states include the greatest number of foreign-born individuals, diversity in the United States is not limited to just a few states and communities. Robust communities of Somali immigrants, for example, exist in such places as Lewiston, Maine; Minneapolis, Minnesota; and San Diego, California. In each wave of immigration, newly arrived individuals and families settle throughout the nation. Often, they find homes near their sponsors, relatives, or other immigrants from their country of origin. In some instances, the availability of work determines where they settle.

The United States has long been a country that offered safe haven to people who leave their home country because of war or oppression. Since 1975, over 3 million individuals entered the United States as refugees (i.e., someone who has fled their country of origin and is unable to return because they have a well-founded fear of persecution; U.S. Citizenship and Immigration Services, 2011). After intensive screening and assessment, those who qualify as refugees are assisted by governmental and nongovernmental agencies to find a place to settle and begin their new life. If family members are already in the United States, new refugees would typically be helped to settle in close proximity. If not, the agencies work to match the needs of the refugees with the resources available in communities across the nation. As a result of this program, many Iraqi refugees who came to the United States between 1983 and 2004 were resettled in Detroit, Chicago, and San Diego (Singer & Wilson, 2007).

LANGUAGE DIVERSITY

The diversity of the United States can also be described in terms of the languages spoken. In both large cities and smaller communities, it is not uncommon to hear a number of different languages. From the 1997–98 school year to the 2008–09 school year, the number of English-language learners in U.S. schools increased by 51%, from 3.5 million to 5.3 million (Education Week, 2011a). In California schools, 50 home languages are spoken (Jepson & de Alth, 2005). Spanish, the most common language, is spoken by 84.5% of English-language learners, followed by Vietnamese (2.3%), Hmong (1.5%), Cantonese (1.5%), and Filipino (1.3%). California is not the only state in which language diversity is an increasingly important feature. Many states have both recent immigrants and long-time residents whose first language is not English. Acknowledgment of the nation's language diversity is becoming more evident as signs, product directions, and public documents are printed in multiple languages; radio and television stations broadcast their messages in Spanish, Chinese, Vietnamese, and a host of other languages; and Americans become aware of the value of a second language.

THE IMPACT OF DIVERSITY ON FAMILIES

The impact of cultural, ethnic, and linguistic diversity is a topic about which there are few generalizations because diversity affects each family and each family member differently. The culture or cultures on which identity is based, the language(s) spoken, and the values, beliefs, and behaviors that are practiced influence each individual's way of thinking, feeling, and interacting. Cultural norms, traditions, and expectations shape each life from before birth through death in subtle and not-so-subtle ways. At a superficial level, events such as holiday celebrations, foods that are served, and the clothing that is worn are all influenced by culture. At more profound levels, beliefs about child rearing, approaches to health care, views about the meaning of life and death, and the values related to family, success, social interaction, social justice, and spirituality are shaped in large measure by deep cultural roots. Within families, children's socialization, the way decisions are made, and who makes those decisions, as well as the way in which power is used or shared, have a profound impact on daily life, aspirations, and opportunities.

Lynch (1998b) has described several cultural continua that represent a range of beliefs about a universal value (see Table 2.1). These continua–interdependence versus independence, nurturance of young children versus independence of young children, time given versus time measured, broadly defined ownership versus specific individual ownership, the importance of harmony versus control–and many other values exist in all known cultures.

However, cultural groups (and individuals within each cultural group) vary in their positions on each of the continua, which results in differences in beliefs and behaviors. Individuals also change their positions on the continua over time based on personal experience, new learning, and life circumstances. As an example, all cultures have beliefs about time and its importance in daily life. In some cultures and for many individuals within it, time as measured by a clock or calendar is of little importance. In other cultures, clocks and calendars are extremely important, and much of life is lived based on specific times and dates. This was clearly illustrated for me when I lived in Indonesia. The concept of time was viewed very differently there than it was viewed in my experience in the United States. In Indonesia, time was freely given rather than parceled out in a predetermined way. Interactions were more often based on the time needed rather than the time allocated. Thus, if a student needed to spend 45 minutes with his or her professor rather than just the allotted 15 minutes, the professor's next obligation would simply begin a half hour later than planned. The words in Bahasa Indonesia used to communicate this flexibility are *jam waktu* ("rubber time"), meaning that time can be stretched or shrunk to accommodate the need at hand, making the clock irrelevant. This view of time contrasts markedly from the United States, where electronic calendars, beeping phones, meeting dates, and scheduled appointments predominate. Neither approach to time is better than the other; they are simply different. However, when two people fall at opposite ends of the time continuum–when one sees time as absolute and the other views time as being flexible–there is likely to be conflict. The same is true for the other continua. Professionals who focus on helping a child achieve independence or individuality may find themselves in conflict with families or family members who emphasize interdependence. This kind of conflict may manifest when an early childhood professional

Table 2.1.   Cultural continua

Extended family and kinship networks	Small unit families with little reliance on the extended families
Interdependence	Individuality
Nurturance of young children	Independence of young children
Time is given	Time is measured
Respect for age, ritual, and tradition	Emphasis on youth, future, and technology
Ownership defined in broad terms	Ownership is individual and specific
Differentiated rights and responsibilities	Equal rights and responsibilities
Harmony	Control

From Lynch, E.W. (1998). Developing cross-cultural competence. In E.W. Lynch & M.J. Hanson (Eds.), *Developing cross-cultural competence: A guide for working with children and their families* (2nd ed., p. 58). Baltimore, MD: Paul H. Brookes Publishing Co.; reprinted by permission.

is encouraging a mother to wean and toilet train her toddler. It may also come into play in later life when family members are being encouraged to "let go" of their young adult by letting him or her live independently or attend college in another city or state. Such separation may seem unthinkable to parents when their older children's families live in the same home or on the same street.

A number of programs from child care to schools to local lending libraries have found themselves at odds with their clients over the ownership continuum. In many cultures, ownership is broadly defined. Relatives, friends, and neighbors share resources with little regard to who purchased the item. In the United States, one of the first words that children learn is *mine,* and this sense of personal ownership continues throughout life. Thus, when a family borrows a toy, book, or compact disc from the library, the expectation from those in charge is that it will be returned. A family, however, who views ownership broadly may pass the item along to someone else and never return it to the library. For the librarian, this is frustrating. Not only does it remove the material from formal circulation, but it depletes the library's resources. The frustration that ensues may result in a very negative image of the family–irresponsible, careless, and untrustworthy–when, in fact, the family was simply operating from a different place on the ownership continuum.

The differences in each family's beliefs and behaviors related to these and other continua influence the impact of diversity on the family and their interactions with others. When family's beliefs and behaviors are closely aligned to those of their associates or professional service providers, the impact is usually minimal. But as differences between a family's beliefs and values and the beliefs and values of others increase, so too does the opportunity for dissonance and conflict. These differences often occur when families and systems interact. The emphasis on procedures, timelines, and specific goals and objectives inherent in most service systems may be at odds with many families' ways of thinking and living. Because the differences in beliefs, behaviors, and life practices vary as much within as between cultural groups, one cannot assume that every individual or family within a cultural group shares the same perspective. However, consideration of the continua can provide a framework for learning more about each family, their values, and the ways in which they act upon those beliefs and values.

Language differences may profoundly affect a family's access to a community and its services because "language is the primary means of access to understanding, relationships, and services" (Lynch, 1998a, p. 32). In the United States, families whose members are English-language learners have fewer opportunities than those who are fluent in English. Imagine that you are just beginning to learn English. Consider how difficult it would be if you had to have an interpreter every time you were trying to find something in a grocery store, speak to your child's teacher, see a physician, or apply for services. Even for families who are fluent in English, the language of service systems is often highly technical and peppered with abbreviations. As a result, linguistic diversity often has a significant impact on a family's daily life, their feelings of acceptance, and the opportunities available to them.

DIVERSITY AND THE SOCIALIZATION OF CHILDREN

In every family, the way in which children are socialized is influenced by cultural and sociocultural norms and traditions. Cultural beliefs and traditions influence whether children are encouraged to be curious or compliant, talkative or quiet, assertive or passive, and reflective or reactive.

The following examples illustrate a wide range of socialization experiences influenced by cultural and sociocultural experiences. Each example is designed to help readers think about the beliefs, values, and experiences that have shaped them and those that shape the families and children with whom they work.

Amy and Marta

Amy and Marta are two newborns who are leaving the hospital with their families for the first time. Amy will go home to a room of her own with a nightlight and teddy bear wallpaper. When she cries, her parents will be attentive up to a point, but they may decide within the first year that sometimes she "just has to cry herself out." Her parents believe in helping children develop their ability to comfort themselves at an early age, individuate, and become more independent.

Marta will eventually share a room with one of her siblings, but for the first 2–3 years of her life she will sleep in her parents' room, often in the bed with them. Whenever she whimpers, cries, or shows any fussiness, she will be held, cuddled, walked, or fed. Her parents are less concerned about independence than interdependence and focus more on nurturance than self-comforting during infancy and early childhood.

Although these very early experiences are mediated by a number of other factors, they will influence each child's behavior. Amy may appear to be more curious and willing to engage with unfamiliar objects and people. Marta may prefer being close to people she knows well and less interested in amusing herself with toys and objects. Such differences are further illustrated in the story of Fernando and Kyle, two boys in the same classroom.

Fernando and Kyle

Fernando's family strongly emphasizes cooperation and the good of the group. Fernando has been taught to think of the group before he thinks of himself, and his home life reflects this value. Kyle's family places a very high value on personal achievement, and he has been raised to be competitive. In their classroom, Fernando and Kyle behave quite differently. Although Fernando almost always knows the answer to the teacher's questions, he is uncomfortable raising his hand because it seems like showing off, especially because he knows correct answers result in praise from the teacher in front of his classmates. Kyle, however, is eager to demonstrate his knowledge and is reinforced by the teacher's praise. From his teacher's point of view, Fernando is shy and nonparticipatory, whereas Kyle is bright and eager. Whether the boys or their teacher are aware of it, the difference in the boys' socialization has shaped their behavior, others' opinions of them, and the opportunities that may come their way.

Linda and Ameetha

Linda was raised to believe that she could do or be anything she wanted to be. Her family encouraged her to play with dolls and trucks, to participate in sports and choir, to attend math camp, and to run for office in various organizations. As an adult, she is running for state senate after 6 years in the state assembly.

Ameetha lived next door to Linda. Her parents were very protective of their daughter. They made sure that her time was spent within the family or with other girls. She deferred to her father and brothers in all decisions, learned how to manage a home and family with skill and grace, and graduated from college. Now Ameetha has two lovely children, takes care of her mother-in-law, teaches a class for girls at their mosque, and contributes her time and talent in support of her husband's role as the mosque's imam. Both Linda and Ameetha are happy that their lives have turned out as they had hoped, and both have lives that were dramatically influenced by their socialization.

Aaron and Greg

Aaron was born 3 months premature and has significant physical disabilities. Soon after his birth, Aaron's parents divorced. From the beginning, Aaron's mother decided to treat Aaron like a typical child. She advocated for Aaron with every school and agency, sought out allies who shared her passion for inclusion, and became a vocal advocate for individuals with disabilities. Last June, Aaron graduated from high school, attended graduation parties, and is enjoying his freshman year at a university approximately 100 miles from home.

Greg also has significant physical disabilities and was brought up by a devoted single mother. Greg's mother felt that one of her primary roles was to protect Greg from a rough-and-tumble world. She sought services that he needed and felt fortunate that he attended a school for children with similar disabilities and participated in activities such as Special Olympics. She was quite devastated when she learned in his freshman year of high school that the sheltered workshop in the community was closing its doors. Since Greg graduated from high school 4 years ago, he has continued to live at home. Most of his day is spent playing computer games and taking an online university course now and then. Although a good community college is nearby and Greg has the cognitive ability and the financial resources to attend, Greg and his mother are afraid for him to venture into that world.

HOW DIVERSITY AFFECTS DAILY LIFE

Although it is difficult to generalize about the impact of diversity on a family or family member, one generalization can be made. When a family's diversity—their culture, race, ethnicity, language, religious beliefs, or sexual preferences—puts them in danger or deprives them of equal access and opportunity, the well-being of the family and its members is in jeopardy. For most individuals and families in the United States, the impact of their culture, ethnicity, and home language appears to be minimal. They go about the tasks of everyday living without thinking about these characteristics or the ways in which they are touched by each of them. For others, these characteristics define who they are and profoundly affect daily interactions with others. More specifically, being white and speaking English significantly enhances the likelihood that individuals will be treated with respect, have their basic needs met, and have more opportunities for material success and advancement. The sections that follow focus on specific areas in which diversity may alter daily life.

Academic Success

According to the Children's Defense Fund (2000, p. 64), "Nearly a half-century after *Brown v. Board of Education* [the U.S. Supreme Court decision that desegregated schools], a student who is Black, Latino, or Native American remains much less likely to succeed in school." Students who are African American are 20% less likely to graduate from high school than their white peers; Latino and American Indian students fare only marginally better (Children's Defense Fund, 2011). Many factors contribute to this disparity, including the differences in school funding from community to community. Studies have shown that schools in which 50% or more of the students are minorities spend slightly more per pupil on average than schools that serve less than 50% minority students (National Center for Educational Statistics, 1996). However, schools with 50% or more minority students typically have less buying power—that is, their dollars do not go as far because they are often located in high-cost, metropolitan areas. In addition, these schools are far more likely to have to pay for additional services, such special programs for low-income students, special education students, and students who are English-language learners. Because school funding is usually dependent to some extent on local property taxes, schools in poorer communities are unable to raise as much money as those in wealthier districts (Education Week, 2011b). Poor schools often have inadequate facilities, materials, and supplies as well as outdated equipment and less-experienced teachers. All too often, these schools serve larger populations of students of color.

Even more insidious than the effect of poverty on achievement is the finding of the landmark report from the College Board National Task Force on Minority High Achievement (1999) that a growing number of teachers have lower expectations for African American, Latino, and American Indian students. School failure frequently leads to dropping out and a continuation of the conditions that lead to poverty. Conversely, the higher the education level attained, the greater the earnings. For example, college graduates earn more than twice as much annually as individuals who have only a high school diploma. Compared to high school dropouts, college graduates earn more than 2.5 times as much annually (Children's Defense Fund, 2011). These differences in income are not transient. Individuals with limited education are disadvantaged throughout their lives. The high school completion rates in 2007–2008 were 61.5% for African American students, 63.5% for Latino/Hispanic students, and 64.2% for American Indian/Alaska Native students, so improvement in educational outcomes and life circumstances continues to be threatened.

These issues cannot be relegated to the problems of poverty alone or the existence of a permanent underclass. The College Board National Task Force on Minority High Achievement (1999) reported another startling finding: Although the number of middle-class African American and Latino students is growing, they are not performing nearly as well academically as their Anglo-American and Asian American middle-class peers. These achievement disparities continue through college, where African American, Latino, and American Indian students earn significantly lower grades than Anglo-American and Asian American students with similar college admissions test scores (College Board National Task Force on Minority High Achievement).

Education is not the only arena in which income disparities may positively or negatively affect daily life. Inadequate housing, lack of access to health care, problems with drug and alcohol addiction, and violent neighborhoods severely undermine the lives of many families. These challenges touch families in all cultural, ethnic, and racial groups; however, people of color—particularly African Americans, Latinos, and American Indians—are disproportionately affected.

Housing

For many individuals and families in the United States, finding a safe place to spend the night has become a daily concern. Homelessness is a critical issue for the 2.5 million people estimated to be homeless in this country (National Alliance to End Homelessness, 2009). Nearly 1 million preschoolers and school-age children were homeless in 2008–2009 (Children's Defense Fund, 2011). This number, however, does not include children whose circumstances prevent them from enrolling in school. Between the 2006–2007 and 2008–2009 school years, the number of school-age homeless children increased by 41% and the number of homeless preschoolers increased by 43% (Children's Defense Fund). African Americans are overrepresented among the homeless, but typically the racial and ethnic composition of homeless people reflects that of the local area.

The bursting of the real estate bubble followed by high rates of long-term unemployment and a recession resulted in many people losing their homes. With these people sometimes unable to afford rent, find support from other family members, or find shelter through charitable organizations, homelessness became widespread for the first time since the Great Depression (National Alliance to End Homelessness, 2009). Unfortunately, projections suggest that without a dramatic change in the nation's economy, the number of people who are homeless will continue to surge. The stereotype of people who are homeless is one of people who sleep on the street, are completely disconnected from the job market, and remain in this situation for years. This stereotype, like all stereotypes, does not accurately portray the homeless population. In fact, homelessness is usually a result of short-term economic descent—the loss of a home, a job, or family support. The recession has put more people on the economic edge, and any unexpected emergency may trigger homelessness (National Alliance to End Homelessness).

Although research on the outcomes of children who are homeless has yielded inconsistent findings (Danseco & Holden, 1998), most agree that being homeless is not optimal for healthy growth and development.

Health Care

In a country with the most technologically advanced health care system, access to affordable health care is a challenge faced by many families. Until 2010, the United States was the only developed nation without a national health care system. The Patient Protection and Affordable Care Act (PL 111-148) for providing health care for all individuals was agreed to, passed by Congress, signed into law, and upheld by the Supreme Court in challenges. The new legislation, which will be phased in over several years, has the potential to provide accessible, affordable health care for all, including low-income families, many of whom are families of color.

As stated in a report by the Children's Defense Fund (2000, p. 26), "To a large extent, health status is still determined by race, language, culture, geography, and economics." Between 2004 and 2006, the infant mortality rate for black infants was 2.3 times higher than for white, non-Hispanic infants; the rates were 1.7 times higher for Asian, Native Hawaiian, and Pacific Islanders and 1.5 times higher for American Indian and Alaska Natives than for white infants (National Partnership for Action to End Health Disparities, 2011). The infant mortality rate for Latino children varies considerably within the Latino population. In 2008, there were 4.5 deaths per 1,000 live births for infants of Central and South American ancestry compared to 8.0 per 1,000 live births for Puerto Rican infants (Federal Interagency Forum on Child and Family Statistics, 2011). Many variables such as education, proximity, transportation, and availability of bilingual providers determine a family's access to health care. Health insurance, however, is the variable that probably has the most significant impact. When children and families are uninsured, they are considerably less likely to receive health care or have positive health outcomes (DHHS, 2011). In 2009, for example, 93% of white, non-Hispanic children were covered by health care at some time during the year compared to 89% of black children and 83% of Latino children (Federal Interagency Forum on Child and Family Statistics).

Racial and ethnic disparities in health are not limited to children. Health concerns continue to be disproportionately distributed throughout adulthood by race and ethnicity. Although death from coronary heart disease has been reduced across all racial and ethnic groups, the mortality rate is higher for African Americans than any other group except Asian American men, who have a higher mortality rate from stroke (National Center for Cultural Competence, 2003). Deaths from cancer are disproportionately high among Latino Americans, but Chinese Americans are five times more likely than individuals from any other group to have liver cancer and Vietnamese American women are five times more likely to have cervical cancer. Diabetes is the seventh leading cause of death in the United States. The likelihood of diabetes is 1.7 times greater for African Americans, 2.0 times greater for Latino Americans, and 2.8 times greater for Alaska Natives and American Indians compared with Anglo-Americans (National Center for Cultural Competence). HIV/AIDS also affects several racial/ethnic groups disproportionately. African Americans accounted for an estimated 44% of new HIV infections in 2009, and Latinos accounted for 20% of new infections in the same year (Centers for Disease Control and Prevention, 2011). When one considers that people of color have less access to affordable and appropriate health care, these statistics are even more sobering. Individuals who have the greatest need for care may not be receiving it.

Drug and alcohol addiction and exposure to neighborhood violence are also more likely for families of color. Issues surrounding these challenges to family functioning and service delivery are discussed in depth in Chapter 6.

Civil Rights and Equality

As long as basic civil rights, equal access, and equal opportunity are not part of each individual's daily experience, some families will continue to be vulnerable. The challenges addressed in the previous section cannot be assumed to be the failures of the families affected. Rather, they are failures of society. Prejudice—both individual and systemic—is at the root of inequality. Until prejudice is no longer a part of the human vocabulary, families and their members will suffer.

THE IMPACT OF DIVERSITY ON SERVICE SYSTEMS

Most service systems were not designed to accommodate the diversity that is common among today's families. Like most businesses, service systems rely on the "typical" consumer and economies of scale to ensure that their already heavy workloads can be managed. Although making service delivery and systems of care culturally competent has been the goal of educational, health, and counseling services for several decades (e.g., Gibbs & Huang, 1989; Hanson, Lynch, & Wayman, 1990; Kalyanpur & Harry, 1999; Lynch & Hanson, 1992, 1998, 2004, 2011; Olds, London, & Wieland Ladewig,

1996; Ponterotto et al., 1995; Wayman, Lynch, & Hanson, 1990), the goal has been difficult to achieve. In some instances, procedures designed to be individualized and responsive to family diversity have become routine in the interests of time. In other situations, administrators and staff do not have the training required to create and maintain culturally competent services that build on family strengths. In addition, culturally competent services may not be recognized as foundational to effective service delivery.

As diversity increases throughout the nation, the need for services for families from diverse cultures, languages, sociocultural backgrounds, and sexual orientations also increases. However, there is a mismatch between the number of service providers and the number of families from diverse backgrounds. Many professional-level service providers are European American. Many of the families with whom they work are not. Although the shortage of human services personnel is great throughout the nation, the shortage of human services professionals from diverse cultural and linguistic backgrounds is even greater. Far more effort needs to be placed on the training, education, recruitment, and retention of professionals from diverse groups. It is not that service providers and those receiving services must be paired by race, language, culture, socioeconomic status, and sexual orientation. However, all service providers should enhance their cross-cultural sensitivity and skills. Also, service systems should work to ensure that their staff members reflect the demographics of the population.

Differences in service utilization between various cultural and racial groups are frequently studied. It is not uncommon to find that families of color are less likely to use health, dental, and early intervention services than their European American counterparts. Potential barriers to utilization were discussed earlier in this chapter, but another barrier is related to the client's comfort with the provider—comfort that goes beyond speaking the same language. Having rapport with the provider and being comfortable with the environment and the bureaucratic procedures associated with the service are also essential to providing services to families from various backgrounds. The accessibility of the professional selected, the client and professional's ability to communicate in a shared language, the availability of information in the preferred language, and the understanding and respect that the professional demonstrates for personal preferences and life circumstances contribute to a client's willingness to use services. For many families of color, low-income families, or English-language learners, services may not seem welcoming—and few go where they do not feel welcome.

The increase in family diversity has significant implications for services and service delivery systems in education, health, and social services. Just as businesses assess consumer needs and preferences and alter their marketing and merchandise to meet evolving needs, so should public service agencies continue to reevaluate their work and their clients.

Each agency and each individual within it has a different level of knowledge, understanding, and competence in relation to culturally competent service delivery, so no single recommendation would be appropriate. A number of service components should be considered when determining where changes may be needed, however. These components, as well as questions and activities to help determine the efficacy of the service delivery being provided, are listed in Table 2.2. They represent a sample of the kinds of questions that agencies, administrators, and staff members can use to evaluate their own systems.

Table 2.2.   Questions and activities to help assess culturally competent service delivery

Staffing
Do the existing staff (including administrators and board members) mirror the diversity of the families served in culture, race, and language?
Have *all* staff members (including administrators and board members) participated in staff development that focused on cultural diversity and cultural competence?
What changes have been made as a result of the training?
What are the outcomes of those changes? What is the evidence for those outcomes?

Service delivery
Is information about the agency available in multiple languages? Is the information available in multiple locations to reach diverse groups? Is the information provided in multiple formats (e.g., brochures, radio or television public service announcements on ethnically focused stations, bilingual/bicultural spokespersons at street fairs)?
Are trained interpreters available whenever needed?
Is there flexibility in location and times of service to match family needs and preferences?
Are different models of service delivery available to match family needs and preferences?
Are services available to meet the unique needs of grandparents, fathers, foster parents, and others in the parenting role?
Where are the sites at which services are provided? Are they accessible to everyone, including those with special needs?
What do service settings look like? Are they clean and well maintained? Do they appear safe? Are there provisions for waiting comfortably, having privacy, and entertaining young children? Do they appear welcoming to diverse groups of families and individuals?
Is there a process for asking families what changes they would like to have made?

Input and evaluation
Does the agency have an advisory group that is representative of the families served?
Does the agency routinely evaluate its services using multiple methods that gather data from diverse groups?
In the past year, what changes have been made in direct response to the advisory group's input? Family input? Community input?

SUMMARY

The nation's demographics paint a colorful picture. The cultural, ethnic, racial, and linguistic diversity among families is increasing throughout the country. The way in which families are organized; their values, beliefs, and behaviors; and what they find meaningful in their lives demand attention and new skills from professionals. Learning about each family's background and life experiences creates a context that professionals can use to better understand the family's perspective—the beliefs and behaviors that they value, their views of health care, spirituality, interpersonal interactions, and the way that they experience the world around them. Understanding these aspects of each family and of the family members within it provides professionals with a framework for developing interventions that are consistent with the family's viewpoints, practices, and preferences. Thus, increasing cross-cultural competence is a critical need within service professions. When working with families, one size does not fit all. Instead, programs and services need to be tailored to fit each family's context. When the match between a family's needs, perspectives, and resources can be made by a service provider, outcomes for children and families will be improved—the ultimate goal of intervention.

ACTIVITIES TO EXTEND THE DISCUSSION

1. **Answer the following questions**. When you have answered the questions, join a small group and share your responses. Consider the range of experiences within the small group.

    • Have you ever lived outside the United States or in another state? Where? For how long? Under what circumstances (e.g., born there, parents worked there, staying with other family members)?

    • Have you ever traveled outside the United States? Where? Under what circumstances (e.g., visiting family, vacationing)?

    • If you have not lived or traveled outside the state or the United States, where is the place that you have been that was most unfamiliar or foreign to you (e.g., a fancy country club, a friend's house where the rules were very different from those of your home)?

    • What did you learn from your experiences that exposed you to a place that was unfamiliar?

    • How did you feel about that experience?

    • If you could go anyplace in the world to learn more about the culture, where would you go? Why?

2. **Participate in an ethnic or cultural event within your own community**. Learn more about the special celebrations, activities, and events in your community that are special to one or more ethnic/cultural/racial groups. Attend the event, activity, or celebration and write a short description of your experience. Include what the event was, why it was important to the particular ethnic/cultural/racial group, and what you learned and how you felt about the experience. You might consider Martin Luther King, Jr. Day celebrations and remembrances, the Chinese Mooncake Festival, the Mexican Day of the Dead, Chinese New Year, Japanese Obon Festival, or any other event in or near your community.

3. **Explore the resources in your community for increasing your own cross-cultural competence**. Locate community organizations that are focused on serving families from diverse backgrounds, attend an event that focuses on one or more cultural or ethnic groups, and learn about the range of religious or spiritually oriented settings in your community that serve diverse groups. Share what you have learned with your classmates.

TO LEARN MORE: SUGGESTED WEB SITES

American Civil Liberties Union
http://www.aclu.org

CLAS: Culturally and Linguistically Appropriate Services
http://clas.uiuc.edu

National Center for Cultural Competence, Georgetown University
http://nccc.georgetown.edu

Southern Poverty Law Center
http://www.splcenter.org

United Nations Documents: Universal Declaration of Cultural Diversity
http://www.un-documents.net/udcd.htm

U.S. Census Bureau: American FactFinder
http://factfinder2.census.gov

REFERENCES

Barrera, I., & Corso, R.M. (2003). *Skilled dialogue: Strategies for responding to cultural diversity in early childhood.* Baltimore, MD: Paul H. Brookes Publishing Co.

Benedict, R. (1934). *Patterns of culture.* Boston, MA: Houghton Mifflin.

Bulbeck, D., Raghaven, P., & Rayner, D. (2006). Races of *Homo sapiens*: If not in the southwest Pacific, then nowhere. *World Archeaology, 38*(1), 109–132.

Centers for Disease Control and Prevention. (2011, August). HIV in the United States: An overview. Retrieved August 3, 2012, from http://www.cdc.gov/hiv/topics/surveillance/resources/factsheets/incidence-overview.htm

Children's Defense Fund. (2000). *The state of America's children: Yearbook 2000.* Washington, DC: Author.

Children's Defense Fund. (2011). *The state of America's children, 2011.* Retrieved November 17, 2011, from http://www.childrensdefense.org/child-research-data-publications/data/state-of-americas-2011.pdf

College Board National Task Force on Minority High Achievement. (1999). *Reaching the top: A report of the national task force on minority high achievement executive summary.* Retrieved November 17, 2011, from http://professionals.collegeboard.com/profdownload/pdf/reachingthe_3952.pdf

Danseco, E.R., & Holden, E.W. (1998). Are there different types of homeless families? A typology of homeless families based on cluster analysis. *Family Relations, 47,* 159–166.

Education Week. (2011a, June 16). *English-language learners.* Retrieved November 7, 2011, from http://www.edweek.org/ew/issues/english-language-learners/

Education Week. (2011b, June 20). *School finance.* Retrieved November 19, 2011, from http://www.edweek.org/ew/issues/school-finance/

El Nasser, H., & Overberg, P. U.S. population growth slowed, still envied. Retrieved November 7, 2011, from http://www.usatoday.com/news/nation/census/2011-01-06-us-population_N.htm

Federal Interagency Forum on Child and Family Statistics. (2011). *America's children: Key indicators of well-being, 2011.* Retrieved July 12, 2012, from http://www.childstats.gov/pdf/ac2011/ac_11.pdf

Gibbs, J.T., & Huang, L.N. (1989). *Children of color: Psychological interventions with minority youth.* San Francisco, CA: Jossey-Bass.

Gollnick, D.M., & Chinn, P.C. (1997). *Multicultural education in a pluralistic society* (4th ed.). Upper Saddle River, NJ: Prentice Hall.

Gollnick, D.M., & Chinn, P.C. (2009). *Multicultural education in a pluralistic society* (8th ed.). Upper Saddle River, NJ: Prentice Hall.

Gordon, M.M. (1964). *Assimilation in American life: The role of race, religion, and national origins.* New York, NY: Oxford University Press

Green, J.W. (1982). *Cultural awareness in the human services.* Upper Saddle River, NJ: Prentice Hall.

Grieco, E.M., & Trevelyan, E.N. (2010). *Place of birth of the foreign-born population: 2009. American Community Survey Briefs.* Retrieved November 7, 2011, from http://www.census.gov/prod/2010pubs/acsbr09-15.pdf

Hall, E.T. (1976). *Beyond culture.* Garden City, NY: Anchor Books.

Hanson, M.J., Lynch, E.W., & Wayman, K.I. (1990). Honoring the cultural diversity of families when gathering data. *Topics in Early Childhood Special Education, 10,* 112–131.

Jepson, C., & de Alth, S. (2005). *English learners in California schools.* San Francisco: Public Policy Institute of California. Retrieved November 7, 2011, from http://www.ppic.org/content/pubs/report/R_405CJR.pdf.

Kalyanpur, M., & Harry, B. (1999). *Culture in special education: Building reciprocal family-professional relationships.* Baltimore, MD: Paul H. Brookes Publishing Co.

Klein, M.D., & Chen, D. (2001). *Working with children from culturally diverse backgrounds.* Albany, NY: Delmar Learning.

Ladson-Billings, G. (1996). "Your blues ain't like mine": Keeping issues of race and racism on the multicultural agenda. *Theory Into Practice, 35*(4), 248–256.

Lee, B.A., Tyler, K.A., & Wright, J.S. (2010). The new homeless revisited. *Annual Review of Sociology, 36,* 501–521. Available from http://www.annual reviews.org

Lynch, E.W. (1998a). Conceptual framework: From culture shock to cultural learning. In E.W. Lynch & M.J. Hanson (Eds.), *Developing cross-cultural competence: A guide for working with children and their families* (2nd ed., pp. 23–45). Baltimore, MD: Paul H. Brookes Publishing Co.

Lynch, E.W. (1998b). Developing cross-cultural competence. In E.W. Lynch & M.J. Hanson (Eds.), *Developing cross-cultural competence: A guide for working with children and their families* (2nd ed., p. 47–86). Baltimore, MD: Paul H. Brookes Publishing Co.

Lynch, E.W. (2011). Developing cross-cultural competence. In E.W. Lynch & M.J. Hanson (Eds.), *Developing cross-cultural competence: A guide for working with children and their families* (4th ed., p. 41–77). Baltimore, MD: Paul H. Brookes Publishing Co.

Lynch, E.W., & Hanson, M.J. (Eds.). (1992). *Developing cross-cultural competence: A guide for working with young children and their families.* Baltimore: Paul H. Brookes.

Lynch, E.W., & Hanson, M.J. (1993). Changing demographics: Implications for training in early intervention. *Infants and Young Children, 6*(1), 50–55.

Lynch, E.W., & Hanson, M.J. (Eds.). (1998). *Developing cross-cultural competence: A guide for working with children and their families* (2nd ed.). Baltimore, MD: Paul H. Brookes Publishing Co.

Lynch, E.W., & Hanson, M.J. (Eds.). (2004). *Developing cross-cultural competence: A guide for working with children and their families* (3rd ed.). Baltimore, MD: Paul H. Brookes Publishing Co.

Lynch, E.W., & Hanson, M.J. (Eds.). (2011). *Developing cross-cultural competence: A guide for working with children and their families* (4th ed.). Baltimore, MD: Paul H. Brookes Publishing Co.

Mather, M., Pollard, K., & Jacobsen, L.A. (2011). *PRB reports on America: First results from the 2010 census.* Retrieved September 9, 2011, from http://www.prb.org/Publications/Reports OnAmerica/2011/census-2010.aspx

McIntosh, P. (1990, Winter). White privilege: Unpacking the invisible knapsack. *Independent School, 49,* 31–36.

Montaigne, M. de. (1580). *Les essais.* Bordeau, France: Simon Millanges.

National Alliance to End Homelessness. (2009). *Homelessness looms as potential outcome of recession.* Retrieved November 17, 2011, from http://www.endhomelessness .org/content/general/detail/2161

National Center for Cultural Competence. (2003). *Policy brief: Rationale for cultural competence in primary care.* Retrieved November 26, 2011, from http://www11.georgetown.edu/ research/gucchd/nccc/documents/Policy _Brief_1_2003.pdf

National Center for Educational Statistics. (1996). *Issue brief: Do districts enrolling high percentages of minority students spend less?* Retrieved November 18, 2011, from http:// nces.ed.gov/pubs/web/97917.asp

National Partnership for Action to End Health Disparities. (2011). *National stakeholder strategy for achieving health equity.* Retrieved November 21, 2011, from http://minority health.hhs.gov/npa/templates/content .aspx?lvl=1&lvlid=33&ID=286

Olds, S.B., London, M.L., & Wieland Ladewig, P. (1996). *Maternal-newborn nursing: A family centered approach* (5th ed.). Boston, MA: Addison-Wesley.

Olson, S. (2001, April). The genetic archaeology of race. *The Atlantic Monthly,* 69–80.

Perry, M.J., & Mackun, P.J. (2001, April). *Census 2000 brief: Population change and distribution 1990 to 2000.* Washington, DC: U.S. Census Bureau.

Pew Hispanic Center. (2011, March). *Census 2010: 50 million Latinos, Hispanics account for more than half of nation's growth in past decade.* Retrieved September 10, 2011, from http://pewhispanic.org/files/reports/140 .pdf

Patient Protection and Affordable Care Act, PL 111-148, 42 U.S.C. §§ 11101 *et seq.*

Ponterotto, J.G., Casas, J.M., Suzuki, L.A., & Alexander, C.M. (Eds.). (1995). *Handbook of multicultural counseling.* Thousand Oaks, CA: Sage Publications.

Royal, C.D.M., & Dunston, G.M. (2004). Changing the paradigm from "race" to human genome variation. *Nature Genetics, 36,* S5–S7.

Singer, A., & Wilson, J.H. (2007, March). *Refugee resettlement in metropolitan America.* Retrieved November 12, 2011, from http:// www.migrationinformation.org/Feature/ display.cfm?id=585

Smith, E., & Sapp, W. (Eds.). (1996). *Plain talk about the Human Genome Project: A Tuskegee University conference on its promise and perils . . . and matters of race.* Tuskegee, AL: Tuskegee University Publications Office.

U.S. Census Bureau. (2011). *Statistical abstract of the United States: 2012.* Retrieved November 7, 2011, from http://www.census.gov/compendia/statab/2012/tables/12s0012.pdf

U.S. Citizenship and Immigration Services. (2011). Refugees and asylum. Retrieved August 3, 2012, from http://www.uscis.gov/

U.S. Department of Energy Genome Programs. (2012). Retrieved August 3, 2012, from http://genomics.energy.gov

U.S. Department of Health & Human Services, Centers for Disease Control and Prevention. (2011). *Health disparities and inequalities report—United States, 2011.* Retrieved November 27, 2011, from http://www.cdc.gov/minorityhealth/CHDIReport.html - CHDIR

Wayman, K.I., Lynch, E.W., & Hanson, M.J. (1990). Home-based early childhood services: Cultural sensitivity in a family systems approach. *Topics in Early Childhood Special Education, 10,* 56–75.

Families in Context

Conceptual Frameworks for Understanding and Supporting Families

Marci J. Hanson

"A family is a circle of caring."

—**Anonymous**

"The family is the association established by nature for the supply of man's everyday wants."
—**Aristotle (as cited in Tripp, 1970, p. 209)**

"Man is a knot, a web, a mesh into which relationships are tied. Only those relationships matter."
—**Antoine de Saint-Exupéry (as cited in Tripp, 1970, p. 536)**

"Call it a clan, call it a network, call it a tribe, call it a family. Whatever you call it, whoever you are, you need one."

—**J. Howard (1978)**

Families come in all shapes and sizes. Regardless of the configuration, the one universal descriptor is that families are diverse in nature. They vary along all dimensions, such as structure and membership, size, beliefs and values, culture, languages spoken, roles and functions, and living arrangements. The concept of family is largely a personal concept. Individuals view their families through their own lenses; members of the same family may offer quite different accounts and perspectives on the workings of their family.

However, families do not exist in a vacuum as a separate unit. Rather, they are embedded in the complex webs of their larger communities, including extended kinship networks, friends, neighbors, work environments, educational organizations, faith communities, and other social networks. Families and the individuals within them influence these communities; in addition, the larger beliefs, values, and practices of these communities affect and define the families within. Service systems and service providers are integral components of these communities, particularly for families whose members experience biological or environmental conditions that affect their abilities to meet individual and family goals and support all family members. The service methods used by practitioners can inhibit a family's ability to function. These practices also can support and enhance the strengths and resources that families can marshal to meet their own needs.

Theoretical and conceptual models provide organizational frameworks for defining the concept of family and understanding how families operate and change. Several key frameworks are highlighted in this chapter because of their influence on the shaping of clinical models of support and services for families: the family systems framework, bio-ecological models, and models of coping and/or adaptation to stress. These frameworks have been applied extensively to the study of families of children with disabilities and risk conditions and have been instructive in identifying and understanding the effect of disability or risk on the family as a whole.

Following this discussion, the transactional model of human development is reviewed in an effort to examine the reciprocal influences within the family context on the development of the individual. This perspective allows one to analyze the more direct influences on the individual's development and the active role of persons in con-structing their own trajectories. The concepts of risk and resilience also are considered to further the understanding of why certain factors and contexts constitute risk for some individuals and families but not for others. Finally, implications for interventions that are designed to support families to function effectively in meeting their own goals and needs are outlined at the close of the chapter. The frameworks selected for these discus-sions focus on emphasizing and enhancing family strengths and resilience.

WHAT IS A FAMILY?

When asked to portray the family with whom she was working for a class assignment, a graduate student responded as follows:

> The family structure . . . reminds me of the days of diagramming sentences. Each clause has its own nouns and verbs, but they all connect to form a complete sentence. What makes this family a complete sentence is the fact that they consider and define themselves as a family.

She continued on to describe this family as including a husband and wife, their children (both from their marriage to each other and from previous marriages), the grandmother (the wife's mother), the grandmother's brother, and the wife's sister and her fiancé. The whole family lived with the grandmother with the exception of the wife's sister and fiancé, who had recently moved out of the home but were considered part of the household. The affiliations among these family members came from blood ties, bonds of marriage, and a shared commitment. Other class members volunteered similar observations; their definitions and descriptions of families varied considerably in terms of the number of people within the family, types of family arrangements, and, in some cases, the formal relationships (e.g., marriage, cohabitation, stepparenting) among the family members. Although these varied descriptions appear to defy the establishment of a common definition, they all contain these common elements of a family: 1) a set of individuals bound together and 2) a shared understanding or commitment to one another among family members.

Many theoreticians and researchers also have attempted to define the core con-cepts that demarcate a family. Individual family members may have strong ties and rela-tionships to individuals in their larger social networks and view them as "like family."

However, White and Klein (2008) identified four features that differentiate families from other social networks, such as friends and coworkers:

1. Families usually last for a longer period of time than other social groups.

2. Families are intergenerational.

3. Relationships among family members include both biological and affinal (e.g., legal) relationships.

4. Relationships among family members link them to a larger kinship network.

Children typically join family units at birth, and the family members in these units constitute the children's caregivers. For most children, entering into and belonging to the family is involuntary. These ties remain in some form over time and link children to a larger network of people (relatives) and family history and traditions (White & Klein, 2008). These features serve to distinguish families from other types of social groups, such as friendship networks. Families may include married partners with children, nonmarried partners with children, single parents with children, adults bound by marriage or other contractual commitments, groups of adults and children living communally, and so forth. Even when a child and his or her parents have all died, relatives such as the child's grandparents may remain bound together in some fashion as a family.

This exercise of attempting to define family underscores the breadth of family possibilities and the range of issues that must be considered by service providers when working with families. Just as the many variations among families must be appreciated, the various contexts in which families reside must be recognized. The functioning and development of the family can be understood only in this broader social context.

CONCEPTUAL MODELS FOR UNDERSTANDING FAMILIES

Several prominent theories and conceptual frameworks have aided the understanding of how families operate and interact within their larger communities. Setting aside the issue of whether these frameworks constitute viable theories, they will be examined as useful models that have greatly influenced ways in which families are viewed and services are construed and implemented. Insights for structuring policies and interventions to support families are derived from these perspectives. Several frameworks are highlighted in this text to explain and interpret the effects of disability and/or risk on the developing child within the family: the family systems model, the bioecological framework, and models of coping and adaptation to stress.

Family Systems Model

The family systems model is one of the predominant theoretical perspectives in family studies and family therapy (Braithwaite & Baxter, 2006; Broderick, 1993; Whitchurch & Constantine, 1993; White & Klein, 2008). This view of the family as an interactive system of individuals also has been advanced as a framework for understanding the roles and relationships among family members as they care for an individual with disabilities or developmental risks (Turnbull, Summers, & Brotherson, 1984; Turnbull & Turnbull, 1990, 1997).

The family systems perspective is based on four fundamental assumptions (White & Klein, 2008). The first assumption is that all parts of the system are interconnected, which implies that all family members are integrally linked with one another. Second, the family as a system only can be understood by viewing it as a whole, rather than in terms of its individual parts or members. In essence, the whole is considered to be greater than the sum of its parts. Third, the family system both affects and is affected by its environment. This notion focuses on feedback—the outputs of the family system and the inputs to that system. The fourth assumption is that the system is not a reality but rather a way of knowing about the family. It is a way of understanding the organization and experiences of families rather than an actual physical phenomenon.

The family is considered, like other social systems, to be a goal-seeking system (Broderick, 1993; White & Klein, 2008). Each family has its own goals and priorities; family members select and mobilize support to meet these objectives. These goals are not static and will be modified as families strive to meet tasks and demands at various points in the life cycle, such as the birth of a child or care for an aging parent. Families likewise differ in the degree to which the individuals within the family jointly define and act together to implement these priorities. Families also are characterized by boundaries that affect their interaction and the flow of information—that is, "permeability" between the family and the outside environment. For instance, families differ markedly in their openness to include or interact with outsiders. All families have their own unwritten internal rules for making changes or transformations and for maintaining and regulating the interactions among family members. Examples include how a husband and wife communicate and treat one another or how parents relate to and discipline their children.

Some families have very rigid rules or codes of behavior for the members (e.g., strict religious beliefs, codes of behavior for how children relate to their elders), whereas others maintain flexible rules and adapt readily to change. Another concept often applied to the systems approach is the notion of equilibrium. Family systems tend to maintain a homeostasis. Like the human body's own internal thermostat, families adjust to inputs or environmental demands to maintain the sense of balance. These practices may govern how the family responds to an outside stress or intervention. Because the family is likened to a system with interacting parts, tremendous variety occurs in the ways in which they adapt to changes and in the feedback loops.

The parts or components of the family also may be understood by an awareness of the subsystems within the family. Subsystems may include the parents, siblings, marital subsystem, parent–child subsystem, extended family members, and so on. An individual's ability to function and meet role obligations in one subsystem (e.g., the parental subsystem) does not necessarily predict one's ability to function comfortably and successfully communicate in another (e.g., the marital subsystem).

A glimpse at the life of Amanda and her parents, Barbara and Roger, will help us examine the family systems model in an attempt to appreciate the complexity of family interactions as well as the many factors that influence families. Through this case study, we enter the life of a couple as they become new parents with their first child.

The Morgan Family

Barbara and Roger Morgan tried for many years to have a child. As time passed and Barbara watched her younger sisters deliver healthy babies, her anxiety about parenthood was amplified. Finally, Barbara and Roger became the parents of a baby girl,

Amanda. Their devotion to Amanda was fueled by their intense desire to have children and Barbara's efforts to become pregnant.

Amanda was born prematurely and experienced a prolonged period of hospitalization after birth. Amanda's difficult delivery and birth experiences necessitated that Barbara take a leave of absence from her job as a nurse at a local university hospital. The round-the-clock care and frequent medical appointments created by Amanda's chronic illnesses and developmental delays became a full-time job for Barbara. The loss of Barbara's income became a source of concern to the family as they struggled to maintain their home mortgage and move from a dual-income to a single-income family. The long hours required by Roger's job were only increased by his need to advance.

The birth of their child also altered the lifestyle that Barbara and Roger had come to expect in their 8 years as a married couple. Their exercise routines, concert going, and outside interests were put on hold as they adapted to having a new baby and meeting her medical and caregiving needs. Family members' and friends' responses to the family's altered circumstances varied. Most were supportive and offered to grocery shop, babysit, and assist when needed. However, several individuals appeared to feel awkward and quit communicating with Barbara and Roger. One friend even suggested that they consider "out-of-home" care for their baby. Although Amanda's birth brought Barbara and Roger tremendous joy and relief at their fulfillment of parenthood, it also brought concerns, lifestyle changes, and new demands.

The family systems model helps us to understand the dynamics of families such as the Morgans. This family is comprised of Barbara, Roger, the new baby Amanda, and extended family members (grandparents, aunts, and uncles). The family's primary subsystems include Amanda and her parents (parent–child), Barbara and Roger together as the marital subsystem, and Barbara and Roger with their parents and other family members (parent–extended family).

As discussed previously, families have boundaries—in other words, their degree of being open or closed to outside influences. Families also differ and have their own rules for operation or change; these rules represent how family members communicate and relate to one another, such as how a husband and wife behave toward one another and make decisions. Barbara and Roger, for instance, were open to adjusting to their new responsibilities by altering their work schedules and commitments, as well as their lifestyles. They were thankful that Barbara's parents could help out occasionally with babysitting and household tasks. Both Barbara and Roger started their marriage as partners who worked outside of the home and shared equally in family responsibilities. Following Amanda's birth, they were able to communicate effectively with one another and adapt (although not without ambivalence and some difficulties) by shifting roles and relationships (e.g., Barbara quit her job to care for Amanda at home). They rearranged their work schedules and outside interests to support the other needs of the family after Amanda's birth. The decreased family income and the increased caregiving demands were counterbalanced by cutbacks in the family's recreational and social activities and expenses.

The family systems approach presupposes that families are influenced by feedback from the outside, such as societal norms to behave or conform in particular ways. In this case, Barbara and Roger responded to the expectations of the medical community and their own parents' judgments about the situation, as well as to feedback from other sources such as their employers and friends. Key important concepts in the family systems model as embodied in this case study are the dynamic and ever-changing influences on the family and family member's interconnectedness and the internal structures that bind them together in responding to these influences.

Application of the Family Systems Approach to Risk/Disability   The family systems approach has been synthesized with special education concepts and applied in work with families of children who are at risk for or have disabilities. Turnbull, Summers, and Brotherson (1984) proposed such a framework, which consists of four components (see Figure 3.1): family characteristics, family interaction, family functions, and family life cycle.

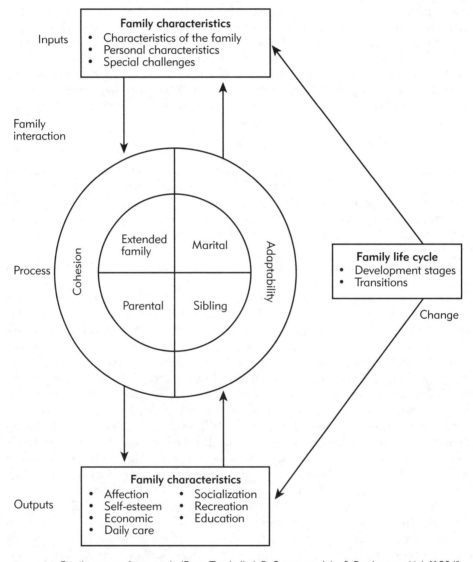

Figure 3.1. Family systems framework. (From Turnbull, A.P., Summers, J.A., & Brotherson, M.J. [1984]. Working with families with disabled members: A family systems approach. Lawrence, KS: RTC/IL, University of Kansas; reprinted by permission.)

Briefly, family characteristics include the personalities of family members, their values and beliefs, cultural background and perspectives, socioeconomic status, disability, health status, and family resources, to name a few. These characteristics are viewed in this schema as input variables into family interaction. The relationships among family members and family subsystems are considered through the component of family interaction. Relationships vary in terms of their adaptability to change in response to stressors or outside influences and also in terms of their cohesiveness (i.e., degree of bonding among members and each member's maintenance of independence within the family). The outputs of family interaction address the fulfillment of family needs through accomplishing family functions. Family functions include meeting economic needs, physical and health care needs, recreation and socialization needs, the need for affection, self-identity needs, and educational/vocational needs. Finally, the family life cycle component addresses the developmental and nondevelopmental changes that affect families over time. These life cycle events may include births, deaths, divorce, change in employment, and change in residence, among others.

Returning to the example of the Morgan family, this framework can be used to understand the family's current roles and relationships. With respect to family characteristics, Barbara and Roger bring to the family their own individual personalities and interests, marital relationship, economic resources and demands, educational backgrounds, and coping styles. Amanda brings her own characteristics, including her personality, temperament, appearance, and developmental challenges and needs. These characteristics or inputs influence the family's interaction and the relationships among members within the various subsystems (e.g., husband–wife, parent–child, extrafamilial subsystem–extended family, others). For instance, these variables have had an impact on the relationship Barbara and Roger have with one another and on the relationships they have with their parents, siblings, and their professional colleagues. These relationships or components of family interaction, in turn, have influenced the family's ability to meet basic needs or functions of the family, such as economic provision, recreational, affectional, social, medical, and so forth.

Although the Morgan family will change as it experiences various transitions and shifts through its family life cycle, this glimpse at life just after Amanda's birth demonstrates the alterations that already have occurred in response to the infant's birth. The family's characteristics are changed by the introduction of a new family member and by the needs of that child. The family's functions are altered in that Barbara must go on leave from her job, and the family's economic resources are reduced although economic demands are increased. The ability to meet these family needs or functions will be determined by interaction variables related to Barbara and Roger's relationship and their relationships with others. This brief example demonstrates the complex interconnections of families and the fact that the family is much more than the sum of its parts.

Implications for Intervention   The family systems model provides a useful focus to both the unit of intervention and to the approach. In this framework, the family is viewed as a whole and members are seen as an interacting unit (Broderick, 1993). Meaningful supports must consider this whole unit and the parts within, in so far as family members affect one another and in turn are affected by outside forces. Simply put, service providers will likely have limited success in implementing any service intervention unless the whole family is considered. This family systems perspective also underscores the recognition of differences among families in their goals, priorities, and means of attaining their objectives, as well as variability in the ways that the family members interact both internally among themselves and as a family with the outside world.

Bioecological Systems Models

Families do not exist as an insular unit. Rather, they are situated within other contexts, such as their communities and the broader societal network. Bioecological models focus on these contexts; emphasis is placed on how individuals and families adapt to changing conditions. White and Klein (2008) outlined the key assumptions of the ecological perspective:

1. Individuals and groups are both biological and social in nature.

2. Humans depend on their environment for survival.

3. Humans are social in nature and depend on others.

4. Human life is finite and time can be seen as both a constraint and a resource.

5. Interactions are spatially organized.

6. Human interaction can be understood at different levels—both at the population level and at the level of the individual.

These tenets underscore the social nature of development and the crucial importance of environmental interactions. The family is typically the primary context for the child's development and that of other members, but this unit is greatly affected by the external contexts with which it interacts.

The ecology of human development postulated by Bronfenbrenner (1979, 1986, 2005) provided an influential model for understanding the relationships between the developing person and the environment. The family is viewed as one component or

ecosystem within the ecological systems described by Bronfenbrenner (1979). This ecological systems framework also provides a model for placing families in the broader context of the ecosystems within which they must interact and the broader social environment. This model is particularly appealing for the study of families of children who have disabilities or are at risk in that it enables one to describe the range of influences on families and the interactions among systems over time (e.g., Beckman, 1996; Bernier & Siegel, 1994; Berry, 1995; Hanson et al., 1998; Kazak, 1989; Odom, 2002; Odom et al., 1996).

Bronfenbrenner (1979) described the ecological environment as a nested set of structures or systems that interact with each another. These structures are the microsystem, mesosystem, exosystem, and macrosystem (see Figure 3.2). Briefly, the microsystem is "a pattern of activities, roles, and interpersonal relations experienced by the developing person in a given setting with particular physical and material characteristics" (Bronfenbrenner, p. 22). For the young child, the family is the primary microsystem. Other microsystems may include child care environments and early education programs. The interrelationships among these microsystems are termed the mesosystem. For young children, these relationships may occur between the home and child care program, home and school, and home and hospital, to name a few. Thus, the mesosystem is a series of microsystems and encompasses the immediate systems with which families and children may interact.

The exosystem level is "one or more settings that do not involve the developing person as an active participant, but in which events occur that affect, or are affected by, what happens in the setting containing the developing person" (Bronfenbrenner,

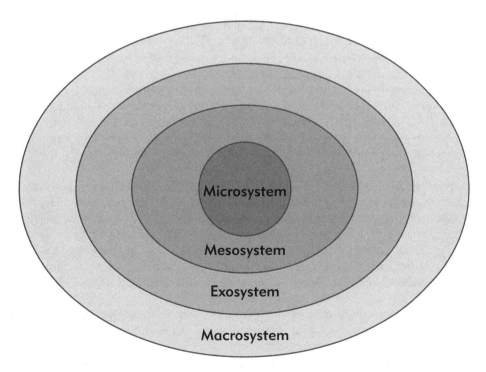

Figure 3.2. Ecological systems framework. (*Source*: Bronfenbrenner, 1979.)

1979, p. 25). Examples for young children include the policies of the child care and education programs and institutions, neighborhoods, families' social networks, parents' employers, and employment policies—all networks outside the family that can have a direct impact on the child and family. At the broader systems level, or macrosystem, are societal and cultural beliefs and values that serve to shape and influence the lower order systems. For the young child, societal and cultural views on childrearing patterns, early education, the meaning of disability, and health and education intervention philosophies and policies (e.g., philosophy of inclusion) all can be found at this macrosystem level.

This model was further expanded to describe the impact of the individual's personal characteristics and the influence of time on development (Bronfenbrenner, 1999, 2005; Bronfenbrenner & Ceci, 1994; Bronfenbrenner & Morris, 1998, 2006). The variable of time can be appreciated both in terms of the effects of the timing of an event on the individual's or family's development and the cumulative effects of an event over time on development. The bioecological systems framework is illustrated through the following discussion of Hwa Hwa and his family.

 ## Hwa Hwa

Hwa Hwa is a 4-year-old boy with Down syndrome who lives with his mother, father, and sister in a city with a large Asian population. The family moved to the United States several years ago from the People's Republic of China. Both of Hwa Hwa's parents work in blue-collar jobs (one works during the day and one works at night) to provide for their family and to meet the high cost of living in this urban area. Hwa Hwa attends a Montessori preschool program; he was one of the children targeted as a good candidate for inclusion because of his friendly personality. One of Hwa Hwa's major developmental needs is speech and language development. Although the program recognizes Hwa Hwa's speech and language needs, and these goals are stipulated on his individualized education program (IEP), the one speech-language pathologist available to the preschool speaks only English and Spanish (the languages spoken by the majority of the children in the program).

The primary microsystem for this child is Hwa Hwa's immediate family. Hwa Hwa's own characteristics (e.g., age, disability, personality) influence his family. His family members also each bring their own personal characteristics of values and beliefs, abilities, personalities, and knowledge and concerns about Hwa Hwa's disability. The other major microsystem at this point in Hwa Hwa's life is his preschool program with its particular philosophy and resources. As he gets older, other microsystems, such as his school and neighborhood, increasingly will come to the fore and exert an impact.

At the mesosystem level, Hwa Hwa's parents interact with his preschool program, his sister's elementary school, and their employers. The preschool program not only welcomes parental involvement but in fact expects it. No one on the staff at the program speaks Cantonese, however. This has a significant negative impact on the communication and relationships between the family and the preschool staff members.

At the exosystem level, several school and employment policies are used to demonstrate this ecological model. The school system that operates the preschool is a strong advocate for inclusion of children with disabilities. Hence, Hwa Hwa is given an opportunity to participate in a neighborhood school with his typically developing peers even though he shows marked developmental delays. The school's lack of employee experience with the Cantonese language, however, affects Hwa Hwa's ability to participate and learn in that environment. Thus, the school's policies and hiring practices have a direct impact on the ability or inability of the program to address or meet Hwa Hwa's developmental and educational needs.

Exosystem issues are evident for the parents as well. Neither parent is allowed time off from his or her job to attend school functions, thus making it difficult for both parents to stay informed regarding the education program and to participate in school activities.

Examined from the broader macrosystem level, this family lives in a community with a large Asian population, and many supports are available to families from this ethnic and linguistic background. Furthermore, the community is known for its liberal policies and support for diverse populations, including people from non–Anglo-European backgrounds and those with disabilities. Although the values and beliefs espoused in the community provide a supportive environment for this family, these beliefs and values have not been enacted for the betterment of the family at the other systems levels through the use of interpreters for the child and family or through involving the parents through culturally appropriate approaches.

This story of Hwa Hwa and his family allows us to examine the interconnections and influences among systems described in this framework. Hwa Hwa and his family are nested within multiple contexts that are interrelated and that exert a profound influence upon one another.

The bioecological systems framework provides a structure for examining and appreciating the broader societal context in which families must function. The family is the primary microsystem for its members. Members are nurtured and cared for in the family home. The family is connected to other microsystems such as schools, community programs, child care programs, and health care systems. These interact with and influence the family and its individual members. These systems, in turn, are influenced by the broader policies and structures of other systems (exosystems), such as the parents' workplace, the medical care system, the education system, and insurance programs, among others.

At the still broader macrosystem level, societal values and policies influence the other priorities, policies, and resources in other systems. Examples include public policies related to diversity (immigration, language supports) and disabilities, including federal legislation pertaining to education and disability rights such as the Individuals with Disabilities Education Act (IDEA) of 1990 (PL 101-476), the Individuals with Disabilities Education Improvement Act of 2004 (PL 108-446), and the Americans with Disabilities Act (ADA) of 1990 (PL 101-336).

Viewing families through the lens of the bioecological systems framework provides a vehicle for examining the multiple and interconnected influences on the family. The family, however, remains the prime context of development particularly for the young child.

Family Niche in Social Systems   Families occupy an important niche in social systems. They are part of a larger kinship network and the family group or system is embedded within the larger ecological culture in which these groups function. The family microculture has been acknowledged and studied as a crucial developmental niche for the child who enters this system with her or his own biological makeup but is influenced by the cultural and social construction of the family environment with its daily routines, activities, priorities, child-rearing practices, beliefs, and caregiver characteristics (Super & Harkness, 1997).

Weisner's (2002, 2005) ecocultural niche perspective expands on the concept developmental niche and focuses on the cultural unit of the family. This ecocultural model is conceptualized around the ways that families interpret meaning and share culture through interactions among caregivers and children in the activities and practices of their everyday routines. This model has been applied to the study of families of children with developmental delays and has been used to examine the ways in which families meet the challenges of these circumstances, accommodate to the needs and demands, and perceive their situations (Gallimore, Weisner, Bernheimer, Guthrie, & Nihira, 1993; Nihira, Weisner, & Bernheimer, 1994; Weisner, Matheson, & Bernheimer, 1996; Weisner, Matheson, Coots, & Bernheimer, 2005).

Implications for Intervention   By the very term *bioecological,* this perspective shines a lens on the family within the larger ecology or context of community and society and reveals the multiple influences upon the family. Emphasis is placed on the interaction of the family unit with the broader world that is construed as dynamic and changing. This perspective also highlights the importance of interactions within families and the cultural influences on family members through family routines and practices, as well as the means by which families address the demands and needs related to risk or disability circumstances. Intervention philosophies and services for families are embedded in these systems in the family's ecology and can exert major influences through the types of services provided and the professional practices implemented.

Adjustment and Adaptation Models for Coping with Stress

The birth or later diagnosis of a child or family member with a disability, illness, or other type of risk condition typically necessitates changes for the family. Most clinical professionals view this change as producing stressful family outcomes. Conceptual models have been proposed for examining families' adaptation and adjustment to these altered life circumstances through the use of coping strategies (Berry & Hardman, 1998; Blacher & Hatton, 2007; Turnbull et al., 1993). These frameworks have been developed to understand the meaning of stress and how it operates in families' lives. Psychological stress has been defined as "a particular relationship between the person and the environment that is appraised by the person as taxing or exceeding his or her resources and endangering his or her well-being" (Lazarus & Folkman, 1984, p. 19). This definition underscores the interaction between personal variables and environmental variables in defining stressors and their impact. It also highlights the importance of the individual's cognitive appraisal of the circumstances.

ABCX Model   A predominant conceptual model designed to understand the impact of stressful events is the ABCX model advanced by Hill (1949, 1958; see Figure 3.3). In this model, factor A refers to the stressor event. Factor A can include both normative stressors (e.g., family adding a new member through the birth of child) and nonnormative stressors (e.g., birth trauma, child's specialized medical needs). Factor B refers to the family resources to meet the stressor, and factor C is the family's appraisal

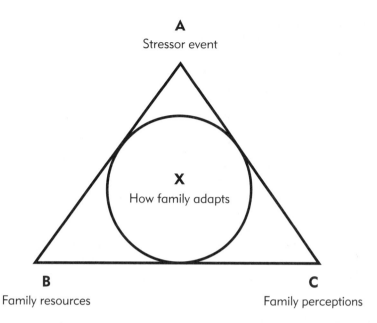

Figure 3.3.   The ABCX model. In this model, factor A (the stressor event) reacts with factor B (the family resources available to meet the stressor) and factor C (the family's appraisal or definition and interpretation of the event) to produce X (the response to the crisis). (*Sources*: Hill, 1949, 1958.)

or definition and interpretation of the event. According to this model, factor C interacts with factors A and B to produce factor X, the family's response to the crisis. To understand how this model is used to look at family adjustments, the example of Judy, Kevin, and their daughter, Samantha, is presented.

Judy and Kevin

Judy and Kevin's second child, Samantha, was born 12 weeks prematurely with the umbilical cord wrapped around her neck. Samantha experienced anoxia and was rushed to the neonatal intensive care unit (NICU) shortly after her birth. Judy and Kevin went home but continued to visit Samantha daily. Judy was able to express milk to bring to her baby and got to hold Samantha in the NICU. Although terrified and saddened by their baby's trauma, Judy and Kevin relied on the support of the professionals and their family and friends, and they longed for the day when they could bring baby Samantha home. This support enabled them to remain confident of Samantha's recovery. The information that they received from professionals also gave them options for services and supports that they could use in the future as needed.

In this case, factor A is the premature and high-risk birth; it includes both normative (birth of a child) and nonnormative (premature birth and illness) stress factors. Factor B, the family's resources, includes the support Judy and Kevin provided each other as well as that given by friends and family who lived close by, good medical care in a facility with a NICU, and sufficient health insurance. Factor C, which is the primary emphasis in this model, is the family's appraisal or interpretation of the stressor event. Because of the supportive resources of the care institutions and family and friends, Judy and Kevin were optimistic about Samantha's future.

Double ABCX Model   McCubbin and Patterson (1982, 1983a, 1983b) expanded the ABCX model in their work with families of children with disabilities and chronic illness. This expanded model is typically called the double ABCX model. In this model, more emphasis is placed on the family's appraisal of the event (the C factor) and also the interactive and additive nature of events. In this expanded model, aA refers to the original stressor and to the pile up of other stresses and strains, and bB denotes the perception of resources. Factor cC alludes to the family's perception of the original stressor event and their appraisal of the demands and their own capacity for managing or meeting these challenges. This model also introduced the concept of sense of coherence (based on Antonovosky, 1979), which refers to the family's ability to balance trust and control (i.e., their ability to know when to trust other authority figures versus when to take charge with their own resources). Consider this model as it relates to the story of Judy and Kevin.

Right before Samantha's birth, Kevin was laid off his job in construction. Judy anticipated that she would not return to her job as a teacher until her children were old enough to go to school. Now she had to consider going back to work to make ends meet for the family. She also worried about Samantha's caregiving because she realized that her daughter might have special needs. The couple's other child, 3-year-old Joshua, had recently been diagnosed with asthma, which had produced new challenges for the family in terms of procuring health services and modifying their home environment to support Joshua's health needs. Thus, Samantha was born into a family that was already grappling with some stressors. Her traumatic birth situation multiplied the concerns of the family (factor aA).

Judy and Kevin sat down and analyzed their situation. They decided that they had enough health insurance to get by and that they could borrow some money from Judy's parents if needed. They also felt comfortable with the medical care and regimen for Joshua. He seemed to have adjusted well to medication and his condition was under control. Kevin met with a friend who promised to help him get a job with another construction company. Both parents recognized the resources they had (factor bB) and planned for how to deploy these resources. They were confident that although times would be tough, they would get through this together and provide the needed care for their children (factor cC). Judy and Kevin felt that they had the abilities and resources to meet the additional challenges that Samantha's condition might produce.

Family Adjustment and Adaptation Response Model   A related model that is useful in understanding families' adjustment to stressors is the Family Adjustment and Adaptation Response model (FAAR; Patterson, 1988, 1989). This model represents an expansion over the previous models in that it examines the family's adaptation and adjustment over time. Thus, the emphasis is placed on the adaptation rather than the stress. Emphasis also is placed on positive, or salutogenic, outcomes. The term *salutogenesis* was coined by Antonovsky (1979, 1993) in his analysis of the study of disease. This term is intended to capture a more constructive orientation to developing healthful (as opposed to disease) states and contrasts with more traditional approaches with a pathogenic orientation to the study of disease.

Like the previous models discussed, the FAAR model stresses the cognitive appraisal or the role of the meanings families assign to events as they shape their responses and adaptation to the crisis. Two different levels of meaning used by families in the adaptation process are considered: situational meanings and global meanings (Patterson, 1988, 1989). Situational meanings include the immediate situation and how a family defines the demands and assesses their capacity to meet them. For instance, the family may have a child who is very sick. Their expectations for how to care for the child, what the child's needs necessitate, and what their resources are all fall into this category. The family's cognitive coping strategies can be used to meet the situational demands. When demands supersede the family's capability to manage them, the family will experience stress. Examples of cognitive coping include recognition of one's self-esteem or efficacy (i.e., knowledge and confidence that one can handle the situation), knowledge that physical resources exist to alleviate the demand (e.g., money, insurance, caregivers), and awareness of characteristics of the individual child and/or parents that may be helpful, such as a responsive or warm personality, assertiveness or perseverance, or the family's ability to work together.

Global meanings, however, transcend the specific situation and refer to a more stable set of beliefs and values. Patterson (1993, p. 227) referred to this as the "family schema." The family schema can be characterized by five dimensions based on the beliefs and meanings reported in research with families of children who were medically fragile.

1. *Shared purpose.* The family has reordered priorities with a greater focus on people and commitment to life.

2. *Collectivity.* The family focuses on working closely together and with others, such as doctors, in meeting the demands of the child.

3. *Frameability.* The family has a new, more optimistic focus or outlook on the characteristics of the child or family as a whole, such as being grateful for what they do have.

4. *Relativism.* Family members feel more tolerant, flexible, and less judgmental.

5. *Shared control.* Parents realize that they have less control over life than they previously thought and often acknowledge a "higher power" in their lives.

The FAAR model includes both the adjustment and the adaptation phases of response. It is in the adjustment phase that the family makes first-order changes in response to the demands (e.g., mother or father takes time off work, couple hires a new caregiver). When the crisis continues, second-order changes are required. During this adaptation phase, the family system is restructured and changes may occur in family roles, functions, or boundaries. For instance, the mother or father may decide to quit employment outside of the home to care for the child. Clearly, this signals a change in family roles and resources.

As families are able to adapt, they may attain a positive perspective of the situation (salutogenesis). Research with families of children who were medically fragile revealed that parents often reported positive aspects of raising their children that included the child's warmth and responsiveness, the tenacity and perseverance of the child (which made the parents want to invest more effort), the family's closeness in pulling together as a unit, the assertiveness skills parents developed and the ability to deal with multiple providers and third-party payers, and the empathy and growth witnessed in their other children (Patterson & Leonard, 1993). These perceptions relate to the situational meanings. At the level of global meanings, family members may believe they are better able to draw from their previous experiences in managing a situation, have confidence in their abilities to be assertive and communicate effectively with other care providers, and are able to amass their resources and supports quickly and effectively (e.g., calling on a neighbor or family member).

The changes that families make in their beliefs and in their behaviors to manage the demands of a disability/illness occur within the "social context of relationships" (Patterson, 1993, p. 235). One can debate whether behavior changes cognitive meanings, cognitive meanings change behavior, or both. Regardless, families of children with disabilities or other special needs may be faced with increased stressors and demands in their lives. These demands by definition can create the need for changes or adjustments. The capacity to change varies across individuals and from family to family. Clearly, not all families have the same resources or the abilities to adapt and thrive. Real limits exist in the degree to which families can change the world in which they live. The emotional reactions of individuals, the behaviors of family members, family members' cognitive beliefs, and the family's external or physical resources all play a role. One can only conclude and appreciate that, in the words of Patterson (1993, p. 236), "Families are complex social units and they vary widely in their adaptive capacities."

Implications for Intervention   Although models aimed at explaining and understanding families' adjustment and adaptation to disability, illness, and risk stem from a view that these factors pose negative sources of stress for families, they have been influential in underscoring the merits of developing systems of support for families. Support has been conceptualized along a broad spectrum from the informal support provided by family, friends, neighbors, and other important persons to the family, to formal systems

of support such as early intervention, social services, psychological services, and health services. Increasingly, this support has been construed as aimed at enhancing family members' self-esteem and sense of efficacy in meeting any challenges of their altered situations.

Summary

Regardless of the framework that is used to understand family dynamics and change, all perspectives share a common focus on the importance of interactions with the environment. Each family member brings his or her own personal characteristics, needs, beliefs, values, and culture to the family, and each family develops its own tacit way of operating. The interactions that family members and the family as a group have with the larger world contribute markedly to shaping the family's practices, outcomes, and trajectory. This malleability can offer a hopeful outlook when families encounter challenges, as all families do.

TRANSACTIONAL MODEL OF DEVELOPMENT

Everything is a transaction; everyone and everything is affecting everyone and everything else (Sameroff, 2009). Contemporary theorists and researchers agree that development is a highly complex process that is influenced by the dynamic interplay between biology and environmental experiences (nature and nurture). Interactions are at the core of this notion. The transactional model helps us to understand these influences and dynamic interactions between biology and experience.

The developmental process is characterized by the mutual reciprocal effects of both the context on the individual and the individual on the context. Although the development of individuals occurs along different pathways, human relationships play an essential role in optimal development and are the building blocks for the development of the young child (Shonkoff & Phillips, 2000). The quality of the home environment and family resources (e.g., basic needs, socioeconomic, psychological and emotional, learning opportunities) exert crucial influences on child development (Shonkoff & Phillips). A strong research base supports the importance of the family context and the active contributions that individuals make to their own development.

The argument for a transactional nature of development was presented in seminal articles by Sameroff (1975) and Sameroff and Chandler (1975). In the latter, these researchers examined developmental outcomes for infants with respect to medical and caregiving risks. This extensive literature review on biological risks and the "continuum of caretaking casualty" (Sameroff & Chandler, p. 218) documented the myriad of risks to the infant from biological problems, including premature delivery and anoxia (i.e., a lack of oxygen delivered to tissue), as well as factors associated with social conditions, such as poor socioeconomic conditions and mothers' physical and mental health. Sameroff and Chandler described and contrasted different developmental models that sought to explain child outcomes according to these factors. They described the main effects model (often called the medical model) that explains development primarily in terms of the individual's constitutional characteristics (e.g., presence of biological damage) or environmental factors (e.g., neglect). In this model, a risk condition (e.g., a birth defect or trauma) is considered to be causally linked as a determinant directly to a developmental outcome. The main effects model was contrasted with models that focus on interactional effects.

A transactional model of development was postulated as the optimal model through which to view development. This transactional model recognizes the "continual and progressive interplay between the organism and its environment" (Sameroff & Chandler, 1975, p. 234) and views the contributions of the individual to his or her own development. In other words, individuals are not viewed as static entities but rather seen as actively engaged in constructing their own worlds. In this sense, the characteristics of a person both transform and are transformed by interactions with the environment. For example, if a baby actively engages her parent by smiling and reaching for her mother's face, the mother will likely feel drawn to the infant and continue the interaction by looking back at the baby, smiling, and talking. Over time, the infant learns how to engage the mother's attention and care and learns to feel secure in that attention, and the mother delights in the baby's responsiveness; these continued interactions will likely foster the baby's competencies in social interaction and communication and also cement the mother's feeling of competence as a parent. For most children and adults, their primary world is their family. Thus, the family and caregiving environments are both affected by the individual family members' characteristics and likewise serve a primary role in shaping their development.

Viewing child and family development through a transactional perspective allows one to understand the complex interactions and transactions that occur. This perspective also guides notions of early intervention goals and focus (Sameroff & Friese, 1990). Using the main effects model, the birth of a baby with biological risks or a genetic anomaly would lead to linear predictions of developmental risks and characteristics. The implications and predictions when using a transactional lens are entirely different and more dynamic. To demonstrate these different explanatory approaches, we will use the example of an individual born with Down syndrome.

Prior to the 1960s, physicians often counseled parents to institutionalize a child with Down syndrome, predicting that the child's developmental prognosis and life expectancy were poor (a viewpoint represented by the main effects model). Today, individuals with Down syndrome attend school, star in television programs, are featured as models in clothing catalogs, work in restaurants and businesses, and write books. What happened? Down syndrome was not cured, and the genetic mysteries that produce Down syndrome have not been solved. Rather, these children and families are given early support that fosters positive transactions. Children now typically begin participating in early intervention regimens in which they are helped to develop more fully and at an advanced rate. These programs foster increased skills whereby children can interact with their environment through more competent and complex communication, exploration, and social interactions. This increased child competence also may affect the parent's own feelings of competence and raise parental expectations for their children's developmental potential. Like an upward spiral, these positive effects lead to positive transactions that, in turn, change the opportunities and expectations in the next phase of development. As individuals with Down syndrome are seen participating in society, the community has more opportunities to develop greater understanding of individuals with Down syndrome and higher expectations for them. As is evident from this example, educational policies, intervention services, and societal expectations can and do enhance the early developmental potential and opportunities of children and their families. Although opportunities are not without bounds or limits, the transactions create a dynamic context for the developing child.

These perspectives are further underscored by research in neuroscience that documents the impact that early experiences (both positive and negative) or the absence of appropriate stimulation has on brain development (Shonkoff & Phillips, 2000; Shore, 1997). Greater understanding of how experience acts on the nervous system to shape early brain growth and development has focused increased attention on identifying the most beneficial learning environments for young children (Bruer & Greenough, 2001). Although these investigations have documented the dynamic interplay between nature and nurture and increased our understanding of brain plasticity, these findings are only beginning to be translated into policy implications and recommendations (Shonkoff & Phillips; Young, 2002).

RISK AND RESILIENCE

Scarcely a day goes by that the news media does not feature a story about risk—children at risk for school failure, toxins released into the environment that constitute health risks, deviant behavior explained in terms of poor parenting, risks of abuse or neglect encountered in an individual's early years, and risks of physical violence in our communities. To be sure, these factors all constitute major risks to human development. As such, it is tempting to focus attention in education, health care, and the social services on what can and does go wrong. However, many things also go right in human development and within families.

What do we mean by the terms *risk* and *resilience?* Researcher Emmy Werner (1990, p. 97) posited the following: "The concepts of resilience and protective factors are the positive counterparts to the constructs of vulnerability (which denotes an individual's susceptibility to a negative outcome) and risk factors (which denote biological or psychosocial hazards that increase the likelihood of a negative developmental outcome)."

In discussing the concept of risk, Rutter (1996, 2000) explained the importance of differentiating between risk indicators and risk mechanisms. Risk indicators are broadly defined variables that are statistically associated with risk. Poverty and homelessness are examples of risk indicators. Although they are strongly associated with risk, these factors do not necessarily in and of themselves create risk for the individuals. Risk mechanisms denote how risk works or the risk process itself that results in the disorder; for instance, a child may be born to a family living below the poverty level and in difficult circumstances (risk indicators). Whether those circumstances lead to actual risks to the individual's development will depend on the risk mechanisms; these mechanisms may include the family's access to medical and health care, the family's extended family and friendship resources, the parent's resourcefulness and support networks, emotional availability of family members, supportive learning opportunities, and other types of resources and supports.

According to Rutter (1996, 2000), the risk process also is greatly influenced by the individual's response to stressors. Each individual responds differently. Rutter cautioned that protection from risk might derive, in some cases, from exposure to risk rather than avoidance of the risk if the individual is able to successfully cope with the event. He likened this process to the effects of inoculations used to build resilience to infections. Some experiences can be seen to have a steeling effect. For example, Rutter observed that, in families growing up in the Great Depression, older children who were given early responsibilities and those who performed these responsibilities successfully fared better in the long run in their capabilities.

Rutter (1996, 2000) also noted that protection from risk is affected by prior experiences and that different factors may operate differently at different periods during the lifespan. For example, experiencing early malnutrition or subnutrition is associated with developing heart disease in later life, whereas being overweight in mid-life increases risk for disease. Rutter (1996, 2000) explained that a particular event might constitute a risk for one person but a protective event for another. For example, adoption usually protects a child from a poor, nonnurturing environment; however, in some cases it may constitute a psychological risk.

Rutter (1996, 2000) highlighted the transactional nature of development by underscoring the need to focus on individualized aspects or experiences rather than broad categories of risk factors. People's characteristics, such as temperament and coping abilities, and attitudes or appraisals of their own abilities, can greatly affect their resilience to risk factors. The importance of an individual's interaction and contribution to his or her own development is evident from this research, as is the importance of the individual's social context in posing risk or providing protection and support.

Families clearly are an important social context for all individuals. A risk condition within the family, such as marital discord or parental mental illness, may exert a profound influence and may affect the members within the family differently, depending on each one's ability to cope with the stressors. Societal influences also can play a major role in supporting both families and the individuals within them.

Several researchers have examined supportive factors, termed *protective mechanisms* by Rutter (1990, 1996) and *protective factors* by Werner (1990). Rutter (1990, 2000) examined different types of protective mechanisms that promote resilient responses to potentially stressful factors. First, he described reducing the risk itself, such as children who are able to distance themselves emotionally from a mentally ill parent or an acrimonious divorce situation. Other examples include parents who avoid drawing a child into a marital conflict, as well as parents who provide adequate parental supervision and monitoring to prevent their children's exposure to or continuance of risk from danger, such as the influence of a negative peer group.

A second protective mechanism was termed by Rutter as preventing or reducing "negative chain reactions" (Rutter, 2000, p. 672). For instance, hostile family exchanges may escalate when hostile comments are made by one of the members. Teaching family members to use humor or other coping strategies to diffuse the situation may lessen the hostility cycles that are likely to occur otherwise. Using effective coping strategies and avoiding damaging coping strategies, such as the use of alcohol or drugs, are other ways family members can reduce negative chain reactions. Third, Rutter described the importance of promoting self-esteem and self-efficacy in individuals. Factors that produce self-esteem and self-efficacy include secure and supportive personal relationships, successful accomplishment of tasks or responsibilities, and the successful use of coping strategies when encountering stresses. Fourth, the act of opening up positive opportunities may be protective, such as in the case of when families with teenagers move to a new town or school and away from high-risk peer groups. Other positive opportunities may include educational and career opportunities, broader choices of relationships with others, and even a change in home environment. Finally, a fifth protective mechanism identified by Rutter is the individual's method of cognitive processing—in other words, how the individual accepts negative experiences and reframes them around positive concepts. Rather than dwelling in denial or deception, the individual with this protective mechanism in place accepts and focuses on the positive aspects of the situation or the experience.

The work of Werner and colleagues (Werner, 1990; Werner, Bierman, & French, 1971; Werner & Smith, 1977, 1989, 1992) also examined risk and protective factors from a transactional perspective. Their core research is based on a landmark longitudinal study of children in Kauai from their prenatal period to adulthood. Findings from this investigation documented that poor developmental outcomes were associated with peri-natal assaults (i.e., difficulties or trauma associated with the birth or delivery), particu-larly when paired with poor environmental conditions. Children who were reared in more favorable environments, however, fared better even if they began life at greater biological risk. Werner and Smith (1992) attempted to identify factors over time that had served as protectors. These general factors (listed from early childhood to later child-hood) include the following:

- Birth order (being first born)

- Activity level (having a high activity level)

- Individual characteristics, such as absence of distressing habits associated with eating and sleeping

- Responsiveness to people

- Ability to display affectionate or cuddly behaviors

- Autonomy

- Positive social orientation

- Advanced self-help skills

- Adequate motor and communication skills

- Strong problem-solving abilities and achievement scores

- Ability to focus attention and control impulses

- Positive self-concept

- High regard for school and future expectations

In addition to individual characteristics, family variables were examined in the Kauai study (Werner & Smith, 1992). The factors that served a protective function were parent's educational level, attention paid to the infant, positive early parent–child relationships, care by other kin, adult coping styles, family coherence demonstrated through shared values, and adult structuring and rule setting at home. Factors outside of the family also served as protective influences, such as the support of other family members, teachers, neighbors, community leaders, and friends. These studies demonstrate the dynamic interplay between the personal characteristics of individuals and families and the broader environment in which they grow and live. Both the immediate family environment and the communities in which families are nested exert a tremendous influence on the children and families.

This research highlights not only areas of influence but also intervention arenas for fostering resilience. The concepts of risk and resilience apply not only to an examination of child development but also to family development and functioning (Singer & Powers, 1993). Families' resilience in adapting to challenges, such as the birth of a child with a disability, has received less attention in the literature than have the risks to family functioning posed by such events. A review of the literature by Patterson (1991) sheds some light on resilience and adaptation in families of children with chronic illnesses. Patterson noted that resilient families

- Maintained their family boundaries and control over their family decisions in the face of interactions with outside forces, such as professionals

- Were able to openly and assertively express feelings and convey communications competently

- Ascribed positive meanings to difficult situations and remained flexible in their roles and tasks

- Demonstrated teamwork within the family and maintained the family as a unit

- Engaged in active problem solving and coping skills

- Maintained social integration through friendships and participation in social networks and activities

- Developed collaborative relationships with professionals

This work identified the importance of the family's responses to demands associated with the illness. Patterson's work also elucidated the importance of a partnership or alliance between family and professionals as the basis for supportive interventions.

IMPLICATIONS FOR SUPPORTIVE INTERVENTIONS FOR FAMILIES

The family support movement has received great attention both nationally and internationally from policy makers and clinicians. Family initiatives also have been brought to the forefront of disability rights and services. These initiatives have raised awareness of the importance of the family as the primary context for children's development. The family unit is now viewed as the major focus of intervention and support services.

Contemporary approaches to family support center on recognizing family strengths and resources. These notions are often in sharp contrast to more traditional approaches or services for families that were characterized by "residualism, professional dominance, and pathology" (Singer & Powers, 1993, p. 4). In other words, supports were traditionally given to a small, residual number of families who were viewed as unable to function without such services (e.g., the traditional welfare system in the United States). Approaches were professionally driven so that families were fitted to the services rather than the reverse. These services were developed around a pathological or problem-oriented approach and interventions were focused on "fixing" families.

The shift in perspective to family support has been applied and expanded to families of children with disabilities (Dunst, Trivette, & Deal, 1988; Singer & Irvin, 1989). Family support is construed in a broader social context and the family unit is recognized as being embedded in other social networks in the ecological framework. Family competencies and capabilities are stressed and the role of professionals has shifted to support, rather than control, over family goals and decisions.

Using a social systems perspective, Dunst, Trivette, and Deal (1994) outlined six principles that reflect this family support philosophy based on views of family competency:

- Enhancement of a sense of community

- Mobilization of resources and support

- Shared responsibility and collaboration

- Protection of family integrity

- Strengthening of family functioning

- Proactive practices in the human services

In this perspective, interventions build on the family's interactions within its community and focus on the resources and informal supports, such as family members and friends, inherent in that family. Interventions are conducted in a manner that enhances families' competencies, recognizes families' values and life ways, and maximizes families' control over decision making and services. This approach allows for a more individualized and flexible system of service delivery that is responsive to the particular needs of families and their cultural and linguistic heritage and preferences. Collaborative partnerships between family members and professionals are at the heart of all interventions delivered in this manner.

This consumer-driven approach to services has been termed a *family-centered approach.* Dunst, Trivette, and Deal (1988, p. 48) identified four essential intervention principles associated with this approach:

1. To promote positive family functioning, focus intervention efforts on "family-identified needs, aspirations, and personal projects."

2. To meet the needs identified by the family, capitalize on family strengths and capabilities as they mobilize their needed resources.

3. To ensure that the family obtains resources to meet their needs, emphasize strengthening existing social support networks and identifying other potential sources of information and assistance.

4. To enhance the family's ability to become self-sustaining in meeting their needs, use helping behaviors that promote the family's ability to gain and use its own competencies and skills to obtain needed resources.

These principles not only provide the nexus of a philosophy of service delivery, but they also offer direct benchmarks for practice. Service providers can examine their own methods and approaches to serving children and families by reflecting on these principles. The story of Kasheen and his family illustrates these principles of family support.

Kasheen

Kasheen was adopted when he was 6 months old, and his parents later discovered that he had been born early and prenatally addicted to drugs. The first years were difficult for his parents as they adapted their home to provide a calming and consistent environment for Kasheen, who was easily excited and difficult to console. At first, they were barely able to leave home without him crying intensely, but over time they were able to participate in neighborhood and family events. Kasheen was able to attend a preschool program at their church when he turned 3. A special education consultant for the school district provided on-site consultation for children with developmental delays. Given his delays in communication and in meeting cognitive developmental milestones, Kasheen qualified for services. Then, suddenly, when Kasheen was only 3½ years old, his father died of a heart attack. At that point, Kasheen and his mother, Nonda, moved in with Nonda's mother to save money on rent, allowing Nonda to have supportive child care when she was at work during the day.

Kasheen's grandmother became a tremendous source of support for both Nonda and Kasheen. Nonda's two sisters, her brother, and their families also lived in nearby communities, and the whole family and neighbors chipped in to provide child care and to take Kasheen to and from school and other appointments.

Now, Kasheen is 6 years old and attends his neighborhood kindergarten. During the early months of the school year, his teachers requested that Kasheen be tested for learning disabilities because of his inability to master early literacy concepts and difficulties following directions and focusing his attention. His teachers reported that even during recess, Kasheen shifted from activity to activity and playmate to playmate without sustaining attention in any one place. The kindergarten teachers were convinced that Kasheen "had learning problems." Nonda followed through with these recommendations, at which point Kasheen was identified as having attention-deficit/hyperactivity disorder (ADHD). The teachers believe that their suspicions were confirmed by the educational psychologist's diagnosis.

Although Nonda welcomed the assessment to learn more about Kasheen's needs, she has found it demoralizing to be told that Kasheen will always have "problems" and that she should ensure that he has a male role model integrally involved in his life. She feels like she is doing the best that she can. This diagnosis came as a blow to Nonda on top of the previous disappointments and challenges that she has experienced.

What types of support have Nonda and Kasheen needed throughout Kasheen's lifetime? What service approaches have and have not been helpful? First, when Nonda and her husband adopted Kasheen, they were faced with caregiving challenges (e.g., crying, inconsolability) that they had not anticipated. Nonda reported that their strong marital foundation and the support of their own families helped them to meet Kasheen's needs. The teachers and other service providers in the preschool early intervention program and preschool helped Nonda by providing her with practical tips and educational information for supporting Kasheen's development at home. They made home visits and actively included Kasheen's grandmother in all planning and delivery of services.

The family also benefited from participating in early intervention services during which teachers and an occupational therapist provided them with information on how to hold and feed Kasheen and how to structure their home environment so that they would be less likely to overtax his senses. Nonda felt less professional support when Kasheen was in kindergarten, however.

If this family is viewed through the lens of the service provider as "the expert" and dispenser of services to individuals in need, one may see a single parent, a child without a father, a child with learning difficulties, and other risk conditions. If one views the family through a different lens that is based on a family-centered approach, different phenomena become apparent. Through this lens, one can see that Nonda and Kasheen have many strengths and resources. Kasheen is able to participate in his local school program and make friends. Nonda is employed and able to support her family. She is also quite capable of gaining access to community resources and services for Kasheen. Furthermore, the family has a tremendously close network of family and friends who are an active and integral part of their lives. Nonda also relies on spiritual guidance from her faith and her faith community. She is confident in that guidance and in her own abilities to see the family through whatever challenges they may encounter. Those teachers, therapists, and other service providers who acknowledged these strengths were able to provide the most support for Nonda and Kasheen. They answered Nonda's questions, provided the specific technical information that she requested to manage and address Kasheen's needs, and helped her to obtain information on school programs in her area. They also told Nonda about a parent-to-parent support network in her community for parents of children with similar needs. Nonda has found this to be another valuable resource for child-rearing tips as well as an avenue to broaden her own friendships.

SUMMARY

When viewing families from various perspectives, the choice is not unlike that posed in the old cliché of viewing the cup as either half empty or half full. Each view leads to a different approach to our lives and/or our work. The approach advocated in this text is to examine the many possibilities for supporting families to fulfill their roles as primary contexts for growth and nurturance for each individual within the family.

The conceptual frameworks for understanding families described in this chapter all illuminate the complex nature of human development and the ever-changing environments in which the individuals and families reside. These models emphasize both the contributions of individuals' characteristics and environmental factors in transforming one another through this dynamic interplay. Although the challenges families may face pose a complex array of service needs, these notions of development also render a wealth of opportunities for change and growth through the provision of resources and supports.

ACTIVITIES TO EXTEND THE DISCUSSION

1. **Describe your family system.** Sketch out the family system for your own family. Identify the family members. What are the subsystems within your family? What are the roles played by family members? Are some roles preferred or easier to play than others? Do these roles ever conflict or seem out of balance? Can you identify some of the unwritten rules that govern the way your family members interact with one another (e.g., which family members make the primary decisions about discipline and child-rearing practices)?

2. **Draw an ecological map of your own family or a family with whom you work.** Describe the major influences at the microsystem, mesosystem, exosystem, and macrosystem levels. Around what individual or family issues do these systems connect or overlap?

3. **Think of a character in a book, movie, or television program that you would describe as resilient.** What characteristics of that individual led you to that conclusion?

4. **Provide an example of the transactional model of development.** Identify a child and family with whom you work. How does the transactional model explain some developmental shift or milestone in the child and family, such as the child being accepted into a local preschool? Use a concrete example and sketch out the direction of influences.

REFERENCES

Americans with Disabilities Act (ADA) of 1990, PL 101-336, 42 U.S.C. §§ 12101 *et seq.*

Antonovsky, A. (1979). *Health, stress and coping.* San Francisco, CA: Jossey-Bass.

Antonovsky, A. (1993). The implications of salutogenesis: An outsider's view. In A.P. Turnbull, J.M. Patterson, S.K. Behr, D.L. Murphy, J.G. Marquis, & M.J. Blue-Banning (Eds.), *Cognitive coping, families, and disability* (pp. 111–122). Baltimore, MD: Paul H. Brookes Publishing Co.

Beckman, P. (Ed.). (1996). *Strategies for working with families of young children with disabilities.* Baltimore, MD: Paul H. Brookes Publishing Co.

Bernier, J.C., & Siegel, D.H. (1994). Attention-deficit hyperactive disorder: A family and ecological systems perspective. *Families in Society, 75,* 142–150.

Berry, J.O. (1995). Families and deinstitutionalization: An application of Bronfenbrenner's social ecology model. *Journal of Counseling and Development, 73,* 379–383.

Berry, J.O., & Hardman, M.L. (1998). *Lifespan perspectives on the family and disability.* Boston, MA: Allyn & Bacon.

Blacher, J., & Hatton, C. (2007). Families in context. In S.L. Odom, R.H. Horner, M.E. Snell, and J. Blacher (Eds.), *Handbook of developmental disabilities* (pp. 531–551). New York, NY: Guilford Press.

Braithwaite, D. O., & Baxter, L.A. (Eds.) (2006). *Engaging theories in family communication: multiple perspectives.* Thousand Oaks, CA: Sage Publications.

Broderick, C.B. (1993). *Understanding family process: Basics of family systems theory.* Thousand Oaks, CA: Sage Publications.

Bronfenbrenner, U. (1979). *The ecology of human development.* Cambridge, MA: Harvard University Press.

Bronfenbrenner, U. (1986). Ecology of the family as a context for human development research perspectives. *Developmental Psychology, 22,* 723–742.

Bronfenbrenner, U. (1999). Environments in developmental perspective: Theoretical and operational models. In S.L. Friedman & T.D. Wachs (Eds.), *Measuring environment across the life span: Emerging methods and concepts* (pp. 3–28). Washington, DC: American Psychological Association Press.

Bronfenbrenner, U. (2005). *Making human beings human: Bioecological perspective in human development.* Thousand Oaks, CA: Sage Publications.

Bronfenbrenner, U., & Ceci, S. (1994). Nature-nurture reconceptualized: A bioecological model. *Psychological Review, 101,* 568–586.

Bronfenbrenner, U., & Morris, P. (1998). The ecology of developmental processes. In R. Lerner (Ed.), *Handbook of child psychology: Vol. I: Theoretical models of human development* (5th ed., pp. 993–1028). New York, NY: Wiley.

Bronfenbrenner, U., & Morris, P.A. (2006). The bioecological model of human development. In R. Lerner (Ed.), *Handbook of child psychology: Vol. 1, Theoretical models of human development* (6th ed., pp. 793–828). Hoboken, NJ: Wiley.

Bruer, J.T., & Greenough, W.T. (2001). The subtle science of how experience affects the brain. In D.B. Bailey, Jr., J.T. Bruer, F.J. Symons, & J.W. Lichtman (Eds.), *Critical thinking about critical periods* (pp. 209–232). Baltimore, MD: Paul H. Brookes Publishing Co.

Dunst, C.J., Trivette, C.M., & Deal, A.G. (1988). *Enabling and empowering families: Principles and guidelines for practice.* Cambridge, MA: Brookline Books.

Dunst, C.J., Trivette, C.M., & Deal, A.G. (1994). *Supporting and strengthening families: Methods, strategies and practices.* Cambridge, MA: Brookline Books.

Gallimore, R., Weisner, T., Bernheimer, L., Guthrie, D., & Nihira, K. (1993). Family responses to young children with developmental delays: Accommodation activity in ecological and cultural context. *American Journal on Mental Retardation, 98,* 185–206.

Hanson, M.J., Wolfberg, P., Zercher, C., Morgan, M., Gutierrez, S., Barnwell, D., et al. (1998). The culture of inclusion: Recognizing diversity at multiple levels. *Early Childhood Research Quarterly, 13*(1), 185–209.

Hill, R. (1949). *Families under stress.* New York, NY: Harper.

Hill, R. (1958). Generic features of families under stress. *Social Casework, 49,* 139–150.

Howard, J. (1978). *Families.* Retrieved April 14, 2012, from http://www.quotationspage.com/quotes/Jane_Howard

Individuals with Disabilities Education Act (IDEA) of 1990, PL 101-476, 20 U.S.C. §§ 1400 *et seq.*

Individuals with Disabilities Education Improvement Act of 2004, PL 108-446, U.S.C. §§ 1400 *et seq.*

Kazak, A. (1989). Families of chronically ill children: A systems and social-ecological model of adaptation and challenge. *Journal of Consulting and Clinical Psychology, 57,* 25–30.

Lazarus, R., & Folkman, S. (1984). *Stress, appraisal, and coping.* New York, NY: Springer.

McCubbin, H.I., & Patterson, J.M. (1982). Family adaptation to crises. In H.I. McCubbin, A.E. Cauble, & J.M. Patterson (Eds.), *Family stress, coping and social support* (pp. 26–470). Springfield, IL: Charles C. Thomas.

McCubbin, H.I., & Patterson, J.M. (1983a). Family stress and adaptation to crises: A double ABCX model of family behavior. In D. Olson & B. Miller (Eds.), *Family studies review yearbook* (pp. 87–106). Beverly Hills, CA: Sage Publications.

McCubbin, H.I., & Patterson, J.M. (1983b). The family stress process: The double ABCX model of family adjustment and adaptation. *Marriage and Family Review, 6,* 7–37.

Nihira, K., Weisner, T., & Bernheimer, L. (1994). Ecocultural assessment in families of children with developmental delays: Construct and concurrent validities. *American Journal on Mental Retardation, 98,* 551–566.

Odom, S.L. (Ed.). (2002). *Widening the circle: Including the child with disabilities in preschool programs.* New York, NY: Teachers College Press.

Odom, S.L., Peck, C.A., Hanson, M.J., Beckman, P.J., Kaiser, A.P., Lieber, J., et al. (1996).

Inclusion at the preschool level: An ecological systems analysis. *Social Policy Report: Society for Research in Child Development, 10*(2 & 3), 18–30.

Patterson, J.M. (1988). Families experiencing stress. The Family Adjustment and Adaptation Response Model. *Family Systems Medicine, 6*(2), 202–237.

Patterson, J.M. (1989). A family stress model: The Family Adjustment and Adaptation Response. In C. Ramsey (Ed.), *The science of family medicine* (pp. 95–117). New York: Guilford Press.

Patterson, J.M. (1991). Family resilience to the challenge of a child's disability. *Pediatric Annals, 20,* 491–499.

Patterson, J.M. (1993). The role of family meanings in adaptation to chronic illness and disability. In A. Turnbull, J. Patterson, S. Behr, D. Murphy, J. Marquis, & M. Blue-Banning (Eds.), *Cognitive coping, families, and disability* (pp. 221–238). Baltimore, MD: Paul H. Brookes Publishing Co.

Rutter, M. (1990). Psychosocial resilience and protective mechanisms. In J. Rolf, A. Masten, D. Cicchetti, D. Nuechterlein, & S. Weintraub (Eds.), *Risk and protective factors in the development of psychopathology* (pp. 181–214). New York: Cambridge University Press.

Rutter, M. (1996). Psychosocial adversity: Risk, resilience, and recovery. Keynote address published in *Making a difference for children, families and communities: Partnerships among researchers, practitioners and policymakers.* Washington, DC: Department of Health and Human Services.

Rutter, M. (2000). Resilience reconsidered: Conceptual considerations, empirical findings, and policy implications. In J.P. Shonkoff & S.J. Meisels (Eds.), *Handbook of early intervention* (2nd ed., pp. 651–682). New York, NY: Cambridge University Press.

Sameroff, A. (1975). Early influences on development: Fact or fancy? *Merrill-Palmer Quarterly, 21,* 267–294.

Sameroff, A. (Ed.) (2009). *The transactional model of development: How children and contexts shape each other.* Washington, DC: American Psychological Association.

Sameroff, A.J., & Chandler, M. (1975). Reproductive risk and the continuum of care taking casualty. In F.D. Horowitz (Ed.), *Review of child development research: Vol. 4* (pp. 187–244). Chicago, IL: University of Chicago Press.

Sameroff, A.J., & Friese, B.H. (1990). Transactional regulation and early intervention. In S.J. Meisels & J.P. Shonkoff (Eds.), *Handbook*

of early childhood intervention (pp. 119–149). New York, NY: Cambridge University Press.

Shonkoff, J.P., & Phillips, D.A. (Eds.). (2000). *From neurons to neighborhoods: The science of early childhood development.* Washington, DC: National Academies Press.

Shore, R. (1997). *Rethinking the brain: New insights into early development.* New York, NY: Families and Work Institute.

Singer, G.H.S., & Irvin, L.K. (1989). *Support for caregiving families: Enabling positive adaptation to disability.* Baltimore, MD: Paul H. Brookes Publishing Co.

Singer, G.H.S., & Powers, L.E. (Eds.). (1993). *Families, disability, and empowerment: Active coping skills and strategies for family intervention.* Baltimore, MD: Paul H. Brookes Publishing Co.

Super, C., & Harkness, S. (1997). The cultural structuring of child development. In J.W. Berry, P. Dasen, & T.S. Saraswathi (Eds.), *Handbook of cross-cultural psychology, Vol. 2: Basic process and human development* (pp. 1–39). Boston, MA: Allyn & Bacon.

Tripp, R.T. (1970). *The international thesaurus of quotations.* New York, NY: Thomas Y. Crowell.

Turnbull, A.P., Patterson, J.M., Behr, S.K., Murphy, D.L., Marquis, J.G., & Blue-Banning, M.J. (Eds.) (1993). *Cognitive coping, families, and disability.* Baltimore, MD: Paul H. Brookes Publishing Co.

Turnbull, A.P., Summers, J.A., & Brotherson, M.J. (1984). *Working with families with disabled members: A family systems approach.* Lawrence, KS: The University of Kansas.

Turnbull, A.P., & Turnbull, H.R. (1990). *Families, professionals, and exceptionality: A special partnership* (2nd ed.). Columbus, OH: Charles E. Merrill.

Turnbull, A.P., & Turnbull, H.R. (1997). *Families, professionals, and exceptionality: A special partnership* (3rd ed.). Columbus, OH: Charles E. Merrill.

Weisner, T. (2002). Ecological understanding of children's developmental pathways. *Human Development, 174,* 275–281.

Weisner, T. (Ed.) (2005). *Discovering successful pathways in children's development.* Chicago, IL: The University of Chicago Press.

Weisner, T., Matheson, C., Coots, J., & Bernheimer, L. (2005). Sustainability of routines as a family outcome. In A.E. Maynard & M.I. Martini (Eds.), *Learning in cultural context* (pp. 41–73). New York, NY: Kluwer Academic.

Weisner, T., Matheson, C., & Bernheimer, L. (1996). American cultural models of early influence and parent recognition of developmental delays: Is earlier always better than later? In S. Harkness & C.M. Super (Eds.), *Parents' cultural belief systems: Their origins, expressions, and consequences* (pp. 496–532). New York, NY: Guilford Press.

Werner, E.E. (1990). Protective factors and individual resilience. In S.J. Meisels & J.P. Shonkoff (Eds.), *Handbook of early childhood intervention* (pp. 97–116). New York, NY: Cambridge University Press.

Werner, E.E., Bierman, J.M., & French, F.E. (1971). *The children of Kauai: A longitudinal study from the prenatal period to age ten.* Honolulu, HI: University of Hawaii Press.

Werner, E.E., & Smith, R.S. (1977). *Kauai's children come of age.* Honolulu, HI: University of Hawaii Press.

Werner, E.E., & Smith, R.S. (1989). *Vulnerable but invincible: A longitudinal study of resilient children and youth.* New York, NY: McGraw-Hill.

Werner, E.E., & Smith, R.S. (1992). *Overcoming the odds: High risk children from birth to adulthood.* Ithaca, NY: Cornell University Press.

Whitchurch, G., & Constantine, L. (1993). Systems theory. In P. Boss, W. Doherty, R. LaRossa, W. Schumm, & S. Steinmetz (Eds.), *Sourcebook of family theories and methods: A contextual approach* (pp. 325–352). New York, NY: Plenum.

White, J.M., & Klein, D.M. (2008). *Family theories* (3rd ed.). Thousand Oaks, CA: Sage Publications.

Young, M.E. (Ed.). (2002). *From early child development to human development: Investing in our children's future.* Washington, DC: The World Bank.

4

Traditional and Evolving Family Roles and Functions

Eleanor W. Lynch

"Things hold. Lines connect in ways that last and last and lives become generations made out of pictures and words just kept."

—Lucille Clifton (as cited in Mullane, 1995, p. 85)

"If the family were a container, it would be a nest, an enduring nest, loosely woven, expansive, and open. If the family were a fruit, it would be an orange, a circle of sections, held together but separable— each segment distinct. If the family were a boat, it would be a canoe that makes no progress unless everyone paddles. If the family were a sport, it would be baseball: a long, slow, nonviolent game that is never over until the last out. If the family were a building, it would be an old but solid structure that contains human history, and appeals to those who see the carved moldings under all the plaster, the wide plank floors under the linoleum, the possibilities."

—Letty Cottin Pogrebin (1983, pp. 25–26)

"The family is resilient, flexible, a survivor. It could probably flourish (and has certainly shown in the past that it can) without the wider society. But if we erode the role of the family, can the wider society flourish?"

—Jo Boyden (1993, p. 23)

What do families do? Why are families important? How have the roles and responsibilities of families changed over time? These are complex questions with no short answers, but this chapter provides a discussion of these issues, as well as their implications for families that include members with disabilities and the professionals who provide services to families. Readers of this chapter may want to consider their own families as a backdrop to the discussion. Did the family you grew up in differ from the family you live with today? How was it different? Do family members have different roles or different responsibilities? How did these changes occur? Were they planned, or did they just happen? Reflecting on the individual, political, and societal influences that have shaped our own families provides a perspective for considering the challenges and changes that families encounter as they evolve.

EVOLVING FAMILY ROLES AND RESPONSIBILITIES

The first question in this chapter was, "What do families do?" The short answer is that they do a lot, which may seem obvious. Consider the myriad things that family members do to survive physically and economically, provide nurturance and guidance, support one another psychologically, relax and play together, and find meaning in life. It is no wonder that families feel stressed. In the United States and throughout the world, families serve multiple functions and are responsible for providing for their members in a multitude of ways.

At the same time that families struggle with meeting their responsibilities, the roles and functions ascribed to families are evolving. This evolution of expectations and aspirations can make family life seem like being on a ship tossed by the waves. Just when comfort and stability are achieved, another wave hits, causing disorientation, loss of balance, and effort and energy to once again find equilibrium. Occupational, social, political, and economic changes have contributed to this evolution, as have industrialization and technological advances. For example, in 1969, 43% of U.S. women worked outside the home; in 2009, 59% of working-age women were in the labor force (Bureau of Labor Statistics, 2011a). Only a handful of countries, such as Canada and Sweden, have as many women in the labor force as the United States, and these figures are expected to increase. Between 1998 and 2018, the percentage of women in the civilian labor force is expected to increase by 9%. The greatest increase (89.8%) is projected to be among women between 65 and 74 years of age, with the second highest increase (61.4%) among women 75 years and older. Over that same period, the numbers of 16- to 19-year-old and 35- to 50-year-old women in the labor force are projected to decrease (Bureau of Labor Statistics, 2011a).

Other figures related to women in the labor force present a more detailed picture that relates to family roles, responsibilities, and routines. In 2010, 70.8% of all mothers with children between 6 and 18 years of age were working or looking for work, slightly below the percentage in 2009 of 71.4%. In 2010, 63.9% of women with a child younger than 6 years participated in the labor force, and 56.5% of women with a child younger than 12 months were in the labor force (Bureau of Labor Statistics, 2011b). Although the percentage of women with children in the labor force has declined slightly in the past several years in these categories, the data show that more than half of women with children work full or part time. Marital status, socioeconomic factors, ethnicity, and educational level all contribute to whether mothers work or remain at home with their children, but there are working mothers representing all life circumstances. As women enter or advance in the work force, their roles and responsibilities increase. The whole family may need to change to accommodate work hours and demands, travel, new child care arrangements, and sometimes relocation. Fathers may expand their domestic and parenting roles to include more time for working in the home, caring for children, or managing the daily activities that keep homes and families running; other family members such as grandparents, aunts, and uncles may be recruited to provide assistance.

As family roles have evolved from men working and women staying at home to care for children and the home, social mores have also changed. The social stigma attached to women who work, especially mothers, is no longer a significant deterrent. Unlike the 1950s, when many people viewed women who worked as abandoning their children and demonstrating that their husbands were unable to provide adequately, it is now assumed that many women will be in the work force. Industrialization was an important contributor to women's increased presence in the work force. Although women throughout the world have always engaged in manual labor, industrialization expanded the availability of work that was less physically demanding. The dramatic

change in the political landscape brought about by the women's liberation movement beginning in the 1960s created opportunities and equal rights for women that
increased the number of women working outside the home and expanded the types
of work available to them. Medical advancements that enable women to control
reproduction have had a profound effect on their ability to become economically
independent and pursue a career. Choices now exist about whether and when to
have children, which provides greater opportunities to plan for career development
and advancement as well as child rearing. More recently, the need for knowledge
workers–those who are employed because of their expertise in a particular field–has
added occupational flexibility for many men and women (Serrat, 2008). As consultants, freelancers, or contract workers on specific projects, knowledge workers can
often determine their own hours and work from their homes, allowing both men and
women to more easily adjust their work life around other family responsibilities.

Economic conditions continue to have a significant influence on the number of
women who work outside the home. As consumer goods, health care, housing, and
education costs increase, so does the need for additional income, making women's
salaries and wages a necessity in many families. These changes have altered the functions in some families. For example, families may have less time to provide for their
children's daily care and recreation and entrust more of those functions to relatives, non-
relative child care providers, after-school programs, organized sports, or camps. When
these options are not available, some children spend more time on their own without
adult supervision.

Data also suggest that men may be feeling considerable pressure as they try to balance work and family responsibilities (Konigsberg, 2011). Part of the pressure comes

from men's own view of the "ideal" man as a successful provider and an involved father, husband/partner, and son (Aumann, Galinsky, & Matos, 2011). Traditional gender roles that were accepted in earlier decades—a woman takes care of family and children and a man provides financial support—are no longer the norm. Instead, financial and domestic responsibilities are divided and shared between husbands and wives or between partners. Since this sharing began on a large scale, the work-family conflict experienced by men in dual-earner households has risen significantly. In 1977, 35% of the men surveyed reported work-family conflict compared to 60% in 2008, whereas 41% of women reported work-family conflict in 1977 compared to 47% in 2008—a change that is not statistically significant (Aumann, Galinsky, & Matos). There are several possible explanations for this difference. Women entered the work force recognizing the added challenges that they were taking on and were in some ways more prepared for those conflicts. Changes in the workplace itself may account for some of the difference, as may changes in family structure. Aumann, Galinsky, and Matos (2011), however, have described this phenomenon as the male mystique, analogous to the feminine mystique coined by Betty Friedan in 1963. They suggest that men are now experiencing the same kind of gender role transition and conflict that women experienced in the 1960s, when women recognized that traditional role expectations were no longer acceptable but that there was little support for making the transition to new roles. Perhaps more important than why men are experiencing increased conflict is the fact that they feel significant pressure; this alone changes the dynamics within the family.

The roles and functions in families with children with disabilities have also evolved as a result of changes in society. Attitudes toward individuals with disabilities have changed dramatically over the years. Formerly institutionalized or otherwise hidden from society, people with disabilities are now included as valued brothers, sisters, colleagues, and friends. The political capital of the Civil Rights movement and the women's movement provided a launching pad for advocacy groups that sought equal rights and opportunities for individuals with disabilities. Political action resulted in a series of precedent-setting laws, such as the Education for All Handicapped Children Act of 1975 (EHA; PL 94-142), which, for the first time, mandated free and appropriate public education for *all* children and youth regardless of their disabilities. This law enabled families to send their children with disabilities to public schools, reducing the educational, economic, and caregiving demands that these families had traditionally borne exclusively. The EHA was reauthorized as the Individuals with Disabilities Education Act of 1990 (IDEA; PL 101-476), which was amended and reauthorized multiple times since then. The laws, however, have not eliminated the need for families' advocacy to ensure that their children receive appropriate programs and services, nor have they reduced the time that is required of families to participate with teachers, therapists, physicians, and others as members of their child's educational, therapeutic, and medical teams.

Additional legislation, such as Section 504 of the Rehabilitation Act of 1973 (PL 93-112) and the ADA of 1990 (PL 101-336), increased rights and opportunities for individuals with disabilities throughout adulthood and across areas unrelated to education. This enabled families to think and plan differently for the needs of their sons and daughters with disabilities. Supported apartments, group homes, and other living options for individuals with disabilities allowed many parents to contemplate an "empty nest" rather than lifelong responsibilities for their son's or daughter's direct care. These laws made it possible for individuals with disabilities to anticipate fair hiring practices, accommodations in the workplace, and independence as adults.

Technology has also been a boon for individuals with disabilities. New technologies have made communication and mobility possible for people whose physical disabilities challenge both of these areas. New knowledge has prevented some disabilities and reduced the impact of others, significantly improving the quality of life for many individuals and their families. The information age of technology has also provided a new array of job opportunities for individuals with disabilities, increasing their vocational and career opportunities as well as opportunities for social interaction and relationships.

FRAMEWORKS FOR UNDERSTANDING FAMILIES

Chapter 3 provided an overview of the theoretical frameworks that have been used to study and understand families. This chapter presents an overview of several theoretical approaches that incorporate family functions in their conceptualization; it then narrows the focus to a detailed discussion of the family systems framework described by Turnbull, Summers, and Brotherson (1984) and Summers, Brotherson, and Turnbull (1988). Their framework and the framework detailed by Seligman and Darling (2007) address family functions as one component of the family system, describe the roles and functions that are expected of families in the contemporary Western world, and elaborate on the ways in which the family system may be affected when it includes a member with a disability.

One conceptual framework used to understand families is the structural functionalism framework. This framework first emerged in the late 1930s (Malinowski, 1939) and incorporates psychological, sociological, and anthropological traditions. It assumes that structures are designed to provide specific functions. From a macrosocial perspective, the family is one of the structures within the larger social system responsible for supporting the social system and contributing to the maintenance of social order. From a microsocial perspective, the family itself can be viewed as a system in which the positions held by family members (e.g., mother, daughter, grandmother, father) and the roles that they play can be studied (Gelles, 1995). The structural functionalism framework assumes that social order is possible because social structures create responsibility for carrying out various tasks or functions. Like other systems theories, the structural functionalism framework assumes that structures are nested in larger systems. However, it has been interpreted from a biological or organic perspective that maintains there is no replacement for the function of a missing structure. That interpretation is now questionable in biology, and it is seldom (if ever) true in families. In families, when a structure is no longer present, another assumes its functions. Consider Pablo's family in the following case study.

Pablo

When Pablo was 4 years old, his mother was killed in an automobile accident. Pablo's father and maternal grandmother assumed responsibility for his daily care, nurturance, and guidance. Pablo's aunts stepped in to provide care when his father had to be out of town on business or just needed time for his own grieving and healing. Over time, Pablo's father was able to adjust his work schedule to be home when Pablo returned from school so that he could take him to soccer practice and be available to meet the needs of a growing boy.

From a strict structural functionalism perspective, the roles and responsibilities of Pablo's mother would have been lost when she died. This was not the case in Pablo's life, however. Although the original structure provided by his mother was missing, the functions that she provided were not. Other family members assumed those roles and ensured that Pablo was loved and well cared for.

Structural functionalism has been replaced by other theories of family, but this chapter acknowledges the theory because of its contributions to underscoring the many functions that families perform daily and throughout an individual's life span. For families and their members to survive, certain jobs have to be done—obtaining financial resources, providing daily care, helping family members stay healthy, finding opportunities for recreation and leisure, and transmitting family values. Each family may accomplish these jobs in different ways, but each family grapples with the jobs by setting priorities and assigning responsibilities or by ignoring or deferring the responsibilities to other individuals, organizations, social institutions, or governmental agencies.

Family Systems Theory

In systems theory, families are viewed as highly complex social systems in which the characteristics, needs, experiences, actions, and reactions of each family member affect every other member as well as the family as a whole. Families are interactive, reactive, and interdependent (Seligman & Darling, 2007). Perhaps the best way to understand family functions is to consider them in the broader context of the family systems framework (Seligman & Darling; Summers et al., 1988; Turnbull et al., 1984). Although this framework was developed to enable professionals and families to consider the ways in which having a child with disabilities may affect the family, it is equally helpful in thinking about all families. The framework includes the following components (Turnbull et al., 1984):

1. *Inputs* made up of the family characteristics, such as the size and constellation of the family, family ideology, and cultural identification

2. *Process,* which is characterized by family interactions, such as the patterns and style of communication, cohesion, and adaptability

3. *Outputs,* which are made up of the family functions mentioned previously

4. *Change* through the life cycle as a result of changes within and outside the family. For a comprehensive review of this model and its components, see Turnbull and Turnbull (2001).

Family Structure One might think of family characteristics as the family's signature—those aspects that make each family different from every other family. Each family is unique. A family's characteristics include the number of individuals in the family and the family constellation, cultural style, and ideological style.

As discussed in the previous chapters, family size and constellation vary dramatically from family to family, as well as over the years as children are born; divorces, remarriages, and blending occur; children leave home and perhaps return; and family members die. Single-parent families, gay and lesbian families, and families in which grandparents are the primary caregivers encounter some challenges common to all families and some challenges that are unique to them. The same is true for families in which a family member has a disability.

Family members' cultural beliefs, values, behaviors, race, the languages spoken, and the traditions and spiritual practices followed are also a part of the family's characteristics. A family's cultural characteristics may influence its members' views of disability. For some, disability may be perceived as a gift from God or an affirmation that the family members have the ability and strength to meet the added challenges. For others, disability may be considered shameful and something to be hidden from view. A family's sociocultural characteristics, such as level of education, socioeconomic status, and geographic locale, often contribute significantly to a family's signature. For many families, their culture, race, or ethnicity have less influence on their lives than their educational level, socioeconomic status, and the area in which they live.

A family's ideology is typically based upon their values, beliefs, traditions, coping behaviors, and culture. Ideology reflects the family's history and the beliefs, values, and ways of viewing the world that have been passed down from one generation to the next (Seligman & Darling, 2007). Although it is rooted in history, like any other family characteristic, it can change. Marriage to someone with a different ideology or exposure to other ways of viewing the world through education, a job, or a move to another part of the country may alter the whole family's ideology or the ideology of one of its members. For example, someone from a cattle-ranching family may change their view of the family occupation when they fall in love with and marry a vegan. The parent of a family in which being bright, well educated, and competitive is critical may find that their perspective has been too narrow as they raise a son who has a significant intellectual disability. Regardless of what a family's ideology is or how it shifts over time and circumstances, it contributes to the family's signature.

Personal characteristics of family members also help to define families, just as families help to determine each member's personal characteristics. A demanding, difficult family member who is alcoholic and abusive has a profound effect on every other member of the family. The effect that such a family member has on individuals within the family may vary dramatically, however. Some family members may gain personal strength and autonomy from learning to cope and negotiate with and/or free themselves from this person's demands and abuse. Other family members may lose all sense of personal control, ambition, and self-esteem; still others will fall somewhere in between. In some families, a member's personal characteristics may include a disability. For example, having a child with autism may bring the entire family together as they love, care for, and advocate for their son, daughter, brother, sister, grandchild, niece, or nephew. In other families, incorporating a child with autism may result in isolation, resentment, or blaming, causing the family to pull apart rather than together. Although every family member's personal characteristics affect every other member of the family, the nature of the impact—like the weather—cannot always be predicted.

Family Interaction   Family interaction is made up of the complex relationships among and between the various subsystems within and outside of the family. Each subsystem is separated by boundaries that help to define interactions. In some families, these boundaries are relatively fluid; in others, they are not. Four subsystems are included in the framework proposed by Turnbull et al. (1984). They include the marital, sibling, parental, and extended family subsystems. As you think of your own family, you may discover that these subsystems overlap, are nonexistent, or fail to describe the way in which your family is structured. To a great extent, subsystems are determined by cultural and sociocultural experiences. For example, the marital subsystem is traditionally composed of a husband and wife. As discussed in Chapter 1, a much wider range of adult partnerships may constitute the marital subsystem. The official sanction of marriage is not available to all couples whose roles are described by this subsystem. The extended family subsystem is equally diverse. For many families, the extended family *is* the family. All members are important participants; no one is considered to be distant as the word *extended* suggests. The sibling subsystem exists within families that have more than one child. In blended families, the sibling subsystem may be divided into additional subsystems representing half brothers and half sisters from previous marriages in addition to those from the current marriage. The parental subsystem is typically the same as the marital subsystem; however, this is not always the case. For example, in some families, grandparents are fulfilling the parenting role when members of the marital subsystem are unable to assume that role. In other families, an older sister or brother may assume a parenting role to ease the burden. In families with a child with disabilities, it is not atypical for brothers and sisters to be involved in some of the parenting tasks, just as older sisters and brothers often participate in parenting a younger sibling.

Regardless of the makeup of the various subsystems, each operates within a range of cohesion and adaptability that is defined by the family. Cohesion is the extent to which families are emotionally bonded to one another as well as the extent to which they feel that they are independent from the family (Seligman & Darling, 2007; Turnbull & Turnbull, 2001). A critical point in any discussion of family cohesion is the cultural identification of the family. No universal norm exists. A family that may seem cohesive to the point of being enmeshed may be typical for the values, beliefs, and behaviors of their culture. Likewise, a family in which members have considerable independence from one another and lead their own lives without ongoing consultation and feedback from the family may be typical for their culture but seem quite unusual to those who come from traditions that are more obviously cohesive. For a more thorough discussion of theoretical, clinical, and research bases of family cohesion, see Olson, Russell, and Sprenkle (1980) and Minuchin and Fishman (1981). For example, a family that is very cohesive—one that depends almost exclusively on family members for social support, recreation, decision making, and so forth—may be less open to intervention from outsiders and see less need for intervention for children or other family members with disabilities. Families whose members have considerable autonomy outside of the family may be more inclined to seek external support and services. Although culture can play a significant role in determining both cohesion and adaptability, each family ultimately plays by its own rules.

According to Turnbull and Turnbull (2001, p. 126), "adaptability refers to the family's ability to change in response to situational and developmental stress." Some families are masterful at dealing with stress and adapting to stressful situations when they arise. Other families have considerably more difficulty in changing to reduce stress or dealing with difficult situations, such as the birth of a child with a disability, job loss, serious illness, or a move to a new community. Families at the extremes in adaptability are those that change so often and so quickly that life is chaotic, as well as those that have become rigid because they cannot change. As in most areas of life, the extremes are not optimal for family well-being. For a more thorough discussion of the theoretical underpinnings of family adaptability, see Olson et al. (1980) and Olson, Sprenkle, and Russell (1979).

Family Functions   In an adaptation developed by Turnbull and Turnbull (2001), the family systems framework describes eight functions that families provide for their members: affection, self-esteem, spiritual, economic, daily care, socialization, recreation, and education. Although discussed in relation to families who have children with special needs, this conceptualization of family functions is relevant to all families. Bristor (1995), whose work has been applied in the field of mental health, listed the following seven responsibilities as functions of families: protection, economic resources, nurturance, mediation, education, adaptation, and continuity. Ronneau (1999) provided another listing of functions in a descriptive study of families who care for children with severe emotional disabilities. The six functions identified for this study included domestic, self-identity, affection, socialization, recreation, and education or vocational needs. Overlap among the models is evident and is highlighted in Table 4.1. Although some individuals and cultures may emphasize the importance of the family's role in certain functions more than in others, the expectation that families will fulfill these functions is nearly universal. The next section of this chapter discusses each of the family functions in greater detail.

Family Life Cycle   The final component in the family systems framework is the family life cycle—the changes over time that typically cause stress and influence family functioning. The traditional model of family follows this evolution: A couple begins as a family without children, followed by years devoted to child rearing and launching children into their own lives; the couple then become empty nesters, enter old age, and lose a partner through death. These benchmarks are part of the developmental life cycle of many families. However, it does not work that way for all families. Many families begin with one or more children. Partners may change over time, or there may never be partners involved in child rearing. Some children are never launched. Empty nesters may take on the parental role again with their grandchildren, or an individual might experience the death of a spouse prior to old age. Regardless of the sequence of occurrence, change and transitions are stressful. Having or adopting a baby, becoming responsible for an elderly parent, getting or losing a job, facing a serious illness, moving to a new community, and experiencing shifts in income (both up and down) are changes that are often accompanied by considerable stress. Even smaller changes, however, take

Table 4.1.   Family functions as identified in the literature

Turnbull, Summers, and Brotherson (1984)	Bristor (1995)	Ronneau (1999)	Hanson and Lynch (2004)
Affection	Protection	Domestic	Love and affection
Self-esteem	Economic resources	Self-identity	Daily care and health maintenance
Spiritual	Nurturance	Affection	
Economic	Mediation	Socialization	Economic support
Daily care	Education	Recreation	Identity development
Socialization	Adaptation	Education or vocational needs	Socialization and guidance
Recreation	Continuity		Educational and vocational development
Education			Recreation, rest, and recuperation

their toll. A substitute teacher at school, a holiday at the child care center, or a parent's need to stay late at work one evening are small changes that can be disruptive for families. The way in which families cope with the stress of change is, in part, determined by the other components of the family systems framework, including family members' characteristics—particularly their cultural affiliation and identity, their range of cohesion and adaptability, and their perception of and ability to fulfill family functions during times of added stress. For a more complete discussion of family life cycle theory, refer to Carter and McGoldrick (1980, 1989).

When viewed as a system, the roles, functions, and impact of individual family members become more clear. Just as a pebble tossed into a pond creates ripples that magnify its influence, each family member affects every other. As you read the next section about specific family functions, consider the ways in which individual family members, the characteristics of the family, their cohesion and adaptability, and their place in the life cycle may affect their ability to fulfill each function.

FAMILY FUNCTIONS

As described previously, authors provide different but overlapping lists of family functions (Bristor, 1995; Onaga, McKinney, & Pfaff, 2000; Ronneau, 1999; Seligman & Darling, 2007; Turnbull et al., 1984). This chapter takes a broad view of family functions and combines and adapts functions listed by several authors. We include seven functions (Hanson & Lynch, 2004):

1. Love and affection

2. Daily care and health maintenance

3. Economic support

4. Identity development

5. Socialization and guidance

6. Educational and vocational development

7. Recreation, rest, and recuperation

Each function is described in the sections that follow, with an emphasis on the ways in which having a child with a disability and family diversity may influence the ways in which functions are performed.

Love and Affection

Perhaps the most basic function of families is to love and show affection for one another. The bond that links family members is often thought to be the strongest of all human interactions, and the axiom that "blood is thicker than water" underscores this belief. Many aspects of love and affection fall within this function, such as the love and intimacy between adult partners in the family, the nurturing and unconditional love given by parents to children, and the special support and caring for older family members or those who have special needs.

Families and family members demonstrate their love and affection for one another in a variety of ways. Some families exhibit considerable physical contact—hugs, kisses, pats, and snuggles. Other families may be less demonstrative but show their love and affection in other ways, from specially prepared meals to fond looks to making remarkable sacrifices to support and care for another family member. Culture, gender, situational variables, and personal preferences all influence the ways in which families show their love and affection.

In all families sometimes and in a few families most of the time, love and affection seem to be absent. An abusive spouse, an angry teenager, or a demanding grandparent is difficult to love when he or she is engaging in these behaviors. Family members may find it more difficult to express love and affection when a child's autism makes her squirm away from hugs or when a conduct disorder causes a child to be combative and destructive. It may take considerable time for members of blended families to love each other and find comfortable ways of showing affection. For some, caring and respect may be the ultimate, and most appropriate, outcome.

Family members who are not psychologically available because of their own mental health problems or addictions have difficulty fulfilling this family function because they cannot engage in the reciprocal interactions that love and affection require (Seifer & Dickstein, 1993). Maternal depression has been studied for its potential for causing psychological unavailability. As emphasized by Clark and Fenichel (2001), when a woman is diagnosed with maternal depression, it does not tell us how that mother is caring for her child. She may be sensitive and responsive, but maternal depression may also cause her to be unable to respond to her child's physical and emotional needs. The extent of maternal depression and the ways in which it is manifested are critical elements in determining the type and intensity of intervention for the mother and other family members. Well-publicized incidents, including one in which a mother allowed her car to roll into a lake with the children inside, illustrate the tragic consequences of ignoring maternal depression.

Regardless of how one perceives a family as an outsider, family bonds are often much stronger than they appear. Blood often is thicker than water, and one can never assume that love and affection are not present.

Daily Care and Health Maintenance

Every family has its daily chores that keep individuals and the household running. Tasks such as grocery shopping, meal preparation, laundry, cleaning, transporting family members, home repairs, running errands, and paying bills consume major portions of the day. Few individuals who work and have families feel that they have adequate time for these routine but necessary activities, which is one of the reasons why so many products and strategies have been developed to save time. Fast food, children's shoes with Velcro fasteners, online banking, automated teller machines at grocery stores and gas stations, washers, dryers, dishwashers, microwaves, and smartphones are all designed to reduce the time spent in daily chores. For two-career families, single parents, and families in the sandwich generation who care for their own children as well as their aging parents, daily responsibilities can be daunting.

Families from collectivist cultures may be more effective at mobilizing resources for daily care because they have a greater pool of people from which to draw (Lynch & Hanson, 2011). Likewise, families with many brothers and sisters, aunts and uncles, grandparents, and cousins nearby may find it far easier to manage the demands of daily life than a single parent struggling in isolation.

Caring for someone with a chronic health or medical problem increases the complexity of daily life as well as the time required for caregiving. This may be especially true for families in which a member has a disability. In Knoll's (1996) study of 48 families in New York State who had children with low incidence disorders and complex medical histories, families reported that their son or daughter needed complete supervision throughout large portions of the day. In addition to the extra time required for daily routines such as bathing, dressing, eating, and sleeping, many children required time-consuming medical procedures as well as scheduled administration of medications and frequent appointments with physicians and therapists. Other disabilities also add time and complexity to a family's daily demands. Children who need considerable structure to accomplish tasks and maintain their behavior require preplanning and support through the most routine tasks. In *Time* magazine, Greenfeld described childhood with his brother Noah, who has autism:

> Noah, who can't speak, dress or go to the bathroom completely unassisted, will always be the center of our family. He never earned that role; his needs dictated it. . . . I accepted the fact that Noah and his problems could fill a battleship of parental duty and obligation, leaving my mother and father too spent to worry about the more banal problems of their normal son. (2002, p. 54)

Other children with disabilities may require frequent occupational, physical, speech-language, or psychotherapy with the attendant issues of scheduling, time, and transportation. Many will require additional time to participate in every activity because of motor problems or cognitive delays that interfere with their responding or understanding. In some instances, the family member with a disability may be a young adult or an aging parent whose needs are equally demanding physically and psychologically. Regardless of family constellation, culture, language, ethnicity, and socioeconomic circumstances, families are responsible for many chores that keep family members healthy and well cared for. Having a child or other family member with a disability often adds to the tasks that must be accomplished and the time and energy that it takes on a daily basis.

Economic Support

Although the standard of living across families in the United States and throughout the world varies markedly, families in the United States are expected to be financially independent. The welfare reform legislation first enacted in 1996 underscores this value—or at least the value that individuals should not be lifelong dependents on government support (Haskins, 2009). In this chapter, financial independence is viewed very conservatively as a living wage—one that enables a family to live above the poverty level (Roston, 2002). This is not a generous wage, nor is it one that most Americans would choose; however, the living wage enables individuals and families to pay for adequate housing, food, and basic health care, with some extra at the end of the month. Although the American society values financial independence, for many families it has proved unattainable. In 2009, approximately 15.5 million children (20%) in the United States were living in poverty (Lee, Levey, & Lazo, 2011). Of those, nearly half lived in extreme poverty, defined as an annual income of half the poverty level—$11,025 for a family of four in that year (Lee, Levey, & Lazo). In 2010, poverty in the United States hit a 50-year high. Families in which parents do not have an education, job skills, or English-language competence have far less access to financial resources. Teenage parents often lack both an education and marketable skills, and many single parents struggle to earn enough to care for themselves and their children. (See Chapter 6 for a comprehensive discussion of the impact of poverty on families.)

Families of children with disabilities—especially disabilities such as autism, intellectual disability, cerebral palsy, and complex medical conditions that require technological support—spend more money on their children with a disability than on their other children (Turnbull & Turnbull, 2001). Extra costs combined with a frequent need for one parent to leave the work force for a period of time to care for or manage the child's care make many families of children with disabilities more vulnerable to economic stress. Many people with children with disabilities find it difficult to ask for help, especially financial help. As Knoll concluded from his study of families of children with complex, low-incidence disabilities over 15 years ago,

> Again and again, the families tell of benefits managers, service coordinators, discharge planners, and social workers whose actions indicate that they regard the families as welfare junkies out to milk the system for everything it's worth. An attitude is conveyed, even in dealing with entitlements and plans to which the parents have long contributed, that the families are the beneficiaries of some benevolent charity and should be happy with what they are given. Families struggling to come to terms with their child's disability and the care demands associated with it find themselves stigmatized, impoverished, and degraded. In a society of rugged individualists they are forced to ask for help, which, in itself, is more than some parents can deal with. (1996, p. 220)

The families whose views Knoll expressed were widely spread across the socioeconomic continuum. They were also culturally, racially, and geographically diverse within the state of New York. But regardless of these differences, they shared a common concern about the ability to provide for their family financially and to support the additional costs associated with their child with a disability.

Identity Development

One of a family's most important responsibilities is to help each member develop his or her own identity. Developing a sense of self, self-esteem, and moral/ethical character that enables a person to contribute constructively as a member of a family, community, and the larger society is one of the most important developmental tasks. Development of one's sense of self begins within the first 12 months of life and is an ongoing process (Roth-Hanania, Busch-Rossnagel, & Higgins-D'Alessandro, 2000). Based on Minuchen (1974), Deason and Randolph (1998, p. 466) suggested that "the family is the laboratory in which the ingredients of belonging and being separate are mixed to produce an identity." Identity development requires opportunities to explore possibilities and try various ways of being and interacting.

Families typically provide the social context that is the most enduring and open to identity exploration (Deason & Randolph, 1998). Identity development occurs as part of overall growth and development. In the majority of families, parents note the qualities, preferences, and characteristics of their children and work to shape those that are consistent with the family's beliefs. For example, a family with strong ties to their church may notice that their daughter enjoys music. To encourage her preferences within the family's beliefs, they may help her download hymns and spirituals for children, take her to concerts featuring religious music, and see that she joins the children's choir at church. Another family may have strong convictions about social justice and human rights. When their son displays a passion for history and geography, they may ensure that he is exposed to documentaries and history books that present multiple perspectives. They may take him along when they volunteer at the migrant community center and encourage him to learn the stories of the children and families that they meet there. In these families, there may be bumps in the road, but identity development occurs rather naturally with only short-term strife. In other families, identity development is fraught with difficulties and poses significant challenges to parents and children alike. In some families, a son or daughter may seem to rebel against all that his or her parents stand for and develop an identity that bears little relationship to other family members. In other families, the adults themselves are still working to develop their self-identity, self-esteem, and moral/ethical character, making it more difficult, if not impossible, to provide the support and guidance that their sons and daughters need in their own search for self.

In research on the outcomes of children of adolescent mothers, low maternal self-esteem and depression—both related to identity development—have been cited as factors that contribute to negative outcomes in children's behavior and developmental outcomes (Osofsky, Hann, & Peebles, 1993). Personal, cultural, sociocultural, and political issues can also challenge identity development. The experiences of children with disabilities may be dramatically different from the experiences of their peers. For example, having a physical disability in a community in which sports define one's place in the social hierarchy is likely to result in a severe challenge to an individual's healthy identity development. Likewise, having developmental delay and/or intellectual disability makes it more difficult to fit into a fast-track, academic world oriented toward achievement.

An individual's race, culture, and/or ethnicity may also make identity development more challenging. In schools, neighborhoods, communities, and countries in which prejudice against certain ethnic, racial, religious, or language groups flourishes, it is more difficult for those who are discriminated against to develop a healthy self-identity. The same is true when poverty is considered. Being impoverished does not contribute to the development of a positive self-identity. None of the characteristics that interfere with the development of a positive self-identity is all encompassing, nor do any of these characteristics alone define the outcomes. They do, however, make it more difficult for children and families alike to fulfill the function of identity development.

Socialization and Guidance

For most young children, families provide the first opportunities for socialization. Finding a place within the family and interacting with an expanding network of family members lays the groundwork for future social interactions. In large, extended families, children's early socialization may occur as they interact with siblings, grandparents, cousins, aunts, and uncles before they interact with individuals outside the family. In smaller families without a nearby extended family or kinship network, children may meet and spend time with family friends and their children early in their development. They may also be exposed to children in playgroups or formal childcare environments. Schools, neighborhoods, camps, civic, and religious activities also provide opportunities for socializing with others and developing social skills.

As children participate in social situations within and outside of the family, their behavior is typically guided by the values and beliefs of their parents or primary caregivers. Guidance may include helping with problem solving, providing advice and feedback, shaping basic beliefs and values, and transmitting spiritual and/or ethical and moral values (Summers et al., 1988). For example, some families believe in the importance of giving to others in tangible ways, and they transmit this value to their children very concretely through activities such as volunteering at a homeless shelter, inviting away-from-home military personnel or international students over for dinner, and helping to build or repair homes for those in need. Through these actions, families are providing guidance for their children. Although the type, extent, and method of providing guidance varies from culture to culture, religion to religion, place to place, and family to family, providing guidance to children as they develop is universal. When guidance provided by family members or caregivers conflicts dramatically with the expectations within the larger cultural milieu, however, success with this family function is threatened.

Providing guidance to a child with a disability may require different skills and approaches. If the disability interferes with the child's understanding, cognitive ability, or judgment, guidance may be more direct and may focus more on transmitting social/behavioral values that are grounded in the family's ideology rather than the ideology itself. For example, instead of exploring *why* taking someone else's toy is not acceptable, they may instead teach their son or daughter not to grab things from other people's hands. It has also been demonstrated that healthy family functioning results in better social skills among children with disabilities (Bennett & Hay, 2007).

Almost all disabilities interfere to some extent with a child's socialization. Physical or sensory disabilities that interfere with play (Diamond & Hong, 2010), communication disabilities that make it difficult to share preferences and/or needs (Hall, 2013), and socioemotional and mental health disabilities interfere with children's abilities to develop social skills (Kingery, Erdley, Marshall Whitaker, & Reuter, 2010). The emphasis on inclusion of children with disabilities underscores the need for social skill development.

Although advocacy efforts and legislation support increased opportunities for inclusive social opportunities, families of children with disabilities are most often responsible for ensuring that these opportunities actually occur (Turnbull & Rueff, 1997).

Educational and Vocational Development

Parents are their children's first teachers. Although it has become somewhat of a cliché, much of what each person knows was first taught or learned at home. Likewise, many of the behaviors that lead to success or failure in the workplace are a product of the child's family environment—persistence, thoughtfulness, curiosity, motivation, and the ability to accept feedback and get along with others are just a few examples. Adolescents' or young adults' first jobs are often the result of family connections. Although families are not expected to provide formal education or vocational training, their ideology, life circumstances, and culture contribute greatly to their children's educational and occupational aspirations and outcomes.

Like the other functions described in this chapter, having a child with a disability or departing from the norm in any other sociocultural dimension may make fulfilling this function more difficult. Until 1975, children with disabilities in the United States were not guaranteed a free public education. Infants and toddlers in the United States were not guaranteed early intervention services until the late 1980s. The ADA, which made discrimination against individuals with disabilities in the workplace illegal, was not passed until 1990. Clearly, family members have had to play a significant role in obtaining education and vocational opportunities for their sons and daughters over many years.

IDEA of 1975 and its subsequent amendments mandate a free appropriate education for individuals from birth through age 22. Although this has been a critical and much-needed piece of legislation, it has not always resulted in the intended benefits. For some, the mandated services have not been easy to obtain, and parents and advocates have continued to fight for their children's needs and rights. For others, local districts and state systems have been far too willing to provide special education services to certain groups, resulting in a serious overrepresentation of children of color in programs and services for individuals with disabilities.

Overrepresentation is particularly evident among African American children and English-language learners. The disproportional representation of students of African American descent in special education, their underrepresentation in programs for gifted students, and the over- and underrepresentation of other students of color has been an area of research and concern for over 40 years (Artiles, Kozleski, Trent, Osher, & Ortiz, 2010). More recently, research has also considered the types of placements—least to most restrictive—in relation to students' cultural and linguistic diversity (Skiba, Polonii-Staudinger, Gallini, Simmons, & Feggins-Azziz, 2006). In the analyses of special education placements, it is evident that African American and American Indian students are overrepresented in special education programs for high-incidence disabilities, such as learning disabilities. Likewise, they are underrepresented in programs for students who are gifted. A study of English-language learners placed in special education programs found that these students also are much more likely to be identified as having learning disabilities or intellectual disabilities than Anglo-American English-speaking peers. Once identified, they were also less likely to be served in either the least restrictive or the most restrictive environment when compared with their Anglo-American peers (Sullivan, 2011). These issues suggest that parents' roles in advocacy continue to be critical to ensure the appropriate education for their sons and daughters with disabilities.

Recreation, Rest, and Recuperation

The enormity of tasks required of families indicates that another important family function is creating time and opportunity for its members to recreate, rest, and recuperate. Each family has its own definitions of these terms. For some, recreation may mean running, working out, or practicing yoga; for others, it may be reading, playing the piano, attending concerts and plays, or playing cards. Rest may be taking a nap or simply doing something different from the typical demands of daily living. Recuperation also takes different forms depending on time, personal preferences, and resources. Whether recuperation involves a cup of hot tea or a vacation in Hawaii, it is critical to healthy functioning for all family members over the long term.

Finding the time, opportunity, and resources for each of these activities may be more difficult when a family member has a disability. Issues of access, acceptance, and sometimes behavior may have to be considered. Is it possible to go to the beach with a child who travels by wheelchair? What will it be like to take a child with loud vocalizations to a restaurant? Can a child who is extremely active sit through storytime at the local library? Although these things may all be possible, when a family member has a disability, issues such as these may complicate a family's ability to have fun together.

Other challenges are lack of time and experience. Caregiving may take more time or skills when a child or any other family member has a disability; it also may be more difficult to find babysitters who are both competent and comfortable with staying with the child while other family members spend time together. The basic lack of free time is an issue for many families, but especially for families of children or aging parents with disabilities. Even when well-trained care providers are available, many families cannot find the time or the energy to go out. Families of children with disabilities may find that rest, recuperation, and recreation are especially difficult to incorporate into their lives.

Families who are impoverished or those in which mental health problems prevail may also be challenged to fulfill this family function. Lack of financial resources limits the options for free time as well as the options for ways to spend that time. Likewise, families with serious mental health issues may be unable to mobilize themselves to engage in family activities.

IMPACT OF CONTEMPORARY SOCIETY ON FAMILY ROLES AND FUNCTIONS

Changes in the economy, health care, legislation, and the political climate exert ongoing influences on the roles that families play, the functions they perform, and the ways in which they are supported or deterred in fulfilling those functions. This section illustrates some of the ways in which family functions have been supported or supplanted by the larger societal context.

Federal and enabling state laws have had a profound effect on the support that families receive in performing the functions ascribed to them. Legislation establishing Head Start in 1965 was one of the first federal efforts to support low-income children and their families in a more comprehensive way. In addition to providing preschool experiences for 3- and 4-year-old children from low-income families, the legislation provided physical and mental health care, nutrition, social services, and opportunities for parents to be involved in their children's education and to develop their own leadership skills (Children's Defense Fund, 2000). More recently, Early Head Start has extended these services down to birth. This support has assisted families for several decades with the functions of daily care and health maintenance, identity development, socialization, and education. Other federal laws have had a significant impact on families' abilities to perform their expected functions. As mentioned previously, IDEA of 1975 required federal and state support for students with disabilities, which released many parents from the full responsibility of providing education for their sons and daughters with disabilities. Although parents, families, and professionals continue to report inadequacies and injustices within the special education system of services, the guarantee of a free and appropriate public education aids in the education, vocational development, and socialization of children with disabilities. It may also contribute to family members' ability to work outside the home to increase their economic self-sufficiency and provide a few hours each day that can be used for recuperation—or at least for attention to tasks other than child care and monitoring.

The home schooling movement has had the opposite effect. Rather than cast parents and family members in the role of overseeing, monitoring, and/or orchestrating their children's education, this movement allows parental education to replace public education. In other words, parents and families take responsibility for the delivery of formal education to their children as a family function. A common rationale is that home schooling is an antidote to public schools that are inadequate. The social and political agenda of home schooling has been questioned and concerns expressed that home schooling may, in fact, threaten the democratic ideals of public education (Apple, 2000). Families who select home schooling may have less time for other family functions, or one parent in a dual-career family may need to leave or substantially alter his or her work hours. For some, home schooling may interfere with the family's ability to provide recreation, rest, and recuperation. For others, eliminating school hours and schedules may increase the time that family members have to be together for relaxation and recreation. In still other instances, the role of parent as teacher may interfere with recreation as every activity becomes a lesson. Regardless of the way each family handles the responsibilities involved, other family functions will be affected.

Welfare reform has also influenced families' abilities to fulfill various family functions, but its effects have been argued as both positive and negative. Designed to increase employment opportunities by increasing the skills of welfare recipients, many questions about the long-term effects on families remain. For example, has job training resulted in employment that is sustainable and sufficient for economic independence? Have child care options for parents in job training or newly acquired jobs been adequate to ensure that young children are receiving high-quality daily care, positive opportunities for identity development, and socialization? Has income been sufficient to provide health care and health maintenance, or have health benefits been lost through welfare reform?

Families in which both parents work have also affected the way in which family functions are performed. Second incomes are always welcome and often a necessity in homes across the nation. On the one hand, families with two wage earners increase the likelihood that there will be adequate financial resources; on the other hand, the demands may reduce their ability to perform other functions effectively. Exhausting schedules may make it more difficult for parents to participate in their children's education, provide opportunities for socialization, and engage in recreation, rest, and recuperation individually or as a family. Conversely, families living in poverty may be very successful in providing love and affection for their children, but they may have significantly reduced options fulfilling other family functions.

The availability of information and increased access, especially through electronic media, has also influenced family functioning. Internet access has provided some families with resources on health care, enabled them to bank and make purchases online, helped them to research educational alternatives, and provided quick access to information about promising vocational pursuits. For some, this may result in additional time spent in such functions as identity development, socialization, love and affection, and recreation, rest, and recuperation. For others, it may simply result in more time spent at the computer.

Medical breakthroughs have also influenced family functions. In 1979, van Eys stated that a number of diseases that were once considered to be terminal are no longer life threatening; rather, they result in chronic illness. That statement continues to be true. As mortality from disease and disability is reduced, morbidity increases. Whether care is provided for a premature infant, a medically fragile child, or an older adult experiencing a host of physical and mental difficulties, chronic illnesses place considerable demands on family members financially and in daily caregiving. These demands often interfere with the performance of other family functions.

The mobility of the population in the United States does not, at first consideration, appear to be related to family functions. However, it has had a rather profound effect. When extended family members lived closer together, greater opportunities existed to share family functions. Grandparents might assist with daily care, the expression of love and affection, and socialization. Aunts, uncles, and cousins might also contribute to child rearing and to supporting each of the family members. As many families have become more dispersed, support for family functions is not so readily available from other family members. Many single parents and couples are on their own and are expected to fulfill all of the familial functions. Every day, families demonstrate that this can be done; however, every day, in families throughout the nation, it takes its toll.

FROM FAMILY FUNCTIONS TO FAMILY ROUTINES: THE ROLE OF PROFESSIONALS

Descriptions of the family systems approach stop at the level of family functions. The six to eight domains of family responsibility provide the big picture—or a macro view—of what families are expected to do. Many professionals, however, interact with parents and families at the micro level—the level that includes family routines. According to Bernheimer and Weisner (2007), family routines are the things that people do from the moment they get up until the time they go to bed. Consider Ben's family.

On school days in 7-year-old Ben's house, his parents get up, shower, and dress. His mother makes breakfast and packs Ben's lunch, while the father wakes Sarah and Ben and helps Ben get dressed and ready for school. Mom drives Ben and Sarah to school on the three days a week when she goes to work at noon. Dad drives the other two days. The parents take turns picking up Ben and his sister from school, taking Sarah to weekly soccer practice, Ben to a weekly therapy session, and running errands. While one of the parents makes dinner, the other parent helps Ben and Sarah with their homework. After dinner, Ben helps Sarah clean up, and the whole family spends about an hour watching a movie or playing games together. At 7:45 p.m., Ben takes a bath, is tucked into bed for a story, and says goodnight. During Ben's bedtime routine, Sarah spends some time texting friends, listening to music, writing in her diary, and deciding what she is going to wear the next day. On weekends, the routines are a bit different, with time spent visiting grandparents, attending Sarah's soccer games, playing with children in the neighborhood, and participating in activities at the temple. It takes considerable organization and energy for Ben's parents to maintain these routines, especially because Ben has cerebral palsy and needs physical assistance to bathe, dress, eat, and move around the house.

Professionals who suggest additional activities for families to incorporate into their already busy and exhaustive schedules must consider how their request fits into the family's routines (McWilliam, 2010). For example, if a therapist asked Ben's family to include at least 30 minutes each day in exercises to maintain and increase his range of motion, it would be difficult to find the time. If, however, the therapist showed Ben's parents how to incorporate these exercises during his bath, at bedtime, and perhaps as he is dressing in the morning, it is much more likely that they will be done. That approach incorporates the additional exercises into existing routines, which makes it easier to perform all of the expected functions. One of the jobs of professionals is to assist families in maintaining the routines that support family functions.

SUMMARY

Families can best be understood as a system that includes the characteristics of the family and its members, their ability to communicate, the way in which they fulfill family functions, and their place in the life cycle. Outside influences have profound effects on families, but families also influence the larger society. Contemporary families are expected to fulfill a wide range of roles and functions. Sometimes these roles and functions are supported by society as a whole–its attitudes, laws, economic structures, and resources. Sometimes the same forces undermine the roles and functions expected of family members. Each family, regardless of its makeup, develops ways to accomplish its work as effectively as possible, but the path is seldom smooth and straight. As circumstances and life situations change, so must families. Strategies for fulfilling family functions often need to accommodate changes within and outside of the family. Families throughout time have demonstrated remarkable abilities to adapt and continue to provide the care, love, and support that is foundational to being a family. One of the roles of professionals in their interactions and interventions with families is to support families to function in healthy, fulfilling ways.

ACTIVITIES TO EXTEND THE DISCUSSION

1. **Consider your own family functions.** Make a list of the things that your family and its members do to survive economically; support one another psychologically; ensure that basic needs for food, shelter, health, and nurturance are met; and find meaning in life.

2. **Think about your own family and the family functions that this chapter discusses.** Which of the functions is most challenging to fulfill in your family? Which is the easiest? Are there other functions that you would add to the list?

3. **Make a list of all of the things that you do on a typical day.** Review the list and indicate which function each one addresses. Are there any activities that do not fit into one of the functions? Share your responses with others in your group.

4. Consider your own routines and what you would have to do if a professional suggested that you do at least 45 more minutes of exercise each day. How would you fit it into your schedule? What would you give up or juggle to find those 45 minutes? How successful do you think you would be?

5. On the Internet, find an article about being a caregiver. It could be about caring for a child or adult with a disability, chronic health problem, or dementia. Read the article and list the main issues that are addressed. Share those issues with at least three other people who read an article about being a caregiver and discuss the similarities and differences in the issues raised in the articles.

TO LEARN MORE: SUGGESTED WEB SITES

ALLIANCE National Parent Technical Assistance Center
http://www.parentcenternetwork.org/national/aboutus.html

Beach Center on Disability
http://www.beachcenter.org/default.aspx

Family and Relationships
http://www.apa.org/helpcenter/family/index.aspx

Frank Porter Graham Child
Development Institute, University of North Carolina
http://www.fpg.unc.edu

Lesbian and Gay Parenting
http://www.apa.org/pi/lgbt/resources/parenting.aspx

Medicare's Caregiver Topics
http://www.medicare.gov/caregivers/caregiver-topics-landing.html

Parenting Resources
http://www.usa.gov/Topics/Parents.shtml

U.S. Department of Health and Human
Services, Administration for Children and Families
http://www.acf.hhs.gov/acf_services.html

REFERENCES

Americans with Disabilities Act of 1990, PL 101-336, 42 U.S.C §§ 12101 *et seq.*

Apple, M.W. (2000). The cultural politics of home schooling. *Peabody Journal of Education, 75,* 256–271.

Artiles, A.J., Kozleski, E.B., Trent, S.C., Osher, D., & Ortiz, A. (2010). Justifying and explaining disproportionality, 1968–2008: A critique of underlying views of culture. *Exceptional Children, 76*(3), 279–300.

Aumann, K., Galinsky, E., & Matos, K. (2011). *The new male mystique.* New York, NY: Families and Work Institute National Study of the Changing Workforce.

Bennett, K.S., & Hay, D.A. (2007). The role of family in the development of social skills in children with physical disabilities.

International Journal of Disability, Development and Education, 54, 381–397.

Bernheimer, L.P., & Weisner, T.S. (2007). "Let me just tell you what I do all day . . .": The family story at the center of intervention and practice. *Infants and Young Children, 20*(3), 192–201.

Boyden, J. (1993). *Families: Celebration and hope in a world of change.* London, UK: Gaia Books.

Bristor, M.W. (1995). *Individuals and family systems in their environments* (2nd ed.). Dubuque, IA: Kendall/Hunt.

Bureau of Labor Statistics. (2011a). *BLS spotlight on women at work.* Retrieved July 8, 2012, from http://www.bls.gov/spotlight/2011/women/pdf/women_bls_spotlight.pdf

Bureau of Labor Statistics. (2011b). Employment characteristics of families, 2010. Retrieved July 8, 2012, from http://www.bls.gov/news.release/famee.nr0.htm

Carter, E.A., & McGoldrick, M. (Eds.) (1980). *The family life cycle: A framework for family therapy.* New York, NY: Gardner Press.

Carter, E.A., & McGoldrick, M. (Eds.) (1989). *The changing family life cycle: A framework for family therapy* (2nd ed.) Boston, MA: Allyn & Bacon.

Clark, R., & Fenichel, E. (2001). Mothers, babies, and depression: Questions and answers. *Zero to Three, 22*(1), 48–50.

Children's Defense Fund. (2000). *Yearbook 2000: The state of America's children.* Washington, DC: Author.

Deason, D.M., & Randolph, D.L. (1998). A systematic look at the self: The relationship between family organization, interpersonal attachment, and identity. *Journal of Social Behavior & Personality, 13,* 465–479.

Diamond, K.E., & Hong, S-Y. (2010). Young children's decisions to include peers with physical disabilities in play. *Journal of Early Intervention, 32*(1), 163–177.

Education for All Handicapped Children Act of 1975 (PL 94-142), 20 U.S.C. §§ 1400 *et seq.*

Friedan, B. *The feminine mystique* (1963). New York, NY: W.W. Norton.

Gelles, R.J. (1995). *Contemporary families: A sociological view.* Thousand Oaks, CA: Sage Publications.

Greenfeld, K.T. (2002, May 6). My brother. *Time, 159,* 54.

Hall, L. (2013). *Autism spectrum disorders: From theory to practice* (2nd ed.). Boston, MA: Pearson.

Haskins, R. (2009, December 18). *The 2010 reauthorization of welfare reform could result in important changes.* Washington, DC: Brookings Institute.

Individuals with Disabilities Education Act of 1990, PL 101-476, 20 U.S.C. §§ 1400 *et seq.*

Kingery, J.N., Erdley, C.A., Marshall, K.C., Whitaker, K G., & Reuter, T.R. (2010). Peer experiences of anxious and socially withdrawn youth: An integrative review of the developmental and clinical literature. *Clinical Child & Family Psychology Review, 13*(1), 91–128.

Knoll, J.A. (1996). Charting unknown territory with families of children with complex medical needs. In G.H.S. Singer, L.E. Powers, & A.L. Olson, *Redefining family support: Innovations in public-private partnerships* (pp. 189–220). Baltimore, MD: Paul H. Brookes Publishing Co.

Konigsberg, R.D. (2011, August 8). Chore wars. *Time, 178*(5). Retrieved August 5, 2012, from http://www.time.com/time/magazine/article/0,9171,2084582,00.html

Lee, D., Levey, N., & Lazo, A. (2011, September 14). U.S. poverty totals hit a 50-year high. *Los Angeles Times,* pp. A1, A15.

Lynch, E.W., & Hanson, M.J. (Eds.). (2011). *Developing cross-cultural competence: A guide to working with children and their families* (4th ed.). Baltimore, MD: Paul H. Brookes Publishing Co.

Malinowski, B. (1939). The group and the individual in functional analysis. *American Journal of Sociology, 44,* 938–964.

McWilliam, R.A. (2010). Assessing families' needs with the routines-based interview. In R.A. McWilliam (Ed.), *Working with families of young children with special needs* (pp. 27–59). New York, NY: Guilford Press.

Minuchin, S. (1974). *Families and family therapy.* Cambridge, MA: Harvard University Press.

Minuchin, S., & Fishman, H.C. (1981). *Family therapy techniques.* Cambridge, MA: Harvard University Press.

Mullane, D. (Ed.). (1995). *Words to make my dream children live: A book of African American quotations.* New York, NY: Doubleday.

Olson, D.H., Russell, C.S., & Sprenkle, D.H. (1980). Circumplex model of marital and family systems II: Empirical studies and clinical intervention. *Advances in Family Intervention Assessment and Theory, 1,* 129–179.

Olson, D.H., Sprenkle, D.H., & Russell, C.S. (1979). Circumplex model of marital and family systems I: Cohesion and adaptability dimensions, family types, and clinical applications. *Family Process, 18,* 3–28.

Onaga, E.E., McKinney, K.G., & Pfaff, J. (2000). Lodge programs serving family functions for people with psychiatric disabilities. *Family Relations, 49,* 207–217.

Osofsky, J.D., Hann, D.M., & Peebles, C. (1993). Adolescent parenthood: Risks and opportunities for mothers and infants. In C.H. Zeanah, Jr. (Ed.), *Handbook of infant mental health* (pp. 106–119). New York, NY: Guilford Press.

Pogrebin, L.C. (1983). *Family and politics: Love and power on an intimate stage.* New York, NY: McGraw-Hill.

Rehabilitation Act of 1973, PL 93-112, 29 U.S.C. §§ 701 *et seq.*

Ronneau, J.P. (1999). Ordinary families–extraordinary caregiving. *Family Preservation Journal, 4*(1), 63–80.

Roston, E. (2002, April 8). How much is a living wage? *Time, 159,* 52–54.

Roth-Hanania, R., Busch-Rossnagel, N., & Higgins-D'Alessandro, A. (2000). Development of self and empathy in early infancy: Implications for atypical development. *Infants and Young Children, 13*(1), 1–14.

Seifer, R., & Dickstein, S. (1993). Parental mental illness and infant development. In C.H. Zeanah, Jr. (Ed.), *Handbook of infant mental health* (pp. 120–142). New York, NY: Guilford Press.

Seligman, M., & Darling, R.B. (2007). *Ordinary families, special children* (3rd ed.). New York, NY: Guilford Press.

Serrat, O. (2008). *Managing knowledge workers.* Retrieved July 8, 2012, from http://www.adb .org/Documents/Information/Knowledge -Solutions/Managing-Knowledge-Workers .pdf

Skiba, R.J., Poloni-Staudinger, L., Gallini, S., Simmons, A.B., & Feggins-Azziz, R. (2006). Disparate access: The disproportionality of African American students with disabilities across educational environments. *Exceptional Children, 72*(4), 411–424.

Sullivan, A.L. (2011). Disproportionality in special education identification and placement of English language learners. *Exceptional Children, 77*(3), 317–334.

Summers, J.A., Brotherson, M.J., & Turnbull, A.P. (1988). The impact of handicapped children on families (pp. 504–544). In E.W. Lynch & R.B. Lewis (Eds.), *Exceptional Children and Adults: An Introduction to Special Education.* Glenview, IL: Scott Foresman.

Turnbull, A.P., & Rueff, M. (1997). Family perspectives on inclusive lifestyle issues for people with problem behavior. *Exceptional Children, 63,* 211–227.

Turnbull, A.P., Summers, J.A., & Brotherson, M.J. (1984). *Working with families with disabled members: A family systems approach.* Lawrence, KS: University of Kansas.

Turnbull, A.P., & Turnbull, H.R. (2001). *Families, professionals, and exceptionalities: Collaborating for empowerment* (4th ed.). Upper Saddle River, NJ: Merrill-Prentice Hall.

van Eys, J. (1979). The normally sick child. In J. van Eys (Ed.), *The normally sick child* (pp. 11–27). Baltimore, MD: University Park Press.

Families with Children with Disabilities

Marci J. Hanson

"It was ability that mattered, not disability, which is a word I'm not crazy about using."

—Marlee Matlin (as cited in Miserandino, 2004)

"Having [a child with a disability] has taught me not to judge others who are different . . . rather find their strengths."

—Parent (as cited in Hanson, 2003b, p. 358)

"He's definitely been a blessing over and over and over again. He's always had a positive attitude. He's taught me what unconditional love is."

—Parent (as cited in Hanson, 2003b, p. 358)

Disability is a part of our lives. A report jointly released by the World Health Organization and the World Bank estimated that 15% of the world's population has a significant physical or intellectual disability, including about 5% of children (Brown, 2011; World Health Organization, 2011). Although the incidence of disability increases with aging, a large number of children also have disabilities. Trends in prevalence data for the United States reveal that approximately one in six children have developmental disabilities and specific conditions, such as autism and attention-deficit/hyperactivity disorder, have increased in recent years (Boyle et al., 2011).

The experience of families in rearing and caring for their children with disabilities has been the subject of articles in the popular press and in scientific journals. Many have emphasized the possibility for negative repercussions related to the disability and documented the increased struggles faced by families in meeting the health, educational, and social needs of their children. In recent decades, this perspective has been replaced by a more comprehensive and balanced approach that considers both positive and negative outcomes and an analysis of family interaction and adaptation when a child has special needs (Blacher & Baker, 2007; Blacher & Hatton, 2007).

To be sure, the presence of disabling conditions can be challenging. However, the notion of disability is a complex phenomenon. The transactional nature of development underscores the importance of each person's interaction with her or his environment. A physical or intellectual condition may be deemed a barrier for one person in one context, but it may not be experienced as a difficulty by another person in a different setting. The ability to walk and the reality of whether an individual uses legs or a wheelchair for mobility, for instance, have little bearing on the person's ability to use a computer or function as a productive member of society.

Current international perspectives on health and disability, as articulated through the International Classification of Functioning, Disability and Health of the World Health Organization (2012), now reflect this more complex and transactional outlook. The revised classification system for describing health status has shifted away from the sole emphasis on a particular physical condition to a broader view of how individuals are able to function and socially participate in their environment. Health and disability factors are viewed from a more social perspective and account for the contexts in which individuals live.

The family is typically the primary context of importance for the child with a disability. This chapter examines the context of the family and the experiences of families as they adapt and adjust to circumstances associated with the disability. The focus is on understanding families' abilities to meet the needs of all family members including the child with disabilities, as well as service delivery models that support and enhance families' strengths and resources in addressing their own family goals and functions.

The cultural and community contexts in which families reside and interact may profoundly influence their abilities to approach challenges posed by their children's health and disability conditions. Developmental disabilities occur in all socioeconomic and ethnic groups. However, a family living in poverty that is struggling to meet the most basic health, safety, and sustenance needs of their children may need more supports and assistance outside the family to address their concerns. Families' living contexts in which disabilities are met with acceptance and community support, on the other hand, may experience different types of needs to meet their families' goals. As we have discussed throughout this text, families' societal contexts can play pivotal roles in supporting or limiting the family's ability to function.

The experiences of families and the opportunities and options that are available to them in rearing and supporting a family member with developmental disabilities or risks is deeply embedded in the values and culture of the society within which the family resides. Race, culture, social class, and language are variables integrally linked to how developmental disabilities are defined and the opportunities provided to children and families (Klingner, Blanchett, & Harry, 2007). Families' interactions with the various contexts in which they are nested (e.g., neighborhood; community; health, education, and social service agencies; government) deeply affect how they adapt to circumstances surrounding disability. As such, the service delivery system must offer a variety of options that are flexible and can be tailored to the variable needs of families in this diverse world. Contemporary options for service delivery reflect a shift away from earlier service models that were primarily professionally driven. Today, service systems typically are more family based and designed to support and enable families to function effectively.

Societal mores have varied over the years and across cultures depending on attitudes and perspectives on the meaning of disability (Berry & Hardman, 1998; Klingner et al., 2007; Safford & Safford, 1996). In ancient times, individuals with disabilities in some societies were cast out or even killed because they were viewed as burdens or nonproductive members of that society. In other societies, they were seen as possessing special powers and links to higher spiritual powers. Although the industrial age gave rise to more humanitarian perspectives and reforms, disability typically was viewed as a disease. Greater focus was given to intervention through medical and/or education regimens, but attempts to "cure" the disability were generally unsuccessful. Societies that placed high value on the economic contributions of its citizenry showed a lack of acceptance toward individuals with disabilities because they doubted the productivity of these individuals. In time, most cultures have embraced social and educational programs for individuals with disabilities. The participation or self-determination of those individuals and their families in defining their own needs and supports has increasingly become the priority.

Societal values and mores also influenced service practices and scientific investigation by clinicians and researchers. For many years, parents—particularly mothers—were blamed for their children's disabilities such as intellectual and developmental disabilities, emotional disturbances, and health problems. For instance, mothers of children with autism were characterized as cold and unresponsive and were viewed by some as being responsible for their children's disorders. Notions promulgated during the eugenics movement (1880–1930) undoubtedly fueled this view of parents as causing their children's disabilities (Turnbull & Turnbull, 1990).

Fortunately, contemporary viewpoints have led to a more informed and just, less linear, and more transactional approach to understanding the nature of human development and to promoting models that support optimal outcomes. They recognize the dynamic nature of the interplay between the child and the family, between the family and the larger world or community, and the importance of interactions among family members. This focus leads to interventions that more closely address family priorities and concerns and identify appropriate points of support.

INITIAL FAMILY EXPERIENCES WHEN A BABY IS BORN WITH A DISABILITY

Most expectant parents have developed a picture in their minds of the child they will have. Wrapped up in these mental images are all the hopes and dreams, cultural values and expectations, family histories, and personal preferences of each parent. When a child is born with or subsequently acquires a disability or disorder, these images, as well as the hopes and expectations, must be revisited and adjusted.

Parents who give birth to a child with a disability often describe their initial reaction as one of feeling shattered, overwhelmed, or devastated. These adjectives underscore the shock, the suddenness, and the comprehensive impact this event can have on the family. They also highlight the sadness and the violation of expectations that the event precipitates. Families may experience trauma when this discrepancy occurs between the ideal or fantasized child and birth experience and the actual child and less optimal birth situation (Bruce & Schultz, 2001; Solnit & Stark, 1961). When the reality of the circumstances does not match parents' hopes and expectations, parents are faced with an altered course for their family.

Clinicians have likened parents' responses to those of people who experience the terminal illness or death of a loved one. Parental response has been described as mourning the loss of the expected child. Using stage models, typically based on the stages of grief described in the work of Kubler-Ross (1969), clinicians have speculated that parents go through a series of responses to the traumatic event that begins with shock and disorganization or disequilibrium (including feelings of denial, anxiety, guilt, anger, depression, fear, blame, and bargaining or shopping for another option or cure) and is followed by acceptance and reorganization.

Although such models can be useful for understanding the range of emotions and feeling states that family members may experience as they grapple with the new knowledge of the child's disability, significant caveats are in order. Some family members may experience these feeling states, whereas others may not. Some may pass through these states, but in a different order. Some individuals may experience these states, but each may take varying amounts of time to go from state to state; for example, individuals may dwell in an emotional state for a long time or for a day. Categorizing family members' responses as lodged in a particular stage based on a limited interaction can be disrespectful, overly simplistic, and poor clinical practice. Rather, service providers must appreciate the tremendous variation in parental reactions as well as the other stresses, strains, and supports that are brought to bear on the situation.

Furthermore, cultural backgrounds and values play a significant role in defining the meaning families place on having children with disabilities (Hanson, Lynch, & Wayman, 1990; Lynch & Hanson, 2011). Just as different cultures stress different child-rearing practices, roles for family members, and family values, the meaning and causation ascribed to disability or risk also vary according to cultural history and background. In some cultures, disability may be attributed to chance, whereas in others it may be seen as a punishment for a sin committed or a taboo violated by one of the parents (e.g., eating the wrong food) or an ancestor (e.g., committing a wrongdoing or crime). In some cultures, the individual with a disability may be seen as virtually possessed by an evil spirit, whereas in other cultures the individual with a disability may be seen as a gift from God and as imbued with special powers or perceptions. The interaction of disability and gender may play a role as well. In some cultures, the birth of a male child is more highly prized than that of a female; in these cultures, if the boy is born with a deformity or disability, the reaction may be particularly adverse. Given the diversity among the families and the variability of cultural responses to the meaning of disability, care must be taken by family service professionals not to jump to rapid conclusions about the family's interpretation or behavior with respect to the meaning of the birth event or disability. Service providers are cautioned not to make assumptions about family responses or the stages that the family will encounter. Stage theories simply do not account for diversity among families, nor do they respect individual differences in responses. They do not acknowledge the transactional nature of family responses and adjustment.

IMPACT OF DISABILITY ON FAMILIES

The preponderance of clinical and research attention has been directed to the negative impact on the family of having a child with a disability. Today, those in the scientific and clinical communities typically incorporate a more balanced perspective, considering the potential positive impact as well as the strengths and resilience of families (Blacher & Hatton, 2007; Blacher, Neece, & Paczkowski, 2005; Hastings & Taunt, 2002; Risdal & Singer, 2004; Summers, Behr, & Turnbull, 1989).

The addition of any new member to the family usually brings not only joy and hope but also some trepidation and stress. Although stress is a part of human existence for all individuals and families, families of individuals with disabilities may be subject to additional stressors created by the risk or disabling conditions (Singer & Irvin, 1989). Families are typically thrust into new interactions with a myriad of professionals in the medical and health care fields, education, and social services. Some of these interactions may relate to highly emotional and draining life and death decisions. Families also are met with increased bills and financial burdens for these services. Parental employment and child care arrangements often are affected by the child's disorder, and the family's routines and activities may be dramatically altered in response to the child's needs. The challenges of caregiving may be overwhelming to primary caregivers, not to mention their impact on interactions with other family members, friends, and acquaintances. The disability, like a rock thrown into a pond, has repercussions that reverberate throughout the elements and routines of the family's life. As one father related, "Adam's our cruise, our new home, our boat. You know over the years, we laugh because every time we would get a down payment [for a house], it would go for Adam" (as cited by Hanson, 2003b, p. 360). Although this family realistically appraised their situation and lamented some of their sacrifices, they also added that they "wouldn't have had it any other way."

A number of research studies have examined stress in relationship to families of children with disabilities. In general, findings comparing these families with those of children who are typically developing find increased stress and greater demands on family functioning and well-being for families with children with disabilities (Beckman, 1991; Dodd, Zabriskie, Widmer, & Eggett, 2007; Dyson, 1991, 1993; Palfrey, Walker, Butler, & Singer, 1989; Winkler, 1988). The type of disability also has been linked to amount of stress and family functioning. Greater stress has been associated with severe physical disabilities (Sloper & Turner, 1993), autism, conduct disorders and behavior problems (Noh, Dumas, Wolf, & Fishman, 1989; Orr, Cameron, Dobson, & Day, 1993; Sanders & Morgan, 1997), intellectual disabilities (Fidler, Hodapp, & Dykens, 2000), and neurological disorders (Hanson & Hanline, 1990). Although it is noteworthy that characteristics and types of disability appear to play a role in the degree to which families experience stress and demands (Hodapp, Ly, Fidler, & Ricci, 2001; Sanders & Morgan, 1997), most studies have not addressed how perceptions may vary by gender and cultural group. Some studies have noted different predominant types of stress for mothers (e.g., caregiving) and fathers (e.g., financial), as well as the effect of family structure (e.g., being a single parent versus having a partner) on stress levels (Bailey, Blasco, & Simeonsson, 1992; Beckman, 1991; Trute & Hauch, 1988). The research studies, as a whole, do establish that many families of children with disabilities encounter additional stressors or demands necessitating changes and reorganization in families' expectations for their children, in the roles and relationships among family members, and in the routines and priorities of the family.

Investigations also have documented the more positive impact on families of having children with disabilities. Reviews have examined these dimensions of positive experiences on family life related to parenting and sibling experiences and have identified factors such as pleasure and satisfaction in caring for and relating to the child, personal growth, and greater purpose in life (Dykens, 2005; Hastings & Taunt, 2002; Stoneman, 2005). These studies have attempted to identify the full range of family experiences; other studies have included families from various cultural groups. Blacher and Baker (2007), for instance, studied families of children with disabilities from both Anglo and Latino backgrounds. They inferred positive impact from the lack of negative views, the fact that parents experienced many of the same joys of child rearing as did families of children without disabilities, and the reports that families experienced unique or special benefits from their parenting experiences, such as greater sensitivity and tolerance. They found positive impact was inversely related to children's behavior problems and that positive impact moderated the relationship between parenting stress and behavior problems. Differences between cultural groups were noted in that Latina mothers reported higher positive impact.

The impact of a child with a disability in the family will vary from family to family. The presence of a disabling condition may add to family demands and necessitate adjustments in family life. However, like any factor, the impact will be enacted differently by different families and will vary over time. Service providers are encouraged to keep this more balanced perspective in mind. Global generalizations about family reactions and needs fail to take into account differences in personal characteristics of family members, including dimensions such as personality dispositions, coping styles, and cultural values and beliefs.

FRAMEWORKS FOR UNDERSTANDING
FAMILIES' EXPERIENCES AND OUTCOMES

To fully appreciate the range of family responses and the circumstances faced by families as they adjust to challenges posed by a disabling condition, it is useful to reflect on the conceptual models (family systems, ecological, and coping/adaptation models) described in Chapter 3. These models all emphasize the dynamic interaction between families and their environment in the processes of adaptation and adjustment to change. Assumptions that the presence of a disabling condition will lead to negative repercussions are not supported. Moreover, emphasis is placed on how families use their resources to adjust and adapt to their altered circumstances (McCubbin & Patterson, 1982; Patterson, 1988, 1989, 1993) and how the family as a unit and individual family members may grow personally from the experience. These changes are deeply influenced by and embedded in the social relationships among family members and their relationships with others, including service providers. Families have different types and amounts of resources, and the meaning they ascribe to challenges and resources will vary. Service providers will be well served to appreciate this diversity in family response and appreciate the individual and unique characteristics of each family's set of circumstances.

SERVICES AND SUPPORT FOR
FAMILIES OF CHILDREN WITH DISABILITIES

All service delivery systems in the fields of health care, education, and social services face challenges related to how best to serve and support families as they adjust to the different or increased demands associated with raising a child with a disability or developmental risk. As discussed throughout this text, service delivery philosophies have shifted away from linear or medical models that directly link the individual's outcome to a disease or disorder to more dynamic approaches aimed at capitalizing on the resources and strengths that individuals and families bring to their situations. It is likely that families have not suddenly developed new strengths and resources. Rather, service providers have made a shift into new roles and relationships with families.

These philosophical shifts and concomitant changes in service delivery models are directly linked to societal values and mores and to beliefs about families. As service providers travel this road of working with families in various capacities, it is important to remember that these values and philosophies drive services. Service providers have personal choices to make along this path with respect to how they behave with families.

Historically, when a child was diagnosed with a disability, parents and other family members were given a prescribed set of activities or directives for where and how to care for their child. Specialists in the various helping professions (i.e., health, education, and social services) functioned as experts and, like orchestra conductors, they assessed the child's difficulties and needs and provided guidance and direction to families.

The importance of parents' involvement in the care and education of their children with disabilities has long been understood, and the roles and relationships of family members in their children's intervention regimens have been paramount. Over the years, parents of children with disabilities have functioned as their children's advocates, political advocates, organization members, teachers, assistant staff members in intervention programs, and program catalysts. Many parents still actively participate in their children's services through these roles. Although parents historically have been seen as crucial to their children's development, they have often been relegated to the role of recipients of services rather than decision makers. These service philosophies can be contrasted with more contemporary program philosophies that emphasize partnerships between parents and professionals, placing the family at the core of the decision-making process (Sandall, McLean, & Smith, 2000).

Family-Centered and Relationship-Based Approaches

Two terms have entered the early intervention service delivery lexicon and best describe the goals of contemporary service philosophy: *family-centered* and *relationship-based* interventions or service delivery models. Both stress the importance of acknowledging the child as living within the context of the family, the family members as the primary decision makers for the child, and the relationships among family members and among family members and professionals as being essential to the intervention and support processes. Family-centered (also referred to as family-focused or family-based) approaches place emphasis on the following (Bailey et al., 1986):

- Helping the family to care for and raise their child with a disability and cope with unique needs

- Helping the family understand the development and needs of the child both as an individual and as a family member

- Promoting parent–child interactions that are sensitive and warm, mutually enjoyable, and appropriate to the child's developmental level

- Preserving and reinforcing the dignity of the family by responding to their needs and desires in all phases of service—assessment, planning, and evaluation

Family-centered models can be contrasted with more traditional approaches in that the focus is on the child within the context of the family, not just on the child. The child's and family's *strengths* and *resources* are highlighted and form the basis for the intervention. Again, this is in contrast to previous approaches that focused on the disability as a pathology or difficulty. Families are placed in the role of decision makers rather than merely as the recipients of decisions made by experts or specialists. This orientation represents a shift in power in the relationship.

The implementation of family-centered services often involves new roles and relationships and "ways of doing business" for professionals who have been trained as experts only. Professionals must continue to maintain and update their knowledge and special expertise and share this information with families. The goals, styles, and methods they use in their delivery of services may be modified somewhat from traditional approaches, however. The following key elements for professional behavior have been identified as essential to the implementation of family-centered services and remain strong underpinnings of clinical service (Edelman, Greenland, & Mills, 1992):

- Recognizing the family as the constant in the child's life, whereas other caregivers and service systems may come and go

- Facilitating collaboration at all service levels between parents and professionals

- Honoring and respecting family diversity in all dimensions—cultural, racial, ethnic, linguistic, spiritual, and socioeconomic

- Recognizing family strengths and the different approaches that families may use in coping

- Sharing unbiased and honest information with family members on an ongoing basis

- Encouraging family-to-family support and networking

- Acknowledging and incorporating the developmental needs of the child and other family members into the service

- Implementing policies and services that promote emotional and financial support for families

- Designing and implementing services that are accessible, culturally and linguistically respectful and responsive, flexible, and based on family-identified needs

The centrality of the relationship between parent and child is emphasized in the expanded concept of relationship-based service approaches. Although typically applied to clinical approaches in infant mental health and early intervention, the relationship-based model underscores the crucial importance of services aimed at supporting and nurturing sensitive and satisfying parent–child interactions and relationships (Mahoney, 2009; Weston, Ivins, Heffron, & Sweet, 1997; see also Chapter 8 in this text). This approach advocates and incorporates partnerships between parents and professionals in the planning and implementation of appropriate services for the child and family.

Enabling and Empowering Families

The family-centered and relationship-based service approaches focus on the child within the context of the family, rather than on the child alone. The family is part of a social system and all parts of the system are interconnected. Empowerment is a helpful concept for guiding service practices with families; empowerment may include a person's access to and control over needed resources, decision-making and problem-solving abilities, and abilities to interact effectively with others to gain the resources they need (Dunst, Trivette, & Deal, 1988). In examining the early intervention context and analyzing the roles of help seekers and help givers, Dunst et al. highlighted the importance of service providers (help givers) in creating opportunities for families (in this case, help seekers) to experience and display their competence. They referred to these experiences as *enabling*. Thus, the major thrust of these family-centered services is to help families become more competent and mobilize their resources.

The assessment and intervention model advocated by Dunst et al. (1988) described four components. The first component is the identification of family needs and aspirations—what the family's priorities are and where the family wants to expend their efforts and resources. The second component is the family's style and functioning—in other words, the unique ways in which that family operates. Third, the family's social network is mapped to identify resources for meeting the family's needs. Finally, the help-giving behavior of the professionals facilitates families' aligning their needs and resources to implement their goals.

Support for families may come from many sources including both formal and informal networks. Formal networks typically include professionals and helping agencies (i.e., education, health, and social services) that are formed to provide assistance to families needing services. Informal networks refer to family members, friends, neighbors, social groups, spiritual leaders, and so forth. Although these informal networks are not formed to provide assistance, they often serve that purpose. For many years, these informal sources of support were often overlooked or underrated. As services have been implemented with a social systems perspective in mind, the importance and power of these informal social support resources to family well-being has come to be recognized (Dunst, Trivette, Gordon, & Pletcher, 1989).

Family Experiences and Service Options

Families of children with disabilities, like all families, face an inordinate number of daily demands. When the child (or any family member) has extra or extraordinary needs for care, the family may be faced with even more challenges. The discussion that follows highlights some of the resources and personal characteristics that have been described

by families as useful or as outcomes of their experiences in parenting a child with a disability. These issues are directly, forcefully, and eloquently described by parents themselves in a number of publications (e.g., Harry, 2010; Naseef, 2001; Spiegle & van den Pol, 1993; Turnbull et al., 1993; Turnbull & Turnbull, 1985).

Growing Personally Families often describe their own personal growth and that of their immediate family members as a result of raising a child with disabilities. It is common for parents to note increases in their abilities to advocate for their children and their own sense of self-reliance and self-esteem. They often take great pride in the challenges they have effectively met and express confidence in their abilities to continue to address the needs of their child and family. Family members also mention the growth they have experienced in terms of helping others and being more receptive to other people who may be different. One mother of a (now adult) child with Down syndrome described her experience of returning to study at a community college. She related with pride that she went out of her way to help foreign students find their way around the college because she understood what it was like to be treated as different and what it was like to be fearful of new challenges. These experiences do not minimize the many difficulties that families may encounter, but they do illustrate the opportunities for personal growth and satisfaction that many family members report.

Developing New Skills and Resources Families of children with disabilities may need and receive a variety of services from formal networks. Caring for a child with a disability typically demands that the parents develop a certain degree of expertise in complex medical jargon and procedures, therapy techniques, and educational protocol. A major goal of most helping agencies is to provide information, education, and training in caring for and educating children with disabilities. Through the use of these informational and education/training resources, family members often become quite knowledgeable in and adept at working with children with that particular disability. They use these skills and expertise to improve their own children's circumstances and also to help other families of children with similar challenges. Increasingly, parents and other family members have become teaching partners in in-service and preservice training programs for professionals in the helping fields. Parents' input and perspectives are highly valuable to new and continuing professionals in training.

Supporting Parent–Child Interactions and Relationships A child with a disability may present many caregiving challenges. Some young children, for example, are hard to soothe. Others, due to their physical disabilities, may remain in rigid postures or fail to make eye contact with their parents. All of these characteristics can affect the way that parents feel about their children and can hamper parents' feelings of competence and enjoyment when interacting with them. Professionals can assist parents to more effectively read and understand their children's signals or cues and respond in a fashion that will enhance interaction and their children's development (Hanson, 1996).

Reducing Stress Family services may be aimed at reducing the family's stress and demands. This may be as simple as a professional being more attentive to the stress of a family and showing care not to pile on programs, services, or appointment demands. It may come in the form of helping parents procure needed services such as respite care, child care, or community programs that will include the child with special needs. In some cases, formal counseling or stress reduction workshops may be useful for the parent, and the professional can assist him or her in finding such services.

Linking to Parent-to-Parent and Community Resources Some families may choose the opportunity to get to know other parents in similar circumstances or parents who have "gone before" them and have experiences to share. Numerous parent-to-parent networks and family resource centers are found throughout the nation, and professionals may help families to link to these networks in their communities (Santelli, Poyadue, & Young, 2001). Similarly, a variety of national, state, and local organizations that range from disability rights organizations to city recreational programs may be useful to families. For more information, visit the National Dissemination Center for Children with Disabilities web site (http://www.nichcy.org).

Again, the role of the professional is to provide parents with the information they need to be able to gain access to these services if they wish. Some parents desire active participation in parent networks and/or other community organizations; others prefer to remain more contained within their immediate family or ethnic, cultural, or spiritual communities. Although information and service options should be made available and accessible to all families in the modality and language of their choice, professionals must respect families' decisions regarding whether or to what degree they wish to participate in these organizations.

Focusing Services on Family Priorities and Strengths

Services that are truly family centered are culturally sensitive and respectful. Implementing these services typically requires a shift in perspective or point of view for most service providers. Rather than starting with professional assumptions about what the family needs or should have based on the challenges posed by the disability, professionals must begin with identifying the family's own priorities and concerns. This focus precludes an a priori view of what impact the disability may have or what services the family may need or desire. Working with families in creating strategies and mapping their resources puts the family in the position of power and responsibility. This perspective emphasizes the strengths and resources that families bring to the table rather than the problems created by the child's disability. The experiences of one family, Gennifer and Demiko, help demonstrate family experiences and service models.

Gennifer and Demiko

Gennifer is a 19-year-old high school dropout and single mother raising her 3-year-old son, Demiko. Demiko was born prematurely and hospitalized for a prolonged period of time at birth. Medical personnel suspect that the premature delivery was related to Gennifer's lack of prenatal care and drug use during pregnancy. Demiko has multiple disabilities including cerebral palsy, speech delays, and visual impairments. Gennifer lives in a large urban area on very little income from her part-time job.

If the story ended here, it would be easy to predict that the outcome for Demiko and Gennifer would not be a very positive one. Many professionals would be tempted to blame Gennifer for Demiko's poor developmental prognosis and prescribe an intensive regimen of therapy and education outside of the home. However, the story does not stop here. Gennifer lives with her mother and her grandmother in her mother's home. All three women love Demiko dearly and spend countless hours tending to him. A home-based early intervention teacher visits their home weekly to help teach them strategies for caring for Demiko and enhancing his development. Together, these women are looking for preschool programs in their local community so that Demiko can begin school. Furthermore, Gennifer no longer uses drugs and has been clean since Demiko's birth. She is also working on her high school general equivalency diploma so that she can get a better job. To be sure, Gennifer and Demiko face many challenges, but they have many resources and strengths even though they are living in poverty and Demiko has severe disabilities.

The outlooks and options available to families are quite different depending on whether the focus is placed on their difficulties and what they lack, or whether the lens is aimed on the strengths and resources that families bring to meet their challenges. All families have strengths and resources; service providers should assist families in identifying these and accessing the supports that they need.

Justin

Justin is an extremely active 6-year-old boy who is passionate about trains and cars. His parents, Lily and Evan, try to capitalize on his interests by filling the house with books and toys about things with wheels. Because Justin is such a picky eater, his parents have continued the "wheel theme" at the dinner table with train placemats and plates; they even try to tempt Justin to eat by cooking wheel-shaped macaroni. Justin attends a local public school in his neighborhood and has been provided special education and related services since he was diagnosed as having an autism spectrum disorder when he was 2½ years old. His first school experience was an early intervention program. Once a week, an early interventionist visited Justin's family home and helped Justin's parents organize family routines to enhance Justin's communication and social skills as well as address his eating difficulties. When he was 3 years old, Justin attended a half-day preschool program where an itinerant special education teacher worked with his parents and the preschool teachers to modify the preschool and home environment to best meet Justin's educational and developmental goals. Evan also took off work for an afternoon each week to take his son to a local playgroup. Now, in his local neighborhood elementary school, Justin continues to receive special education services. Justin's parents are thankful for the expertise and assistance of teachers and other specialists who have taught them how to support Justin's development so that he can participate in school and have friends.

NATIONAL POLICIES FOR CHILDREN
WITH DISABILITIES AND THEIR FAMILIES[1]

Children with disabilities, like Justin and Demiko, typically need educational and developmental services that are specifically tailored to meet their individual needs. Their families also need support to learn how to address their youngster's own special needs. This

---

[1]A portion of the discussion on disability policy is adapted from Hanson (2003a).

section provides an overview of primary policies in the United States that are designed to address the needs of individuals with disabilities. These laws and policies have their foundation in years of experience and advocacy by professionals and parents of children with disabilities. Prior to the 1970s, some children in the United States were denied a public school education because they had disabilities. Family and advocate-initiated litigation, court decisions, national legislation, research studies, and family grassroots advocacy efforts all served to change this perspective dramatically. The 14th Amendment to the U.S. Constitution guarantees equal protection for all citizens under the law and establishes the right to not be discriminated against for an unjustifiable reason such as race or disability. This amendment was central to establishing a legal remedy for this inequity in educational opportunities for children with disabilities. For a historical discussion and review of public polity related to developmental disabilities, the reader is referred to Turnbull, Stowe, Turnbull, and Schrandt (2007).

Several key laws have provided far-reaching guarantees and rights for individuals with disabilities. This legislation charted policies and services to ensure that individuals with disabilities received equal protection under the law and public education. They also have ensured that families are active participants in educational programs. These laws are briefly reviewed, with special emphasis given to IDEA and its components for family involvement in children's educational planning and implementation.

Americans with Disabilities Act

ADA of 1990 is a landmark piece of legislation with crucial implications for access and education for children with disabilities. The ADA is a federal civil rights law that ensures that people with disabilities have access to all entities (including child care for young children). It gives individuals with disabilities civil rights protection like those provided to people on the basis of race, sex, national origin, and religion, and it requires that reasonable accommodations be made to allow everyone to participate in the services and opportunities offered.

Section 504 of the Rehabilitation Act of 1973

Section 504 of the Rehabilitation Act of 1973 is a civil rights law that prohibits discrimination on the basis of disability. In education, it continues to play an important role because it also applies to students with disabilities who may not be eligible for special educational services under other laws, such as IDEA. The definition of disability is defined more broadly and applies to those that have a physical or mental impairment that substantially limits one or more major life activities.

Assistive Technology Act

The Assistive Technology Act of 1998, amended in 2004 as Public Law 108-364, ensures that individuals with disabilities have access to assistive technology devices and services. The use of assistive technology for people with disabilities can improve individuals' access and the ability to function in school, home, work, and the community.

Individuals with Disabilities Education Act and Amendments

Access to public education and special education services and supports were realized for school-age children through another piece of landmark legislation, the Education for All Handicapped Children Act of 1975 (PL 94-142; see Braddock [1987] and Turnbull [1986] for reviews of federal policies and the development of this law in the United States). This law subsequently was modified to apply to all preschool-age children with disabilities and, through state discretionary programs, to children with disabilities from birth through 2 years. This legislation was retitled as IDEA of 1990 (PL 101-476) and was subsequently amended in 2004 (PL 108-446).

   IDEA Foundational Core Principles   IDEA provides the framework for educational policies and services for children with disabilities and their families. Six principles are core to this framework:

1. *Free and appropriate public education.* This provision requires that special education and related services be provided to children at public expense and that these services meet the standards of the state educational agency. A policy of "zero reject" is inherent in this law that precludes public schools from excluding children with disabilities. Furthermore, services are to be "appropriate" to the individual needs of each child.

2. *Appropriate evaluation.* This law stipulates many conditions related to evaluation: a "full and individual initial evaluation," the requirement of parental consent for the initial evaluation, evaluation by a team of professionals, assessment in the child's native language or mode of communication, the use of multiple measures rather than a single instrument to determine eligibility, and the provision for reevaluations. Furthermore, evaluation activities are to include data gathering information pertinent to the child's involvement and progress in the core general education curriculum, and evaluation procedures must be nondiscriminatory.

3. *Development of an individualized education program (IEP).* IDEA requires that an IEP be developed for each child with a disability. IEPs must state the child's current level of educational performance; measurable child goals; specified special education and related services; the dates, frequency, location, and duration of services;

and transition services to the next educational environment. The IEP is developed through a team approach that includes the child's parents and appropriate professionals. The child's strengths and the parents' concerns for enhancing the child's education are taken into consideration. For children from birth through 2 years of age, the individualized plan is termed the individualized family service plan (IFSP). These plans are described in greater detail in a subsequent section.

4. *Education provided in the least restrictive environment (LRE).* Children with disabilities must be provided an appropriate education designed to meet their individual needs in environments in which the children are educated with their peers without disabilities to the maximum extent possible. The intention of the law is to maximize the opportunities for children with disabilities to be educated with their peers and in their neighborhood communities. The emphasis is on creating services and supports that allow children to have access to and participate in the general education curriculum. For young children, the LRE is typically referred to as *natural environment* and may include the children's homes, as well as other settings in which children received care, such as child care programs.

5. *Parent participation in decision making.* Parents have the right to review their child's educational records, and parental informed consent is required for children's initial evaluation and placement. Parents can actively participate in all aspects of the evaluation, placement, and education process, and they have the right to challenge or appeal any decision related to the identification, evaluation, or placement of their child.

6. *Procedural safeguards to protect the rights of parents and their child with a disability.* IDEA outlines safeguards to ensure that the rights of children with disabilities and their parents are protected, including parents' access to educational records, right to request a due process hearing, and right to appeal the hearing decision and bring civil action to appeal a hearing decision. Rights and requirements related to discipline are specified in the law as well.

Family Roles and Services for Children   IDEA essentially establishes a national policy and infrastructure for a system of service delivery across the United States. Central to this service system is the recognition of the unique role that families play in children's development. Two primary components or parts of IDEA are reviewed: the Early Intervention Program for Infants and Toddlers with Disabilities, Part C of IDEA, which covers services to children from birth through age 2, and Part B of IDEA, which covers services to children from ages 3 through 22 years.

Early Intervention Program for Infants and Toddlers with Disabilities   In 1986, the U.S. Congress established the Early Intervention Program for Infants and Toddlers with Disabilities. The law was based on the recognition of "an urgent and substantial need" to enhance the development of infants and toddlers with disabilities, reduce education costs by minimizing the need for special education through early intervention, minimize the likelihood of institutionalization of individuals with disabilities, maximize independent living, and enhance the capacity of families to meet their children's needs.

The Program for Infants and Toddlers with Disabilities (Part C of IDEA) is a federal discretionary grant program that assists states in planning, developing, and implementing a statewide system of early intervention services for infants and toddlers with disabilities, ages birth through 2 years, and their families. The statute and regulations for Part C stipulate state requirements for implementing this comprehensive, coordinated, multidisciplinary, and interagency service delivery program.

For states to participate in the program, they must ensure that early intervention will be available to every eligible child. The law defines an eligible infant or toddler with a disability as follows (IDEA, 2004, 20 U.S.C.):

> An individual under 3 years of age who needs early intervention services because the individual (i) is experiencing developmental delays, as measured by appropriate diagnostic instruments and procedures in one or more of the areas of cognitive development, physical development, communication development, social or emotional development and adaptive development; or (ii) has a diagnosed physical or mental condition which has a high probability of resulting in developmental delay.

States may, at their discretion, also serve children who are at risk of experiencing substantial developmental delay as defined by that state. Thus, definitions of eligibility vary considerably across states.

In implementing the program, the governor of each state designates a lead state agency to administer the program. A variety of agencies may function as the lead agency including education, health, human services, social services, developmental disabilities, and rehabilitation service agencies. Despite state differences with respect to child eligibility criteria and the state's lead agency of administration, several elements must be stipulated in each state's plan. These common elements are the minimum components required of a statewide comprehensive system for early intervention for infants and toddlers with special needs (IDEA Part C, 20 U.S.C. §1435[a], as cited by National Early Childhood Technical Assistance System, 2012a):

- Definition of developmental delay

- Appropriate early intervention services based on scientifically based research

- Timely and comprehensive multidisciplinary evaluation of needs of children and family-directed identification of the needs of each family

- Individualized family service plan and service coordination

- Comprehensive child find and referral system

- Public awareness program

- Central directory of services, resources, and research and demonstration projects

- Policies and procedures for personnel standards and development

- Single line of authority in a lead agency designated or established by the governor for carrying out 1) general administration and supervision, 2) identification and coordination of all available resources, 3) assignment of financial responsibility to the appropriate agencies, 4) development of procedures to ensure that services are provided in a timely manner pending resolution of any disputes, 5) resolution of intra- and interagency disputes, and 6) development of formal interagency agreements

- Policy pertaining to contracting or otherwise arranging for services

- Procedure for securing timely reimbursement of funds

- Procedural safeguards

- System for compiling data on the early intervention system

- State interagency coordinating council

- Policies and procedures to ensure that, to the maximum extent appropriate, early intervention services are provided in natural environments

The range and types of services that are funded through this program are varied and represent services from many different disciplines. These services may include the following (20 U.S.C. §1400):

> (i) Family training, counseling, and home visits; (ii) special instruction; (iii) speech-language pathology and audiology services and signed language and cued language services;(iv) occupational therapy; (v) physical therapy; (vi) psychological services; (vii) service coordination services; (viii) medical services only for diagnostic or evaluation purposes; (ix) early identification, screening, and assessment services; (x) health services necessary to enable the infant or toddler to benefit from the other early intervention services; (xi) social work services; (xii) vision services; (xiii) assistive technology devices and assistive technology services; and (xiv) transportation and related costs that are necessary to enable an infant or toddler and the infant's or toddler's family to receive another service.

Family-centered services are to be provided in the child and family's natural environment. Thus, services may be provided in a range of environments that include the child's home and community locations, such as a child care or infant/toddler program.

A description and overview of this law and its components is provided by the National Early Childhood Technical Assistance Center (2012a). Updates to regulations and state services also are available (Danaher, Goode, & Lazar, 2011).

Part B of IDEA   Children and youth from 3–22 years receive special education and related services under Part B of IDEA that are administered through state and local education agencies. The provisions of due process, nondiscriminatory testing and evaluation, IEP, and placement in LREs that were reviewed earlier are applied to educational services. Important provisions of the law also acknowledge the role of parent involvement, particularly in programs for young children with disabilities, highlight strengthening the role of parents, and ensure meaningful opportunities for parents to participate in their child's education at school and home.

Eligibility criteria for a child with a disability under Part B of IDEA include the following conditions: intellectual disabilities, hearing impairments (including deafness, speech, or language impairments), visual impairments (including blindness), serious emotional disturbance, orthopedic impairments, autism, traumatic brain injury, other health impairments, specific learning disabilities, deaf-blindness, or multiple disabilities. For children from ages 3 to 9 years, the state and local educational agency may, at their discretion, also serve children with developmental delays as defined by that state; this may include delays in the areas of physical, cognitive, communication, social or emotional, or adaptive development.

A wide range of services may be considered in special education service delivery systems. These types of services include assistive technology devices and services, audiology, counseling services, early identification and assessment, medical services of diagnosis or evaluation, occupational therapy, parent counseling and training, physical therapy, psychological services, recreation, rehabilitation counseling services, school health services, social work services in schools, special education, speech pathology, and transportation.

Educational environments are typically more broadly construed for young children than they are for school-age children. For children younger than kindergarten age, educational environments may include child care and Head Start programs as well as school programs. Head Start is a key environment for services. The Head Start program was established in 1965 through provisions in the Economic Opportunity Act of 1964 (PL 88-452). A primary focus was to provide early educational and social services for young children from low-income families in an effort to provide them with a head start and to break the cycle of poverty. The Economic Opportunity Act subsequently was amended to require that at least 10% of the enrollments in Head Start be children with disabilities and that their specialized services be provided in these programs. As such, these Head Start service options have had a major impact in expanding inclusive services for young children. Head Start also has had, from its inception, a strong family and community focus, and it has emphasized multidisciplinary service provision and coordination. These are crucial components of services for children with disabilities.

Key Education Service Delivery Concepts Under IDEA   IDEA addresses a number of key concepts and components. The primary elements are outlined and briefly discussed.

Individualized Education Programs for Children   Under the law, all children with disabilities are required to have an IEP/IFSP. The IEP consists of a written statement that includes the child's present level of academic achievement and functional performance; measurable annual goals and a description of how the child's progress will be measured; special education and related services, supplementary aids and services, and program modifications or supports needed to enable the child to meet educational goals and participate with other children; an explanation of the extent, if any, to which the child will not participate with nondisabled children in the regular classroom; individual accommodations that may be needed to measure achievement and performance; the date for beginning services and the frequency, location, and duration of those services and modifications. An IEP team includes the child's parents, general education teacher, special education teacher, representative of the local educational agency, and other individuals who may have knowledge of or expertise regarding the child.

Under Part C, infants and toddlers and their families receive an IFSP. The IFSP includes written statements of the infant's or toddler's present levels of physical, cognitive, communication, social or emotional, and adaptive development; the family's resources, priorities, and concerns relating to enhancing the development of the child; the major outcomes expected and the criteria, procedures, and timelines used to determine progress; specific early intervention services; the natural environments in which early intervention services will be provided, including a justification if services will not be provided in a natural environment; the time, place and duration of the services; who pays for the services; the identification of the service coordinator who oversees the implementation of the IFSP; and the steps to be taken to support the transition of the toddler to preschool or other appropriate services. A model form for the IFSP is provided by the U.S. Department of Education (http://idea.ed.gov/part-c/search/new).

These individualized plans are fundamental to services for children with disabilities. Education plans and the delivery of services are designed to meet each child's unique needs, and systems of accountability are stipulated. Challenges have centered around the provision of appropriate and meaningful assessments, establishing parent–professional partnerships for planning and implementation, ensuring parents' meaningful roles while individualizing for each family's cultural and linguistic background and preferences, and exercising professional teamwork in developing and providing services.

Family-Centered Service Delivery Models In family-centered service delivery models, the full and active participation of parents and family members is encouraged, particularly in early intervention service delivery systems for infants, toddlers, and preschoolers. IDEA and its regulatory procedures formalized due process procedures and requirements for involving families in decisions regarding their child's assessment, placement, and education program planning and implementation.

The roles of families and the many ways in which families can be involved in their children's education programs have taken various forms and shifted over the years. At times, emphasis has been placed on notions of parents as teachers, parents as advocates, and parents as assistants in classrooms. Of course, one size does not fit all. Families differ in terms of their family membership or structure, family roles, culture and linguistic background, faith backgrounds, values and belief systems, resources, and the family's priorities and concerns for their children. So too do they differ in the roles and preferences for their involvement.

Family-centered or family-focused services refer not only to a philosophy of services, but also to a set of recommended practices in the field of early intervention (Bruder, 2000; Sandall, McLean, & Smith, 2000). These services describe a cluster of practices, including providing respectful and culturally sensitive family services, identifying families' concerns and priorities for their children, obtaining families' informed consent and participation in the decision-making process regarding service decisions for their children, and implementing practices that empower families and support and enhance families' development and competencies.

Inclusion, Least Restrictive Environments, and Natural Environments The law specifies that services should be provided to the maximum extent possible in educational environments in which children with disabilities are educated with children who do not have disabilities. It further stipulates that children should be removed from such an environment only when the nature or severity of the child's disability is such that the education cannot be achieved adequately in the general education environment with supplemental aids or services. This provision is often referred to as education in the least restrictive environment. Different terms, such as *mainstreaming* and *integration,* have been used over the years to describe the participation of children with disabilities in educational environments with their typically developing peers. Today, the practice is typically termed *inclusion.*

The intent is similar for infants and toddlers, although the language of the law differs somewhat. The Part C program for infants and toddlers states that services should be provided to the maximum extent appropriate in natural environments. Such environments include the child's home and community environments in which children without disabilities participate.

The provision of the children's individualized and specialized services within their homes and community and school programs requires careful planning, teamwork, administrative support, flexibility, and family involvement. Learning opportunities abound in daily routines and family and community activities. Particularly in the early years, interventionists are challenged to adapt activities, curricula, and environments and forge new working relationships to meet the needs of children with disabilities in a range of environments (Bruder & Dunst, 2000; Dunst, 2007; Guralnick, 2001; Odom, 2002; Sandall, McLean, & Smith, 2000; Sandall & Schwartz, 2008).

Transitions   A child's life is characterized by crucial transitions, particularly for children born at risk. These transitions are defined as "points of change in services and personnel who coordinate and provide services" (Rice & O'Brien, 1990, p. 2). The first transition may occur as the child moves from care in the hospital to the family's home. Subsequent transitions for children with disabilities include the transitions from home into infant/toddler services, from infant/toddler services into preschool, and from preschool to kindergarten to elementary school and so forth. Transitions can be stressful for families under the best of circumstances. Because in many states different agencies are responsible for early intervention services for infants/toddlers than for preschool/school-age education services, these transitions may be particularly challenging. Interagency agreements and transition procedures, support for families from key personnel, preparation of children for the transition, information exchange procedures between the sending and receiving services and personnel, and staff training and preparation for transition are but a few of the areas targeted for careful planning and support in order to ease transitions for children and their families (Hanson, 2005; Rosenkoetter, Hains, & Fowler, 1994).

Personnel Preparation and Interdisciplinary Team Models   Professional standards and personnel licensure, certification, and credentialing requirements may differ by state and also across professions based on the standards set by each professional discipline. Thus, considerable variability can be found across states, although all must adhere to provisions for a comprehensive system for professional development.

Most professional groups have expanded curricula at both the preservice and in-service levels to address competencies related to serving young children and their families, and many have separate certification or add-on training programs in pediatric or early care. Creative and cross-disciplinary approaches are needed, however, for personnel development across health, education, and social service fields (Winton, McCollum, & Catlett, 2008).

The range of service needs experienced by children with disabilities and their families bridge professional disciplines. Only through collaborative team models can these service needs be fully addressed. In early intervention, the transdisciplinary team model is considered the most optimal for service delivery. The transdisciplinary team model highlights a team approach through which "role release" is practiced, in that one or a few professionals are the primary individuals responsible for implementing a child's program with assistance, consultation, and continuous skill training and development from the full spectrum of team members representing various disciplines. This team approach requires careful collaboration across professional service providers and requires time and resource allocation for training and planning, as well as commitments and effective working relationships among professionals (Hanson & Bruder, 2001).

Parents and other family members are crucial members of any intervention/education team. Including families in a respectful, culturally sensitive, and family-centered way has necessitated adaptations and shifts in preservice and in-service personnel preparation for professionals. Most programs now actively seek and involve families in these training regimens.

Service Coordination and Interagency Collaboration   Service coordination is a mandated service under Part C of IDEA, and it is to be provided at no cost to families.

It is defined as an "active, ongoing process that assists and enables families to access services and assures their rights and procedural safeguards" (National Early Childhood Technical Assistance Center, 2012b). Early intervention team members must jointly provide assessment, intervention, and evaluation activities in a partnership with the child's family and enable families to obtain the various services they need (Bruder & Bologna, 1993). Active and collaborative cross-disciplinary working relationships and interagency coordination are needed regardless of the child's age and special needs. Such collaboration forms an important element in providing support to families.

Benefits of IDEA   The passage of IDEA has provided an unprecedented opportunity in the United States to establish a unified service delivery system to address the complex needs of children with disabilities and their families. A child's individualized service needs and goals and the active inclusion and participation of the child's family are at the core of policies and procedures. The legislation has provided the necessary infrastructure for developing a system that spans the United States and incorporates the full range of service delivery agencies, structures, and professional disciplines that deliver education services. It has afforded the means to cross boundaries of agencies and professions in order to serve the diverse needs of children and their families. By the same token, the comprehensive nature of this legislation also has produced tremendous challenges related to interagency coordination, teaming and collaboration, and the provision of full and meaningful participation options for families in a manner that is congruent with family priorities and needs.

SUMMARY

Although having a family member with a disabling condition may have a great impact on a family, many of the challenges these families face are the same or similar to those of other families. In other words, parents of children with disabilities should be viewed as parents first, just as their children with disabilities should be viewed as children first. When the child has a disability, however, it may create the need for more supports or specialized services to enable the child and family to participate in normative family events and routines.

As service providers reflect on their views about families and families' perspectives on parenting children with disabilities, they must be vigilant and keep in mind the impact of cultural and societal values in shaping these service priorities and approaches. Families are nested within the contexts of their neighborhoods and communities as well as the larger society in which they live. The policies, laws, values, and priorities of these communities help shape the experiences that families will have and the services and supports that will be available to them and desired by them.

Most individuals and families readjust and adapt to the new challenges presented to them by the presence of a disability. As the literature previously reviewed has suggested, families who have a member with a disability are often even inspired to reach out to others and develop a sense of their roles in the "greater good" of their communities. For instance, as one mother reflected, "I guess the hardest part has been to figure out what his little niche is. And I think maybe it's just that he's a teacher [of others]" (as cited by Hanson, 2003b, p. 364). Regardless of a family's goals, professionals can best help families by engaging in practices that facilitate the family's sense of competence and confidence and the family's abilities to determine the services and resources that they will need throughout their journey.

"Once we got over the dismay and shock at the hospital and picked up our shattered dreams and hopes, we began the slow process of reorienting and reorganizing those dreams and hope into a different set of rules, a different lifestyle. No, maybe our little boy with Down syndrome wouldn't be able to realize some of those high dreams we had composed before his birth, but with a little reshuffling (and a lot of hard work) he will be able to realize other dreams that we are composing day by day. So the song will have different words and a different melody, but will still be a masterpiece."

—Timothy and Marilyn Sullivan (as cited in Hanson & Harris, 1986, p. 8)

ACTIVITIES TO EXTEND THE DISCUSSION

1. **Mapping supports.** Identify a difficulty or issue of significance with which you or a family member is grappling. Develop a map or outline of the resources and supports that you have for addressing this concern. Try to consider the broad range of resources and supports that are available to you and the ways in which they are interconnected. Sketch out or display your "map" of these resources and supports much as you would an organizational chart for a business or corporation. Draw lines to show how they may be interconnected.

2. **Imagine how it feels.** To envision the experience for families as they encounter new stresses in their daily lives, try this activity with a friend or colleague. Ask your partner to make a list of all the stressors the family may encounter (e.g., car breaks down, child care provider moves away, illness in the family, parent loses job). With each stressor or demand, have your partner place a balloon in your arms. Before long you will find it difficult to manage or juggle the many balloon "stressors." Suddenly the balloons will start to drop or pop, creating even more chaos and instability for you as you struggle to keep them in order and afloat. While this task graphically displays the juggling act, it cannot possibly do justice to the emotional experience of coping with these issues, especially with a loved one such as one's child.

3. **Mapping supports and resources for a family in your clinical practice.** If it is comfortable and appropriate, work with a family in your clinical practice to map out the supports and resources that they have to address identified needs. For example, they may have extended family members and/or neighbors and friends who help out with child care, errands, and picking up children after school. Professionals may provide valuable services with respect to medical needs and educational needs. A local agency may provide information on housing options. As the discussion continues, professionals and families can identify and appreciate the many formal and informal supports that may be available to families.

TO LEARN MORE: SUGGESTED WEB SITES

National Dissemination Center for Children with Disabilities
http://www.nichcy.org

National Early Childhood Technical Assistance Center
http://www.nectac.org

Office of Special Education and Rehabilitative Services
http://www2.ed.gov/about/offices/list/osers/index.html

U.S. Department of Education
http://www.ed.gov

REFERENCES

Americans with Disabilities Act (ADA) of 1990, PL 101-336, 42 U.S.C. §§ 12101 *et seq.*

Bailey, D., Blasco, P.M., & Simeonsson, R.J. (1992). Needs expressed by mothers and fathers of young children with disabilities. *American Journal on Mental Retardation, 97,* 1–10.

Bailey, D., Simeonsson, R., Winton, P., Huntington, G., Comfort, M., Isbell, P., . . . Helm, J.M. (1986). Family-focused intervention: A functional model for planning, implementing, and evaluating individualized family services in early intervention. *Journal of the Division for Early Childhood, 10,* 156–171.

Beckman, P.J. (1991). Comparison of mothers' and fathers' perceptions of the effect of young children with and without disabilities. *American Journal on Mental Retardation, 95,* 585–595.

Berry, J.O., & Hardman, M.L. (1998).*Lifespan perspectives on the family and disability.* Boston, MA: Allyn & Bacon.

Blacher, J., & Baker, B. (2007). Positive impact of intellectual disability on families. *American Journal on Mental Retardation, 112,* 330–348.

Blacher, J., & Hatton, C. (2007). Families in context: Influences on coping and adaptation. In S. Odom, R. Horner, M. Snell, & J. Blacher (Eds.), *Handbook of developmental disabilities* (pp. 531–551). New York, NY: Guilford Press.

Blacher, J., Neece, C., & Paczkowski, E. (2005). Families and intellectual disability. *Current Opinion in Psychiatry, 18,* 507–513.

Boyle, C., Boulet, S., Schieve, L., Cohen, R., Blumberg, S., Yeargin-Allsopp, M., et al. (2011). Trends in the prevalence of developmental disabilities in U.S. children, 1997–2008. *Pediatrics, 127*(6), 1034–1042.

Braddock, D. (1987). *Federal policy toward mental retardation and developmental disabilities.* Baltimore, MD: Paul H. Brookes Publishing Co.

Brown, D. (2011, June 9). *Report: 15 percent of world population is disabled.* Retrieved July 12, 2012, from http://www.washingtonpost.com/national/report-15-percent-of-world-population-is-disabled/2011/06/09/AGZcqBNH_story.html

Bruce, E.J., & Schultz, C.L. (2001). *Nonfinite loss and grief: A psychoeducational approach.* Baltimore, MD: Paul H. Brookes Publishing Co.

Bruder, M.B. (2000). Family-centered early intervention: Clarifying our values for the new millennium. *Topics in Early Childhood Special Education, 20,* 105–115, 122.

Bruder, M.B., & Bologna, T.M. (1993). Collaboration and service coordination for effective early intervention. In W. Brown, S.K. Thurman, & L. Pearl (Eds.), *Family-centered early intervention with infants and toddlers: Innovative cross-disciplinary approaches* (pp. 103–127). Baltimore, MD: Paul H. Brookes Publishing Co.

Bruder, M.B., & Dunst, C.J. (2000). Expanding learning opportunities for infants and toddlers in natural environments: A chance to reconceptualize early intervention. *Zero to Three, 20*(3), 34–36.

Danaher, J., Goode, S. & Lazara, A. (Eds.). (2011). *Part C updates* (12th ed.). Chapel Hill, NC: National Early Childhood Technical Assistance Center.

Dodd, D., Zabriskie, R., Widmer, M., & Eggett, D. (2007). Contributions of family leisure to family functioning among families that include children with developmental disabilities. *Journal of Leisure Research, 41,* 261–286.

Dunst, C.J. (2007). Early intervention for infants and toddlers with developmental disabilities. In S. Odom, R. Horner, M. Snell, & J. Blacher (Eds.), *Handbook of developmental disabilities* (pp. 161–180). New York, NY: Guilford Press.

Dunst, C.J., Trivette, C.M., & Deal, A.G. (1988). *Enabling and empowering families: Principles and guidelines for practice.* Cambridge, MA: Brookline Books.

Dunst, C.J., Trivette, C.M., Gordon, N.J., & Pletcher, L.L. (1989). Building and mobilizing informal family support networks. In G.H.S. Singer & L.K. Irvin (Eds.), *Support for caregiving families: Enabling positive adaptation to disability* (pp. 121–141). Baltimore, MD: Paul H. Brookes Publishing Co.

Dykens, E. (2005). Happiness, well-being, and character strengths: Outcomes for families and siblings of persons with mental retardation. *Mental Retardation, 43,* 360–364.

Dyson, L.L. (1991). Families of young children with handicaps: Parental stress and functioning. *American Journal on Mental Retardation, 95,* 623–629.

Dyson, L.L. (1993). Response to the presence of a child with disabilities: Parental stress and family functioning over time. *American Journal on Mental Retardation, 98,* 207–218.

Economic Opportunity Act of 1964, PL 88-452, 42 U.S.C. §§ 2701 *et seq.*

Edelman, L., Greenland, B., & Mills, B.L. (1992). *Family-centered communication skills: Facilitator's guide.* St. Paul, MN: Pathfinder Resources.

Education for All Handicapped Children Act of 1975, PL 94-142, 20 U.S.C. §§ 1400 *et seq.*

Fidler, D., Hodapp, R., & Dykens, E. (2000). Stress in families of young children with Down syndrome, Williams syndrome, and Smith-Magenis syndrome. *Early Education and Development, 11,* 395–406.

Guralnick, M.J. (Ed.). (2001). *Early childhood inclusion: Focus on change.* Baltimore, MD: Paul H. Brookes Publishing Co.

Hanson, M.J. (1996). Early interactions. In M.J. Hanson (Ed.), *Atypical infant development* (2nd ed., pp. 235–272). Austin, TX: PRO-ED.

Hanson, M.J. (2003a). National legislation for early intervention: United States of America. In S. Odom, M.J. Hanson, J. Blackman, & S. Kaul (Eds.), *Early intervention practices around the world* (pp. 253–279). Baltimore, MD: Paul H. Brookes Publishing Co.

Hanson, M.J. (2003b). Twenty-five years after early intervention: Follow up of children with Down syndrome and their families. *Infants and Young Children, 16,* 354–365.

Hanson, M.J. (2005). Ensuring effective transitions in early intervention. In M.J. Guralnick (Ed.), *A developmental systems approach to intervention: National and international perspectives* (pp. 373–398). Baltimore, MD: Paul H. Brookes Publishing Co.

Hanson, M.J., & Bruder, M.B. (2001). Early intervention: Promises to keep. *Infants and Young Children, 13*(3), 47–58.

Hanson, M.J., & Hanline, M.F. (1990). Parenting a child with a disability: A longitudinal study of parental stress and adaptation. *Journal of Early Intervention, 14*(3), 234–248.

Hanson, M.J., & Harris, S.R. (1986). *Teaching the young child with motor delays.* Austin, TX: PRO-ED.

Hanson, M.J., Lynch, E.W., & Wayman, K.I. (1990). Honoring the cultural diversity of families when gathering data. *Topics in Early Childhood Special Education, 10*(1), 112–131.

Harry, B. (2010). *Melanie, bird with a broken wing: A mother's story.* Baltimore, MD: Paul H. Brookes Publishing Co.

Hastings, R., & Taunt, H. (2002). Positive perceptions in families of children with developmental disabilities. *American Journal on Mental Retardation, 107,* 116–127.

Hodapp, R., Ly, T., Fidler, D., & Ricci, L. (2001). Less stress, more rewarding: Parenting children with Down syndrome. *Parenting: Science and Practice, 1,* 317–337.

Individuals with Disabilities Education Act (IDEA) of 1990, PL 101-476, 20 U.S.C. §§ 1400 *et seq.*

Individuals with Disabilities Education Act (IDEA) of 2004, PL 108-446, 20 U.S.C. §§ 1400 *et seq.*

Klingner, J., Blanchett, W., & Harry, B. (2007). Race, culture, and developmental disabilities. In S. Odom, R. Horner, M. Snell, & J. Blacher (Eds.). *Handbook of developmental disabilities* (pp. 55–75). New York, NY: Guilford Press.

Kübler-Ross, E. (1969). *On death and dying.* New York, NY: Macmillan.

Lynch, E.W., & Hanson, M.J. (2011). *Developing cross-cultural competence: A guide for working with children and their families* (4th ed.). Baltimore, MD: Paul H. Brookes Publishing Co.

McCubbin, H.I., & Patterson, J.M. (1982). Family adaptation to crises. In H.I. McCubbin, A.E. Cauble, & J.M. Patterson (Eds.), *Family stress, coping and social support* (pp. 26–47). Springfield, IL: Charles C Thomas.

Mahoney, G. (2009). Relationship Focused Intervention (RFI): Enhancing the role of parents in children's developmental intervention. *International Journal of Early Childhood Special Education, 1,* 79–94.

Miserandino, D.M. (2004). Matlin, Marlee. *The celebrity café.* Retrieved from http://thecelebritycafe.com/interviews/marlee_matlin_2004_08.html

Naseef, R.A. (2001). *Special children, challenged parents: The struggles and rewards of raising a child with a disability* (Rev. ed.). Baltimore, MD: Paul H. Brookes Publishing Co.

National Early Childhood Technical Assistance Center. (2012a). *Part C.* Retrieved from July 12, 2012, from http://www.nectac.org/partc/partc.asp

National Early Childhood Technical Assistance Center. (2012b). *Service coordination under*

Part C. Retrieved July 12, 2012, from http://www.nectac.org/topics/scoord/scoord.asp

Noh, S., Dumas, J.E., Wolf, L.C., & Fishman, S.N. (1989). Delineating sources of stress in parents of exceptional children. *Family Relations, 38*, 456–461.

Odom, S.L. (Ed.). (2002).*Widening the circle: Including the child with disabilities in preschool programs*. New York, NY: Teachers College Press.

Orr, R.R., Cameron, S.J., Dobson, L.A., & Day, D.M. (1993). Age-related changes in stress experienced by families with a child who has developmental delays. *Mental Retardation, 1*, 171–176.

Palfrey, J.S., Walker, D.K., Butler, J.A., & Singer, J.D. (1989). Patterns of response in families of chronically disabled children: An assessment in five metropolitan school districts. *American Journal of Orthopsychiatry, 59*, 94–104.

Patterson, J.M. (1988). Families experiencing stress. The Family Adjustment and Adaptation Response Model. *Family Systems Medicine, 6*(2), 202–237.

Patterson, J.M. (1989). A family stress model: The Family Adjustment and Adaptation Response. In C. Ramsey (Ed.), *The science of family medicine* (pp. 95–117). New York, NY: Guilford Press.

Patterson, J.M. (1993). The role of family meanings in adaptation to chronic illness and disability. In A.P. Turnbull, J.M. Patterson, S.K. Behr, D.L. Murphy, J.G. Marquis, & M.J. Blue-Banning (Eds.), *Cognitive coping, families, and disability* (pp. 221–238). Baltimore, MD: Paul H. Brookes Publishing Co.

Rice, M.L., & O'Brien, M. (1990). Transitions: Time for change and accommodation. *Topics in Early Childhood Special Education, 9*(4), 1–14.

Risdal, D., & Singer, G.H.S. (2004). Marital adjustment in parents of children with disabilities: A historical review and meta-analysis. *Research and Practice for Persons with Severe Disabilities, 29*, 95–103.

Rosenkoetter, S.E., Hains, A., & Fowler, S.A. (1994). *Bridging early services for children with special needs and their families: A practical guide for transition planning*. Baltimore, MD: Paul H. Brookes Publishing Co.

Safford, P.L., & Safford, E.J. (1996). *A history of childhood and disability*. New York, NY: Teachers College Press.

Sandall, S.R., McLean, M.E., & Smith, B.J. (2000). *DEC recommended practices in early intervention/early childhood special education*. Longmont, CO: Sopris West.

Sandall, S.R., & Schwartz, I.S. (2008). *Building blocks for teaching preschoolers with special needs* (2nd ed.) Baltimore, MD: Paul H. Brookes Publishing Co.

Sanders, J., & Morgan, S. (1997). Family stress and adjustment as perceived by parents of children with autism or Down syndrome: Implications for intervention. *Child & Family Behavior Therapy, 19*, 15–32.

Santelli, B., Poyadue, F.S., & Young, J.L. (2001). *The parent to parent handbook*. Baltimore, MD: Paul H. Brookes Publishing Co.

Singer, G., & Irvin, L.K. (1989). Family caregiving, stress, and support. In G.H.S. Singer & L.K. Irvin (Eds.), *Support for caregiving families: Enabling positive adaptation to disability* (pp. 3–25). Baltimore, MD: Paul H. Brookes Publishing Co.

Sloper, P., & Turner, S. (1993). Risk and resistance factors in the adaptation of parents of children with severe physical disability. *Journal of Child Psychology and Psychiatry, 34*, 167–188.

Solnit, A.J., & Stark, M.H. (1961). Mourning and the birth of a defective child. *Psychoanalytic Study of the Child, 16*, 523–537.

Spiegle, J.A., & van den Pol, R.A. (Eds.). (1993). *Making changes: Family voices on living with disabilities*. Cambridge, MA: Brookline.

Stoneman, Z. (2005). Siblings of children with disabilities: Research themes. *Mental Retardation, 43*, 339–350.

Summers, J., Behr, S., & Turnbull, A. (1989). Positive adaptation and coping strengths of families who have children with disabilities. In G.H.S. Singer & L.K. Irvin (Eds.), *Support for caregiving families: Enabling positive adaptation to disabilities* (pp. 27–40). Baltimore, MD: Paul H. Brookes Publishing Co.

Trute, B., & Hauch, C. (1988). Building on family strength: A study of families with positive adjustment to the birth of a developmentally disabled child. *Journal of Marital and Family Therapy, 14*, 185–193.

Turnbull, H.R. (1986). *Free appropriate public education: The law and children with disabilities*. Denver, CO: Love Publishing Co.

Turnbull, A.P., Patterson, J.M., Behr, S.K., Murphy, D.L., Marquis, J.G., & Blue-Banning, M.J. (Eds.) (1993). *Cognitive coping, families, and disability*. Baltimore, MD: Paul H. Brookes Publishing Co.

Turnbull, H.R., Stowe, M.J., Turnbull, A.P., & Schrandt, M.S. (2007). Public policy and developmental disabilities: A 35-year retrospective and a 5-year prospective based on the core concepts of disability policy. In S. Odom, R. Horner, M. Snell, & J. Blacher (Eds.), *Handbook of developmental disabilities* (pp. 15–34). New York, NY: Guilford Press.

Turnbull, A.P., & Turnbull, H.R. (1985). *Parents speak out: Then and now.* Columbus, OH: Charles E. Merrill.

Turnbull, A.P., & Turnbull, H.R. (1990). *Families, professionals, and exceptionality: A special partnership* (2nd ed.). Columbus, OH: Charles E. Merrill.

Weston, D.R., Ivins, B., Heffron, M.C., & Sweet, N. (1997). Formulating the centrality of relationship in early intervention: An organizational perspective. *Infants and Young Children, 9*(3), 1–12.

Winkler, L.M. (1988). Family stress theory and research on families of children with mental retardation. In J.J. Gallagher & P.M. Vietze (Eds.), *Families of handicapped persons: Research, programs, and policy issues* (pp. 167–195). Baltimore, MD: Paul H. Brookes Publishing Co.

Winton, P.J., McCollum, J.A., & Catlett, C. (Eds.) (2008). *Practical approaches to early childhood professional development: Evidence, strategies, and resources.* Washington, DC: ZERO TO THREE.

World Health Organization. (2011). *World report on disability.* Retrieved August 7, 2012, from http://www.who.int/disabilities/world _report/2011/en/index.html

World Health Organization. (2012). *International Classification of Functioning, Disability and Health (ICF).* Retrieved July 12, 2012, from http://www.who.int/classifications/ icf/en/

6

Families Living in Poverty

Marci J. Hanson

"Poverty demoralizes."

—Ralph Waldo Emerson (1860, p. 90)

"It is not an ennobling experience. Poverty entails fear, and stress, and sometimes depression; it means a thousand petty humiliations and hardships."

—J.K. Rowling (2008)

"If a free society cannot help the many who are poor, it cannot save the few who are rich."

—John F. Kennedy, Jr. (1961)

Poverty pervades every aspect of the life of an individual and a family. Income deprivation influences whether families can meet the most basic needs for food and shelter. It affects the health of family members. Poverty influences human relationships and stresses parents' abilities to care for and raise their children. Poverty can exert a particularly devastating influence on children's development, and it is disproportionately represented across particular cultural and ethnic groups. With limited access to resources that others take for granted and exposure to more perilous living conditions, some individuals' lives are rendered more difficult and at risk. Persons living with economic hardships are more likely to have physical and mental health concerns. Children growing up in low-income families are more likely to endure compromised child development.

The effects of childhood poverty have been documented extensively with respect to academic and school outcomes. Children growing up in poverty begin school behind their peers who have more means, and they often continue to demonstrate lower skill performance during their schooling (Duncan & Magnuson, 2011). The effects of environmental conditions associated with growing up in poverty are especially troubling for very young children who are undergoing rapid and important brain development. Timing, thus, may be an issue. Harmful circumstances that occur early in a child's life during this particularly sensitive and vulnerable period of development may constitute even greater risk from neglect or exposure to harm (Duncan & Magnuson).

The 2010 census revealed that the official U.S. poverty rate was 15.1%; this figure represents 46.2 million people (DeNavas-Walt, Proctor, & Smith, 2011). Using a new supplemental poverty measure (SPM) that takes into account government benefits such as nutritional supplements, medical costs, and housing subsidies, the poverty rate increases to 49 million Americans, or 16% of the population (Short, 2011). These facts are particularly alarming when one reflects on the official classification system, which defines the federal poverty line as $22,113 for a family of four and as $24,343 using the new SPM. Poverty rates have been increasing for most population groups, with the real median income declining for both White and Black households—even those who are not classified as "poor" (DeNavas-Walt, Proctor, & Smith). Over 15.5 million children, or nearly one quarter of children in the United States, are growing up in low-income families (Chau, Thampi, & Wight, 2010a, 2010b, 2010c; Wight, Chau, & Aratani, 2011). Of these children, 9% live in families considered to be at the extreme poverty level (less than 50% of the federal poverty line). The rate of poverty varies widely across the country, but these data indicate that black, American Indian, and Hispanic children are disproportionately affected.

This chapter explores the meaning of poverty, how poverty affects family and child outcomes, and how transactional models of development help family service providers to understand and support family adjustment and adaptation. Although associations of poverty with damaging developmental outcomes are well documented in the research literature, the pathways whereby income deprivation influences an individual child or family are complex. Lack of access to resources (e.g., adequate meals, health care, learning environments) or exposure to deleterious conditions (e.g., neighborhood violence) can snowball and lead to conditions such as health concerns, depression and mental health issues, less responsive caregiving, and compromised educational and learning opportunities. The supports and resources that are provided to children and families can influence these pathways; they can provide the mechanisms and opportunities to strengthen families' abilities to cope and adapt to stressful circumstances.

THE FACES OF POVERTY

Poverty has many faces. The stories that follow suggest the range of American families who struggle through economic hardships, as well as the multiple effects created by economic deprivation on families. Some families are able to overcome these difficulties, whereas others succumb to the overwhelming uphill battle. Begin by considering these different families, all of whom struggle with economic hardship to care for their children.

These families exemplify the many faces of poverty. As discussed briefly in Chapter 1, poverty is found across all geographical regions, races, and family constellations, although higher percentages of families living in poverty are found in certain groups. Low-income families are more likely to be headed by a single parent (usually a mother), reside in a city, and have not graduated high school. In addition, although a larger number of people living in poverty are Anglo-American, a larger percentage of African Americans, American Indians, and Hispanic/Latinos are poor (Dalaker, 2001).

Cecilee

Mary Anne and her daughter, Cecilee, who has cerebral palsy, share dinner with her large family every Sunday when the family meets after church. Mary Anne and her daughter live in a small trailer behind her mother's house and most of Mary Anne's relatives live within 5 miles of them. Mary Anne feels fortunate to have her family close by. Someone is almost always available to care for Cecilee for a short time or give her a ride to her Head Start class or to a medical appointment. Mary Anne is unemployed; she recently was laid off from her custodial job at a nearby paper plant. The long hours spent working at night had been difficult for her, but now she is faced with unemployment and no income. When Mary Anne is out searching for work, Cecilee's grandmother tries to take care of Cecilee, but her arthritic condition prevents her from being able to lift or move to assist Cecilee.

Hernandez Family

Graciela and Arnoldo Hernandez scramble to keep food on the table and a roof over their heads. Graciela works during the morning and afternoon and then rushes to retrieve their son from preschool and prepare the family meal before Arnoldo goes off to his night job. They are worried about the health and safety of their three young children. They confess to the family support coordinator from their child's school that their apartment is full of rats. However, they do not want to complain for fear of being evicted. They try to keep the children off the floor and keep them close at night.

Ge

Ge is a 7-year-old girl who has a visual impairment. Ge's father, Ly Chia, and her mother, Mai Dao, immigrated to the United States from Laos and settled in a small farm community. Her family was forced to subsist on welfare after the economic recession that shut down many local factories in their new community. Ly Chia's brother lives nearby. He manages to feed his own family from the produce of his small farm and to help Ly Chia's family as well. Ge is in first grade and is bussed to school with her 9-year-old brother, while her 3-year-old sister remains at home during the day. Ge's brother helps her navigate and get to her classroom, where she receives specialized services for her visual impairment.

Lamont

Lamont's family lives in a large, urban area. When Lamont was born at City Hospital, Jonalene, his mother, was told that he had Down syndrome and that he would need pediatric care and an early intervention program. She and her husband, Carl, took him back to the hospital emergency room several times over the next year—once when he fell off the bed and stopped breathing, and again when he had a fever and was coughing and wheezing so much that they were afraid he would die. A public health nurse came to visit the family's small apartment and helped them to get connected to a local agency that provides services to infants with disabilities. Jonalene fully intended to get Lamont registered in the program, but she and her husband split up and she had to leave the apartment. She was forced to move from shelter to shelter. Just finding a roof over their heads and getting a hot meal each day became her daily existence.

José

Arely and her 16-year-old son José immigrated to the United States 10 years ago. They share a small apartment with Arely's sister and her son in a suburban area. Both sisters send whatever money they can to relatives in El Salvador who were left homeless by an earthquake. Arely typically works 12 hours per day, and often 6 days per week, cleaning houses. She is extremely worried about her son, who was expelled from high school after threatening another student. She finds solace and support in her church; she goes every Sunday (her one day off of work) and several nights a week to pray.

Dawn

Floyd and Nancy Marshall have two children, Dawn and David. Dawn's birth was fraught with difficulties, and she sustained brain damage during delivery. Subsequently, she had numerous hospitalizations and health complications. Floyd works at the local mill and earns minimum wage while Nancy tries to earn a few dollars here and there by helping to care for elderly neighbors or children. Making ends meet each month is a challenge. The family has borrowed money from Nancy's parents, and they have relied on the assistance of people in their community on more than one occasion. They often express exasperation over the fact that their hard work does not seem to get them ahead or even on par with their family's needs.

Children and Poverty

Over 15 million children live in poverty (under the official poverty line of $22,113 per year for a family of four); that number increased by 33% between 2000 and 2010 (Wight, Chau, & Aratani, 2011) to represent 21% of all children. When the new supplemental poverty measure is used to calculate the proportion of children living in poverty, the percentage drops to 18% (Short, 2011). This reduction is due to the inclusion of family resources from in-kind benefits, such as targeted government programs aimed at nutritional supplements (Supplemental Nutrition Assistance Program), children's health care, housing supplements, and child care. Nine percent of children (6.8 million children) have families who live in extreme poverty (i.e., at less than 50% of the federal poverty level or less than $11,000 for a family of four people; Wight et al.). The poverty rate for infants and toddlers is higher than for any other age group (Krutsinger & Tarr, 2011; Wight et al.). Immigrant families are likely to live in poverty (27%), and the poverty

rates for children vary by race/ethnicity: 36% for Black/African American children, 34% for American Indian children, 33% for Latino children, 15% Asian children, and 12% for White children (Wight et al.).

Studies show that families typically need at least twice the income level at the poverty line (more than $44,000 for a family of four) to make ends meet (Chau, Thampi, & Wight, 2010c). It is noteworthy that some 42% of children live in families at this level (twice the poverty level), which is considered low income. The concerns of these families typically mirror those for families considered to be "poor" and include issues of underemployment or unemployment, child care, and health care.

As is evident, a large number of children live in poverty in the United States. These conditions influence their exposure to risk conditions and reduce their access to environmental conditions for optimal learning and development.

Poverty and Race/Ethnicity

Using 2010 census data, the official poverty rates by race/ethnicity are as follows (Short, 2011):

- Whites: 13.1% (31,959,000 people)

- Blacks: 27% (10,741,000 people)

- Asians: 12.1% (1,737,000 people)

- Hispanics of any race: 26.7% (13,346,000 people)

Poverty rates have been increasing across the board for most racial and ethnic groups in the United States. However, the new SPM formula that takes into account government benefits (e.g., nutritional supplements, medical costs, housing subsidies) shows the greatest increase for Hispanics, with the poverty rate shifting from 26.7% using the official measure to 28.2% with the SPM (Short, 2011). The use of the SPM measure shows a reduction in the poverty rate for Blacks (from 27.5% to 25.4%) due to participation in social programs.

Census reports also document the association of race and ethnicity with health disparity indicators such as family composition (e.g., single parents), food insecurity, health insurance coverage, environmental factors (e.g., exposure to secondhand smoke, lead poisoning), health and dental care, and health issues including asthma, obesity, and learning and behavioral problems (Seith & Kalof, 2011). Factors of race and ethnicity also are associated with gaps in school readiness (Brooks-Gunn, Rouse, & McLanahan, 2007). These associations and disparities are disturbing given that an increasing number of children of color are living in poverty.

Poverty and Disability

The links between poverty and disability are also compelling. Findings from the Institute for Women's Policy Research analysis of disabilities among families reported that low-income families are nearly 50% more likely to have a child with a disability or a severe disability than are higher income families. Furthermore, they reported that families receiving welfare benefits have an even higher likelihood of having at least one child with a disability: 20% of all families receiving welfare benefits have a child with a disability; of these families, 13% have a child with severe disabilities (Lee, Sills, & Oh, 2002). In addition, this analysis found that single-mother families were more likely to have a child with a disability than were two-parent or single-father families. Disability rates were also higher for single mothers in low-income families than for single mothers with higher incomes. Approximately 29% of these low-income single mothers had a disability and 17% had a severe disability (as contrasted with 17% and 5%, respectively, for higher income single mothers). The percentages were even more startling for single mothers receiving welfare or Temporary Assistance for Needy Families—38% of these women had a disability and 25% were reported to have a severe disability (Lee et al., 2002).

Other reviews related to welfare reform and disabilities estimated that 30%–40% of families receiving welfare had either a mother or a child with some level of disability (Loprest & Acs, 1996; Meyers, Lukemeyer, & Smeeding, 1996). A study conducted by Fujiura and Yamaki (2000) gathered prevalence data that revealed a relationship between poverty and risk for disability. The conditions of poverty that may lead to disability or chronic illness and the provision of resources to low-income families who have members with disabilities, however, have largely been overlooked in research and policy formation (Rosman & Knitzer, 2001). Recommendations for addressing the needs of these families who receive welfare and who have family members with disabilities have been made to expand access to health care, child care, and vocational training and secure income maintenance through Supplemental Security Income (Birenbaum, 2002).

Historical Trends in Poverty Rates

Poverty rates undeniably are linked to social and political time periods (e.g., the Great Depression) and to the corresponding shifts in family characteristics and societal pressures and opportunities. The increase in mother-only households is often cited as causally linked to increased poverty rates for children. However, the link may not be so linear or clear cut as is often thought. Although lower income levels typically characterize mother-only households, the low earnings of fathers and employment insecurity remain prime contributors to increases in poverty as well (Hernandez, 1997). In addition, analyses suggest that these issues (e.g., low salaries) may indirectly influence poverty and family trends by necessitating that mothers work outside the home to increase family income; thus, perhaps they contribute to separation and divorce (Hernandez). The issue is not so much family structure as it is the economic and employment experiences and opportunities for both mothers and fathers.

Poverty rates for families and children have varied over the past decades. In a study of poverty between 1998 and 2000 (Dalaker, 2001), the average rates over the 3-year period for various populations were the following: 11.9% for all races, 25.9% for American Indian/Alaska Natives, 23.9% for Blacks, 23.1% for Hispanics, 11.3% for Asian/Pacific Islanders, and 9.9% for Whites (7.8% for white, non-Hispanic). The overall poverty rate dropped between 1999 and 2000, undoubtedly due to a strong economy. With the economic downturn in the early 21st century, more families and children began living in impoverished circumstances. The percentage of children living in low-income families increased from 37% in 2000 to 42% in 2009 (Chau, Thampi, & Wight, 2010c). The risks posed to the well-being of these families and children are many and comprehensive. Duncan and Magnuson (2011), citing studies of child achievement and adult employment, argued that the effects of poverty in childhood on later development are particularly compelling and influential.

WHAT IT MEANS TO BE POOR

In the discussion thus far, the definition of poverty has centered on income level as defined by the official federal poverty line for a family of four. Policy makers and social scientists, however, have hotly debated the characteristics used to define poverty or economic deprivation. Income alone hardly paints the whole picture. In fact, these numbers and percentages are conservative markers for children and families living in poor economic resource conditions. The official measure has failed to take into account key government programs that affect family income, changes in standards for living, job expenses, medical costs, changes in family situations, and geographic variations in expenses (Short, 2011). A 1988 study by Hagenaars and de Vos (as cited in McLoyd, 1998a) described different methods for defining poverty: absolute poverty, in which one does not have the minimum required for basic needs such as food, clothing, and housing; relative poverty, in which one has less than others in terms of what is typical for most members of that society; and subjective poverty, in which a person feels that he or she does not have enough to get along.

The absolute poverty marker refers to the official poverty line as determined by the Social Security Administration in the 1960s; it is the most commonly used marker for policy and research. This marker provides thresholds for families of different sizes and compositions and was calculated to represent the cost of a minimum diet multiplied by three. A number of difficulties are associated with this marker. First, it fails to adjust for geographic location in living costs and variation in support programs, such as food stamps and Medicaid. In addition, pretax income is used to determine who is below the threshold of poverty. Also, this marker does not reflect the poverty gap—in other words, how far below the threshold the family falls. For a history of the official poverty measure, see Fisher (1997). For more information on measuring income and poverty, see Citro and Michael (1995), Fass (2009), and Short (2011).

Other definitions offer a broader view of economic deprivation than that based on a somewhat arbitrary cash marker of family income. In some research studies, socioeconomic status (SES) has been used to categorize individuals. Components such as the father and mother's occupations, education levels, and certain lifestyle variables also have been included. Both the concepts of poverty income and SES, however, are viewed as ongoing and linked to conditions such as unemployment or low wages (McLoyd, 1998a). Therefore, they may fail to account for events in the family's life that produce economic deprivation. For example, an employed person may experience a sudden loss or drop in income. Although this may not push the individual into poverty, the impact of the economic hardship affects the individual's and the family's functioning and dynamics. The issues of the timing and terms of poverty are not always considered in research and policy studies. Undoubtedly, living in persistent poverty has a different impact on children and their families than does living through bouts of poverty. In addition, statistics reveal that race and ethnicity interact with the persistence of poverty. African American and Latino children experience higher rates of poverty; they also are more likely to live in poverty for longer time periods than Anglo-American children (Brooks-Gunn, Duncan, & Maritato, 1997). Thus, family circumstance and structure, parental education, time, and degree of poverty all may exert a profound effect on a family's economic well-being. These issues, coupled with how individual family members perceive or experience their economic circumstances, make it difficult to tease apart indicators or markers for poverty.

Regardless of the definition of poverty used, most definitions do not begin to capture the many differences in day-to-day living practices that children and families experience when existing under economically deprived conditions–particularly those that persist over years. Such challenges run the gamut from a lack of basic necessities (e.g., food, clothing, housing) to irregular work or work schedules, lack of family support, lack of child care, insufficient access to health care, safety issues, exposure to stressful living conditions, and psychological stress, among many others. Similarly, ethnic and cultural factors interact with these issues, as well as the timing of poverty and chronicity of this deprivation. The many factors and dimensions make poverty difficult to define and study. Policy makers and social scientists do concur that the effects of poverty are pervasive and potentially devastating.

IMPACT OF POVERTY ON THE WELL-BEING OF CHILDREN AND FAMILIES

Although many families manage to overcome adverse circumstances, living in poverty unleashes a set of factors and events that pose great risk to the well-being and development of children and their families. A proliferation of research in the 1990s analyzed the impact of poverty on development (Brooks-Gunn & Duncan, 1997; Brooks-Gunn, Duncan, & Maritato, 1997; Brooks-Gunn, Klebanov, & Duncan, 1996; Duncan & Brooks-Gunn, 1997; Huston, 1991; Huston, McLoyd, & Garcia Coll, 1994; McLoyd, 1998b) and extensively documented the type and range of potentially deleterious effects. Highlights from this research are briefly reviewed with respect to what is known about the impact on child development and family functioning.

Poverty and Child Development

Given the crucial importance of early experience to an individual's development, it is alarming that so many children are growing up under circumstances that may place their development at risk. In a landmark policy and scientific publication on the science of early childhood development, Shonkoff and Phillips (2000, p. 275) noted, "One of the most consistent associations in developmental science is between economic hardship and compromised child development."

Children living in impoverished conditions may be at greater risk of exposure to a variety of risks including inadequate nutrition, environmental toxins, impaired parent–child interaction, trauma and abuse, lower quality child care, and drugs and substance abuse by parents (Krutsinger & Tarr, 2011; National Center for Children in Poverty, 1999). These factors further increase the risk of developmental impairment for children.

Because nearly one in five young children in the United States lives in poverty, the urgency of this issue is apparent (Chau, Thampi, & Wight, 2010c). Scientific evidence on early brain development underscores the importance of experience in the early years to the child's emotional, intellectual, and physical development (Shore, 1997). Advances in neuroscience research have documented the course of early brain development and highlighted the sensitive period for optimal brain development in the earliest years (including prenatal development) of the child's life. During these early years, exposure to environmental stimulation has a profound effect on brain growth and development. Likewise, early exposure to risks, such as those factors previously listed, also may impede brain development.

In this light, consider again the risk factors identified by the National Center for Children in Poverty (1999; see Figure 6.1). Malnutrition in children is associated with

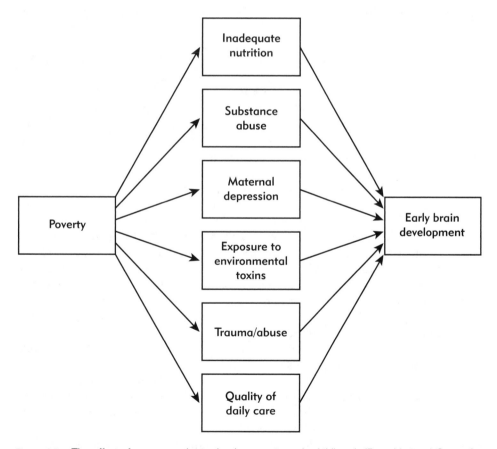

Figure 6.1. The effect of poverty on brain development in early childhood. (From National Center for Children in Poverty [1999]. *Poverty and brain development in early childhood* [p. 1]. Retrieved from http://www.nccp.org/publications/pdf/text_398.pdf; reprinted by permission.)

delays in physical growth and motor skills development, lower test scores in subsequent years on academic subjects, social withdrawal, and, as a result, lower expectations from parents and teachers. Research studies substantiate the link between degree of poverty and degree of malnutrition (Brown & Pollitt, 1996). Substance abuse during and after pregnancy also has been demonstrated to produce deleterious effects on brain development (Mayes, 1996). Exposure to toxins such as lead also can damage or stunt brain growth (Seith & Isakson, 2011). Furthermore, children who experience trauma or abuse in their early years may have difficulties forming attachments, and they may display more anxiety and depression. The stressors associated with poverty create more trauma for these children (Brooks-Gunn et al., 1995).

The quality of care also is important to children's well-being, particularly children's emotional and intellectual development. Mothers who suffer from depression are less likely to provide appropriate and needed stimulation and interactions with their infants, resulting in deficits such as lowered activity levels, withdrawal behaviors, and shorter attention spans (Belle, 1990). Positive interactions and exposure to learning environments influence how the brain develops. Poor child care and parent–child interactions likely impede a child's development, whereas high-quality child care experiences have been linked with enhanced child development (Burchinal, Lee, & Ramey, 1989; Cost, Quality and Child Outcomes Study Team, 1995). Children living in poverty are disproportionately exposed to risks, and thus their well-being is seriously threatened.

An extensive body of research literature has documented the association between poverty and child outcomes. Family income can dramatically affect outcomes for children and adolescents, and these negative effects are more apparent for some outcomes than for others. In addition, these outcomes are linked to the depth and duration of poverty (Brooks-Gunn & Duncan, 1997). Descriptive studies have linked poverty conditions to teenage pregnancy, low academic achievement, and juvenile delinquency (Brody et al., 1994; McLeod & Shanahan, 1993; Sampson & Laub, 1994). Furthermore, low income has been associated with socioemotional difficulties, including conduct disorders, anxiety, and depression (Bank, Forgatch, Patterson, & Fetrow, 1993; Dodge, Pettit, & Bates, 1994; McLoyd, Jayaratne, Ceballo, & Borquez, 1994; Pinderhughes et al., 2001).

Brooks-Gunn and Duncan (1997), using data from large-scale, national, cross-sectional databases, provided a comprehensive analysis of the links between family income and child outcomes. The data sets analyzed included the Panel Study of Income Dynamics, the National Longitudinal Survey of Youth (NLSY), Children of the NLSY, National Survey of Families and Households, the National Health and Nutrition Examination Survey, and the Infant Health and Development Program (IHDP). Outcomes were examined in the areas of physical health (low birth weight, growth stunting, lead poisoning), cognitive ability, school achievement, emotional and behavioral outcomes, and teenage out-of-wedlock childbearing.

Brooks-Gunn and Duncan (1997) noted that different indicators of risk or well-being were found at different periods in the child's life (e.g., birth to 2 years, early childhood from ages 3 to 6, late childhood from ages 7 to 10, early adolescence from ages 11 to 15, late adolescence from ages 16 to 19). With respect to physical health, their analyses revealed that children from low-income families were less likely to be in excellent health. Children born to mothers with low incomes also were more likely to have low birth weights—a factor itself associated with potential health, cognitive, and behavioral difficulties in future development. Furthermore, children living in poverty were more likely to manifest growth stunting and experience lead poisoning.

With regard to cognitive abilities, Brooks-Gunn and Duncan (1997) noted that children living in poverty were 1.3 times more likely than children who were not living in poverty to experience developmental delays and learning disabilities. In a related study using the NLSY and IHDP data sets, children from families with lower incomes scored lower on standardized tests of IQ, verbal ability, and achievement (Smith, Brooks-Gunn, & Klebanov, 1997). In that study, the effects of poverty were found at each of the ages tested between 2 and 8 years. Furthermore, duration of poverty was found to be a crucial variable. Children who lived in persistent poverty (i.e., for more than 4 years) fared worse than those who never lived in poverty, and they scored 6–9 points lower on cognitive assessments. It is also noteworthy that these negative effects appeared to grow stronger as the children got older (as demonstrated on the Peabody Picture Vocabulary Test–Revised [Dunn & Dunn, 1981] as a measure for the IHDP sample). Effects of income also were shown as early as age 2 for the IHDP children. In addition, the severity or magnitude of poverty appeared to affect children's outcome on cognitive measures. Children in the lowest income group (i.e., family income less than 50% of the poverty level) scored 7–12 points lower than children from families who had low incomes but not at the lowest poverty level. The effect of poverty was noted to have some relationship to school achievement in the older age groups as well (Brooks-Gunn & Duncan). Poverty was shown to exert a small but negative impact on graduation rates and years of schooling attained. An increase in family income in the early years was associated with more years of schooling completed, however.

Emotional and behavioral child outcomes were also analyzed (Brooks-Gunn & Duncan, 1997). Children who were poor were found to experience emotional and behavioral difficulties more frequently than children who were not poor. Both externalizing behaviors (e.g., aggression, fighting, acting out) and internalizing behaviors (e.g., anxiety, social withdrawal, depression) were studied. Again, results revealed that children growing up in persistent poverty were more likely to experience both externalizing and internalizing behavior problems than were children who had not grown up in persistent poverty (IHDP sample; Duncan, Brooks-Gunn, & Klebanov, 1994). Children who experienced short-term poverty also demonstrated more behavior problems, but the effects were not as great as for those in persistent poverty. Although studies demonstrated a link between poverty and emotional outcomes, the effects of poverty were not as large in this area as for cognitive outcomes (Brooks-Gunn & Duncan). Other research studies have noted effects on socioemotional development and diminished adaptive functioning (e.g., relationships with peers, self-esteem, behavior problems, vulnerability to depression) for children living in poverty (McLoyd, 1990, 1997). Brooks-Gunn and Duncan also examined the relationship of income to out-of-wedlock teenage births. Findings revealed that the timing and duration of poverty did not seem to exert an effect, although the rate of teenage out-of-wedlock births was nearly three times higher for teenagers from low-income families than for teens not living in poverty.

In research on poverty, it is difficult to ferret out the effects of income poverty from other interacting variables, such as timing of poverty and family structure. With respect to timing, these data (Smith, Brooks-Gunn, & Klebanov, 1997) did not reveal differences on cognitive indices. It must be noted that the time periods were short (within the early years), however, and also that these negative outcomes were apparent by the age of 2. Brooks-Gunn and Duncan (1997) cited additional data that the timing of family income level affected a child's years of schooling completed. They found that family income levels in the child's early years (younger than age 5) were more strongly linked to number of school years completed than were family income levels when children were between the ages of 5–10 or between the ages of 11–15. They noted further that a $10,000 increase in mean family income between birth and 5 years was associated with an additional full year of school attained for children from low-income families.

The Effect of Family Structure on Income Levels

The impact of family structure as it relates to family income levels and child developmental outcomes has been of interest. Understanding the effect of different family structures and family shifts in response to changing societal programs (e.g., welfare reform) and values is complex. Research suggests that the family structure makes a difference, and growing up in families characterized by disruption does produce negative developmental consequences (McLanahan, 1997).

In the study by Smith et al. (1997), family structure did not influence outcomes for either of the two samples across ages when income levels were controlled. In the NLSY sample, however, when income level was *not* considered, the situation of living in a female-headed household and the introduction of another new parent into the family were both associated with lower verbal ability scores for young children. According to Booth and Dunn (1994), these findings are in accord with others, suggesting that remarriage or first marriage for a never-married mother may bring stresses. Although surveys indicate that the number of single-parent households has declined in recent years, troubling new reports indicate that more children (particularly African American children in cities) are living in households with no parent (e.g., living with relatives, friends, or foster families; "More Kids," 2002).

ECONOMIC WELL-BEING AND FAMILY VARIABLES

Economic hardship also has been associated with effects on family variables—parenting behavior, parental and family functioning, marital relationships, and family processes (Brody et al., 1994; McLoyd, 1990; Pinderhughes et al., 2001). One study was conducted on a large sample of families in a rural Midwest region characterized by economic difficulty; the authors found economic stress was linked to marital and family conflict and conflicts between parents and their adolescent children (Conger, Ge, Elder, Lorenz, & Simons, 1994).

Other research has expanded knowledge of the relationship between economic hardship and family and child functioning to include more diverse samples. For example, this phenomenon was examined in a study with an ethnically diverse, low-income sample of children who were African American and Hispanic and who lived in families headed primarily by single mothers (Mistry, Vandewater, Huston, & McLoyd, 2002). Results of this research confirmed that economic stress affected parenting behavior due to adverse effects on parental psychological well-being. Parents reported feeling less effective or capable in child disciplinary situations and were observed to be less affectionate in parent–child interactions. These less optimal parenting practices were associated with higher ratings of behavior problems for children and lower teacher ratings for positive child social behavior. Thus, a family economic stress model was used to understand the impact of poverty on families and children. Although economic hardship has been strongly associated with family stress, variables such as family ethnicity, work history, geographical location and density (urban versus rural), and community and personal resources may play crucial roles in determining how families actually respond to economic distress (McLoyd, 1990). Living in poverty challenges the abilities of families and parents to support and care for themselves and their children (McLoyd).

Pathways or Mechanisms of Influence

As is evident from the research reviewed, living in poverty can exert powerful negative influences on family functioning and children's developmental outcomes. Of interest are the pathways or mechanisms whereby income levels influence child outcomes. Brooks-Gunn and Duncan (1997) discussed five potential pathways: health and nutrition, home environment, parental interactions with children, parental mental health, and neighborhood conditions. Each pathway is briefly considered and implications for practice are presented later in this chapter.

Poor health can result from living under adverse economic conditions. Health concerns also can serve as a pathway through which other child outcomes are affected. For instance, low birth weight and increased levels of lead in the blood in young children are both associated with deleterious consequences such as lower scores of cognitive ability in later years. Recurrent ear infections and consequent hearing loss have also been associated with lower IQ scores for children regardless of family's income level. Goldstein (1990) suggested that low birth weight, lead, anemia, and recurrent ear infections may have accounted for up to 13%–20% of the difference in IQ scores between 4-year-old children in families who were considered to be "poor" or "nonpoor" in the study.

Studies also have revealed links between adverse child outcomes for children living in poverty and measures of home environment. Typically, researchers have used the Home Observation of Measurement of the Environment (HOME) Inventory (Caldwell & Bradley, 1984) to study this phenomenon. The HOME scale assesses learning materials in the home, maternal warmth toward the child, and parent experiences with the child. An overview of the research in this area (Brooks-Gunn & Duncan, 1997) suggested that elements of the home environment accounted for a significant portion of the effect of income level on children's outcomes in cognitive ability. Studies have determined that approximately half of the effect of poverty level on children's IQ scores can be explained by its effect on learning experiences in the home (Bradley, 1995).

Moving beyond an examination of home environmental issues such as materials and activities, studies also have linked dimensions of parent–child interactions to child outcomes and poverty. As reviewed by Brooks-Gunn and Duncan (1997), parenting practices affect child achievement and adjustment. Some studies have suggested that in families living in poverty, parents may be more likely to use harsh punishment and display lower quality parent–child interactions. For example, a study on young children's mental health noted that children in homes characterized by poverty were spanked more than those in higher income homes (McLeod & Shanahan, 1993).

Parental mental health is noted as another potential pathway through which poverty affects child outcomes (Brooks-Gunn & Duncan, 1997). Less favorable physical and mental health status is associated with poverty. In turn, parents experiencing conditions associated with poorer mental health, such as depression, are less likely to provide quality learning experiences for their children and to engage in optimal parent–child interactions.

Finally, poverty may serve as a mechanism for potentially altering child outcomes in the way that it affects neighborhoods (Brooks-Gunn & Duncan, 1997; Levanthal & Brooks-Gunn, 2000, 2003). Certainly, neighborhood environments characterized by violence, crime, and limited resources for enhancing child development (e.g., playgrounds, child care, school facilities) may interfere with families' abilities to support one another and their children. Such factors are likely to be associated with adverse child outcomes. Although family effects may exert a more direct link to child outcomes, the neighborhood effects may indirectly contribute to child outcomes, particularly in the school-age years (Chase-Lansdale & Gordon, 1996; Chase-Lansdale et al., 1997). The research suggests that families are the key agents for child outcomes, but neighborhood circumstances may play an increasing role on children's outcomes as they age, particularly when children venture out of the home during school age and beyond (Brooks-Gunn, Duncan, & Aber, 1997a).

EXAMINING RISKS AND SUPPORTS
THROUGH TRANSACTIONAL AND ECOLOGICAL MODELS

Scientific inquiry has shifted from "asking *whether* family resources affect child development to asking *why* research shows so consistently that they do" (Shonkoff & Phillips, 2000, p. 267). As such, the impact of poverty on children and families is perhaps best examined and understood through transactional and ecological models that underscore the importance of the child's and family's interactions with the larger world. These models provide a structure through which the complex array of factors and circumstances associated with living under economic hardship can be viewed and the interplay between characteristics of children/families and the environments in which they live can be better understood. The previous discussion of pathways suggests the importance of this dynamic, transactional process.

Schorr painted a portrait of how a myriad of factors—all influenced by poverty—can place child development in jeopardy:

> The child in a poor family who is malnourished and living in an unheated apartment is more susceptible to ear infection; once the ear infection takes hold, inaccessible or inattentive health care may mean it will not be properly treated; hearing loss in the midst of economic stress may go undetected at home, in day care, and by the health system; undetected hearing loss will do long-term damage to a child who needs all the help he can to cope with a world more complicated than the world of most middle-class children. When this child enters school, his chances of being in an overcrowded classroom with an overwhelmed teacher further compromise his chances of successful learning. Thus, risk factors join to shorten the odds of favorable long-term outcomes. (1988, p. 30)

As this scenario so vividly portrays, children and families living in poverty face increased risks for poor developmental outcomes. These risk factors interact with one another to transform the developmental possibilities for individuals. Mediating factors help to illuminate how poverty is related to adverse developmental outcomes and also how protective factors can serve to support the well-being of children and families.

Reconsider for a moment the transactional model described in Chapter 3. This model helps explain the outcomes in the previous example. It illustrates how environmental factors (e.g., malnutrition, substandard living conditions) can lead to negative developmental consequences for the child (e.g., developmental delay caused by loss of hearing from ear infection). These consequences, in turn, can transform the child's development and lead to other outcomes. This child's undiagnosed hearing loss will likely lead to less participation in school activities and lessons, poorer interactions with peers, and difficulties communicating with important adults in his environment, such as his teacher. These factors produce a transaction: The child's development is negatively affected or transformed such that the child is less likely to be able to interact with or benefit from important aspects of his environment. Furthermore, other characteristics of the child's environment, such as overcrowded schools, poor or inappropriate teaching methods, inadequate or inappropriate health care, and/or lack of diagnostic and intervention services, can exacerbate the negative consequences to the child. From this simple example, one can witness that the child whose development is already at risk is placed in an environment that is less likely to benefit or structure the child's learning. The result is a negative spiral of repercussions. The transactional model therefore helps shed light on the mechanisms or pathways through which impoverishing conditions can act to influence child and family functioning and developmental outcomes.

For the young child at a crucial point in brain development, living in poverty is associated with many short-term risks; when these risks accumulate and interact, they can produce long-term and major consequences. Such factors include the impact on physical health (e.g., poor health and infectious disease, lower vaccination rates, greater rates of asthma and anemia), family effects (e.g., parental depression, maltreatment, exposure to alcohol and substance abuse), and environmental factors (e.g., lack of access to safe play spaces, lead exposure, increased exposure to community and interpersonal violence; Krutsinger & Tarr, 2011).

The number and types of risks faced by children and families also influence the total impact of these risks on development and functioning. The health and developmental status of the infant and quality of the home environment interact with family economic circumstances; the more risks the child and family face, the more likely it is that negative outcomes will arise (Sameroff, 1983, 2009; Sameroff, Seifer, Barocas, Zax, & Greenspan, 1987). Economic circumstances, because of the long and overarching layering of risk conditions, can exert a major influence such that children born into families who are not poor fare better than do those born into impoverishment, even when their biologic or health status is more compromised. Children who are born with biologic risks (e.g., prematurity, low birth weight) and also are born into poverty potentially face a double hazard for even worse developmental outcomes (Escalona, 1982; Parker, Greer, & Zuckerman, 1988).

A common saying is often true: The rich get richer and the poor get poorer. This quip reflects the chronic nature and devastating effects of poverty. Indeed, families often are said to live in a cycle of poverty. This cycle of poverty will likely continue and intensify if children and families are not supported to escape its effects. Given the magnitude and range of negative effects on children and families associated with poverty, research and policy efforts have been directed toward identifying these needed supports.

Studies have provided clues for supportive interventions that minimize potential deleterious outcomes for children and families living in poverty. For instance, research demonstrated that the developmental outcomes of premature, low birth weight (LBW) children living in poverty were linked to the quality of their caregiving environment (Bradley et al., 1994). Children whose outcomes were more favorable received caregiving that was more responsive, accepting, organized, and stimulating than did children with less optimal developmental profiles. Although the majority of LBW infants in this sample who were born into poverty conditions had poor developmental prognoses, several factors appeared to offset the potential for harm. The dimensions of the caregiving environments that appeared to serve as protective factors included parental responsivity, acceptance of the child's behavior, variety of stimulation, availability of toys and materials, and adequate space for privacy and exploration. Thus, some of the same pathways or mechanisms that conspire to produce negative repercussions also can lead to more positive outcomes.

These pathways or mechanisms occur at all levels of families' ecological contexts. Using the terminology proposed by Bronfenbrenner (1979, 1999) and Bronfenbrenner and Morris (2006) that was reviewed in Chapter 3, these contexts and potential areas of support and intervention are examined. At the microsystem level of the child and family within the home environment, characteristics of children and/or parents that may add stress include biologic risk conditions of a child at birth, disability, and chronic illness, to name a few. Parental issues also may contribute positively to the child and family's functioning. These variables include parental mental health and sensitivity, coping strategies, parent–child interaction styles and techniques (e.g., positive disciplinary techniques, provision of learning activities and stimulation, responsivity), appropriate parental expectations, and marital and family functioning. At the mesosystem level are the influences of the neighborhood, child care resources, schools, health care facilities, houses of worship, and other community agencies charged with providing direct services to families. These formal and informal institutions are activated based on the family's desire and ability to gain support and resources from them. These community contexts can promote children's abilities to actively explore their environments and participate in stimulating learning opportunities (e.g., exposure to language, print, numbers) and provide families with safety and security to do their jobs as caregivers and nurturers. Government and community agencies (e.g., health, educational, social service, employment, housing) and other legislative and regulatory networks are considered exosystem contexts that influence children and families through the policies and programs that they provide and the priorities that they establish. Indeed, census data on reduction of poverty in some groups (Short, 2011) documents the value of these programs that provide crucial supports such as nutrition supplementation, health care, housing, and child care.

Finally, at the most global or macrosystem level are societal attitudes and values regarding poverty, ethnic and/or racial groups, and families' lifestyles and structures. The impact of broader cultural and societal values such as the freedom from racism, acceptance of different family structures and practices, and compassion towards others creates a climate that has a profound effect on the institutions that more directly and daily influence children and families. Each of these levels of the ecological context for families reveals a potential intervention point to support individual children and their families living in poverty.

SUPPORT FOR CHILDREN AND FAMILIES LIVING IN POVERTY

What can be done to prevent, ameliorate, and/or counteract the effects of poverty? It is beyond the scope of this text to consider or debate the myriad of government and community programs that have been attempted in an effort to prevent or overcome poverty in the United States. Politicians and policy makers will continue to debate appropriate interventions to mitigate the effects of poverty, including education and employment programs, wage increases, food programs, nutrition supplements, health care, housing subsidies, child care, and early education programs (Devaney, Ellwood, & Love, 1997). Some families have long historical roots in poverty that extend generation after generation, living in neighborhoods characterized by economic distress and hopelessness, lack of education or opportunities to advance, and lack of access to the systems and services to pull themselves up. Other children and families have been thrust into poverty suddenly by a parent's loss of employment or reduction in earning, the loss of a parent, and/or a change in family structure. For some families, helping members to earn more and receive supplements to earned income (e.g., child support payments/contributions from absent parents) can reduce poverty (Plotnick, 1997). But for many, the complexity of their life circumstances requires radical shifts to change their economic fate.

At times, it is overwhelming to contemplate where to begin to support children and families who face the effects of poverty every hour of every day. What, for instance, can education, health care, and social service personnel do as professionals and as individuals to assist these children and families as they face their economic hardships? Although there are no simple solutions, avenues of hope and intervention are available through activating and supporting families and informal support networks, and through relationship-based professional commitments of the helping services.

Characteristics of interventions that are likely to be supportive for families who live in poverty include helping parents and other family members to feel more efficacious in their abilities to nurture and care for their children, develop self-esteem, become more responsive caregivers, respond with warmth and affection to their children, provide stimulating learning opportunities and activities in the home, acquire appropriate developmental and behavioral expectations for their children, and foster harmonious family relationships. These interventions likely will facilitate secure attachments between parents/caregivers and children, build self-esteem for both, and enhance adult–child relationships and interactions. McLoyd (1997) noted that emotional support for families and policies that help families to overcome concrete problems will often go a long way toward alleviating the stresses associated with poverty and the resulting mental health issues of depression, punitive parenting style, and psychological distress.

A re-examination of the circumstances faced by the six families introduced at the beginning of this chapter illustrates some types of support for families living in poverty.

Mary Anne, the mother of 4-year-old Cecilee, for example, feels fortunate to live near her family members, who give her emotional and physical support in caring for her daughter. Her spiritual faith and the friendship and support of people at her church are important to her. Mary Anne and Cecilee also benefit from the more formal supports found in the Head Start program, the local special education system, and medical specialists with whom they work. Mary Anne is also seeking child care so that she can return to work to earn a living.

For the Hernandez family, formal supports are pivotal. The members of this family have a strong emotional bond with one another. However, they need assistance to procure safe housing and provide their family with secure living conditions. Ge's family members also rely on each other and on the emotional and financial support of close family, their farm community, and the community of Laotians that live nearby to help them through their hard times. They are able to survive on their limited economic resources due to these supports.

The story of Lamont and his mother, Jonalene, elucidates the importance of health care and early intervention community services. The availability of these services literally saved Lamont's life when he was ill and provided the needed education and health services to address his developmental and health needs. This family also depends on formal supports such as shelter, health care, and food to help them exist until Jonalene can find a job and gain economic independence for her family.

The support of close family and community is evident in the other families as well. Arely relies on her sister's family and her church, and Floyd and Nancy look to their neighbors and family for loans and work opportunities. Each family also benefits from the resources offered through local schools, social services, and health care facilities. Service providers cannot give families the monetary support and resources that they need to move beyond life in impoverished conditions. But service practitioners can support these families by acknowledging and encouraging families to use their informal resources and sources of support, such as kinship, friendship, cultural/linguistic, and faith-based communities.

Acknowledging the competence that families bring to addressing their own needs only facilitates their abilities to care for themselves. When more formal interventions or services are needed, professionals can assist families to obtain information about what is available and how to gain access to the services. Once these resources are identified, professionals can help families navigate the service maze in order to receive the services they need. Providing referrals and assistance in obtaining housing, food stamps/nutrition supplements, job programs, quality child care, mental health services, housing, legal services, and services in the family's primary language can be invaluable to these families. Although poverty presents daily challenges and remains a heavy burden for most of these families, supportive service providers can help to lighten that load.

SUMMARY

Family income level can exert a profound and substantial influence on the development and well-being of children and families. Indeed, the landscape of opportunity for children and families is transformed by economic hardship. Evidence suggests that family income may be one of the most powerful influences on children early in their lives (Duncan, Yeung, Brooks-Gunn, & Smith, 1998). The impact of poverty is not universal or evenly distributed demographically, although it does touch all races, ethnicities, ages, and geographical regions. Rather, the effects of poverty are disproportionately experienced by certain groups such as young children, children living in single-parent families, and children who are African American, American Indian/Alaska Native, and Hispanic/Latino. In his book *The Souls of Black Folk* (1903), author W.E.B. Du Bois underscored the disparity experienced by these families in a land of plenty: "To be a poor man is hard, but to be a poor race in a land of dollars is the very bottom of hardships" (as cited by Tripp, 1970, p. 712).

The ways in which poverty exacts its toll are becoming better understood. Poverty is linked more clearly with some adverse consequences than with others, particularly with children's cognitive and achievement outcomes. The duration of poverty also is significant. Living in persistent, long-term poverty likely has more devastating consequences than experiencing poverty for shorter periods of time. The degree or severity of economic hardship also is a factor: The more adverse the conditions, the more negative are the consequences that an individual experiences. Timing, too, may play a role, with the experience of poverty in the earliest years having a greater impact than during adolescence or later years. Children experiencing poverty early on and living in extreme poverty for a long period of time are likely to suffer the worst outcomes. Children who are born at risk or with disabilities and who also are born into families living in poverty are considered to be at "double jeopardy." The interaction of biologic factors with the myriad of environmental factors associated with living in impoverished conditions multiplies the risk for adverse outcomes.

Access to health care, social services, quality affordable child care, quality educational programs, and disability services as needed are of critical importance to families living in conditions of economic distress. Typically, the complexities of the risks these children and families' life situations pose necessitate these services even more. Interventions must also center on fostering conditions that offer families the opportunity to live in neighborhoods that are safe from violence and crime and that are free from racial/ethnic/religious discrimination. These goals are more likely to be achieved by strengthening neighborhood infrastructures and encouraging the participation and input of those that live there (Brooks-Gunn, Duncan, & Aber, 1997a, 1997b).

Prevention and reduction in poverty are critical investments for this nation. The reduction in childhood poverty could result in profound advantages in almost every area of life: Children's success in school and increased ability to learn, better child health, less child hunger and malnutrition, and social-emotional well-being.

Although it is one of the richest nations in the world, the United States has a higher rate of poverty than most industrialized nations (Rainwater & Smeeding, 1995). The potential for pervasive and devastating consequences for children and families living in persistent poverty is great in our country. Service providers should renew their commitment to designing programs and policies to alleviate conditions that lead to poverty and to support families in sustaining themselves under troubling circumstances.

Inscribed at the base of the Statue of Liberty in New York is the following poem:

Give me your tired, your poor,
Your huddled masses yearning to breathe free,
The wretched refuse of your teeming shore.
Send these, the homeless, tempest-tost to me:
I lift my lamp beside the golden door.

−Emma Lazarus (1883)

This poem pays tribute to the United States as the haven of the oppressed and gateway to opportunity. May we continue to work to make it so.

ACTIVITIES TO EXTEND THE DISCUSSION

1. **Put yourself in their place.** Imagine that you live in a family of three and that your family's total annual income is less than $14,000. What adaptations would your family have to make? What priorities would you choose? How would you make these choices? What types of support and services would you seek? To truly identify how hard this is, do the math and make an actual budget for your imaginary family.

2. **Think of the impact.** Think of one of the families with whom you work that you know to be struggling with poverty. How has their economic hardship had an impact on their family? When you discuss the family's issues, be sure to change the family members' names and identifying characteristics to ensure confidentiality.

3. **Draw an "ecological map."** For the family you described in Activity 2, draw an ecological map. What specific elements of their lives are affected by their economic struggles at each level of the ecological framework? In your picture, put the family in the center circle. Place circles listing all their family tasks and functions all around the family. Highlight those that are affected by impoverished circumstances. At the outer edges of the map, indicate what sources of support or resources could be brought to bear to assist and support the family to meet their tasks and functions. Connect these supports and resources to the needs using a solid line for those that exist and a dotted line for those that are needed but not available.

4. **Dare to dream.** Consider again the family that you described in Activity 2. If you could activate any possible services and resources for them, what would those services and supports be? As a service provider, how could you help them find those resources?

TO LEARN MORE: SUGGESTED WEB SITES

Children's Defense Fund
http://www.childrensdefense.org/child-research-data-publications/

National Center for Children in Poverty
http://www.nccp.org/

REFERENCES

Bank, L., Forgatch, M.S., Patterson, G.R., & Fetrow, R.A. (1993). Parenting practices of single mothers: Mediators of negative contextual factors. *Journal of Marriage and Family, 55*, 371–384.

Belle, D. (1990). Poverty and women's mental health. *American Psychologist, 45*(3), 385–389.

Birenbaum, A. (2002). Poverty, welfare reform, and disproportionate rates of disability among children. *Mental Retardation, 40,* 212–218.

Booth, A., & Dunn, J. (1994). *Stepfamilies: Who benefits? Who does not?* Mahwah, NJ: Lawrence Erlbaum.

Bradley, R.H. (1995). Environment and parenting. In M. Bornstein (Ed.), *Handbook of parenting* (pp. 235–261). Mahwah, NJ: Lawrence Erlbaum.

Bradley, R.H., Whiteside, L., Mundfrom, D.J., Casey, P.H., Kelleher, K.J., & Pope, S.K. (1994). Early indications of resilience and their relation to experiences in the home environments of low birthweight, premature children living in poverty. *Child Development, 65,* 346–360.

Brody, G.H., Stoneman, Z., Flor, D., McCrary, C., Hastings, L., & Conyers, O. (1994). Financial resources, parent psychological functioning, parent co-caregiving, and early adolescent competence in rural two-parent African-American families. *Child Development, 65,* 590–605.

Bronfenbrenner, U. (1979). *The ecology of human development: Experiments by nature and design.* Cambridge, MA: Harvard University Press.

Bronfenbrenner, U. (1999). Environments in developmental perspective: Theoretical and operational models. In S.L. Friedman & T.D. Wachs (Eds.). *Measuring environment across the life span: Emerging methods and concepts* (pp. 3–28). Washington, DC: American Psychological Association Press.

Bronfenbrenner, U., & Morris, P.A. (2006). The bioecological model of human development (pp. 793–828). In R. Lerner (Ed.), *Handbook of child psychology: Vol. 1, Theoretical models of human development* (6th ed.). Hoboken, NJ: Wiley.

Brooks-Gunn, J., Rouse, C., & McLanahan, S. (2007). Racial and ethnic gaps in school readiness. In R. Pianta, M. Cox, & K. Snow (Eds.), *School readiness and the transition to kindergarten in the era of accountability* (pp. 283–306). Baltimore, MD: Paul H. Brookes Publishing Co.

Brooks-Gunn, J., & Duncan, G.J. (1997). The effects of poverty on children. *The Future of Children: Children and Poverty, 7*(2), 55–71.

Brooks-Gunn, J., Duncan, G.J., & Aber, J.L. (Eds.). (1997a). *Neighborhood poverty: Vol. I. Context and consequences for children.* New York, NY: Russell Sage Foundation.

Brooks-Gunn, J., Duncan, G.J., & Aber, J.L. (Eds.). (1997b). *Neighborhood poverty: Vol. II. Policy implications in studying neighborhoods.* New York, NY: Russell Sage Foundation.

Brooks-Gunn, J., Duncan, G.J., & Maritato, N. (1997). Poor families, poor outcomes: The well-being of children and youth. In G.J. Duncan & J. Brooks-Gunn (Eds.), *Consequences of growing up poor* (pp. 1–17). New York, NY: Russell Sage Foundation.

Brooks-Gunn, J., Klebanov, P., & Duncan, G. (1996). Ethnic differences in children's intelligence test scores: Role of economic deprivation, home environment, and maternal characteristics. *Child Development, 67,* 396–408.

Brooks-Gunn, J., Klebanov, P., Liaw, F., & Duncan, G.J. (1995). Toward an understanding of the effects of poverty upon children. In H.E. Fitzgerald, B.M. Lester, & B. Zuckerman (Eds.), *Children of poverty: Research, health, and policy issues.* New York, NY: Garland Publishing.

Brooks-Gunn, J., Rouse, C., & McLanahan, S. (2007). Racial and ethnic gaps in school readiness. In R. Pianta, M. Cox, & K. Snow (Eds.), *School readiness and the transition to kindergarten in the era of accountability* (pp. 283–306). Baltimore, MD: Paul H. Brookes Publishing Co.

Brown, L., & Pollitt, E. (1996). Malnutrition, poverty and intellectual development. *Scientific American, 274*(2), 38–43.

Burchinal, M., Lee, M., & Ramey, C. (1989). Type of day care and preschool intellectual development in disadvantaged children. *Child Development, 60*(1), 128–137.

Caldwell, B., & Bradley, R.H. (1984). *Home observation for measurement of the environment.* Little Rock, AR: University of Arkansas, Center for Research on Teaching and Learning.

Chase-Lansdale, P.L. & Gordon, R. (1996). Economic hardship and the development of five- and six-year olds: Neighborhood and regional perspectives. *Child Development, 67,* 3338–3367.

Chase-Lansdale, P.L., Gordon, R.A., Brooks-Gunn, J., & Klebanov, P.K. (1997). Neighborhood and family influences on the intellectual and behavioral competence of preschool and early school-age children. In J. Brooks-Gunn, G.J. Duncan, & J.L. Aber (Eds.), *Neighborhood poverty: Vol. I. Context and consequences for children* (pp. 79–118). New York, NY: Russell Sage Foundation.

Chau, M., Thampi, K., & Wight, V. (2010a). *Basic facts about low-income children, 2009: Children under age 3.* Retrieved July 10, 2012, from http://www.nccp.org/publications/pdf/download_377.pdf

Chau, M., Thampi, K., & Wight, V. (2010b). *Basic facts about low-income children, 2009: Children under age 6.* Retrieved July 10, 2012, from http://www.nccp.org/publications/pdf/download_378.pdf

Chau, M., Thampi, K., & Wight, V. (2010c). *Basic facts about low-income children, 2009: Children under age 18.* Retrieved July 10, 2012, from http://www.nccp.org/publications/pub_975.html

Citro, C., & Michael, R. (Eds.) (1995). *Measuring poverty: A new approach*. Washington, DC: National Academies Press.

Conger, R.D., Ge, X., Elder, G.H., Lorenz, F.O., & Simons, R.L. (1994). Economic stress, coercive family process, and developmental problems of adolescents. *Child Development, 65,* 541–561.

Cost, Quality and Child Outcomes Study Team. (1995). *Cost, quality, and child outcomes in child care centers*. Denver, CO: University of Colorado at Denver, Department of Economics.

Dalaker, J. (2001). *Poverty in the United States: 2000. Current population reports: Consumer income*. Washington, DC: U.S. Census Bureau, U.S. Department of Commerce.

DeNavas-Walt, C, Proctor, B., & Smith, J. (2011). *Income, poverty, and health insurance coverage in the United States: 2010*. Washington, DC: U.S. Government Printing Office.

Devaney, B.L., Ellwood, M.R., & Love, J.M. (1997). *The future of children: Children and poverty, 7*(2), 88–112.

Dodge, K.A., Pettit, G.S., & Bates, J.E. (1994). Socialization mediators of the relation between socioeconomic status and child conduct problems. *Child Development, 65,* 649–665.

Duncan, G.J., & Brooks-Gunn, J. (Eds.). (1997). *Consequences of growing up poor*. New York, NY: Russell Sage Foundation.

Duncan, G.J., Brooks-Gunn, J., & Klebanov, P.K. (1994). Economic deprivation and early childhood development. *Child Development, 65,* 296–318.

Duncan, G. J., & Magnuson, K. (2011, Winter). The long reach of early childhood poverty, *Pathways*. Retrieved July 10, 2012, from http://www.stanford.edu/group/scspi/_media/pdf/pathways/winter_2011/PathwaysWinter11_Duncan.pdf

Duncan, G.J., Yeung, W.J., Brooks-Gunn, J., & Smith, J. (1998). *American Sociological Review, 63*(3), 406–423.

Dunn, L.M., & Dunn, L.M. (1981). *Peabody Picture Vocabulary Test-Revised*. Circle Pines, MN: American Guidance Service.

Escalona, S.K. (1982). Babies at double hazard: Early development of infants at biologic and social risk. *Pediatrics, 70,* 670–676.

Emerson, R.W. (1860). *The conduct of life*. Cambridge, MA: The Riverside Press.

Fass, S. (2009). *Measuring poverty in the United States*. New York, NY: National Center for Children in Poverty.

Fisher, G.M. (1997). *The development of the Orshansky poverty thresholds and their subsequent history as the official U.S. poverty measure*. Retrieved August 12, 2012, from http://www.census.gov/hhes/povmeas/publications/orshansky.html

Fujiura, G.T., & Yamaki, K. (2000). Trends in demography of childhood poverty and disability. *Exceptional Children, 66*(2), 187–199.

Goldstein, N. (1990). *Explaining socioeconomic difference in children's cognitive test scores*. Cambridge, MA: Malcolm Wiener Center for Social Policy.

Hernandez, D.J. (1997). Poverty trends. In G.J. Duncan & J. Brooks-Gunn (Eds.), *Consequences of growing up poor* (pp. 18–34). New York, NY: Russell Sage Foundation.

Huston, A.C. (1991). *Children in poverty: Child development and public policy*. New York: Cambridge University Press.

Huston, A.C., McLoyd, V.C., & Garcia Coll, C. (1994). Children and poverty: Issues in contemporary research. *Child Development, 65,* 275–282.

Kennedy, J.F. (January 20, 1961). *Inaugural address*. Retrieved July 10, 2012, from http://www.americanrhetoric.com/speeches/jfkinaugural.htm

Krutsinger, A., & Tarr, N. (2011). *Poverty fact sheet: Implications for infants and toddlers*. Retrieved June 30, 2011, from http://www.zerotothree.org/public-policy/pdf/poverty-fact-sheet-5-10-11-final.pdf

Lazarus, E. (1883). "The new colossus." Statue of Liberty. New York.

Lee, S., Sills, M., & Oh, G.T. (2002). *Disabilities among children and mothers in low-income families*. Retrieved July 10, 2012, from http://www.iwpr.org/publications/pubs/disabilities-among-children-and-mothers-in-low-income-families

Leventhal, T., & Brooks-Gunn, J. (2000). Neighborhoods they live in: The effects of neighborhood residence on child and adolescent outcomes. *Psychological Bulletin, 126,* 309–337.

Leventhal, T., & Brooks-Gunn, J. (2003). Children and youth in neighborhood contexts. *Current Directions in Psychological Science, 12,* 27–31.

Loprest, P., & Acs, G. (1996). *Profile of disability among families on AFDC*. Washington, DC: The Urban Institute.

Mayes, L. (1996, June). *Early experience and the developing brain: The model of prenatal cocaine exposure*. Paper presented at the invitational conference, Brain Development in Young

Children: New Frontiers for Research, Policy, and Practice, Chicago, IL.

McLanahan, S.S. (1997). Parent absence or poverty: Which matters more? In G.J. Duncan & J. Brooks-Gunn (Eds.), *Consequences of growing up poor* (pp. 35–48). New York, NY: Russell Sage Foundation.

McLeod, J.D., & Shanahan, M.J. (1993). Poverty, parenting and children's mental health. *American Sociological Review, 58,* 351–366.

McLoyd, V.C. (1990). The impact of economic hardship on black families and children: Psychological distress, parenting, and socioemotional development. *Child Development, 61,* 311–346.

McLoyd, V.C. (1997). The impact of poverty and low socioeconomic status on the socioemotional functioning of African-American children and adolescents: Mediating effects. In R. Taylor & M. Wang (Eds.), *Social and emotional adjustment and family relations in ethnic minorities* (pp. 7–34). Mahwah, NJ: Lawrence Erlbaum Associates.

McLoyd, V.C. (1998a). Children in poverty: Development, public policy, and practice. In I.E. Sigel & K.A. Renninger (Eds.), *Handbook of child psychology: Vol. 4. Child psychology in practice* (5th ed., pp. 135–208). New York, NY: Wiley.

McLoyd, V.C. (1998b). Socioeconomic disadvantage and child development. *American Psychologist, 53,* 185–204.

McLoyd, V., Jayaratne, T.E., Ceballo, R., & Borquez, J. (1994). Unemployment and work interruption among African American single mothers: Effects on parenting and adolescent socioemotional functioning. *Child Development, 65,* 562–589.

Meyers, M.K., Lukemeyer, A., & Smeeding, T.M. (1996). *Work, welfare, and the burden of disability: Caring for special needs of children in poor families, Income Security Policy Series, Paper No. 12.* Syracuse, NY: Center for Policy Research, Maxwell School of Citizenship and Public Affairs, Syracuse University.

Mistry, R.S., Vandewater, E.A., Huston, A.C., & McLoyd, V.C. (2002). Economic well-being and children's social adjustment: The role of family process in an ethnically diverse low-income sample. *Child Development, 73,* 935–951.

More kids living with no parent. (2002, July 29). *San Jose Mercury News,* p. A4.

National Center for Children in Poverty (1999, June). *Poverty and brain development in early childhood.* Retrieved on August 12, 2012, from http://www.nccp.org/publications/pdf/text_398.pdf

Parker, S., Greer, S., & Zuckerman, B. (1988). Double jeopardy: The impact of poverty on early childhood development. *Pediatric Clinics of North America, 35,* 1127–1241.

Pinderhughes, E., Nix R., Foster, E., Jones, D., & the Conduct Problems Prevention Research Group (2001). Parenting in context: Impact of neighborhood poverty, residential stability, public services, social networks, and danger on parental behaviors. *Journal of Marriage and the Family, 63,* 941–953.

Plotnick, R.D. (1997). Child poverty can be reduced. *Children and Poverty, 7*(2), 72–87.

Rainwater, L., & Smeeding, T. (1995, August). *Doing poorly: The real income of American children in a comparative perspective. Luxembourg Income Study Working Paper No. 127.* Syracuse, NY: Maxwell School of Citizenship and Public Affairs, Syracuse University.

Rosman, E.A., & Knitzer, J. (2001). Welfare reform: The special case of young children with disabilities and their families. *Infants and Young Children, 13*(3), 25–35.

Rowling, J.K. (2008, June 5). *The fringe benefits of failure, and the importance of imagination.* Harvard Commencement Address, Cambridge, MA.

Sameroff, A. (1983). Developmental systems: Context and evolution. In P.H. Mussen (Series Ed.) & W. Kessen (Vol. Ed.), *Handbook of child psychology: Vol. 1. History, theory and methods* (pp. 238–294). New York, NY: Wiley.

Sameroff, A. (Ed.) (2009). *The transactional model of development: How children and contexts shape each other.* Washington, DC: American Psychological Association.

Sameroff, A., Seifer, R., Barocas, R., Zax, M., & Greenspan, S. (1987). Intelligence quotient scores of 4-year-old children: Social-environmental risk factors. *Pediatrics, 79,* 343–350.

Sampson, R.J., & Laub, J.H. (1994). Urban poverty and the family context of delinquency: A new look at structure and process in a classic study. *Child Development, 65,* 523–540.

Schorr, L. (1988). *Within our reach: Breaking the cycle of disadvantage.* New York, NY: Anchor Books.

Seith, D., & Isakson, E. (2011). *Who are America's poor? Examining health disparities among children in the United States.* New York, NY: Columbia University, National Center for Children in Poverty. Retrieved August 12, 2012, from http://www.nccp.org/publications/pub_995.html

Seith, D., & Kalof, C. (2011). *Who are America's poor? Examining health disparities by race and ethnicity.* New York, NY: Columbia University, National Center for Children in Poverty. Retrieved August 12, 2012, from http://www.nccp.org/publications/pub_1032.html

Shonkoff, J.P., & Phillips, D.A. (Eds.). (2000). *From neurons to neighborhoods: The science of early childhood development.* Washington, DC: National Academies Press.

Shore, R. (1997). *Rethinking the brain: New insights into early development.* New York, NY: Families and Work Institute.

Short, K. (2011). *The Research Supplemental Poverty Measure: 2010. Population reports.* Retrieved July 10, 2012, from http://www.census.gov/prod/2011pubs/p60-241.pdf

Smith, J.R., Brooks-Gunn, J., & Klebanov, P. (1997). Consequences of living in poverty for young children's cognitive and verbal ability and early school achievement. In G.J. Duncan & J. Brooks-Gunn (Eds.), *Consequences of growing up poor* (pp. 132–189). New York, NY: Russell Sage Foundation.

Tripp, R.T. (1970). *The international thesaurus of quotations.* New York, NY: Thomas Y. Crowell.

Wight, V.R., Chau, M., & Aratani, Y. (2011). *Who are America's poor children? The official story.* New York, NY: National Center for Children in Poverty.

Family Life at Risk

Pressure from Outside and Turmoil Within

Eleanor W. Lynch

"The family is one of nature's masterpieces."

—George Santayana (1905, p. 35)

"Life in itself is neither a good nor an evil; it is the scene of good and evil."

—Seneca (as cited in Gardner & Reese, 1975, p. 107)

"Sometimes we love with nothing more than hope. Sometimes we cry with everything except tears. In the end, that's all there is: love and its duty, sorrow and its truth."

—Gregory David Roberts (2003, p. 465)

All families have challenges—times of sadness and loss, concerns in the present, and worry about the future. All families also have times of joy, hope, optimism, and contentment. For most families, the positive times outweigh the negative; the family maintains its equilibrium and functions successfully. For other families, negative events, experiences, and feelings exceed the positive. Balance is never achieved, and family life unravels. In some instances, external events or experiences such as extended unemployment, natural disasters, bankruptcy, or exposure to violence alter the family's positive trajectory, resulting in changes in family resources as well as family dynamics. In other instances, the proclivities of one or more of the family members, such as an addiction or abuse, cause the family to lose its purpose and sustainability. Whatever the cause, when families fail to fulfill the functions that are expected of them, the consequences can be profound.

This chapter focuses on the risks involved in addiction, violence, trauma, loss, and disability. The ways in which these life circumstances affect families are described along with promising practices in prevention and intervention. The information presented is often disheartening. For service providers who focus on the positive, many of the situations described may be difficult to imagine or consider. This chapter is included because many service providers encounter these situations daily; it is highly likely that others will, at some time, be exposed to the consequences of these risks in families with whom they work, among their acquaintances and colleagues, or within their own families. Many of these risks transcend the stereotypes of the popular press; in numerous instances, it is clear that the adage "bad things happen to good people" is often true. If professionals are to provide support to families who face the challenges of addiction, violence, trauma, and loss, service providers need to understand the problems and their solutions.

ADDICTION AND VIOLENCE

Addiction and violence are topics that fill headlines and prisons, that break up families and break hearts. They are also concerns that touch the entire population—men and women, children and adults, rich and poor, urban and rural. However, like many risks, the negative effects fall disproportionately on groups with limited resources and often on populations of color. Their impact on families is profound in economic, social, and medical terms; their relationship to disability and risks in development is becoming increasingly clear.

Research, statistics, and recommendations related to addiction and violence abound. The indicators and the outcomes are clear, but comprehensive prevention and intervention efforts that can stem the tide of negative effects are often lacking. Addiction and violence put the lives of families and family members at extreme risk. Recall, for example, the family systems framework described in Chapters 3 and 4. Consider the ways in which drug addiction and violence affect the family system. What might these problems do to communication within and outside the family? How would they affect the functions that families are expected to perform? In what ways might the family life cycle be altered by violence or addiction? The following sections discuss addiction, family violence, child abuse, and neglect; their impact on families; as well as promising practices in prevention and intervention practices of promise.

Addiction

The words *addiction* and *physical dependence* are often used interchangeably, but groups such as the American Pain Society, the American Society of Pain Medicine, the American Society of Addiction Medicine, and the Liaison Committee for Pain and Addiction argue that they are not the same (Heit & Gourlay, 2009). Physical dependence can be defined as an expected neurological adaptation to chronic exposure to a drug or class of drugs. Physical dependence occurs when the body adapts to the drug and requires the drug to function. Drugs of this nature range from illicit drugs such as heroin to common prescription drugs for blood pressure and even laxatives (Berkow, Beers, & Fletcher, 1997). Addiction is a more complex, multidimensional phenomenon that incorporates biological, psychological, and psychosocial elements that result in compulsive use of the drug or involvement in the activity. Using these definitions, substances or activities that do not cause physical dependence may still meet the criteria for addiction: psychological dependence, with the desire to continue to take the drug or engage in the activity because of its pleasurable effects or the reduction in tension and anxiety that occur (Berkow et al.).

In this chapter, addiction and substance abuse are both used to refer to an individual's overwhelming involvement with a drug or other activity—involvement that interferes with daily life, the ability to make sound judgments, and the ability to care adequately for oneself and others. Alcohol, nicotine, cocaine, marijuana, heroin, and prescription drugs fall into this category, as do gambling, some sexual behaviors, and even Internet use. Addictive behaviors pose serious risks to families because they become all consuming and more important than anything else in the addict's life.

Addictions to and abuse of drugs–both legal and illegal–also pose significant health threats. For example, needle sharing in intravenous drug use is associated with HIV; nicotine addiction is a major cause of emphysema and lung cancer; amphetamine abuse results in increased blood pressure and heart rate, which can lead to heart attacks and strokes; and a woman's alcoholism or long-term use of nicotine, cocaine, marijuana, or methamphetamines may lead to negative health and developmental outcomes for her children (Berkow et al., 1997; Minnes, Lang, & Singer, 2011). The need to obtain drugs or engage in the addictive activity is often associated with or results in criminal behaviors. In 2004, the Bureau of Justice reported that 17% of state prisoners and 18% of federal prisoners had committed their most recent offense to obtain money for drugs (U.S. Department of Justice, 2010). Federal Bureau of Investigation data from 2008 indicate that there were 14 million arrests. Of these arrests, 12.2% were for drug abuse violations–the most common category of arrests for crime (Crime in the United States, 2009). The population of incarcerated individuals reflects the same pattern. According to statistics from the Bureau of Justice, 20% of state prisoners and 53% of federal prisoners are incarcerated because of a drug offense. Multiple studies of drug use, arrests, and convictions indicate that drug users are more likely to commit crimes than are nonusers (Spiess & Fallow, 2000), and some of these crimes are violent. In 2008, approximately 4% of all homicides were drug related (U.S. Department of Justice, 2009).

Finally, when addiction becomes all consuming or substance abuse becomes pervasive, addicts and abusers are unable to put the needs of others above their own. They become unavailable to others physically and psychologically, and parenting or partnering in a relationship become secondary to everything else. The negative outcomes are clearly articulated by the DHHS:

> Alcohol and illicit drug use are associated with child and spousal abuse; sexually transmitted diseases, including HIV infection; teen pregnancy; school failure; motor vehicle crashes; escalation of health care costs; low worker productivity; and homelessness. Alcohol and illicit drug use also can result in substantial disruptions in family, work, and personal life. (2010, p. 33)

Addiction has been defined as "the compulsive activity and overwhelming involvement with a specific activity" (Berkow et al., 1997, p. 440). Orford (2001, p. 18) considers addiction to be a problem of excessive appetite for an activity or substance, stating that in addiction the appetite is "so strong that a person finds it difficult to moderate the activity despite the fact that it is causing harm." Although illegal drugs, alcohol, and nicotine typically come to mind when one thinks of addictions, any substance or activity that is excessive and difficult to moderate in spite of negative consequences is considered addictive. Eating, gambling, sexual behaviors, exercise, and Internet use can be considered as addictions if the individual is compulsively involved in them and finds it difficult to alter his or her behavior in spite of detrimental effects. One study examined the prevalence of addiction to Second Life, a sophisticated three-dimensional virtual world, and found that approximately one third of participants met the criterion for or were at risk for Internet addiction (Gilbert, Murphy, & McNally, 2011). It remains to be determined whether the American Psychiatric Association's forthcoming *Diagnostic and*

Statistical Manual of Mental Disorders, Fifth Edition, will include non–drug-related behaviors, such as compulsive gambling and compulsive Internet use, among the list of recognized disorders. Regardless of this decision, many people engage in non–drug-related activities to an extent that is harmful to themselves and their families. Although Orford's broader model of addiction is controversial, it directly addresses the primary concern of this book—families and their resilience in the presence of risk.

Drugs of Choice in Substance Abuse and Addiction To understand families' challenges related to addiction, it is important to know more about the most common types of substance abuse and addiction—the drugs that are used and their effects. This section discusses legal and illegal drugs that are commonly abused, are associated with visits to hospital emergency rooms, can profoundly affect family functioning, and are positively correlated with disability in infants and young children.

Alcohol When one imagines addiction and its consequences, it is common to think of gangs, guns, and back-alley transactions. This image is in stark contrast to a bright, well-appointed living room with people chatting over a martini or glass of wine after work. The second image, however, is not always as pleasant or benign as it sounds. In the United States, nearly 17.6 million adults have alcoholism or alcohol problems (National Institutes of Health, 2012). These individuals crave alcohol, cannot stop drinking once they start, are physically dependent, and need to drink greater and greater amounts to feel the effects that they seek (National Institute on Alcohol Abuse and Alcoholism, 2012). Alcohol is easily accessible and inexpensive when compared to many other addictive drugs, making it available to teens and even younger children who binge drink (i.e., occasionally drink excessively). More men than women abuse alcohol, but abuse among women has increased in recent years (Enoch & Goldman, 2002).

The causes of alcoholism are unknown, but both biological and social theories related to the addiction continue to be investigated. The biological children of parents with alcoholism are more likely to develop alcoholism than are the adopted children of parents with alcoholism, suggesting some genetic predisposition. There is also evidence that the brains of individuals with alcoholism are less sensitive to the effects of alcohol and less easily intoxicated than individuals without alcoholism (Berkow et al., 1997; National Institute of Alcohol Abuse and Alcoholism, 2012).

Personality traits and environmental factors are also associated with alcoholism. Individuals with alcoholism tend to be more isolated, lonely, shy, depressed, dependent, hostile, self-destructive, impulsive, and sexually immature than individuals without alcoholism (Elkins, King, McGue, & Iacono, 2006; Porter & Kaplan, 2011). In terms of social factors, individuals with alcoholism are more likely to come from homes with one parent absent and have disturbed relationships with their parents. These factors often occur within a larger context of poverty, limited education, psychiatric illness, and inadequate treatment options. However, the puzzle is not easily solved. Do these factors lead to alcoholism or are they its result? Regardless of the answer, alcoholics come from all strata of society, ethnicities, educational levels, and income levels. The consequences of alcohol abuse and alcoholism are profound, including its effects on the developing fetus. It is also the drug that is closest to home in many families—one that does not take sophisticated strategies to intervene, one that we can all have a part in controlling.

Nicotine As a legal, easily accessible, and heavily marketed drug, nicotine is one of the most commonly used addictive drugs throughout the world. In the United States, nicotine addiction occurs most commonly from smoking cigarettes. Although the number of people who smoke cigarettes has dropped in recent years with stop-smoking campaigns, antismoking legislation, and treatment options, the number of smokeless tobacco users has increased (National Institutes of Health, 2011). Like alcohol, nicotine addiction can be found among adults and youth, men and women, and across all ethnicities.

The immediate effects of nicotine are not dissimilar to other addictive drugs—a rush, high, or kick caused by the release of adrenaline and glucose. Heart rate, blood pressure, and respiration also increase along with dopamine levels in the areas of the brain that control pleasure and motivation (DHHS, 2001). The long-term effects of nicotine addiction should no longer be surprising: cancer, emphysema, chronic asthma, heart disease, stroke, aneurysms, and vascular disease. It has now become clear that smokers are not the only ones whose health is affected by their habit. According to the Centers for Disease Control and Prevention, no level of secondhand smoke or environmental tobacco smoke is risk free (Centers for Disease Control and Prevention, 2011). Infants and children are at particularly high risk for serious health problems caused by secondhand smoke. Infants are at greater risk for death from sudden infant death syndrome, and children of smokers get sick more often, have more frequent asthma attacks, more ear infections, and more surgeries to put tubes in their ears for drainage (Centers for Disease Control and Prevention).

Although nicotine is as addictive as alcohol, heroin, and cocaine, it is seldom associated with dramatic, downward economic spirals or loss of home and family. This casual consideration of nicotine addiction does not, however, align with the facts. Both the economic and personal costs are significant. Between 2000 and 2004 in the United States, loss in productivity attributable to cigarette smoking and exposure to secondhand smoke amounted to nearly $97 million dollars (Adhikari, Kahende, Malarcher, Pechacek, & Tong, 2008). Of even deeper concern are the mortality figures. Every year between 2000 and 2004, an estimated 443,595 people (269,655 men and 173,940 women) died as a result of smoking. The three leading causes of death were lung cancer, ischemic heart disease, and chronic obstructive pulmonary disease. Smoking during pregnancy resulted in the death of an estimated 776 infants in each of those years. Exposure to secondhand smoke is estimated to have caused 49,400 deaths annually from lung cancer and heart disease, and 736 deaths each year were the result of residential fires caused by smoking. Losing a mother, father, or child prematurely is always a tragedy, but loss from a preventable disease is even more devastating. Like alcohol addiction, nicotine addiction is common in many homes. It is something many people live—and die—with. It is preventable and treatable, and its reduction would account for significant reductions in many other life-threatening diseases as well as a reduction in premature births among mothers who smoke.

Illegal Drugs   It is likely that no one begins using drugs with the intent of becoming addicted. However, all too often, casual drug use changes from an occasional, pleasurable high to a physical need and compulsion—an escalating desire that becomes more important and more powerful than everything else in life. Food, health, cleanliness, safety, the smile of one's child, or the love of a caring parent may not compete with the drive for the next high; thus, little by little, life may change completely. The 2010 National Survey on Drug Use and Health, which examined the rate of drug use in the previous month, indicated that 10.1% of 12- to 17-year-old children were using illegal drugs. Among 18- to 25-year-olds, illegal drug use was 21.5%; among those age 26 and older, 6.6% were drug users. These figures all represent increases in drug use over the previous year. In 2010, 5.8% of 50- to 59-year-olds used illegal drugs (Substance Abuse and Mental Health Services Administration, 2011).

None of the consequences of addiction are positive, so why is addiction so prevalent? Addiction is the result of multiple, complex, and interacting variables. Personality, social, economic, and physiological variables contribute to each individual's reactions to drugs. These variables may predispose individuals to addiction or serve as protective factors that reduce the likelihood of addiction. Although it is not possible to predict the outcomes for an individual, a number of societal variables are associated with risky behaviors that often lead to addiction. For adults, lack of opportunity, unemployment, poverty, limited access to treatment, violence at home and in the neighborhood, and association with substance abusers contribute to drug abuse and addiction.

Marijuana, heroin, cocaine, and methamphetamine are four of the most commonly used illegal drugs along with an ever-changing array of "club drugs." Each drug causes somewhat different effects and each individual's response to a drug is different, but all have significant health risks. All are addictive and can pose serious risks to a mother and her developing fetus during pregnancy (Milligan et al., 2011). For additional information about illegal drugs, their effects, and their health risks, see the resources listed at the end of this chapter.

Prescription Drugs   Prescription drugs are some of the most important tools in modern medicine. They act to prevent disease, reduce pain, and diminish the effects of illness. Many people avoid illness because of prescription drugs, and many others are made more comfortable when they are ill because of the medicines that have been prescribed. From acne to asthma and hay fever to heart disease, prescription drugs can dramatically improve both the quality and length of life. However, despite the good that they do, an estimated 20% of the U.S. population has abused prescription drugs.

Abuse of prescription drugs takes a number of forms: using drugs prescribed for someone else, altering the prescribed dose, using the medication in a manner that does not correspond with the way it was prescribed, or using the drug simply to experience the feelings that it produces (National Institute on Drug Abuse, n.d.). According to current data, the incidence of prescription drug abuse is increasing (National Institutes of Health, n.d.). Although prescription drugs are misused by individuals of all ages, their misuse is especially common among young people. Narcotic painkillers, sedatives and tranquilizers for anxiety and sleep disorders, and stimulants for ADHD are all commonly abused addictive drugs (Mayo Clinic Staff, 2010).

Prescription drugs can be found in many households. Typically, they are prescribed for someone for a legitimate medical need, but unfinished drugs often remain in the house. Stored in a cabinet or drawer and often forgotten, they are easily accessible and tempting to teens experimenting with drugs or adults with drug habits. Even when prescription drugs are appropriately disposed, online pharmacies and pharmacies outside the United States make it easy to obtain prescription drugs without a prescription (Mayo Clinic Staff, 2010). The consequences of abuse of these drugs have resulted in an increase in emergency room visits, admissions for treatment, and deaths from overdose (National Institute on Drug Abuse, 2011). Like all of the addictive substances discussed, abuse of prescription drugs poses significant health hazards.

Treating Drug Abuse and Addiction   The consequences of drug abuse and addiction on families are often devastating: violence, loss of resources, frequent interactions with the police and justice systems, and limited options for treatment and recovery. The loss of one's home as a safe haven and the loss of trust in loved ones are perhaps as undermining to well-being as the loss of material possessions. The consequences of drug addiction and abuse threaten every aspect of family life and make the successful performance of family functions close to impossible. Because of this, considerable effort has been made to develop prevention and treatment programs that work.

Large-scale evaluations of drug prevention and treatment programs have been conducted, and the conclusion is that treatment is effective. However, like so many evaluations of educational and social programs, it is still unclear which programs work for which individuals and under what conditions. Among the models that have been shown to be effective are therapeutic communities, pharmacological treatment, outpatient without drugs or pharmacological management, and inpatient treatment (Office of National Drug Control Policy, 1996). Prevention strategies with young people have included prevention education, opportunities to develop alternative drug-free activities, identifying substance abuse problems early and referring for treatment, building community-based interventions, and working with schools and other institutions to create an environment that reduces risk factors and enhances protective factors (Office of National Drug Control Policy, 2009). Recent efforts in treatment have focused on evidence-based approaches, including pharmacotherapies and behavioral therapies (National Institute on Drug Abuse, 2009). Finally, for any prevention strategy or treatment to work, it has to be available to those who need it when they need it. Making options available, accessible, and culturally competent continue to be challenges to systems and to professionals in those systems that work with and care about families.

Remarkably, many individuals face extremely difficult circumstances and escape addiction. For young people, the risks and protective factors are clear. According to the National Institute on Drug Abuse (2002), the following factors increase the risk of drug abuse among youth:

1. Chaotic home environments, especially those in which parents have mental illness or are substance abusers

2. Lack of parent–child attachment and nurturing

3. Shy or aggressive classroom behavior that is inappropriate

4. School failure

5. Poor social coping skills

6. Friendships and affiliations with peers who display deviant behavior

7. Perception that drug use is acceptable

As might be anticipated, risks that often lead to drug abuse also lead to other forms of antisocial behavior, such as delinquency, youth violence, leaving school, risky sexual behaviors, and teen pregnancy.

Conversely, a number of protective factors help prevent drug abuse and other antisocial behavior. These factors, as identified by the National Institute on Drug Abuse (2002), include the following:

1. Family bonds that are strong and positive

2. Parental monitoring of children's behavior and activities and that of their children's peers

3. Clear, consistently enforced rules of conduct within the family

4. Parental involvement in children's lives

5. School success and strong bonds with community institutions, such as school, church, temple, or synagogue

6. Acceptance of conventional norms about drug use

There are opportunities to prevent or reduce substance abuse and addiction as well as opportunities to help those abusing drugs to change. For this to happen, however, healthy families and supportive communities are requisites.

Violence

Violence is part of nearly every newscast and is featured prominently in online headlines. Primetime television, movies, computer and video games, comics, and cartoons are rife with acts of random and targeted violence; in many genres, guns figure prominently. It should therefore not be surprising that 10.2 out of every 100,000 people were killed by firearms in 2007 in the United States (Florida, 2011). A state-by-state analysis provides a much more refined view. Hawaii had the lowest rate, with 2.6 deaths per 100,000; the rates for New York and New Jersey were 5.0 and 5.2, respectively. At the other end of the spectrum, the District of Columbia had 21.7 deaths for every 100,000 residents, with rates of 20.2 in Louisiana, 18.5 in Mississippi, 17.8 in Alaska, and 15.1 in Arizona (Florida). Gun deaths, whether from homicide, suicide, accidents, or in self-defense do not just occur among adults. According to the Children's Defense Fund (2001, p. xxii), when children under age 15 in the United States are compared to children the same age in 25 other industrialized countries combined, U.S. children are "9 times more likely to die in a firearms accident, 11 times more likely to commit suicide with a gun, 12 times more likely to die from gunfire, and 16 times more likely to be murdered with a gun." Too often, where there are guns, there is violence; all too often, children are caught in the crosshairs.

Gun violence and other types of violence in schools, neighborhoods, and communities have punctuated lives throughout the nation in recent years. Statistics from the Federal Bureau of Investigation (2010) suggest that a violent crime occurred every 25.3 seconds in 2010—one murder every 35.6 minutes, one rape every 6.2 minutes, a robbery every 1.4 minutes, and an aggravated assault every 40.5 seconds; therefore, it is clear that there is violence in communities. These numbers are clearly worthy of the best efforts of service providers, individually and collectively, to understand and prevent future occurrences; however, the broad topic of community violence is outside the scope of this book. The following sections focus on violence at home—usually violence against women and children. Although domestic violence is frequently nested in society's larger problems, this chapter focuses on what happens to those who are battered, abused, and maltreated and the ways in which that affects families and their ability to function.

Domestic Violence Violence between domestic partners or former partners accounts for much of the abuse in America's homes. In domestic violence, both men and women are perpetrators, but women are more likely to be victims than men. Between 1998 and 2002, nearly 75% of victims of family violence were women, and approximately 75% of those committing the violence were men (Durose et al., 2005). Although the rate of domestic violence fell between 1993 and 2002, it still accounted for 11% of all reported and unreported violence. A woman is victimized by an intimate partner every 52 seconds and a man is victimized by an intimate partner every 3.5 minutes (U.S. Department of Justice, n.d.). Adding to the toll is the fact that violence is almost always underreported (Watts & Zimmerman, 2002). Victimization includes a number of behaviors: hair pulling, hitting, slapping, kicking, beating, rape, and threatening or hurting with a knife, gun, or other weapon. Violence against women is typically not an isolated incident, but rather an ongoing pattern of behavior over months, years, and decades (Watts & Zimmerman).

Physical and sexual violence are not the only forms of abuse that occur in many of these destructive relationships. Verbal and psychological abuse such as name calling, preventing the partner from having contact with family and friends, jealousy, and possessiveness often co-occur and can change women's perceptions of their own worth, their relationships, and their rights and place in the larger world (Johnson & Ferraro, 2000). These altered perceptions contribute to the inability to leave an abusive relationship. However, contrary to what is sometimes suggested in the popular press and reports of research, many women do leave to protect themselves and their children (Johnson & Ferraro). It may take several attempts, temporary safe housing, legal advocacy, personal counseling, and supports provided by service agencies, but women do leave.

Johnson and Ferraro (2000) detailed four types of partner violence. First, they described common couple violence, which is typical of a more generalized pattern of control. This sort of violence occurs in specific arguments in which one or both partners lash out at the other. It typically does not accelerate over time, is generally confined to a low level of violence, and is likely to be mutual. Intimate terrorism describes a pattern of behavior that is based on the desire to control the partner. It is usually just one strategy of control used in the relationship, but it is often characterized by violence, psychological abuse, escalation over time, and serious injury. Intimate violence is usually practiced by only one partner. The pattern of abusive behavior in which a partner fights back has been labeled as violent resistance. Most often attributed to women and sometimes resulting in death or serious injury, little research has been conducted on it. It is this sort of violence that is often used in a self-defense plea in homicide cases. Some relationships are defined by mutual combat between partners who are both violent and controlling—mutual violent control.

Who batters women? What is known about men who treat their partners with aggression and abuse? Jacobson and Gottman (1998) studied couples involved in violent relationships. Through interviews, observations during conflict, psychometric evaluations, and observations during arguments in the laboratory, at least two types of men seemed to emerge. One type, labeled in the study as "cobras," could be called sociopathic. They seemed to be completely detached physiologically from vicious verbal attacks on their partners. Even in the heat of these vicious verbal attacks, their heart rate and other physiological measures did not change; they also had a history of violent and antisocial behavior. The other type, referred to as "pit bulls," was physiologically attuned to what was occurring during heated, vicious arguments but can be described as dependent and needy. These data suggest that abusive men have personalities and preestablished patterns of behavior that are likely to lead to abusive relationships with women. Given the longstanding nature of these personality traits and types, in many instances, abuse should be no surprise (Johnson & Ferraro, 2000).

Findings from a landmark survey indicate that rates of assault against women differ by race/ethnicity. The Violence Against Women Survey (Tjaden & Thoennes, 1998) illustrated that American Indian/Alaskan Native women are significantly more likely to report that they were victims of rape or assault than white non-Hispanic, African American, and Asian/Pacific Islander women. Latino women are less likely to report that they have been raped than non-Latino women, but the percent of physical assaults not including rape were similar between the groups. The reasons for these differences cannot be accounted for by the information gathered in the study. The differences may be artifacts of small sample size for American Indian/Alaskan Natives and Asian/Pacific Islanders. They may be the result of different cultural variables, immigration, and comfort in reporting. They may also speak to deeper cultural and sociocultural issues and the nation's ability to address inequities across groups. It does, however, appear that race/ethnicity may be a factor that makes some women more vulnerable to abuse than others. Important next steps are to determine why these differences occur and to find ways to reduce abuse in all relationships.

Effects on Abused Women   The most obvious outcomes of violence are the negative physical and psychological effects on women: injury, pain, hospitalization, recuperation, embarrassment, fear, and depression. Abuse limits women's options for education, work, and even leaving the house. It also limits women's ability to create alone (or with a partner) a safe haven for their children. It is not uncommon for some abusers to prevent their wives or partners from obtaining or maintaining a job or career. Their controlling tactics are often insidious, including depriving the partner of transportation, beatings before a job interview, turning off the alarm clock, harassment at work, and failing to be available for child care as promised (Johnson & Ferraro, 2000).

In a qualitative study conducted by Levendosky (2000), women in abusive relationships discussed the effects of domestic violence on their parenting. The majority reported that their parenting suffered because of the violence. Women described lack of energy, physical illness and injury, and anger as results of abuse that interfered with parenting. Even in the face of these challenges, a number of women marshaled their resources to protect and provide for their children. They used their circumstances to support positive parenting. For example, some reported being more empathetic toward their children and their needs because of their own experiences. Others put considerable effort into helping their children develop self-esteem so that the children would be less likely to be victims of abuse.

Effects on Children   Children who witness violence are also affected by it. Depression, anxiety, poor problem solving, psychosomatic complaints, and low self-esteem are common (Szyndrowski, 1999). Among a representative, national sample of teenagers in the United States, respondents who were exposed to violence reported considerably poorer health than those who had not been exposed (Boynton-Jarrett, Ryan, Berkman, & Wright, 2008). At the most basic level, children who witness violence may have difficulty forming secure attachments, making it difficult to establish and maintain relationships later in their lives (Levendosky & Graham-Bermann, 2001). These patterns of behavior often persist, as evidenced by data indicating that women in college who recall violence between their parents are less socially competent, more depressed, and have lower self-esteem (Henning, Leitenberg, Coffey, Bennett, & Jankowski, 1997). Individually or in combination, these characteristics often interfere with school success.

Of even greater concern are the long-term outcomes for children who witness abuse. Children who witness abuse are at risk for becoming direct victims of the violence and at risk for posttraumatic stress disorder. Children who witness domestic violence learn that violence is a part of intimate relationships, and there is no countervailing force that teaches other ways of communicating and solving problems (Groves, 1996). Victimization places children at risk for delinquency, criminal acts, and violent criminal behavior (National Institute of Mental Health, 2000). Although direct links are difficult to determine because of associated variables, it would not be surprising to find that witnessing violence places children at similar risk. Direct effects of violence on children who are abused are discussed in a later section of this chapter.

The transmission of violence is frequently discussed in the literature. Transmission is believed to have both environmental and genetic components. In other words, children who witness or experience violence and those who live in homes where violence is condoned are in environmental settings in which models of behavior put the child at risk for later violence as a victim or a perpetrator. It is also thought that there may be genetic predispositions to personality and behavioral types that are characteristic of abusers. Children exposed to violence at home and in the community have a higher risk of becoming either a victim or perpetrator of violence as adults (Anderson & Cramer-Benjamin, 1999; Stith et al., 2000). Likewise, men whose childhoods were spent in homes where there was domestic violence have been reported to be more likely to be violent as husbands and partners than those who have not grown up with violence (Johnson & Ferraro, 2000).

Effects on Society　Homelessness is a serious and thus far intractable problem in the United States. In one study, at least half of homeless women were forced onto the streets and into shelters because of extreme violence against them in their homes (Zorza, 1991). In another interview study of homeless women and women living in low-income housing, one third reported that they had experienced severe physical violence from their current or most recent partner (Browne & Bassuk, 1997). According to the National Coalition for the Homeless (2009), 63% of homeless women are victims of domestic violence. Because battering is a crime, the effects on police departments, courts, jails, and parole officers are also significant. Every dollar spent on the crime of battering subtracts from the resources available for prevention and treatment. At another level, the modeling of violence in the home has a range of incalculable costs. If home is not safe, what is? If those closest to us cannot be trusted, who can be trusted?

Preventing Domestic Violence　Domestic violence is not a simple one-dimensional problem. It is a problem that is a result of many interconnected factors and issues. It requires attention and coordinated approaches that involve prevention and intervention at the individual, community, societal, and political levels. As the statistics demonstrate, there is no quick fix. In fact, one of the hallmarks of the progress in this area is getting society to accept the fact that battering is not "the woman's problem." Domestic violence must become unacceptable in homes and communities, and learning that violence in the home is unacceptable should begin early. Families need opportunities to learn child-rearing techniques that do not include physical punishment and to learn communication and problem-solving skills that do not rely on physical force or verbal abuse.

As society's tolerance of abuse decreases, it will be critical to support programs for batterers and ensure that programs are available and accessible. Otherwise, violence will become an even more private and unyielding problem. As with Alcoholics Anonymous, the problem of alcoholism is not condoned, but treatment for it is. This must become equally true for perpetrators of domestic violence. Programs must be delivered to meet the diverse characteristics—cultural, racial, educational, economic, life experience—of those they serve.

In addition to treating batterers, partners and their children must have alternatives that keep them safe and help them regain their sense of control and personal efficacy. Temporary shelters, protection, job training, child care, education, psychological counseling, legal advocacy, and social support are essential to support women leaving violent relationships. Because of the relationship between substance abuse and domestic violence, programs that prevent and treat drug addiction and alcoholism are also keys to reducing domestic violence. Another component in reducing death and serious injury in domestic violence is to tackle an additional public health challenge—the availability and use of guns (Drazen, Morrissey, & Curfman, 2008; Glantz & Annas, 2009). Making guns unavailable has the potential to eliminate or at least reduce access to weapons that are often a part of intimate partner terrorism and violence.

These programs and services are not cheap, nor is it easy to develop them in coordinated and collaborative ways that maximize resources and effectiveness. They are, however, essential if the service providers are serious about the problem, the importance of families, and their ability to function effectively. Interventionists trained to work in family-centered ways have a great deal to contribute to improving their own community's response to family violence. Knowledge of community resources, the ability to work as team members, and advocacy skills are as important to reducing family violence as they are to providing effective intervention with individual families and children.

CHILD ABUSE AND NEGLECT

There were an estimated 3.3 million referrals of suspected child abuse and neglect in the United States in fiscal year 2010—on average, one every 10 seconds—which involved the health, safety, and welfare of an estimated 6 million children (DHHS, 2011; Childhelp, n.d.). Nearly 2 million of the referrals were screened in and 1,793,724 (90.3%) were responded to with an investigation. More than 400,000 of the reports were substantiated, with nearly another 25,000 reports found to be indicated (DHHS). Three fifths of the reports were made by professionals, such as teachers, social services staff, police officers, and attorneys.

Child abuse is pervasive and occurs across all income levels, ethnic and cultural groups, educational levels, and religions. Anglo-American (44.8%), African American (21.9%), and Hispanic (21.4%) children make up 88% of all abused children (DHHS, 2011). In 2010, states reported 1,537 known fatalities due to abuse or neglect; the DHHS (2011) estimated the total number to be 1,560. Children under 12 months were most likely to be victims of abuse, and nearly 80% of those who died were younger than 4 years of age. The perpetrators of child abuse and neglect do not necessarily conform to stereotypes. More than half (53.6%) of the perpetrators were women; 45.2% were men. Of the perpetrators who were parents, over 80% were the biological parent of the victim (DHHS). More than one third of those who abused or neglected children were 20 to 29 years of age; more than 80% were between 20 and 49 years of age. Although birth parents are more likely to physically abuse their children than others, the statistics differ in cases of sexual abuse. Half of the children who were sexually abused were molested by someone other than a parent or someone in a parenting role; one fourth were sexually abused by a birth parent, and one fourth were sexually abused by someone other than a parent or parent substitute. An alarming finding was that sexual abuse perpetrated by a birth parent was more likely to result in a serious injury or impairment than abuse by a nonparent (Sedlack & Broadhurst, 1996).

Child maltreatment includes neglect, medical neglect, physical abuse, sexual abuse, and psychological maltreatment. In the National Incidence of Child Abuse and Neglect Studies commissioned by U.S. Congress (Sedlak & Broadhurst, 1996), standardized definitions were used in the determination of child abuse and/or neglect: The harm standard was met when children had already suffered harm from abuse or neglect, and the endangerment standard was met when children had already experienced abuse or neglect that puts them at risk for harm. In the 2010 statistics, 78.3% of abused and neglected children were neglected, 17.6% were physically abused, 9.2% were sexually abused, 8.1% suffered psychological maltreatment, and 2.4% experienced medical neglect. More than 10% experienced other forms of abuse; in less than 1% of cases, the cause was unknown (DHHS, 2011). The percentage of boys and girls who are physically abused is very similar; however, the rate of sexual abuse is greater for girls than boys (Children's Bureau Administration on Children, Youth, and Families, 2002). Conversely, boys are more likely to suffer serious physical injury from abuse and significantly more likely to be emotionally neglected than girls (Sedlak & Broadhurst). In 2010, 16% of abused children were reported to have a disability (DHHS, 2011).

Many children who experience abuse and neglect are living in poverty (Child Welfare League, 1999; Sedlak & Broadhurst, 1996). Risks for children in families earning less than $15,000 per year in 1993 were significantly greater for every type of maltreatment than children from families earning $30,000 or more (Sedlak & Broadhurst). It has been hypothesized that poverty increases stress on family members, which in turn makes abuse more likely. Although there is a relationship between poverty and abuse, however, the vast majority of people who are living in poverty do not abuse or neglect their children. The relationship of poverty to other social factors related to child abuse, such as transient residence, lower levels of education, and higher rates of substance abuse and mental illness, may help to explain the risks for abuse and neglect faced by children living in poverty. The relationship to substance abuse is particularly striking, with almost half of the substantiated cases of child abuse and neglect related to a parent's abuse of alcohol or drugs (Child Welfare League, 1998).

These facts and findings are difficult to comprehend in a country that describes its children as its most precious resource. In 2010, 1,560 children died from abuse or neglect (DHHS, 2011). In contrast, 162 police officers—individuals who put themselves in harm's way on a daily basis—were killed in the line of duty (Flaherty, 2010). These numbers put the scope of the problem of child abuse in somber perspective.

Child Abuse, Neglect, and Disability   A national study funded by the National Center on Child Abuse determined that 14.1% of the children who had been maltreated had one or more disabilities (American Academy of Pediatrics, 2001). Children with disabilities are at greater risk for child abuse and neglect than children without disabilities. Children with disabilities were 1.8 times more likely to be neglected, 1.6 times more likely to be physically abused, and 2.2 times more likely to be sexually abused than children without disabilities (American Academy of Pediatrics). Like estimates of domestic violence, the numbers of children with disabilities who are abused is likely to be underreported. This is especially likely because child protective services workers who are typically on the front line of child maltreatment cases are not trained to recognize disabilities. Numbers may also be higher because of the inability of some children and youth with disabilities to provide any corroborating information of their experiences.

The causes of child maltreatment for children with disabilities do not differ dramatically from the causes for children without disabilities. However, children with disabilities typically place higher physical, emotional, and financial demands on caregivers (America Academy of Pediatrics, 2001). These extra demands and the additional stressors of children with special needs may be overwhelming to some parents whose frustration and inability to cope are turned on the child (Hibbard & Desch, 2007).

Sexual abuse, like the sexual abuse of all children, has other origins. Children with disabilities may have an increased number of caregivers and personal assistants who have intimate contact with them, providing increased opportunities for sexual molestation. On the positive side, when multiple caregivers are involved, it may be more likely that one will discover and report the abuse (American Academy of Pediatrics, 2001). Children and youth with disabilities may not have knowledge of appropriate and inappropriate sexual behavior. It may not be included in their educational curriculum nor taught by parents or other caregivers. This makes it even more difficult for children to know about appropriate boundaries and tell someone when they are being sexually abused. Societal attitudes may also contribute to increased risk of abuse. Beliefs that individuals with disabilities are less important than others, are asexual, or do not feel pain, or that all caregivers are good and saintly people, may interfere with recognition and reporting of abuse (Administration for Children and Families, 2011a).

Family attitudes may also affect the likelihood of abuse or neglect. Those who view the child as unacceptably different, an embarrassment, or a punishment for their own behavior may be more likely to engage in abuse and neglect or ignore abuse perpetrated by others (Burrell, Thompson, & Sexton, 1994; Rycus & Hughes, 1998). As with all other forms of domestic violence and abuse, parents with other serious problems such as alcoholism and drug abuse are more likely to abuse their son or daughter with a disability than parents who do not have such problems

Effects on Children   Like domestic violence, the immediate outcomes of the physical and sexual abuse of children are physical injury, pain, disability, and death. Negative psychological and cognitive outcomes have been well documented following experiences of victimization and witnessing abuse. They include fear, sadness, bleakness, aggression, learning problems, and depression (Osofsky, 1996, 2000). Children who are abused tend to think less of themselves, to feel guilty, and to feel that they have no control over their own lives—beliefs that can have long-term, negative consequences.

Effects in Adulthood   Abused children who grow up do not leave their childhoods behind. Abuse suffered as a child follows the child into adulthood. Both retrospective and prospective studies of mental health outcomes attest to the risks inherent in childhood abuse and neglect. The relationship is not one to one. Being abused or neglected as a child does not mean that adult outcomes will be negative; however, it does increase the likelihood of mental health problems in adulthood (MacMillan, Fleming, Streiner, & Lin, 2001). In a 20-year prospective study, adult men who were physically or sexually abused or severely neglected as children were found to have diagnoses of antisocial personality disorder and more symptoms of the depressive disorder referred to as dysthymia as adults compared with matched controls (Horwitz, Widom, McLaughlin, & White, 2001). Dysthymic disorders are characterized by a depression that begins in early life and alters one's personality. Individuals with this type of depression are usually gloomy, pessimistic, unable to enjoy life, self-deprecating, lethargic, introverted, and hypercritical (Berkow et al., 1997). Adult women who experienced abuse and/or neglect as children are more likely to be dysthymic, have antisocial personality disorders, and report more problems with alcohol abuse and dependence than their matched controls (Horwitz et al.). Women exposed to physical and verbal abuse as victims or as observers of their mother's battering were more likely to engage in risky sexual behaviors such as early intercourse and having 30 or more lifetime sexual partners. As the number of categories of childhood abuse increases (e.g. abuse, neglect, witnessing of violence against their mothers), so may the likelihood that women engage in risky sexual behaviors (Hillis, Anda, Felitti, & Marchbanks, 2001). The relationship between childhood abuse and neglect and adult outcomes is complex, but it is certainly a contributor to greater risk and less-than-optimal outcomes.

Effects on Society   The economic costs are perhaps the least of the concerns that surround child abuse and neglect, but it would be naive to ignore the financial burden that child abuse and neglect place on communities. Abuse and neglect tax our hospitals, clinics, courts, jails, and community services. Every hour treating a child who has been injured, terrified, or disabled as a result of abuse is an hour that child will not spend playing, learning, and developing a positive sense of self. These costs are immeasurable and have serious long-term consequences that exacerbate the problem, as pointed out previously. At a deeper level, hurting children affects who we are as a society. If the youngest and most vulnerable cannot be protected from interpersonal violence, there is little that can be claimed in terms of compassion and social justice. A society in which the problem is growing rather than abating is one that has considerable work remaining to be done.

Preventing Child Abuse and Neglect   Child abuse and neglect results from a multiplicity of personal, social, cultural, political, and societal problems. Prevention cannot be achieved without addressing each individually and each as part of a larger set of issues. Prevention of child abuse and neglect, like other areas of prevention, can be conducted at three levels: primary, secondary, and tertiary. Primary prevention calls attention to the problem by informing the public and decision makers and its scope and the needs that exist. Secondary prevention focuses on children and families that are known to be at risk for child maltreatment, such as children of substance-abusing parents, families reported for domestic violence, extremely low-income families, and families of children with disabilities. Programs directed to these families may include parent education, substance abuse treatment programs, respite care for families of children with disabilities, and information and referral services for low-income families. The focus of tertiary prevention is on families in which neglect and abuse has already occurred and on the children who have been victimized. Mental health workers may provide intensive counseling to family members and children may be removed to safer environments (Administration for Children and Families, 2011b).

In addition to this three-pronged approach to prevention, issues that are deeply embedded in society, such as racial discrimination, gender inequity, economic disparity, and the condoning (if not glorification) of violence, must be examined. Each contributes to the conditions that allow child abuse to occur. Each individual and each community must reflect upon and make the changes that will improve the chances of protecting children.

TRAUMA, LOSS, ILLNESS, AND DISABILITY

In the 21st century, there are dramatic ways in which life has improved: individual freedom, advanced health care, increased equality, greater knowledge, and rapid communication. All kinds of devices make lives easier and increase the opportunities to learn and stay connected with one another. Yet even in the richness of this environment, there is trauma and loss. Although trauma is most often thought of as a physical phenomenon and loss is most often thought of in relation to the death of a loved one, both are related to change and have a significant psychological impact. Even changes that are positive, such as getting the job you have always wanted or trying a new sport, can be traumatic. A child's first day of kindergarten or a move to a new city can result in sadness and a sense of loss. Usually, people are able to handle the trauma, loss, and the accompanying feelings; typically the trauma and losses in a person's life do not all occur at once. There is time, space, and help available to deal with one loss before being confronted with another. For some individuals, however, the trauma or losses that they experience are so profound or so close together that finding a path through the fear, anger, and grief seems impossible. When this occurs, it becomes increasingly difficult to fulfill family functions. This section discusses several different life circumstances that often precipitate trauma and loss.

Families in the Military

Men and women in the U.S. military and reserves are engaged in wars, peacekeeping, nation building, and disaster relief throughout the world. In the 21st century, full-scale combat in Afghanistan and Iraq has lasted for more than a decade. Natural

disasters such as the tsunami in the Indian Ocean, Hurricane Katrina, the earthquake in Haiti, and the tsunami and nuclear disaster in Japan have all used the personnel and expertise of U.S. military forces. All of these missions—including the stress, danger, and distance of soldiers from loved ones—take their toll on the men and women in the military and their families at home. As a result, military families are at risk for trauma and loss.

More than half of active-duty personnel are married. Nearly 40% are married with children, and 5% are single parents. Among families with children, most children are younger than 5 years. Although men still make up the largest portion of active duty personnel (86%), women comprise 14%. In the Selected Reserve and National Guard (those who are prepared for deployment), nearly 50% are married; 34% are married with children, with most children ranging from 12 to 18 years of age, and 9% are single parents (Office of the Deputy Under Secretary of Defense, 2010).

Military families typically adapt very well to frequent relocations, deployments, and demanding responsibilities, and many thrive in the military lifestyle. However, a growing body of evidence shows that multiple wartime deployments, the amount of direct exposure to combat, and psychological and physical wounds result in much higher levels of stress for those involved and family at home (Mogil et al., 2010; Sheppard, Malatras, & Israel, 2010). Increased stress within the family affects the children. Emotional unavailability, depression, posttraumatic stress, and absence due to long hospitalizations for treatment and rehabilitation combine to make it more difficult to meet children's needs. Studies are beginning to find that instances of child maltreatment may increase, children may have more mental health problems, and school performance may decline (Saltzman et al., 2011).

As more research is being done on the family outcomes of combat veterans, the recommended approach to support and treatment is family focused (Arata-Maiers & Stafford, 2010; Gewirtz, Erbes, Polusny, Forgatch, & DeGarmo, 2011; Mogil et al., 2010). Support for families at home during multiple long-term deployments is an important component. Child care, opportunities to talk and socialize with others who understand the stress, and financial assistance all contribute to strengthening families on the home front. When those at home are safe and secure, the men and women who are deployed have less to worry about.

Support for returning veterans and their families is another component of assistance. After any long separation, things change at home. Usually the partner at home has taken on additional roles and responsibilities, children may have developed different patterns of behavior, and everyone has to redefine his or her place in the family. For those who return with injuries, the services, supports, and redefinition may be considerably more challenging. The multiple needs of military personnel who return with posttraumatic stress disorder and/or combat injuries affect every member of the family and require long-term support, care, and community resources.

Families and Financial Loss

Compared to loss of life and limb, financial loss would seem to be far less traumatic. However, since the banking crisis and beginning of the recession in 2008, financial loss has been a significant contributor to many families' inability to fulfill their expected functions. Losing a job, a home, health care, life savings, and a way of life can be catastrophic. Long-term unemployment and hopelessness about the future for oneself or one's family often leads to depression and all of the challenges to day-to-day functioning that are a part of being depressed. According to the Brookings Institution, one in nine children had an unemployed parent due to the recession in 2010. These children are more likely to experience homelessness, suffer from child abuse, fail to complete high school or college, and live in poverty as adults than are other children (Isaacs, 2010). Financial losses have increased the number of families who are homeless or close to it because of unemployment or foreclosure. Food insecurity has increased, and the dynamics within families have changed. (For a thorough discussion of poverty and its consequences, please refer to Chapter 6.) For some, the ability to connect and parent effectively has been compromised. For others, financial loss has brought families together, increased their commitment to one another, and increased the number of fathers caring for their children on a regular basis (Berman, 2011).

The new group of individuals and families struggling financially differs from those who have lived in poverty. Middle-class families who had lived comfortable lives and had contributed to charitable causes may have never imagined that unemployment or serious financial difficulty would cause them to need the programs and services to which they once contributed. Families who were already living from paycheck to paycheck were suddenly catapulted over the edge without any backup resources to sustain them. Both groups were faced with daily concerns about food, shelter, and paying the bills.

Providing assistance to these families is complex and especially challenging for several reasons. First, professionals unaccustomed to working with families on issues related to income and financial resources may not be knowledgeable about available community resources. Second, many individuals who are newly and suddenly living in poverty are embarrassed by their situation and reluctant to share their need for help. Third, many families do not meet eligibility requirements for long-established programs and services. In addition, demands on existing programs and services have been overwhelming.

Given these constraints, what can professionals do to assist? The first step is to learn more about the resources available from one's own organization and the community. Certain charities, faith-based groups, and civic organizations have resources that can be used for emergency assistance. They, in turn, have connections to organizations that provide longer-term aid as well as to legislated programs and services. Compiling a list of organizations, summaries of what each one can provide, eligibility information, and a contact name and number is a good starting place. If and when a family member mentions a need or asks about services, information should be immediately available. Once professionals have gained knowledge about resources, they might organize events that include speakers from various organizations that provide assistance. Making this a routine parent night, community event, or coffee hour with child care provided may encourage families to attend and learn in an environment in which they do not have to disclose their own circumstances. Although this approach will attract some families, many will not have the time, emotional resources, or energy to attend a meeting when they are under so much stress. To reach these families, professionals and their organization may elect to send information about available resources to all families. When each child takes information home from school or when it is mailed to all families, no family is singled out or has to share information that they would prefer to keep private. Finally, being available if and when a family asks for help, listening to their concerns and their needs, and following through on providing assistance are critical components when addressing any family's needs.

Illness and Disability

The economic downturn is not the only cause of financial loss. Illness that requires expensive care, hospitalizations, long-term treatment, and unemployment is also a contributor to financial insecurity in many families. Whether it is cancer, a stroke, or a severe accident, the costs are emotionally and financially enormous. For families that are uninsured or underinsured, the cost of medical care can plunge them into poverty. The birth of a child with a disability may also change the economic outlook for families. If one partner has to quit work to care for the child or if the costs of care are not covered by insurance, the family is suddenly without the necessary resources to sustain themselves. (For a comprehensive discussion of families and the impact of disability, please refer to Chapter 5.) Mental illness may also be the cause of financial loss. Depression and unpredictable behavior can make it difficult to obtain and retain a job; costly, prolonged treatment with uncertain outcomes combine to make an upward career path unattainable for many. (For a more information on mental illness and its effects on families, please refer to Chapter 8.)

Financial loss, whatever its cause, puts additional stress and strain on families at almost all economic levels. As discussed throughout this chapter and others, families in very stressful situations or in crisis find it much more difficult to fulfill the family functions that support healthy growth and development of the family and the children within it.

SUMMARY

Drug abuse, addiction, family violence, child abuse and neglect, trauma, loss, and disability are a part of life for many families. Their costs and human consequences are devastating, and their prevention continues to be elusive. Substance abuse and violence affect every component of the family system. The family structure often changes as members come and go physically and psychologically. Healthy communication and acceptable boundaries among subsystems are thwarted, and the family's ability to carry out its functions is severely challenged. Even the family life cycle is affected because of changing roles, extended illnesses, incarcerations, deployments, and the transience of caregivers. Trauma and loss of all kinds affect families and their ability to function successfully. The pain, both physical and psychological, of trauma and the sadness that accompanies loss can make family members unavailable to one another, thus interfering with healthy interactions that support growth and development. All of the risks discussed in this chapter are complex, and each is embedded within larger legal, political, and policy issues. No single professional, agency, or organization can resolve all of the challenges that these risks present to families, but concerted efforts at the personal and professional levels can help to build a society that works to reduce risk and support families when they need help.

ACTIVITIES TO EXTEND THE DISCUSSION

1. **Form a small group to discuss the effects of substance abuse on families.** Using the family systems framework, describe the ways in which family functions might be affected by a parent with alcoholism. After you have considered and recorded the possibilities, do the same for a family in which a teen has alcohol problems.

2. **Learn more about your own community's approach to domestic violence.** Find statistics online or from agencies that describe the scope of domestic violence in

your community. What local programs are available to assist victims? Are there any programs designed to help prevent domestic violence?

3. **Search the Internet for information about child abuse and neglect.** How is it defined? What national studies or interventions are being conducted? What are states doing to prevent child abuse and neglect? What local resources are available to help prevent child abuse and neglect?

4. **Invite a veteran to talk with the class about his or her experiences as part of a military family.** Ask the speaker to talk about the supports offered to military families during deployment. Find out what supports he or she wishes had been available. Learn more about what reintegration into civilian life is like.

TO LEARN MORE: SUGGESTED WEB SITES

American Bar Association
Commission on Domestic and Sexual Violence
http://www.americanbar.org/groups/domestic_violence/resources/statistics.html

Mayo Clinic: Posttraumatic Stress Disorder
http://www.mayoclinic.com/health/post-traumatic-stress-disorder/DS00246

MedlinePlus: Child Abuse
http://www.nlm.nih.gov/medlineplus/childabuse.html

The Military Family Research Institute at Purdue University
http://www.cfs.purdue.edu/mfri/public/about/mission.aspx

Military Homefront
http://www.militaryhomefront.dod.mil/

National Institute on Drug Abuse
http://www.drugabuse.gov/

National Institutes of Health
http://www.nih.gov/

PubMed Health: Alcoholism and Alcohol Abuse
http://www.ncbi.nlm.nih.gov/pubmedhealth/PMH0001940/

REFERENCES

Adhikari, B., Kahende, J., Malarcher, A., Pechacek, T., & Tong, V. (2008). Smoking-attributable mortality, years of potential life lost, and productivity losses–United States, 2000–2004. *MMWR Weekly, 57*(45), 1226–1228.

Administration for Children and Families. (2011a). *Child maltreatment 2010.* Retrieved August 4, 2012, from http://www.acf.hhs.gov/programs/cb/pubs/cm10/

Administration for Children and Families. (2011b). *Preventing child abuse and neglect.*

Retrieved August 4, 2012, from http://www
.childwelfare.gov/preventing/

American Academy of Pediatrics. (2001). Assessment of maltreatment of children with disabilities. *Pediatrics, 108,* 508–513.

Anderson, S.A., & Cramer-Benjamin, D.B. (1999). The impact of couple violence on parenting and children: An overview and clinical implications. *American Journal of Family Therapy, 27,* 1–20.

Arata-Maiers, T.L., & Stafford, E.M. (2010). Supporting young children in combat-injured families. *Zero to Three, 31*(1), 22–28.

Berkow, R., Beers, M.H., & Fletcher, A.J. (Eds.). (1997). *The Merck manual of medical information: Home edition.* Whitehouse Station, NJ: Merck Research Laboratories.

Berman, J. (2011, December 8). Recessional taking its toll on America's family relationships: Study. Retrieved March 4, 2012, from http://www.huffingtonpost.com/2011/12/08/recession-family-relationships_n_1136464.html

Boynton-Jarrett, R., Ryan, L.M., Berkman, L.F., Wright, R.J. (2008). Cumulative violence exposure and self-rated health: Longitudinal study of adolescents in the United States. *Pediatrics, 122*(5), 961–970.

Browne, A., & Bassuk, S.S. (1997). Intimate violence in the lives of homeless and poor housed women: Prevalence and patterns in an ethnically diverse sample. *American Journal of Orthopsychiatry, 67,* 262–278.

Burrell, B., Thompson, B., & Sexton, D. (1994). Predicting child abuse potential across family types. *Child Abuse and Neglect, 18,* 1039–1049.

Centers for Disease Control and Prevention. (2011). *Health effects of secondhand smoke.* Retrieved February 8, 2012, from http://www.cdc.gov/tobacco/data_statistics/fact_sheets/secondhand_smoke/health_effects/index.htm

Child Welfare League. (1998). *Alcohol and other drugs survey of state child welfare agencies.* Washington, DC: Author.

Child Welfare League. (1999). *Child abuse and neglect: A look at the states, CWLA's 1999 stat book.* Washington, DC: Author.

Childhelp. (n.d.). *National child abuse statistics.* Retrieved February 18, 2012, from http://www.childhelp.org/pages/statistics

Children's Bureau Administration on Children, Youth, and Families. (2002). *Summary of key findings from calendar year 2000.* Retrieved

August 4, 2012, from http://www.childwelfare.gov/calendar/materials/ncands_10.cfm

Children's Defense Fund. (2001). *Yearbook 2001: The state of America's children.* Washington, DC: Author.

Drazen, J.M., Morrisssey, G.D., & Curfman, G.D. (2008). Guns and health. *New England Journal of Medicine, 359*(5), 517–518.

Durose, M.R., Harlow, C.W., Langan, P.A., Motivans, M., Rantala, R.R., Smith, E.L. (2005). *Family violence statistics including statistics on strangers and acquaintances.* Retrieved February 18, 2012, from http://bjs.ojp.usdoj.gov/content/pub/pdf/fvs02.pdf

Elkins, I.J., King, S.M., McGue, M., Iacono, W.G. (2006). Personality traits and the development of nicotine, alcohol, and illicit drug disorders: Prospective links from adolescence to young adulthood. *Journal of Abnormal Psychology, 115*(1), 26–39.

Enoch, M-A., & Goldman, D. (2002). *Problem drinking and alcoholism: Diagnosis and treatment.* Retrieved February 7, 2012, from http://www.aafp.org/afp/2002/0201/p441.html

Federal Bureau of Investigation. (2010). Crime in the United States, 2010. Retrieved February 16, 2012, from http://www.fbi.gov/about-us/cjis/ucr/crime-in-the-u.s/2010/crime-in-the-u.s.-2010/offenses-known-to-law-enforcement/crime-clock

Flaherty, M.P. (2010, December 28). Officer line of duty deaths up in 2010. Retrieved February 18, 2012, from http://voices.washingtonpost.com/crime-scene/around-the-nation/officer-line-of-duty-deaths-up.html

Florida, R. (2011, January 13). The geography of gun deaths. Retrieved February 16, 2012, from http://www.theatlantic.com/national/archive/2011/01/the-geography-of-gun-deaths/69354/

Gardner, J.W., & Reese, F.G. (Eds.). (1975). *Quotations of wit and wisdom.* New York, NY: W.W. Norton.

Gewirtz, A.H., Erbes, C.R., Polusny, M.A., Forgatch, M.S., & DeGarmo, D.S. (2011). Helping military families through the deployment process: Strategies to support parenting. *Professional Psychology: Research and Practice, 42*(1), 56–62.

Gilbert, R.L., Murphy, N.A., & McNally, T. (2011). Addiction to the 3-dimensional internet: Estimated prevalence and relationship to real world addictions. *Addiction Research and Theory, 19*(4), 380–390.

Glantz, L.H., & Annas, G.J. (2009). Handguns, health, and the second amendment. *New England Journal of Medicine, 360*(22), 2360–2365.

Groves, B.M. (1996). Children without refuge: Young witnesses to domestic violence. *Zero to Three, 16*(5), 29–34.

Heit, H.A., & Gourlay, D.L. (2009). DSM-V and the definitions: Time to get it right. *Pain Medicine, 10*, 784–786.

Henning, K., Leitenberg, H., Coffey, P., Bennett, T., & Jankowski, M.K. (1997). Long-term psychological adjustment to witnessing interparental physical conflict during childhood. *Child Abuse and Neglect, 21*, 501–515.

Hibbard, R.A., & Desch, L.W. (2007). Maltreatment of children with disabilities. *Pediatrics, 119*(5), 1018–1025.

Hillis, S.D., Anda, R.F., Felitti, V.J., & Marchbanks, P.A. (2001). Adverse childhood experiences and sexual risk behaviors in women: A retrospective cohort study. *Family Planning Perspectives, 33*(3), 206–211.

Horwitz, A.V., Widom, C.S., McLaughlin, J., & White, H.R. (2001). The impact of childhood abuse and neglect on adult mental health: A prospective study. *Journal of Health and Social Behavior, 4*(2), 184–201.

Isaacs, J.B. (2010). Families of the recession: Unemployed parents and their children. Retrieved March 4, 2012, from http://www.brookings.edu/papers/2010/0114_families_recession_isaacs.aspx

Jacobson, N., & Gottman, J. (1998). *When men batter women: New insights into ending abusive relationships.* New York, NY: Simon & Schuster.

Johnson, M., & Ferraro, K.J. (2000). Research on domestic violence in the 1990s: Making distinctions. *Journal of Marriage and Family, 62*, 948–964.

Levendosky, A.A. (2000). Mothers' perceptions of the impact of woman abuse on their parenting. *Violence Against Women, 6*, 247–275.

Levendosky, A.A., & Graham-Bermann, S.A. (2001). Parenting in battered women: The effects of domestic violence on women and their children. *Journal of Family Violence, 16*(2), 171–192.

MacMillan, H.L., Fleming, J.E., Streiner, D.L., & Lin, E. (2001). Childhood abuse and lifetime psychology in a community sample. *American Journal of Psychiatry, 158*, 1878–1883.

Mayo Clinic Staff. (2010). *Prescription drug abuse.* Retrieved February 12, 2012, from http://www.mayoclinic.com/print/prescription-drug-abuse/DS01079/

Milligan, K., Niccols, A., Sword, W., Thabace, L., Henderson, J., & Smith, A. (2011). Birth outcomes for infants born to women participating in integrated substance abuse treatment programs: A meta-analytic review. *Addiction Research and Theory, 19*(6), 542–555.

Minnes, S., Lang, A., & Singer, L. (2011). Prenatal tobacco, marijuana, stimulant, and opiate exposure: Outcomes and practice implications. *Addiction Science & Clinical Practice, 6*(1), 57–70.

Mogil, C., Paley, B., Doud, T.D., Havens, L., Moore-Tyson, J., Beardslee, W.R., et al. (2010). Families overcoming under stress (FOCUS) for early childhood: Building resilience for young children in high stress families. *Zero to Three, 31*(1), 10–16.

National Coalition for the Homeless. (2009). *Domestic violence and homelessness.* Retrieved February 18, 2012, from http://www.nationalhomeless.org/factsheets/domestic.html

National Institute on Alcohol Abuse and Alcoholism. (2012). *FAQs for the general public.* Retrieved August 4, 2012, from http://www.niaaa.nih.gov/alcohol-health

National Institute on Drug Abuse. (n.d.). *Prescription drugs.* Retrieved February 13, 2012, from http://www.drugabuse.gov/drugs-abuse/prescription-medications

National Institute on Drug Abuse. (2002). *Risk factors and protective factors in drug abuse prevention.* Retrieved July 3, 2002, from http://www.drugabuse.gov/publications/preventing-drug-abuse-among-children-adolescents/chapter-1-risk-factors-protective-factors

National Institute on Drug Abuse. (2009). *Principles of drug addiction treatment: A research-based guide.* Retrieved February 16, 2012, from http://www.drugabuse.gov/publications/principles-drug-addiction-treatment/evidence-based-approaches-to-drug-addiction-treatment

National Institute on Drug Abuse. (2011). *What is prescription drug abuse? Research reports: Prescription drugs: Abuse and addiction.* Retrieved February 13, 2012, from http://www.drugabuse.gov/publications/research-reports/prescription-drugs/what-prescription-drug-abuse

National Institute of Mental Health. (2000). *Child and adolescent violence research at the NIMH.* Retrieved August 6, 2012, from http://www.nimh.nih.gov/health/topics/

child-and-adolescent-mental-health/children-and-violence.shtml

National Institutes of Health. (n.d.). *Prescription drug abuse.* Retrieved February 12, 2012, from http://www.nlm.nih.gov/medlineplus/prescriptiondrugabuse.html

National Institutes of Health. (2011). *Nicotine addiction and withdrawal.* Retrieved February 8, 2012, from http://www.nlm.nih.gov/medlineplus/ency/article/000953.htm

National Institutes of Health. (2012). *Alcoholism.* Retrieved February 7, 2012, from http://www.nim.nih.gov/medlineplus/alcoholism.html

Office of National Drug Control Policy. (1996). *Treatment protocol effectiveness study.* Retrieved July 1, 2002, from http://www.whitehousedrugpolicy.gov//treat/shanprot.html

Office of National Drug Control Policy. (2009). Evidence-based approaches to drug addiction treatment. In *Principles of drug addiction treatment: A research-based guide* (2nd ed.). Washington, DC: Author.

Office of the Deputy Under Secretary of Defense. (2010). *Demographics 2010: Profile of the military community.* Retrieved February 20, 2012, from http://www.militaryhomefront.dod.mil//12038/Project Documents/MilitaryHOMEFRONT/Reports/2010_Demographics_Report.pdf

Orford, J. (2001). Addiction as excessive appetite. *Addiction, 96,* 15–32.

Osofsky, J.D. (1996). Introduction. *Zero to Three, 16*(5), 5–8.

Osofsky, J.D. (2000). Treating traumatized children: The costs of delay. *Zero to Three, 20*(5), 20–24.

Porter, R.S., & Kaplan, J.L. (2011). *Alcoholism.* Retrieved February 7, 2012, from http://www.merckmanuals.com/professional/special_subjects/drug_use_and_dependence/alcohol.html

Roberts, G.D. (2003). *Shantaram.* New York, NY: St. Martin's Press.

Rycus, J.S., & Hughes, R.C. (1998). *Field guide to child welfare: Vol. III. Child development and child welfare.* Washington, DC: Child Welfare League of America.

Saltzman, W.R., Lester, P., Beardslee, W.R., Layne, C.M., Woodward, K., & Nash, W.P. (2011). Mechanisms of risk and resilience in military families: Theoretical and empirical basis of a family-focused resilience enhancement program. *Clinical Child and Family Psychology Review, 14*(3), 213–230.

Santayana, G. (1905). *Life of reason, reason in society.* New York, NY: Charles Scribner's Sons.

Sedlak, A.J., & Broadhurst, D.D. (1996). *Executive summary of the third National Incidence Study of Child Abuse and Neglect.* Washington, DC: National Clearinghouse on Child Abuse and Neglect Information.

Sheppard, S.C., Malatras, J.W., & Israel, A.C. (2010). The impact of deployment on U.S. military families. *American Psychologist, 65*(6), 599–609.

Spiess, M., & Fallow, D. (2000). *Drug-related crime fact sheet.* Rockville, MD: Office of National Drug Control Policy, Drug Policy Information Clearinghouse.

Stith, S.M., Rosen, K.H., Middleton, K.A., Busch, A.L., Lundenberg, K., & Carlton, R.P. (2000). The intergenerational transmission of spouse abuse: A meta-analysis. *Journal of Marriage and Family, 62,* 640–655.

Substance Abuse and Mental Health Services Administration. (2011). *Results from the 2010 National Survey on Drug Use and Health: Summary of National Findings.* Retrieved February 12, 2012, from http://www.oas.samhsa.gov/NSDUH/2k10NSDUH/2k10Results.htm

Szyndrowski, D. (1999). The impact of domestic violence on adolescent aggression in the schools. *Preventing School Failure, 44,* 9–12.

Tjaden, P., & Thoennes, N. (1998). *Prevalence, incidence, and consequences of violence against women: Findings from the National Violence Against Women Survey.* Washington, DC: National Institute of Justice and Centers for Disease Control and Prevention.

U.S. Department of Health and Human Services. (2001). *Nicotine addiction.* Retrieved July 3, 2002, from http://www.drugabuse.gov/researchreports/nicotine/nicotine.html

U.S. Department of Health and Human Services. (2010). *Healthy people 2010.* Washington, DC: Government Printing Office.

U.S. Department of Health & Human Services. (2011). *Child Maltreatment 2010.* Retrieved February 18, 2012, from http://www.acf.hhs.gov/programs/cb/stats_research/index.htm - can

U.S. Department of Justice. (n.d.). *Crime clock.* Retrieved February 16, 2012, from http://ovc.ncjrs.gov/gallery/posters/pdfs/Crime_Clock.pdf

U.S. Department of Justice. (2009). *2008 crime in the United States: Arrests.* Retrieved August

4, 2012, from http://www2.fbi.gov/ucr/cius2008/arrests/index.html

U.S. Department of Justice. (2010). *Impact of drugs on society*. Retrieved August 6, 2012, from http://www.justice.gov/archive/ndic/

Watts, C., & Zimmerman, C. (2002). Violence against women: Global scope and magnitude. *The Lancet, 359,* 1232–1237.

Zorza, J. (1991). Woman battering: A major cause of homelessness. *Clearinghouse Review, 25,* 421.

8

Infant/Family and Early Childhood Mental Health

Marie Kanne Poulsen

> *"Perhaps the greatest social service that can be rendered by anybody to this country and to mankind is to bring up a family."*
>
> **—George Bernard Shaw (1928)**

> *"Feelings of worth can flourish only in an atmosphere where individual differences are appreciated, mistakes are tolerated, communication is open, and rules are flexible—the kind of atmosphere that is found in a nurturing family."*
>
> **—Virginia Satir (n.d.)**

The social and emotional well-being of each child is the area of development that is commonly identified as most important to parents. Yet, it is not addressed by professionals with the same degree of consideration and planning that is currently being accorded the acquisition of cognition, language, motor skills, and self-help skills.

Consider the following vignettes:

Ethan, age 9 months, hears the front door open and calls out, "Mama." By the time his mother enters the room, Ethan has pulled to a stand and extended his arms to be picked up.

Derek, age 24 months, is called to lunch and wants to run around while he eats his sandwich. When his mother says he must sit down at the table to eat, Derek starts to whine. His mother remarks that it is sometimes hard to stay seated and continues her conversation about lunch and dessert. Derek regroups and takes his seat.

Melanie, age 3, goes to the park with her mother. She shyly stays by her mother's side until a boy named Joshua comes up to greet her. Joshua offers Melanie a ball and soon they are running toward the slide. Looking back to her mother for reassurance, she gingerly climbs the tall ladder and bravely descends the slide.

In these cases, Ethan eagerly initiates engagement with his mother. Derek is learning to manage his emotions to comply with developmentally appropriate expectations. Melanie initially clings to her mother, but eventually joins others in play and takes the initiative to explore, discover, and learn the joys of going down a slide. Infants and young children who are socially and emotionally healthy initiate engagement with the important people in their lives. They respond to developmentally appropriate directives or when other children approach them, and they learn to manage their emotions. They take the initiative to participate in new experiences. In this manner, the child develops an efficacious sense of self and cultivates the resilience to reach his or her full potential, to cope with the everyday challenges of growing up, and to tolerate disappointments, frustrations, and hardship.

The key component in each vignette is the parent–child relationship. Ethan's attachment to his mother is the basis for his eagerness to connect to her once again. Derek's mother serves as a coregulator of his emotions as she provides the support that helps Derek learn to manage his disappointment in not getting his own way. This support enables Derek to respond to developmentally appropriate expectations of behavior. Melanie's mother provides a secure base that allows her to venture and engage in new experiences.

THE FIELD OF INFANT/FAMILY AND EARLY CHILDHOOD MENTAL HEALTH

The infant/family and early childhood mental health movement is based on several significant tenets:

1. The foundations of infant/family and early childhood mental health center on robust health, responsive nurturing relationships, and guidance.

2. The dyadic nature of early relationships calls for the mental health of infants to always be viewed in the context of family stability and family supports.

3. Approaches to intervention are strength based, with a focus on infant and family abilities and adaptive capacities while attending to vulnerabilities (Greenspan & Meisels, 1996).

4. Infant/family mental health is an interdisciplinary interagency community responsibility (Shonkoff & Phillip, 2000).

Michael Trout (1988), in his seminal work, emphasized that infant/family mental health is an interdisciplinary responsibility that reaches beyond the traditional mental health practitioner's scope of practice. This is in acknowledgment of the numerous determinants of infant and early childhood social and emotional well-being. There are several important biological and psychosocial factors that are critical to the development of mother–infant relationships, the regulations of emotions and behaviors, and developmental mastery. They include robust neurobehavioral health, good nutrition, secure attachment to primary caregivers, experiential opportunity, and coping capacity grounded in family stability, and maternal emotional well-being. Infant mental health and well-being can be compromised when any one of these determinants is in jeopardy (see Figure 8.1).

The ultimate goal of the field is to build a community system of care in which community health, mental health, early care and education, early intervention and special education, social service programs, and faith-based and family organizations collaborate with families to provide integrated family-centered services and supports that build and enhance child competency and well-being.

Continuum of Infant/Family and Early Childhood Mental Health Care

With the increase of early childhood research demonstrating the heightened impact of nurturing relationships, there is the realization that the community needs to offer families

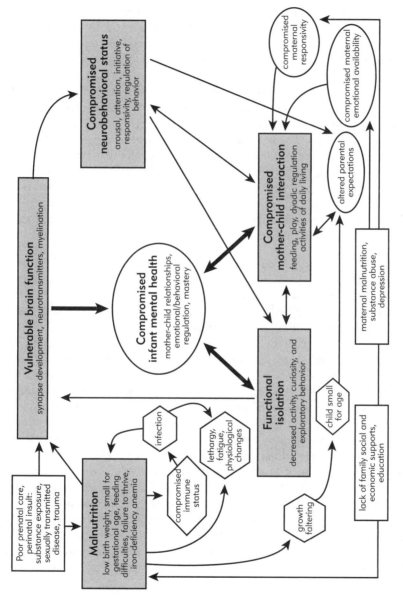

Figure 8.1. Pathways to vulnerable socioemotional development. (From University of Southern California, University Center for Excellence in Developmental Disabilities at Children's Hospital Los Angeles; reprinted by permission.)

various levels of support to strengthen the home and parent–infant relationships. The overall charges of the field are to promote social and emotional development; provide preventive intervention services when there are vulnerabilities, disorders, or disabilities that affect young children's mental health; and to provide infant/family and early childhood mental health treatment when the intensity of concern reaches the level of a psychiatric disorder.

Promotion of Infant/Family and Early Childhood Mental Health   Consider the case of Marla, whose supportive husband has to travel frequently due to a business promotion. She recently gave birth to her first child. Marla, who is an only child, has never been around babies. Her baby cries several times during the night, and Marla is worried that her baby is unhappy. She is lost about what to do.

Universal promotion calls for the community to provide developmental guidance programs that support families and other caregivers to understand child development and develop mindfulness about the importance of relationships and the inner world of infants and young children. The field promotes an infusion of early childhood mental health understanding into the traditional parenting programs that are offered through birthing hospitals, Mommy and Me programs, parenting programs, preschools, and adult education. Many faith-based and parenting organizations offer parents a community that provides parenting guidance and social support. Organizations such as ZERO TO THREE: National Center for Infants, Toddlers, and Families, offer parents and professionals information related to infant and young child mental health and well-being.

Preventive Intervention Programs   Jordan was a medically fragile, low birth weight infant. He is a sensitive baby who cries when his teenage mother sings to him, extends when she tries to cuddle, and turns away when her face comes too close to him. His mother remarks that Jordan does not like her. He is receiving early intervention services to address his neurobehavioral vulnerabilities.

Early intervention services provided by members of a transdisciplinary team help Jordan's mother to understand his sensitivities and give her strategies to care for her baby. An occupational therapist helps her to position Jordan in ways that make it easier for him to cuddle. An infant special educator and Jordan's mother practice ways to communicate to Jordan and discover that Jordan can tolerate his mother humming to him. A psychologist, using interaction guidance principles, videotapes Jordan and his mother. Together, they look at her interactions with Jordan and discover that Jordan only turns away when his mother gets too close and uses a loud voice. They also discovered what makes Jordan smile and how often he actually cooed back to her in response. Jordan's mother now understands the sensitivity of his nervous system and realizes how connected her baby actually is to her.

Communities are urged to provide targeted preventive intervention services for infants and young children who exhibit neurobehavioral, social, or emotional perturbations that interfere with the development of rich relationships, self-regulation, initiative, coping skills, and play, as well as for families in need of parenting supports, social connections, or concrete resources. Caregiving strategies and correcting attributions of Jordan's behavior are important to the infant/family mental health of Jordan and his mother.

Infant/Family and Early Childhood Mental Health Treatment

Anna is 2 years old. She has been in three foster placements, but she was recently reunified with her mother, who is concerned that they are "no longer connected." When Anna falls down, she whimpers for a while and then goes about her business. When she is hungry, she stands by the refrigerator rather than asking her mother for milk. She no longer approaches adults to get her needs met. Anna's language development and cognitive abilities are at age expectancy. An interdisciplinary assessment rules out developmental delays as a contributor to her behavior. Anna awakens several times a night. Anna's mother is becoming exasperated with her behavior and wonders if Anna is trying to punish her. Anna's mother admits that she is "terribly stressed out" due to worries about her 4-year-old son who is acting out, as well as about keeping her apartment after the rent was raised.

Mental health treatment is called for when infants and young children have disturbances that significantly interfere with the child's capacity to eat or sleep, sustain relationships, or regulate their emotions and behavior, as well as when parents are struggling extensively with caregiving or family stability. The goal always is to strengthen the child–parent relationship that provides the organizing force for healthy development.

Because parents are the critical determinants of a child's well-being, mental health services are best provided within the framework of parent–professional partnerships, parent–child relationships, and the circumstances that influence those relationships. Within the service delivery systems, the traditional approach has been to focus on the needs of the child *or* the needs of the caregivers. A paradigm shift from traditional approaches calls for the focus to be on the parent–child relationship. Anna and her mother will be seen together in therapy.

Child mental health foundations are based on the quality of the relationships of all involved: child–parent, parent–provider, and child–provider. Meaningful relationships will only develop when there is mindfulness regarding the nature of interactions. There should be a constant focus on how infants and young children emotionally experience the world and how mothers and fathers are experiencing their roles of parenthood.

The implementation of relationship-based service delivery derives from reflective practice that encourages perspective taking. Providers must be constantly mindful of the emotional complexity of working with infants and young children, as well as of the responsibility of forming meaningful partnerships with parents. Providers need to hold in mind both the parent's and the child's emotional experience of the world and their emotional experience of each other. Responsive and respectful relationships among adults and children are deemed the hallmark of quality mental health service delivery (Pawl & St. John, 1998).

Through self-reflection, providers explore their own feelings and ways of understanding the feelings and needs expressed by parents and by a young child's adaptive and nonadaptive behaviors. It is imperative that the provider holds in mind the vast differences in child-rearing values, beliefs, and practices held by families; providers should remain careful not to judge differences based on their own backgrounds, values, and training.

When intervention services are provided in the home, providers need to be keenly aware of the role of boundaries and how they contribute to the roles that are established between provider and parent. Going into someone's home creates an intimacy not found in center-based settings. Careful reflections must be explored to make decisions related to boundary dilemmas within the sociocultural expectations of families served.

Why the Interest Is Early Childhood Mental Health

The increasing interest in the field of infant/family and early childhood mental health comes from several points of urgency. They include concerns regarding a preacademic emphasis on school readiness, preschoolers with mental health problems, parental voices for services, legislative mandates, and infant brain research.

School Readiness   New emphasis on preparing children for kindergarten often focuses on literacy and numeracy (IDEA, 2004). School readiness, however, involves so much more than knowing the alphabet. For a child to be successful in school, he or she needs to master "learning to learn" behaviors that require considerable self-regulation. The kindergarten child will need to learn to sit still when wanting to play. The child has to concentrate even when worried about things at home or distracted by the commotion in the classroom. Importantly, a child needs to persist instead of becoming discouraged. Young children need to know how to recognize their own feelings and learn acceptable ways to express them, as well as how to calm themselves when becoming upset. They need to be able to initiate with peers, cooperate in play, and deal with the peer conflicts that are part of growing up. The keys to learning success are grounded in the early trusting relationship between a mothering figure and infant. It is only from this firm base that the toddler develops the courage to explore and learn, to eventually manage emotions and behavior, and then to cope with early education expectations (see Figures 8.2 and 8.3).

Between 9.5% and 14.2% of children younger than 5 years experience socioemotional problems that harmfully impact their functioning, development, and school readiness (Brauner & Stephens, 2006). A study of young children in preschool identified that expulsion rates for this age group are three times higher than expulsion rates for students in kindergarten through 12th grade (Gilliam, 2005). Preschool children are being expelled because their biting, hitting, and crying behaviors indicate that they are unable to cope with behavioral expectations inherent in group care. Consequently, there has been increased attention to the early identification, preventive intervention, and mental health treatment for emotionally and behaviorally troubled young children (Substance Abuse Mental Health Services Administration, 2010).

Family Voices   Parents are requesting support relating to their infants' and toddlers' social, emotional, and behavioral development. A study of socioemotional problems of

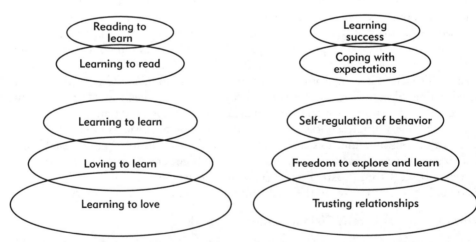

Figure 8.2. Quality early care: steps to school readiness. (From University of Southern California, University Center for Excellence in Developmental Disabilities at Children's Hospital Los Angeles; reprinted by permission.)

Figure 8.3. Quality early care: keys to learning success. (From University of Southern California, University Center for Excellence in Developmental Disabilities at Children's Hospital Los Angeles; reprinted by permission.)

infants and toddlers receiving Part C early intervention services found that up to 25% of them were identified by their parents as being over active, anxious, showing signs of depression, and/or having difficulty with social interactions. However, only 4% of the infants and toddlers were identified as having socioemotional difficulties by their Part C providers (Hebbeler, Spiker, Bailey, Scarborough, & Mallik, 2007). Frequently, parental concerns are not dealt with until they have become serious enough to cause child disturbance and family turmoil, or meet the level of a mental health disorder.

IDEA Part C Reauthorization   In 2004, with the reauthorization of IDEA Part C federal legislation for serving infants and toddlers with disabilities, there was a mandate that states must make child/family social, emotional, and behavioral well-being a service priority. States must measure and report the socioemotional outcomes of infants and toddlers with disabilities in their state performance plans to receive funding (IDEA, 2004).

Infant Brain Development Research   There has been an explosion of infant research defining the significance of early caregiving experience on brain development, infant/family and early childhood mental health, and developmental outcomes (National Scientific Council on the Developing Child, 2007). The field of infant/family and early childhood mental health addresses the relationship of early childhood nurturing experiences to the development of the brain, the capacity for relationships, and the regulation of emotions and behavior.

INFANT MENTAL HEALTH: INSIGHTS FROM INFANT BRAIN RESEARCH

The 1997 White House Conference on infant brain research lent neuroscientific credibility to the assertions of John Bowlby (1988) and other child specialists that attachment and mother–infant relationships play the central role in a child's development. Research has linked the biology of infant brain development with the experiential circumstances that influence it. Early infant experiences shape emotional and behavioral development, temperament, neurochemistry, and the architecture of the brain. A key message was that interpersonal interaction, not sensory stimulation, is the key to infant and early childhood healthy development. This provided new insights into an infant and early childhood service system that had focused primarily on the acquisition of developmental milestones.

Early attachment provides the basis for empathy, intimacy, and the development of a conscience (Thompson, 2008). Infants who grow in a climate of solitude and harshness will learn to expect that it is better to shy away from others and loneliness is safer after all. Early experience conveys both what the world thinks of them and how the child should think of himself (Pawl & St. John, 1998). Both positive and negative early experiences become memory stored in the right brain and guide how the young child subsequently interprets experience, relates to others, and responds to loving, challenging, and distressing events (Bowlby, 1988). Nurturing parent–infant interactions, combined with appropriate developmental guidance and low household stress, provide the foundation for healthy brain development, emotional health, positive social relationships, and an optimal developmental trajectory. The child sees his or her parent as a protector and the world as a safe place.

Infant brain research has demonstrated that early child–parent relationships provide the biological basis for the development of resilience that enables a child to better cope with the challenges faced. Using computerized images of the brain, neuroscientists have provided evidence that environmental conditions and early caregiving experiences have an impact on brain chemistry and influence how the intricate circuitry of the brain is wired (Schore, 1997). The development of a child is formed by a vigorous and continuous intertwining of biology and experience.

Research has demonstrated the role of the caregiving environment in the development of the child's stress management system. A lack of nurturance and/or the presence of toxic stress can affect the architecture of the brain, influencing the regulation of emotions and behaviors and the growing child's capacity to cope with developmental and behavioral expectations (Shonkoff & Phillips, 2000). Studies also demonstrated that the presence of nurturing supportive adults could lower the stress response system that includes heart rate, blood pressure, and stress hormones (National Scientific Council on the Developing Child, 2005). Luby and Myers (2012) studied the role of maternal nurturance when preschoolers are placed in the frustrating situation of having to wait before choosing a brightly wrapped package. Mothers who offered support to help their children regulate their emotions and behavior were deemed as nurturing. When the children were between the ages of 7 and 10 years, researchers performed magnetic resonance imaging of the brain. They found that maternal support in early childhood significantly modified the development of an area of the brain central for stress management and emotional regulation. Children with nurturing mothers had a hippocampus that was 10% larger than the hippocampi of children of mothers rated as not nurturing.

Keys to Understanding Infant, Toddler, and Early Childhood Resilience

- Relationships are central to child development.

- Early caregiving influences the neural circuitry of the brain.

- Infants and young children absorb family stress.

- Extreme stress is toxic to the architecture of the brain.

- Nurturing relationships buffer toxic stress effects.

Source: Center for the Developing Child at Harvard University (2010).

SETTING THE STAGE: INFANT MENTAL HEALTH IN CONTEXT OF FAMILY WELL-BEING

Because infant and early childhood mental health is contingent on early nurturing dyadic relationships, it becomes essential to address family well-being. The DHHS (2009) and the Center for the Study of Social Policy (Stapleton, McIntosh, & Corrington, 2010) have led national initiatives by addressing seminal family protective factors that provide the underpinning for infants and young children to thrive.

The promotion of mental health in infancy centers on ensuring that parents have the information and supports they need to enhance the interactions between parent and child and to forge dyadic relationships. There are universal biologically based trajectories in the development of parent–child relationships (Bowlby, 1988). However, parent–infant relationships exist within and always are affected by the larger social and cultural context of family and community. Parenting must always be appreciated within diverse cultural child-rearing goals, beliefs, and practices (Bernstein, Harris, Long, Lida, & Has, 2005).

Within its sociocultural framework, effective parenting is more easily conveyed in the context of emotional supports, financial stability, and family harmony. Five protective aspects that support child and family well-being are parental nurturance and parent–child attachment, knowledge of child development and child-rearing, parental resilience in managing everyday stressors and recovering from occasional crises, social connections, and concrete supports (DHHS, 2009).

Nurturance and Attachment

The cornerstone of early childhood mental health is based on responsive, sensitive parent–infant interactions that result in an intimate attachment. Tender loving care between primary caregiver and infant provides the neurological and emotional foundations for later relationships and the self-regulation of emotions and behavior. As we saw previously with Ethan, Joshua, and Melanie, warm responsive interactions between mother and infant lay the foundation for all subsequent meaningful relationships; they also serve as a buffer when the infant or young child is overwhelmed by situations or circumstance. For that reason, Anna and her mother needed mental health treatment to repair their attachment connections.

Knowledge About Child Development and Child Rearing

Parent-mediated developmental guidance is essential for children to develop social and emotional competencies. Young children thrive when there is a balance of warm responsiveness and developmentally appropriate limits in dangerous behaviors and nonadaptive expressions of emotion. Child development knowledge and concomitant parenting skills do not come naturally as one assumes parenthood. Good parenting is not an innate talent. Traditionally, parenting practices have been passed on from generation to generation and by the community in which new mothers live. However, due to societal changes, many of the time-honored supports to help mothers and fathers become parents are no longer available. In the past eras of large families, most women had experience with infants, either their younger siblings or the children of their older siblings. Today, people have smaller families, and often the first baby ever held by a new mother is her own. In addition, the traditional neighborhood life that provided a built-in "community of moms" is disappearing as mothers have entered the workforce, with 64.2% of women with children younger than 6 years employed outside the home (U.S. Bureau of Labor Statistics, 2009). With high mobility in many parts of the United States, young parents may be isolated from extended family and that concomitant guidance and support. In addition, 41% of babies are born to single mothers who may not have the economic, social, and emotional support of a partner (National Center for Health Statistics, 2009). As in the example of Marla presented earlier, she had social and emotional support from her husband, but they both badly needed assistance in knowing more about child development and child rearing.

Social Connections

Runyan et al. (1998) described the importance of social capital—the benefits derived from personal social relationships that influence the parenting process. Social capital includes the presence of two parents or parental figures in the household, social support for the maternal caregiver, neighborhood support, and church/temple/mosque attendance. The authors also noted that when a family has more than two children, parental energy is more divided and will need added supports.

Parenting benefits from the social support of family, friends, and neighbors. Social connections buttress the parenting process in dealing with caregiving situations related to guidance, limits, and discipline, as well as providing assistance in times of need. Mothers in the workforce are often not members of a neighborhood community who can counsel and support each other in the parenting process. Research has documented that the lack of social supports is deleterious to positive parenting and family well-being (Zolotor & Runyan, 2006).

In the previous example, although Marla's husband is emotionally supportive, his long work hours leave Marla isolated for many days at a time. Social connections with other mothers could provide Marla with emotional support and child-rearing advice.

Parental Resilience

All families face everyday stressors and occasional adversity. When parents are emotionally resilient, they are able to solve problems, deal with stress, and recover from crisis. Managing their worries allows parents to more effectively deal with the challenges of being a parent and lessens the likelihood of directing any frustrations at other people, including their children. Helping parents to recognize and address the psychological and physiological signs of stress by seeking support can help them to build their capacity to cope and enhance family stability. Anna's mother, for instance, needed assistance in addressing the psychological impact of stress on her health, her own well-being, and her capacity to be emotionally available to her children.

Concrete Supports in Times of Need

Parent–child relationships are more likely to flourish in the context of family security. Household stability is predicated on access to health care, food, clothing, housing, and transportation to ensure the health, mental health, and development of their children. Caring for the well-being of the family as a whole is an essential component in ensuring infant and early childhood mental health. Linkages to services and supports in the community are part of infant/family and early childhood mental health scope of work (Fraiberg, 1980). Assisting Anna's mother in accessing concrete supports for her family is an important part of the family's mental health treatment plan.

ATTACHMENT AS THE CORNERSTONE OF INFANT/FAMILY AND EARLY CHILDHOOD MENTAL HEALTH

Attachment is the profound long-lasting emotional connection that develops between an infant and mother; it is the basis for all human connectedness. Infants can only grow and thrive in the context of meaningful relationships. Through early intimate predictable mother–infant caregiving relationships, Ethan developed an internal working model of emotional connectedness, a sense of self, and a sense of how the world works. He learned that the world is nurturing and trustworthy rather than turbulent and unpredictable. With nurturing care, Ethan has learned to turn to his mother to have needs met. When Ethan's mother enters the room, he expects a positive response. With time, Ethan readily will also reach out for comfort, solace, attention, and object attainment.

Attachment theory, which was first postulated by Bowlby (1988), holds that infants are biologically wired to forge an emotional tie to their caregivers. An infant's inborn capacity for eye contact, cooing, smiling, reaching, and following loved ones with his eyes are clear signaling behaviors that promote interactions and attachment to his parents. However, the development of an easy attachment is based on a "goodness of fit" between mother and child. Mother–infant attachment evolves effortlessly when the infant is healthy, has a robust nervous system, and an easygoing temperament, as well as when the mother is healthy, has an internal working model of mothering based on her own relationship history, and has enough social, emotional, and economic support (Fraiberg, 1980). Rich attachment emerges when the mother has mindfulness of her infant's internal emotional state, can read and respond to her infant's cues, and responds consistently and contingently to her baby's eye contact, smiles, and coos. The critical element in mother–infant interaction is the shared emotional experience, which is contingent on the well-being and emotional availability of each member of the dyad (see Figure 8.4).

The quality of the mother–infant relationship is contingent on the emotional availability of both mother and child. The circumstances that support mother–child relationships and optimal development are multifaceted. Biological, environmental, and psychosocial circumstances readily impact each member of the dyad's emotional availability to engage

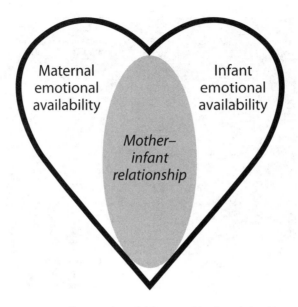

Figure 8.4. Emotional availability: requisite for relationship.
(From University of Southern California, University Center for
Excellence in Developmental Disabilities at Children's Hospi-
tal Los Angeles; reprinted by permission.)

meaningfully with each other. Either member of the mother–infant dyad can facilitate or
impede the development of attachment and meaningful interactions. An infant born prematurely or at very low birth weight may have difficulty arousing or calming enough to engage
without extra help. A mother preoccupied by worries may take excellent physical care of her
infant, but may not be in an emotional state to note the nuanced cues of her baby.

Bowlby (1988) describes how at birth hormones are released that promote intense
alertness in the infants, enhancing responsiveness to mother. Healthy robust infants easily exercise their inborn capacities to respond to tender, loving care. Fetal heart rate (Kisilevsky, Hains, & Lee, 2003) and a one-month-old infant's non-nutritive sucking pattern
differ depending on whether a recording of mother's voice or that of a stranger is heard
(Mehler, Bertoncini, & Barriere, 1973). A healthy newborn is able to nestle to his or her
mother's body and learn to come to alert attention to her voice, search for her face, and
(at 6 weeks) engage with a smile. Contingent social engagement occurs when mothers
respond to their babies' cries as babies thus learn that the world is a trusting place and
intense needs will be met. As attachment is established, 3-month-old infants will recognize a photograph of their mothers' faces when compared to strangers (Barrera & Maurer,
1981) and more readily smile as their mother approaches than when a stranger does.

Gradually infants increase their focused attention and begin to readily initiate interactions with others. Through maturation and positive interactions in nuclear intimate relationships, infants increasingly learn to dance the dance of reciprocity in engagement and
play. Infants spontaneously imitate those who are important to them with responsive smiles
and coos. Through eye gaze, vocalizations, and gestures, they learn to ask for attention,
solace, acknowledgment, and whatever else they need. Long before language becomes well
developed, older infants and toddlers lift their arms, shake their heads, point, eye gaze, and
vocalize to clearly communicate their needs to a responsive caregiver. Older infants gradually

learn to use joint attention to get needs met using eye gaze, pointing, and vocalizing. In this manner, infants learn they are effective and can affect the world.

Research has affirmed that parental warm responsiveness is positively related to secure attachment in toddlerhood (Kassow & Dunst, 2007). From this secure base of attachment, the toddler has the emotional fuel to venture into the world of play and gradually develops the initiative to explore, discover and learn, engage with others, and respond to behavioral expectations and disappointments without falling apart (Ainsworth, Blehar, Water, & Wall, 1978). As emotionally healthy preschoolers, children gain the confidence to initiate interactions with peers, respond to them when approached, and adventure alone or with them into the world of play.

Attachment, Self-Regulation, and the Expression of Emotions

A critical component of early childhood mental health is the young child's capacity to self-regulate, express and manage his emotions and behavior, cooperate with others, and learn to cope with frustrations and disappointment and to resolve conflicts without falling apart. Healthy infants and young children show a wide range of emotions including, joy, rage, devastation, and sadness. A child's capacity to manage emotions takes time and is related to crossing points of the robustness of the biological system, the nature of experience, and the quality of the protective nurturance that comes from attachment. When parents respond to infant distress signals in a predictable and nurturing manner, the building blocks for an internal means of emotional regulations are put in place. Parental responsive nurturance helps to establish connections in the brain that support the child's capacity to adaptively express and regulate emotions (Shore, 1997).

Healthy infants have innate abilities to self-regulate in terms of sleeping, eating, self-consolation, activity, and engagement. Infants are born with a wide range of regulatory mechanisms that have a neurological basis and provide infants the neurobehavioral capacity to adapt to their environment. Infant studies on brain–behavior relationships have brought new appreciation to the role of these inhibitory or reactive mechanisms in the brain that provide the foundation for adaptations that guide and organize emotional, social, and behavioral development.

Regulatory mechanisms that provide for a wide range of neurobehavioral competencies account for individual differences in how infants establish feeding and sleeping patterns, learn to control states of alertness, maintain a balanced sensory threshold, recover from stress, organize behaviors, and develop reciprocal social interactions with the significant persons in their lives (Poulsen, Finello, Provance, Picl, & Reynolds, 2005). Although there is an inborn predisposition for self-regulation, infants and young children do not learn how to manage their feelings and regulate their behavior on their own. Self-regulation stems from parental coregulation. Parents play a significant role in setting up the neural circuitry that helps children learn to regulate (Perry & Pollard, 1997).

Emotionally, a newborn with dyadic supports develops the capacity to focus, attend, and connect. Healthy infants frequently are able to control their beginning whimpers and calm themselves. With maternal support providing coregulation, the infant gradually develops physiological regulation as he or she establishes arousal, alertness, sleeping, feeding, and self-soothing patterns when crying is more than a whimper. Mothers may undress their babies to bring them to a state of alertness that will enable them to engage and to feed. Conversely, mothers may swaddle their babies or reduce external light and noise to help them calm. Goodman (2005) noted that it is likely that parenting behavior shapes the infant's internal working model of self, and their relationships influence the infant's capacity to adapt to developmentally appropriate expectations.

The goals of self-regulation for the toddler and preschooler are for young children to develop the ability to match one's emotional responses and behaviors to the cultural expectations of the situation, have a balance among emotions during everyday activities, and inhibit outbursts when asked to comply with demands that are not to their liking (Kopp, 1992). With enough experience in adult-initiated and child-initiated interactions, the older infant and toddler learn to look to adults for permission, prohibition, recognition, and praise. Suppose an older infant cruises the coffee table and comes upon an adult-cherished item for which he has heard "no-no" a hundred times. He reaches for it and pauses, looking to the adult for information as if to say, "Should I or shouldn't I?" This is the very beginning of learning to "look for the look." The child is using the adult for permission or prohibition. Of course, he may not comply with his mother's admonition, but he is learning to look for the look, which is the beginning of using social cues for the regulation of behavior.

Suppose the toddler explores his world and ends up in the other room, where he calls out, "Mama." If his mother answers, he resumes his play and explorations. If his mother does not answer, he toddles back to check that she is still there and then goes about his business. The toddler is still using his mother as a secure base that is not quite internalized. Attachment to his mother has provided the secure base that supports learning to regulate his behavior. When the 2-year-old child is alone and trying to master stringing beads, he may become easily frustrated and move on to another toy. However, if he has an adult encouraging him, he may stay focused for a longer time; thus, the child learns that when one stays with a task, it can be mastered. Caregiver support therefore enables the child to expand his attention and persistence, while at the same time developing self-mastery. These developmental competencies lay the groundwork for school readiness.

INFANT AND EARLY CHILDHOOD STRESS, NEUROBEHAVIORAL SENSITIVITY, DISTRESS PRONENESS, AND THE DYSREGULATION OF BEHAVIOR

New insights on the role of stress in an infant's and young child's life come from infant brain development and early childhood research (National Scientific Council on the Developing Child, 2005). The genesis of stress may be internal due to the neurobehavioral sensitivity related to perinatal factors and genetic predispositions or external environmental factors, such as harsh experiences or separation and loss of someone loved. The effects of adversity not only influence brain development but also affect learning capacities, adaptive behaviors, and lifelong physical and mental health (American Academy of Pediatrics, 2012).

Typical stressors in a young child's life may include events such as being separated from mother, meeting new people, being denied a desired toy or sweet, fearing the dark or the neighbor's pet, being overwhelmed by too much noise and commotion, or starting a new child care program. Robust infants and young children can handle a certain amount of stress without becoming overwhelmed. When infants and young children experience sensitive care, they are less likely to physiologically respond to minor stress (Goulet, 1998). A modicum amount of stress may alert a variety of neurochemical and hormonal systems throughout the body, leading to brief increases in heart rate and mild elevations in the hormonal systems. Some stress is not harmful when there is repair.

When there is a supportive adult available, there is a quick recovery from acute stress. In this manner, a child builds resilience and the capacity to cope with everyday stress.

Cortisol is a stress hormone that becomes active in the brain. Elevated and decreased levels of cortisol impact the child's regulation of emotions and behavior, reflecting the state of the child's stress management system. In the past, cortisol could only be measured by sampling a child's blood. However, now that it can be measured by sampling a child's saliva or urine, there has been an increasing body of research on this stress-induced hormone. Salivary cortisol mirrors the levels of biologically active cortisol circulating in the blood (Obradovic, Bush, Stamperdahl, Adler, & Boyce, 2010). Cortisol levels elevate as an alarm reaction to a stressful event, resulting in the young child crying and searching for the attachment figure for solace or comfort. Typically, the presence of a responsive caregiver quickly reduces the physiological responses. In a seminal study, Nachmias, Gunnar, Mangelsdorf, Parritz, and Buss (1996) demonstrated that nurturing caregivers could prevent elevations in cortisol in toddlers, even when the young child is temperamentally fearful or anxious. Responsive caregiving buffers the effects of stress, as tender loving care raises the serotonin level that lowers cortisol stress hormone, leading to a fading of the alarm response. Through experiencing and recovering from small stressors, the young child develops the capacity to manage uncomfortable events. In this manner, small stressors can be growth promoting as the child learns to develop mastery of unpredictable situations.

Toxic Stress Leading to Distress Proneness

Self-regulation does not come easily for all children. Biologically reactive children are more vulnerable to stressful experiences, and even the most resilient children can be traumatized by harsh experiences. When children experience chronic stress, their cortisol levels remain elevated for extended periods of time. Continued exposure to cortisol is related to the destruction of neurons and reduction in the number of synapses in the brain. An overabundance of cortisol becomes toxic, affecting the architecture of the brain, which can lead to lifelong problems in learning, behavior, and physical and mental health (Center on the Developing Child, 2010).

Data from infant brain research confirm that chronic or multiple biological and/or psychosocial circumstances can result in a child who develops a hypersensitive nervous system that becomes distress prone. The child with a vulnerable stress-management system experiences the world in a more sensitive manner and will tend to overinterpret and overreact to typical childhood events. When punishment, instead of environmental adaptations, is used as a means to address a child's nonadaptive behavior, the overreactivity will become further entrenched (see Figure 8.5).

Evidence suggests that high levels of stress in the earliest years can actually undermine brain development (National Scientific Council on the Developing Child, 2005). A vulnerable stress management system sets up the child to perceive events to be threatening and to experience events as catastrophic, leading to a surge of stress hormones and lingering distress reactions.

At the toxic stress level, brain cells and connections between brain cells are destroyed. When stress is chronic, the repeated experiences become encoded in implicit memory as expectations of what the world is about. The infant or child lives in a high state of alertness. The child's stress management system thus responds at a lower threshold to events that may be felt as benign to others. Thus, the child becomes distress prone. Chronic stress due to internal sensitivities, external disruptions, or neglect leads

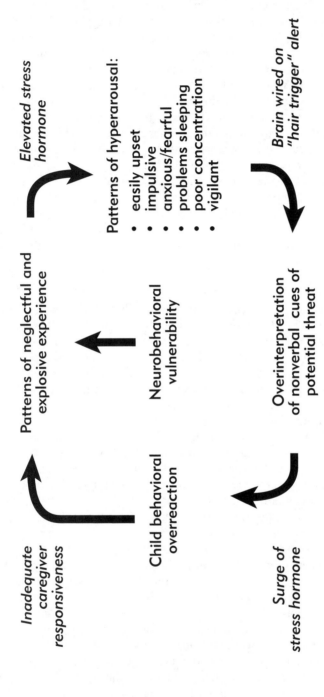

Figure 8.5. Impact of mismatched caregiving on brain and behavior. (From University of Southern California, University Center for Excellence in Developmental Disabilities at Children's Hospital Los Angeles; reprinted by permission.)

to nonadaptive dysregulated behavior in children. This breakdown in nervous system sensitivity may lead to a highly reactive child. Infants, toddlers, and preschoolers may demonstrate behavioral extremes. Young children may respond to chronic stress with unabated crying, aggression, noncompliance, and temper tantrums (Kahana-Kalman, 2000). Very young children who are terrified, distracted, or enraged for no apparent reason may be unable to self-regulate enough to feel merely scared or irked. Other infants and young children who experience chronic toxic stress may close up and no longer express their emotions. Posttraumatic stress disorder describes a state of emotional disturbance stemming from maltreatment, neglect, medical procedures, separations, loss, or chronic hyperarousal from discordant environments.

A variety of biological and experiential stressors can affect the sufficiency of inhibitory and reactive mechanisms and undermine self-regulation, including health problems, disabilities, and family crises. An infant may be born with sufficient mechanisms to withstand the usual perturbations of childhood, in which case it would take an extremely harsh environmental influence or traumatic experience for inhibitory and reactive mechanisms to be affected and behavioral dysfunction to become evident. Conversely, a genetic or congenital biological deficit in regulatory mechanisms may be significant enough to give rise to behavioral disorders even in the absence of negative environmental influences. The issue remains how much of social, emotional, and behavioral vulnerability or disorder is due to biological deficit and how much is due to a biological vulnerability that has been exacerbated by negative experiential influences that perhaps could have been ameliorated.

Biological Influences on the Stress Management System and Behavior

Biological vulnerability embraces the notion that biological circumstances can make a person susceptible to developing emotional disturbances, but the circumstance itself does not cause it. A highly sensitive overreactive nervous system can set the child up for nonadaptive ways of dealing with the world if enough guidance and support are not available to help with self-regulation. Behaviors such as impulsivity, disobedience, aggression, and a lack of compliance to typical discipline are thought to arise from an overloaded stress management system requiring interpersonal supports and environmental modifications. There are several biological circumstances that may influence the social, emotional, and mental health of infants and young children, including temperament, perinatal distress, malnutrition, developmental delays, and health care needs.

Temperament and the Regulation of Behavior   Infants are born with different constitutionally based ways of experiencing and responding to the world. Temperament refers to biologically based patterns of emotional reactions, including sensitivity and intensity of reaction, emotional regulation, activity, and sociability (Bates & Wachs, 1994). In the classic work by Thomas and Chess (1977), nine categories of temperament were defined: activity level, biological regularity, approach or withdrawal in new situations, adaptability, threshold of responsiveness, intensity of reaction, quality of mood, distractibility, and attention span and persistence. The categories have been clustered into three constellations of temperamental characteristics that include the easy child, the slow-to-warm-up child, and the difficult child. Children described as difficult have sensitive temperaments that often lead to irregular sleep, picky eating, frequent fussiness, and tantrums. They may be less adaptive, more emotionally intense, and less sociable than their peers with easy temperaments. They also may be more challenging for parents and caregivers. Children who are highly reactive, especially when raised in a discordant environment, are more vulnerable to developing an emotional or behavioral disorder. Other temperamental traits may also place the child's mental health at risk. Children with unaddressed shyness, inhibitions, or slow-to-warm up temperament patterns may be predisposed to developing an anxiety disorder. Infants and young children with difficult/sensitive or inhibited temperamental traits need understanding and a supportive environment to thrive.

Temperamental characteristics can be exaggerated when there is a poor fit between the child's temperamental capacity to cope with a situation and rigid demands that are made without appropriate modifications for the child. In one study, the mental health of the mother and her level of distress accounted for 24% of the variance in perceived infant difficult temperament (Mautymaa, Puura, Luoma, Salmelin, & Tamminen, 2006). Thomas and Chess (1977) cautioned that temperament alone should not be viewed as the cause of emotional or behavioral problems. Temperament is only one of a number of biological and environmental factors that influence social, emotional, and behavioral development. Children with similar temperamental risk characteristics may have varying developmental trajectories depending on the psychosocial environment in which they are reared.

Perinatal Distress   Infants born with low birth weights, with prenatal exposure to toxic substances, or to mothers who have experienced stress during pregnancy may have higher levels of cortisol, leading to more neurobiological sensitivities (Field, Hernandez-Reif, Diego, Schanberg & Kuhn, 2005). There is a continuum of possible developmental outcomes for infants with perinatal distress, ranging from children who are seriously compromised and developmentally disabled to those who have milder dysfunction affecting attention, learning, and self-regulation to those who are healthy robust children. No single factor is predictive of the infant's developmental trajectory. However, the notion of cumulative risk has led to the appreciation that greater numbers of both infant and maternal biological and family psychosocial risk factors result in a greater risk to positive development.

Many infants who experience perinatal distress are hypersensitive to being uncovered, touched, dressed, bathed, or picked up. Noise, movement, or bright lights may be enough to set them off with excessive high-pitched haunting cries. Inexperienced parents may read these as "leave me alone" cues instead of "help me" signals. Because of early compromised health, development, or neurobehavioral status, infants may experience and respond in unexpected ways to their parents' nurturance. Parents may have difficulty reading and responding to their infants' more muted or sporadic emotional cues or to their toddlers' reactions to seemingly benign situations. Babies with neurobehavioral vulnerabilities may have all their whimpers develop into howls of distress. Dysregulated infants will not have the capacity to focus, attend, and connect without caregivers' special help. In the absence of interventions to address regulatory special needs, infants and young children will continue to be hyperreactive or hyporeactive to the events of their lives. Parents may have difficulty understanding and responding to their toddlers' and preschoolers' overreactions to seemingly nonthreatening situations. The single most important influence on the outcome of children with perinatal vulnerabilities is the psychosocial environment in which they are raised. Without intervention, vulnerable toddlers and preschoolers may struggle to develop task mastery and thus have more difficulty developing a sense of self-efficacy that promotes autonomy, initiative, and resilience.

Malnutrition and Exposure to Toxins   Young children who are undernourished or have iron-deficiency anemia demonstrate more irritability, emotional unresponsiveness, fearfulness, lethargy, and mental apathy, thus resulting in decreased sustained attention and lack of persistence in task completion and interpersonal engagement (Corapci, Calatroni, Kaciroti, Jimenez & Lozoff, 2010). Lead exposure from children ingesting chips of lead-based paint or playground soil from high-traffic or industrial areas has been associated with poor focused attention and aggressive behavior (American Academy of Child and Adolescent Psychiatry, 2004; Schantz, Widholm, and Rice, 2003).

Infants and Young Children with Delays and Special Health Care Needs   Infants and young children with special needs include children with neurobehavioral vulnerabilities, developmental delays, mental health disorders, chronic illness, learning problems, or out-of-home placement. The emotional and social competencies of many infants, toddlers, and young children with vulnerabilities or disabilities are age appropriate (Powell & Dunlap, 2010). However, many young children with special needs face more challenges than their more robust peers. Many children with special needs are experiencing neurobehavioral characteristics that increase their susceptibility to environmental stressors.

Young children with developmental delays may communicate with others with less frequency and show marked differences in joint attention and communicative responses (Windsor, Reichle & Mahowald, 2009). Preschool children with developmental delays and disabilities may have a higher incidence of problem behavior than typically developing children. Biological vulnerabilities, peer rejection, and lack of coping skills contribute to the increase of emotional difficulties (Jacobstein, Stark, & Largo, 2007). Crnic, Hoffman, Gaze, and Edelbrock (2004) noted that children with developmental disabilities engaged in fewer peer interactions and more solitary play; they also are less successful in engaging with positive peer interactions. These children tend to be less compliant in response to adult directions, more active, and more distractible.

Infants and very young children with special needs have the capacity to better emotionally cope with biological vulnerabilities and psychosocial circumstances if they are provided with a climate of nurturance, developmentally appropriate expectations, special caregiving strategies, and opportunities for self-mastery—and if their parents and caregivers are provided with supports in the caregiving process (Guralnick, 2011). It is important to note that the socioemotional vulnerability of the child with disabilities may be compounded by overprotection from parents and limited experience with peers. These circumstances call for increased developmental guidance and inclusive early care and education settings.

Family Crises: Experiential Influences on the Stress Management System

Shonkoff (2010) emphasized the role that family adversity has in the development of young children who absorb the stressors a family is experiencing. Family economics, domestic stability, immigration status, and mental health circumstances contribute to the complexity of family lives and can influence the emotional availability of family members. Stressful family and community circumstances can affect a parent's emotional state, influence the quality of parent–child relationships and children's mental health, and affect the trajectory of a child's behavioral, social, and emotional development, thus resulting in a potential wide array of internalizing and externalizing behaviors (Cooper, Masi, & Vech, 2009).

Economic Hardship   An analysis of the 2010 census showed that 37% of young families with children were living below the poverty line, which is the highest level on record for this group (Center for Labor Market Studies, 2011). With poverty comes an increase in food insecurity, frequent moves, and unsafe neighborhoods. Overwhelmed families may find it difficult to provide consistent, predictable, nurturing interactions with their children. Children who grow up in families dealing with economic adversity frequently exhibit elevated cortisol levels (National Scientific Council on the Developing Child, 2005). Researchers have underscored how the stressful and traumatic conditions of poverty may become translated into brain function changes, impede learning and behavior, and affect the child's capacity to succeed (Duncan, 2010).

Young children in homeless families are more likely to have lower birth weights than other children. The combination of biological vulnerability and family stress exponentially affects the course of emotional and behavioral development (National Center on Family Homelessness, 2009). In recognition of the vulnerability of young children in poverty, Part C of the IDEA of 2004 mandated outreach to homeless shelters.

Domestic and Family Discord   The development and persistence of early behavior problems commonly results when the family lacks harmony and stability (Shonkoff, 2010). Even when the young child is not a direct recipient of domestic violence, the exposure can have a traumatic effect. It is estimated that 15.5 million children live in families in which domestic violence occurs annually, with 7 million of those children witnessing severe domestic violence (McDonald, Jouriles, Ramesetty-Mikler, Caetano, & Green, 2006). Infants as young as 1 month of age can sense when their parents are angry or depressed. This can result in the development of a fearful child or in distorted relationships where the infant or child no longer expects that adults will support and protect them. Clinical data suggest that young children who were traumatically exposed to bitter discord or violence may demonstrate aggressive and acting out behaviors. Children who witness chronic domestic discord or violence are at increased risk for depression, aggression, and posttraumatic stress disorder (Buka, Stichick, Birdthistle, & Earls, 2001). Part C of IDEA of 2004 mandated outreach to domestic violence shelters to identify infants and toddlers needing early intervention services.

Family Disruptions, Child Maltreatment, Separation, and Loss   Babies as young as 3–4 months can experience symptoms of depression when separated from their mothers (Luby, 2000). Young children are capable of lasting grief and disorganized behavior in response to early separation and loss. Military deployment, incarceration, illness, death, and divorce have a profound effect on a child's well-being and should always be addressed. The experience of separation and loss can be as traumatizing as physical abuse and can have a profound influence on the trajectory of emotional development (Cicchetti, 2004).

Young children who experience trauma through physical maltreatment or neglect have high cortical levels that affect impulse control and emotional and behavioral control. Areas of the brain that were activated by the original trauma or chronic neglect can be immediately triggered when a potential threat is perceived (Perry & Pollard, 1997). There is considerable evidence that infants, toddlers, and young children who have experienced physical abuse have lower social competence, show less empathy for others, have difficulty recognizing other's emotions, and show deficits in language ability and school achievement (National Scientific Council on the Developing Child, 2005).

Out-of-Home Placement   Almost 200,000 infants and young children come into contact with the child welfare system each year, of which over 76,000 are removed from their families (Melmed, 2011). Out-of-home placement is always a traumatizing event. According to a National Center for Children in Poverty report, infants in foster care have a higher rate of behavioral problems, developmental delays, and health problems (Cooper, Banghart, & Aratani, 2010).

The trauma of separation and loss is compounded by multiple placements within the foster care system. Adults are not interchangeable. Disruptive placements deprive infants and very young children of the continuity of responsive care that is so critical for the development of attachment, leaving thousands of young children with unacknowledged and often misinterpreted grief. Many such young children are denied the opportunity for sustained rich attachments, a recorded history about self, memories of childhood rituals, and a sense of belonging. They may respond to the adults in their lives by withdrawal and overcompliance or by disruptive and challenging behaviors. It is extremely important that the behavior of a child who has experienced separation and loss be viewed within the lens of grief, anxiety, and sadness rather than solely matching behaviors to the traditional diagnoses of attention deficit, oppositional defiance, and hyperactivity.

From a mental health perspective, if a change of placement occurs, there must be a transition plan with a careful inventory of the young child's preferences, fears, and meaningful rituals, as well as a gradual timeframe for the infant and child to transition from one primary caregiver to another. When there is reunification with the biological parent, child–parent psychotherapy is recommended. This gives the mother the assistance to understand how her child's behavior may have changed due to developmental maturation and the trauma that accompanies separation and loss. It supports developmentally appropriate interactions, as well as guides the child and mother in creating a joint narrative of the traumatic experiences while working toward resolution (Lieberman, Van Horn, & Ippen, 2005).

Maternal Depression   Infants of depressed mothers show early evidence of neurobehavioral vulnerabilities. Field et al. (1990) in their seminal work analyzed face-to-face videotapes of mother–infant interactions. Mothers who were struggling with depression tended to spend less time looking at, touching, and talking to their infants and more often looked at their children with a somber countenance. As a result, infants of depressed mothers become less responsive to all adults, even those who are not depressed. Young children whose mothers are experiencing depression during their early years tend to have increased cortisol reactions and dysregulated behavior to adverse family conditions that can extend into middle childhood (Ashman, Dawson, Panagiotides, Yamada, & Wilkins, 2002).

Maternal History of Broken Relationships   In her seminal work, Selma Fraiberg (1980) addressed the impact of early relationships on one's capacity to form and sustain subsequent relationships. The concept of "ghosts in the nursery" illustrates how past relationships of the caregiver can influence how new relationships between parent and child are likely to form. The way parents interpret and then respond to their infants' behavior is often influenced by their own personal histories. A history of positive early relationships bodes well for the new dyad. Conversely, if a mother has an early history of harsh or broken relationships, the attachment process may face serious hurdles, calling for extra help to change the parenting model experienced as a child. A mother who has experienced a series of rejections may misinterpret her toddler walking away from her as a personal rebuff and as a result limit reaching out to her child.

INFANT/FAMILY AND EARLY CHILDHOOD MENTAL HEALTH PROMOTION, PREVENTIVE INTERVENTION, AND TREATMENT

A significant developmental task of early childhood is to adapt to cultural expectations of behavior. All young children at times behave in ways that prove to be challenging to parents, teachers, and caregivers. Young children go through periods of dysregulation that may include fears, anxieties, shyness, aggression, tantrums, and oppositional or testing behaviors–behaviors that are considered to be normal perturbations of childhood. Caregiver response to such behaviors will influence how the young child learns more or less adaptive ways of dealing with the world. Many common behavioral concerns that parents have are transient in nature or a reflection of the typical range of infant and young child behavior. The goal of the service provider is to help parents and caregivers appreciate their children's emotional experience of the world. Behaviors are ways of communicating how children are managing the developmental expectations placed upon them. For example, chronic childhood tantrums are usually a reaction to stress and frustration rather than the result of what is often ascribed to the child as being spoiled, manipulative, or "babyish."

The promotion of infant/family and early childhood mental health provides developmental guidance in response to common parental concerns about typical child behavior, such as food refusal, inconsolable crying, hitting, biting, tantrums, and not sleeping through the night. Developmental guidance also addresses common parenting practices that may interfere with children's social, emotional, and behavioral development, such as giving the child a bottle in response to every distress, sneaking away without saying good-bye when leaving the house, biting a child back to teach a lesson, and permitting excessive television viewing and electronic games.

Key developmental strategies for the promotion of infant/family and early childhood mental health includes guiding parents and caregivers to spend pleasurable adult–child time for intimate relationships to emerge, to acknowledge and encourage the expression of feelings, and to differentiate feelings and behavior. The provision of routines, meaningful rituals, and clear expectations of behavior provide predictability and a sense of security and safety for the child (Poulsen et al., 2005).

Challenging Behaviors and Early Childhood Mental Health Preventive Intervention

Challenging behaviors are those that impede the development and maintenance of reciprocal, positive, and nurturing relationships with parents and caregivers (Smith & Fox, 2003). For some infants and young children, nonadaptive behavior is repeated to the extent that it interferes with the forming relationships, coping with behavioral expectations, and/or learning. Behaviors that are challenging in infancy include feeding problems, sleep disturbances, excessive crying, and inconsolability. Infants at risk or with disabilities may give muted or sporadic engagement cues. Families with infants may need infant/family services or supports when there is excessive crying, sleeping patterns that have not developed by later infancy, or feeding issues. Professionals with infant/family mental health expertise may partner with parents in discovering, interpreting, and responding to their infants' developmental and emotional cues. A critical component of infant/family and early childhood mental health preventive intervention is to partner with the parent to build on strengths and provide developmental guidance.

Toddlers and preschool-age children who present challenges related to low frustration tolerance, fears, temper tantrums, and aggression to peers might need altered adult interactions and environmental modifications to support their development. Young children who were born with low birth weights or were prenatally exposed to substances may have prolonged neurobehavioral immaturities in the toddler/preschool years that require preventive intervention approaches that modify the environment to help them self-regulate.

Children with language, social, sensory, regulatory, motor, and cognitive delays and disabilities are at higher risk for mental health distress in preschool due to immature self-regulation secondary to delays, frustration relating to an impoverished felt-sense of self-mastery, and/or difficulties in relating to their peers and the significant adults in their lives. Early interventionists with an understanding of early childhood mental health can infuse resilience-building strategies into the therapies that are being provided. The importance of parent-mediated therapeutic strategies cannot be overestimated. Parental involvement is considered a necessary component of early intervention. Mahoney (2009) noted the common contention that without parent participation and responsiveness, early intervention services are likely to be ineffective.

Early childhood mental health preventive intervention provides developmental guidance for inexperienced parents, addresses vulnerabilities that may place a child's social and emotional well-being at risk, and strengthens protective factors that are linked to a child's well-being. Preventive intervention from an infant/family and early childhood mental health perspective has its grounding in relationship-based interventions. Key strategies for infant/family and early childhood mental health preventive intervention includes supporting parents and caregivers to understand the young child's emotional experience of the world, how emotional experience is expressed in nonadaptive behaviors, and how relationship-based interventions are critical in the development of resilience. Strategies also include the importance of identifying and modifying environmental and emotional triggers that affect the child, as well as how to protect infants and young children from overstimulation (Poulsen et al., 2005).

Preschool mental health consultation includes the development of partnerships among parents, teachers, child care providers, and mental health consultants to address challenging behaviors of children in early care and education programs. The goals of mental health consultation are to provide information and strategies that strengthen the healthy social and emotional development of children, to support staff and families in creating prosocial learning and home environments, to engage families and staff in developing individualized behavioral support plans, and to refer children and families to community mental health when appropriate (Allen, Brennan, Green, Hepburn, & Kaufman, 2008). It is critical that parents and early care and education staff work together in addressing challenging behaviors so that there is mutual understanding of the child's needs and shared approaches in helping the child learn to cope with behavioral expectations.

Serious Externalizing and Internalizing Behaviors and Infant/Family and Early Childhood Mental Health Intervention and Treatment

For infants, mental health disorders might be reflected in physical symptoms. Psychological disturbance in infancy may take form in excessive spitting up, poor weight gain, slow growth, and failure to thrive. Lack of eye contact and social reciprocity in cooing and smiling always need to be assessed. Signs of older infant/young toddler psychological disturbance also include persistent inconsolable crying, excessive rocking or head banging, persistent sleep disturbance, chronic apathy, and no differentiation in affectionate response between familiar and unfamiliar persons.

For toddlers and preschool-age children, emotional disturbances are expressed as either internalizing emotional issues or externalizing behavioral issues. Many concerns are transient. However, when the observed behaviors are extensive, chronic, and pervasive and interfere with the child's adaptive functioning, a diagnosis of a disorder is made. Both internalizing and externalizing disorders can be observed at an early age. Externalizing behaviors of concern include persistent, severe, out-of-control, and inconsolable temper tantrums; dangerously aggressive, self-injurious, or impulsive behavior; and constant noncompliance. These externalizing problems are regularly recognized and addressed (Belden, Thomson, & Luby, 2008). However, there is a group of serious internalizing problems that may go unnoticed, particularly in group care. These problems include young children who have a restricted range of affect, tend to have excessive fears, are withdrawn and show little initiative, do not approach caregivers to have needs met, regularly avoid relating to peers, or respond fearfully when approached by others (Egger & Angold, 2006).

When behaviors are not transitory and interfere with a child's or a family's well-being, a family-centered assessment and treatment plan needs to be developed. Infants and young children with serious social, emotional, and behavioral disorders need to be referred to community mental health services.

Infant and early childhood family interaction guidance and psychotherapy focus on enhancing interactions between a child and parent(s), translating the emotional experience of the child for parents, and/or modifying parental expectations and attributions of their child's behavior. Joint parent–child sessions may be interspersed with individual sessions with the parent. An array of infant/family and early childhood mental health services should be available to complement parent–child interaction guidance or parent–child psychotherapy. Additional available supportive services include developmental guidance, parental social supports, therapeutic preschool, and intense home visiting services. When families are struggling with poverty, unemployment, domestic disruptions, and substance use or mental illness, they need to be linked to services in the community.

Mental health treatment is called for when the extent of the concerning behavior meets a level of medical necessity. Medical necessity is required for private and public health insurance funding of infant/family and early childhood mental health treatment. Medical necessity requires the presence of a mental health disorder as defined by the *Diagnostic and Statistical Manual of Mental Health Disorders, Fourth Edition* (DSM-IV; American Psychiatric Association, 1994), plus that treatment is of clinical need and can alleviate symptoms, prevent further deterioration, improve functioning, and assist in restoring normal development in a child (American Association of Community Psychiatrists, 2011). Whereas a DSM-IV mental health diagnosis is required currently for reimbursement of private and public insurance, a more appropriate diagnostic understanding can be gleaned from the *Diagnostic Classification of Mental Health and Developmental Disorders of Infancy and Early Childhood, Revised Edition,* which addresses mental health and developmental disorders specifically for infants, toddlers, and very young children and provides a developmental framework within the context of primary relationships to make a diagnosis (ZERO TO THREE, 2005).

SUMMARY

The foundations of infant/family and early childhood mental health center on robust health, responsive nurturing relationships, and guidance within the context of family stability and family economic and social supports. When the foundations are solid, parent–child relationships and the developmental trajectory toward emotional and social health evolves with relative ease. However, when either member of the dyad is experiencing unaddressed biological and/or psychosocial vulnerabilities, additional supports are needed to assist parents.

Professionals in the field of infant/family and early childhood mental health assert that it is the responsibility of the community to see that support is accessible for parents in their roles as nurturers and guides of infants' and young children's well-being. The role of early childhood mental health promotion is to assure that all families have access to information and strategies to create nurturing home environments that will strengthen the healthy social and emotional development of their infants and young children. For example, Marla and her young son benefited by participating in a community Mommy and Me program that provided parenting information, developmental guidance, and social support. The multidisciplinary early intervention team provided Jordan and his mother with a program that infused an infant/family mental health focus. An occupational therapist, special educator, and psychologist provided preventive intervention by assisting Jordan's mother in reading her infant's cues, understanding his special needs, and learning special caregiving strategies that helped Jordan learn to cuddle. They also linked Jordan's mother to teenage mother supports in the community.

When social, emotional, and behavioral concerns reach a significant level, such as in the case of Anna, child–parent psychotherapy can be offered to enhance the interactions between the two and to help a parent understand his or her child's emotional experience of the world. Child–parent psychotherapy can be paired with developmental guidance, parental emotional supports, and links to concrete resources to help alleviate the financial stresses that affect the family.

ACTIVITIES TO EXTEND THE DISCUSSION

1. **Schedule a conversation with the parent(s) of a child under 12 months of age and ask them to describe the types of information and support that they would like to have regarding parenting.** Also ask them to describe the information and support that they have received. You may add other questions, but be sure to ask the following:

   • Before your child was born, what kinds of experience did you have in caring for an infant?

   • What kinds of information and support have you received as a new parent? For example, if you had questions about your child's crying or eating or sleeping, was there someone to talk with?

- Is there any information or support that you would have liked to have had that wasn't available?

Summarize the information you have gleaned from this discussion and work with classmates or colleagues to outline the policies and the components of a support system that would be beneficial to new parents in your community.

2. **Identify and review two online resources that provide information designed for parents about parenting and caring for young children.** Your review should include the following: name and web site URL; who sponsors the site; what the focus is (e.g., general parenting information, health care, infant and early childhood development, answers to new parents' common questions and concerns); and the level of sensitivity to diverse family structures, child ability levels, cultures, and child-rearing preferences. Finally, indicate whether you would or would not recommend this web site and why.

3. **Think about people you know who have young children or about the families of your friends.** Are there any child-rearing practices, such as discipline, that differ from those of your own family? What are they? Would those practices have been effective and positive in your family? Why or why not?

REFERENCES

Ainsworth, M.S., Blehar, M.C., Waters, E., & Wall, S. (1978). *Patterns of attachment: A psychological study of the strange situation.* Hillsdale, NJ: Lawrence Erlbaum.

Allen, M.D., Brennan, E., Green, B., Hepburn, K., & Kaufman, R. (2008). Early childhood mental health consultation: A developing profession. *Focal Point, 22*(1), 21–24.

American Academy of Child and Adolescent Psychiatry. (2004). *Lead exposure in children affects brain and behavior.* Retrieved July 15, 2012, from http://www.aacap.org/galleries/FactsForFamilies/45_lead_exposure_in_children_affects_brain_and_behavior.pdf

American Academy of Pediatrics. (2012). The lifelong effects of early childhood adversity and toxic stress. *Pediatrics, 129,* 232–246.

American Association of Community Psychiatry. (2011). *Clinical and administrative tools/guidelines: Principles for defining medical necessity in mental health treatment.* Retrieved June 20, 2012, from http://www.communitypsychiatry.org

American Psychiatric Association. (1994). *Diagnostic and statistical manual of mental health disorders* (4th ed.). Washington, DC: Author.

Ashman, S.B., Dawson, G., Panagiotides, H., Yamada, E., & Wilkins, C.W. (2002). Stress hormone levels of children of depressed mothers. *Development and Psychopathology, 14*(2), 333–349.

Barrera, M.E., & Maurer, D. (1981). Recognition of mother's photographed face by the three-month-old infant. *Child Development, 52*(2), 714–716.

Bates, J., & Wachs, T.D. (Eds.) (1994). *Temperament: Individual differences at the interface of biology and behavior.* Washington, DC: American Psychological Association.

Belden, A.C., Thomson, N.R., & Luby, J.L. (2008). Temper tantrums in healthy versus depressed and disruptive preschoolers: Defining tantrum behavior associated with clinical problems. *Journal of Pediatrics, 151*(16), 117–122.

Bernstein, V.J., Harris, E.J., Long, C.W., Lida, H., & Has, S.L. (2005). Issues in multicultural assessments of parent-child interactions: An exploratory study from the starting early smart collaboration. *Applied Developmental Psychology, 26,* 241–275.

Bowlby, J. (1988). *A secure base: Parent-child attachment and healthy human development.* New York, NY: Basic Books.

Brauner, C.B., & Stephens, B.C. (2006). Estimating the prevalence of early childhood serious emotional/behavioral disturbance: Challenges and recommendations. *Public Health Report, 121,* 303–310.

Buka, G.C., Stichick, T., Birdthistle, I., & Earls, F. (2001). Youth exposure to violence: Prevalence, risks and consequences. *American Journal of Orthopsychiatry, 71*(3), 298–310.

Center for the Developing Child at Harvard University. (2010). *The foundations of lifelong health are built in early childhood*. Boston, MA: Harvard University.

Center for Labor Market Studies. (2011). *The impact of rising poverty on the nation's young families and their children, 2000–2010*. Boston, MA: Northeastern University.

Cicchetti, D. (2004). An odyssey of discovery: Lessons learned from three decades of research on child maltreatment. *American Psychologist, 59*(8), 731–740.

Cooper, J.L., Banghart, B., & Aratani, Y. (2010). *Addressing mental health needs of young children in the child welfare system*. New York, NY: National Center for Children in Poverty.

Cooper, J.L., Masi, I., & Vech, J. (2009). *Social-emotional development in early childhood: What every policymaker should know*. New York, NY: National Center for Children in Poverty.

Corapci, F., Calatroni, A., Kaciroti, N., Jimenez, E., & Lozoff, B. (2010). Longitudinal evaluation of externalizing and internalizing behavior problems following iron-deficient anemia in infancy. *Journal of Pediatric Psychology, 126*(4), 884–894.

Crnic, K., Hoffman, C., Gaze, C., & Edelbrock, C. (2004). Understanding the emergence of behavior problems in young children with developmental delays. *Infants & Young Children, 17*(3), 223–235.

Duncan, G.J. (2010). Early-childhood poverty and adult attainment, behavior and health. *Child Development, 81*(1), 306–325.

Egger, H.L., & Angold, A. (2006). Common emotional and behavioral disorders in preschool children: Presentation, nosology, and epidemiology. *Journal of Child Psychology and Psychiatry, 47*, 313–337.

Field, T., Healy, B., Goldstein, S., Perry, S., Bendell, D., Schanberg, S., et al. (1990). Behavior- state matching and synchrony in mother-infant interactions of nondepressed versus depressed dyads. *Developmental Psychology, 26*, 7–14.

Field, T., Hernandez-Reif, M., Diego, M., Schanberg, S., & Kuhn, C. (2005). Cortisol decrease and serotonin and dopamine increases following massage therapy. *International Journal of Neuroscience, 115*, 1397–1413.

Fraiberg, S. (1980). *Clinical studies in infant mental health: The first year of life*. New York, NY: Basic Books.

Gilliam, W.S. (2005). *Prekindergarteners left behind: Expulsion rates in state prekindergarten programs. FCD policy brief series, no. 3*. New York, NY: Foundation for Child Development.

Goodman, G.S. (2005). Wailing babies in her wake. *American Psychologist, 60*(8), 872–881.

Goulet, M. (1998). *How caring relationships support self-regulation*. Toronto: George Brown College.

Greenspan, S.I., & Meisels, S.J. (1996). Toward a new vision of developmental assessment of infancy and young children. In S.J. Meisels & E. Fenichel (Eds.), *New visions for developmental assessment of infancy and young children* (pp. 11–26). Washington, DC: ZERO TO THREE.

Guralnick, M.J. (2011). Why early intervention works: A systems perspective. *Infants & Young Children, 24*(1), 6–28.

Hebbeler, K., Spiker, D., Bailey, D., Scarborough, S., & Mallik, S. (2007). *Early intervention for infants and toddlers with disabilities and their families: Participants, services and outcomes*. Menlo Park, CA: SRI International.

Individuals with Disabilities Education Act (IDEA) of 2004, PL 108-446, 20 U.S.C. 1400 *et seq.*

Jacobstein, D.M., Stark, D.R., & Laygo, R.M. (2007). Creating responsive systems for children with co-occurring developmental and emotional disorders. *Mental Health Aspects of Developmental Disabilities, 10*(3), 91–98.

Kahana-Kalman, R. (2000, Summer). *Maternal depression and child development. Early Intervention Training Institute Newsletter*. New York, NY: Rose F. Kennedy Center.

Kassow, D.Z. & Dunst, C.J. (2007). *Characteristics of parental sensitivity related to secure infant attachment*. Asheville, NC: Winterberry Press.

Kisilevsky, B.S., Hains, M., & Lee, K. (2003). Effects of experience on fetal voice recognition. *Psychological Science, 14*(3), 220–224.

Kopp, C. (1992). Emotional distress and control in young children. *New Directions for Child and Adolescent Development, 55*, 41–56.

Lieberman, A., Van Horn, P., & Ippen, C.G. (2005). Toward evidence-based treatment: Child-parent psychotherapy with preschooler's exposed to marital violence. *Journal of the American Academy of Child and Adolescent Psychiatry, 44*, 1241–1248.

Luby, J. (2000). Depression. In C. Zeanah (Ed.), *Handbook of infant mental health* (pp. 296–382). New York, NY: Guilford Press.

Luby, J., & Myers, R. (2012). Maternal support in early childhood predicts larger hippocampal volume at school age. *Proceedings of the National Academy of Science, 109*(8), 2854–2859.

Mahoney, G. (2009). Relationship Focused Intervention (RFI): Enhancing the role of parents in children's developmental intervention. *International Journal of Early Childhood Special Education, 1,* 79–94.

Mautymaa, M., Puura, K., Luoma, I., Salmelin, R.K. & Tamminen, T. (2006). Mother's early perception of her infant's difficult temperament, parenting stress and early mother-infant interaction. *Nordic Journal of Psychiatry, 60*(5), 379–386.

McDonald, R., Jouriles, E.N., Ramisetty-Mikler, S., Caetano, R., & Green, C.E. (2006). Estimating the number of American children living in partner violent families. *Journal of Family Psychology, 20*(1), 137–142.

Mehler, J., Bertoncini J., & Barriere, M. (1973). Infant recognition of mother's voice. *Perception, 7,* 491–497.

Melmed, M.E. (2011). A call to action for infants and toddlers in foster care. *Zero To Three, 31*(3), 29–34.

Nachmias, M., Gunnar, M.R., Mangelsdorf, S., Parritz, R., & Buss, K.A. (1996). Behavioral inhibition and stress reactivity: Moderating role of attachment security. *Child Development, 67*(2), 508–522.

National Center for Health Statistics. (2009). *Changing patterns of non-marital childbearing in the United States.* Hyattsville, MD: Author.

National Center on Family Homelessness. (2009). *America's youngest outcasts: State report card on child homelessness.* Retrieved July 15, 2012, from http://www.homelesschildren america.org/findings.php

National Scientific Council on the Developing Child. (2005). *Excessive stress disrupts the architecture of the brain: Working Paper #3.* Retrieved June 16, 2012, from http://www.developingchild.net

National Scientific Council on the Developing Child. (2007). *The science of early childhood development.* Retrieved June 18, 2012, from http://www.developingchild.net

Obradovic, J., Bush, N.R., Stamperdahl, J., Adler, N.E., & Boyce, W.T. (2010). Biological sensitivity to context: The interactive effects of stress reactivity and family adversity on socioemotional behavior and school readiness. *Child Development, 81*(1), 270–289.

Pawl, J., & St. John, M. (1998). *How you are is as important as what you do.* Washington, DC: ZERO TO THREE: National Center for Infants, Toddlers, and Families.

Perry, B.D., & Pollard, D. (1997). *Altered brain development following global neglect in early childhood.* Presented at the annual meeting of the Society for Neuroscience, New Orleans, LA.

Poulsen, M.K., Finello, K.M., Provance, E., Picl, J., & Reynolds, V. (2005). *The 3Rs of early childhood: Relationships, resilience and readiness.* Sacramento, CA: Center for Prevention and Early Intervention.

Powell, D. & Dunlap, G. (2010). *Family-focused interventions for promoting social-emotional development in infants and toddlers with or at risk for disabilities: Roadmap to effective intervention practices #5.* Tampa, FL: Technical Assistance Center on Social Emotional Intervention for Young Children.

Runyan, D.K., Hunter, W.M., Socolar, R.S., Amaya-Jackson, L., English, D., Landsverk, J., et al. (1998). Children who prosper in unfavorable environments: The relationship to social capital. *Pediatrics, 101*(1), 12–18.

Satir, V. (n.d.). Retrieved from betterparenting. com/25-inspirational-parenting-quotes.

Schantz, S.L., Widholm, J.J., & Rice, D.C. (2003). Effects of PCB exposure on neuropsychological function in children. *Environmental Health Perspectives, 111*(3), 359–376.

Schore, A. (1997). *Affect regulation and the origin of self.* Hillsdale, NJ: Lawrence Erlbaum.

Shaw, G.B. (1928). *The intelligent woman's guide to socialism and capitalism* (p. 25). Piscataway, NJ: Transaction Publishers. Retrieved from http://www.nccp.org/publications/pdf/text_389.pdf;.

Shonkoff, J. P. (2010, August 3). *Keynote address: Early childhood 2010: Innovation for the next generation.* Washington, DC.

Shonkoff, J.P., & Phillips, D.A. (Eds.). (2000). *From neurons to neighborhoods: The science of early childhood development.* Washington, DC: National Academies Press.

Shore, R. (1997). *Rethinking the brain: New insights into early development.* New York, NY: Families and Work Institute.

Smith, B.J., & Fox, L. (2003). *Systems of service delivery: A synthesis of evidence relevant to young children at risk or who have challenging behavior.* Retrieved July 2, 2012, from http://www.challengingehavior.org

Stapleton, K., McIntosh, J., & Corrington, B. (2010). *Allied for better outcomes: Child welfare and early childhood.* Washington, DC: Center for the Study of Social Policy.

Substance Abuse Mental Health Services Administration. (2010). *Addressing the mental health needs of young children and their families.* Washington, DC: Author.

Thomas, A., & Chess, S. (1977). *Temperament and development*. New York, NY: Brunner/Mazel.

Thompson, R.A. (2008). Early attachment and later development: Familiar questions, new answers. In J. Cassidy & P.R. Shaver (Eds.), *Handbook of attachment theory, research and clinical applications* (2nd ed., pp. 348–365). New York, NY: Guilford Press.

Trout, M. (1988). Infant mental health: Monitoring our movement into the 21st century. *Infant Mental Health Journal, 9*(3), 191–200.

University of Southern California, University Center for Excellence in Developmental Disabilities, Children's Hospital Los Angeles.

U.S. Bureau of Labor Statistics. (2009). *Labor force participation of women and mothers, 2008. Current population survey data*. Washington, DC: U.S. Department of Labor.

U.S. Department of Health and Human Services. (2009). *Strengthening families and communities*. Washington, DC: Author.

White House Conference on Early Childhood Development and Learning. (1997, April 17). What new research on the brain tells us about our youngest children. Washington, DC: Author.

Windsor, J., Reichle, J., & Mahowald, M.C. (2009). Communication disorders. In C.H. Zeanah (Ed.), *Handbook of infant mental health* (3rd ed., pp. 318–331). New York, NY: Guilford Press.

ZERO TO THREE. (2005). *Diagnostic classification of mental health and developmental disorders of infancy and early childhood* (Rev. ed.). Washington, DC: Author.

Zolotor, A.J., & Runyan, D.K. (2006). Social capital, family violence and neglect. *Pediatrics, 117*(6), 1124–1131.

9

Creating Family–
Professional Alliances

Eleanor W. Lynch

"Professionals are people, too. They have good days and bad days. They work long hours that are emotionally draining. They've chosen their profession because they care deeply about children, and nurse the same hopes for your child that you do. You each have your own—partial—expertise. Together you form a complete team."

—Robin Simons (1987, p. 51)

"I cannot describe the assessment in any great detail. Like the first conversation with our pediatrician, of which I could only remember certain features against a hazy background, this assessment remains in my memory like an impressionist painting upon which a student of realism has superimposed six or seven contrasting strokes."

—Beth Harry (2010, p. 70)

"As a staff, the professionals should strive to make the parents an integral part of the intervention team. Parents should be welcomed, needed members of any therapeutic team providing services to their child [with a disability]."

—Gay S. McDonald (1978, pp. 126–127)

This is a book of encouragement; it is about the resilience of families and about the ways in which families and professionals can work together to improve their lives and the lives of children. The importance of these alliances has been recognized in the literature for many years, but partnerships of all kinds are easier to describe than to create and maintain. Tension between families and professionals is not unusual; in fact, some tension is a healthy result of the different roles that family members and professionals play in the lives of children. Parents and family members know their children better than anyone else. They understand the needs of their family system and the beliefs and behaviors that they value and by which they live. On the one hand, family members are typically the child's best advocate because they are trying to meet the child's needs rather than balance the child's needs against larger social, political, and economic needs that professionals confront within their organizations, communities, and states. Professionals, on the other hand, bring advanced knowledge and skill training, extensive experience, and a range of tools and techniques that have been honed over time. They know more children and families than a family by itself will probably meet in a lifetime. Although family service professionals are often strong advocates for the children and families that they serve, most work within a bigger picture of priorities and needs than those of a family or child alone. Sometimes, admittedly, for family service professionals the bigger picture takes precedence.

This chapter discusses family–professional tensions and alliances in the context of a family-centered approach to intervention from the perspectives of research and practice. It defines the goals and principles of family-centered service, dispels the myth that professionals have little to contribute in this approach, and discusses family–professional roles and relationships. It describes evaluation as an important tool in determining whether family-centered practices are being implemented and discusses ethical practice and professional codes of conduct as the underpinnings of service delivery. The chapter concludes with suggestions for putting effective partnerships into practice.

A SHORT HISTORY OF CHANGE IN FAMILY–PROFESSIONAL RELATIONSHIPS

Family-centered services have become the gold standard of early intervention systems, programs, and services since the mid-1980s. In a review of early education programs and outcomes, Bronfenbrenner (1975) concluded that active parent involvement was a major contributor to the success of these programs. In his book *The Future of Children* (1975), Nicholas Hobbs, eminent child psychologist, asserted that the true role of intervention programs was to marshal socializing agents within the family, neighborhood, and community as a way of strengthening families and their functioning. That assertion was more fully described in a later book by Hobbs et al., *Strengthening Families* (1984). The notion of using informal supports rather than formal supports was viewed as a more natural, normalized way of assisting families. The emphasis on the importance of families and of determining family needs from the family's point of view emerged as central to child health care (Baird, 1997).

Fields such as child health care adopted this new model, and research and ideology in areas such as early intervention began to shift. Building on their research with families, philosophy, and evolving notions of best practice, Dunst (1985) and others (Bailey et al., 1986; Dunst, Trivette, & Deal, 1988) challenged the traditional view of child-directed services as the optimal model for early intervention. Turnbull, Summers, and Brotherson's (1984) contributions to the application of family systems theory to families of children with disabilities or children at risk for disabilities moved the field forward in both philosophy and practice. (See Chapters 3 and 4 for details of the family systems framework.) The Education of the Handicapped Act Amendments of 1986 (PL 99-457) (retitled as the IDEA Amendments of 1997 [PL 105-17]) gave planning grants to states to develop early intervention services for families with children from birth to 3 who have, or who are at risk for, disabilities. It also mandated free and appropriate public education for preschoolers with disabilities. The new legislation and its subsequent amendments (IDEA, 2004) created a vehicle for putting new ideology into practice through the IFSPs for children birth through age 3. The IFSP gives families a central role in determining services and the ways in which they are delivered (Hauser-Cram, Upshur, Krauss, & Shonkoff, 1988). It also underscores the need for systems, programs, and individual service providers to rethink their approach to serving children and families.

This rethinking changed the locus of services from children alone to children in the context of their families. Determining family priorities and needed supports became as important as child-centered activities, approaches, and interventions. Family-centered approaches incorporate family support in service delivery, and family support emphasizes family strengths (Dunst, Trivette, Starnes, Hamby, & Gordon, 1993; Singer & Powers, 1993). Professional contributions to family support typically enhance families' well-being and competence, as well as model and teach relationship skills. Professionals must reflect ethical behavior in all interactions, employ strategies for training specific skills and behaviors, and demonstrate knowledge and ability to teach strategies that enhance supports. Optimally, they must display a commitment to collaborative partnerships and place value on the power of self-help groups (Singer & Powers). These skills are foundational to family-centered practices, and wisdom from the family support movement provided evidence that families were quite capable of identifying their own needs.

This view has been reinforced by research in subsequent years in which families of children with disabilities were asked about their own needs and preferences related to information gathering and services. In a qualitative study that examined parents' and professionals' expectations of family outcomes in early intervention and the preferences of each group for gathering information about family strengths and needs, Summers et al. (1990) found that family members looked to early intervention professionals to provide emotional support and friendship. Contrary to professional training curricula that emphasize professional distance and boundaries, these findings underscore the value of personal, informal relationships between professionals and family members when parents are first learning that their son or daughter has a disability. The study also found that early interventionists and early intervention programs were expected to provide information, assist in linking families with other families in similar situations, and help parents and other family members develop skills that would facilitate later relationships with service systems. Professionals were also expected to help parents develop the skills necessary to work more effectively with their son or daughter with disabilities. This last point is critical, for it has been so frequently omitted as programs have attempted to become family centered. Although the role of professionals in family-centered practice has changed, its importance and value have not.

In a similar qualitative study, parents' primary expectation for early intervention was accurate information, positive reactions, and uncensored information about what is available so that parents can decide (Able-Boone, Sandall, & Frederick, 1990). Family members expressed their desire to have the knowledge that would empower them to make informed decisions. This study, too, supported families' desire for professionals who are knowledgeable and who bring their knowledge and skills to the partnership.

In addition to participating in research conducted by professionals, parents and other family members have developed models and approaches to services that underscore the many tenets of family-centered practice (Santelli, Poyadue, & Young, 2001). Parents throughout the country have developed parent-to-parent networks. In parent-to-parent networks, a trained, supportive parent of a child with a disability or risk condition provides information and emotional support as needed to a matched parent who requests assistance (Singer et al., 1999). The veteran parent is often available around the clock for questions, conversations, and emotional support (Santelli, Turnbull, Sergeant, Lerner, & Marquis, 1996). The veteran and referral parents are often matched by children's disability or risk condition, the children's ages, or the even geographic proximity of the families. Parent-to-parent programs have been cited as particularly valuable in providing information and emotional support for families of children with disabilities (e.g., Meyer, 1993; Santelli, Turnbull, Lerner, & Marquis, 1993; Santelli et al., 1996; Turnbull & Turnbull, 2001). The opportunity to talk with someone who has "been there" is often an invaluable resource for families who are encountering new feelings, new demands, and new systems. Parent-to-parent programs do not include professionals and do not represent models of family–professional collaboration. Instead, they underscore the importance of personal contact and knowledge of daily life with a child with disabilities or serious risks—something that most professionals have not experienced.

As additional research on family-centered approaches to service delivery has been conducted, its validity as an approach has been confirmed. In a meta-analysis consisting of eight studies representing 910 toddlers and their families, data suggested that a family systems model of intervention positively affected parent–child interactions and child development (Trivette, Dunst, & Hamby, 2010). Effectiveness of the approach is, in part, dependent not only on the training and skills of professionals but also on their ability to connect emotionally with family needs (Brotherson et al., 2010) and a supportive administrative structure (Epley et al., 2010).

Cognitive Coping

Cognitive coping, according to Turnbull and Turnbull (1993, p. 1), entails "thinking about a particular situation in ways that enhance a sense of well-being." The ability to reframe a situation that is negative or is perceived to be negative in a more positive light is another way to define cognitive coping. Parent-professionals—recognized researchers who are also parents of children with disabilities—have driven research on cognitive coping in the area of developmental disabilities. Contrary to societal views and much of the literature in the field of developmental disabilities, many families feel enriched by their son, daughter, brother, or sister with a disability (Harry, 2010; Turnbull, 2009; Turnbull, Patterson, Behr, Murphy, Marquis, & Blue-Banning, 1993). Expressing these feelings of being enriched by living with, learning from, and loving a child with a disability is an example of cognitive coping. The research on cognitive coping underscores the family-centered principles of empowerment and respect for family perspectives.

A Realignment of Priorities and Ways of Working Together

The professional literature in early childhood special education is replete with guidelines and recommendations for implementing family-centered approaches, but the shift from child-focused to family-centered services has not been easy (Murray & Mandell, 2006; Sandall, Hemmeter, Smith, & McLean, 2005). It was akin to a shift in planetary alignment—all elements within the model now relate differently to one another. This new family-centered approach required that professionals and parents alike develop new ways to work together. As stated by Vacca and Feinberg:

> The new paradigm requires that early interventionists learn to adapt to the culture and aspirations of the families with whom they work. A unidirectional strategy in which parents are expected to become acculturated to the world of the early interventionist is replaced by a bidirectional system in which both the clinician and family learn from and adapt to each other. (2000, p. 41)

Although a family-centered approach remains the gold standard, it continues to be challenging to implement, plagued by misunderstanding, and in need of further research, especially in relation to family outcomes (Dempsey & Keen, 2008).

WHAT DOES FAMILY CENTERED REALLY MEAN?

Several tenets characterize family-centered practice (e.g., Bailey, Raspa, & Fox, 2012; Baird, 1997; Dunst et al., 1988; Hanson, 1996; Hanson & Lynch, 1995; Lynch & Hanson, 2011):

1. It recognizes parents or primary caregivers as experts on their child.

2. It acknowledges the family as the ultimate decision maker for their child and family.

3. It views the family as the constant in the child's life and the service providers and systems in their life as transitory.

4. It respects and works to support family priorities, their goals for service, and the extent to which they choose to be involved.

5. It values trusting, collaborative relationships between parents and professionals.

6. It works to ensure culturally competent services.

7. It includes a focus on capacity building within the family.

To help implement family-centered programs and services, administrative structures need to be based upon a clear vision, possess an organizational climate that nurtures collaborative teamwork, balance professional autonomy with accountability, and have adequate, flexible resources (Epley et al., 2010). The goals of family-centered practices are to strengthen the relationship between the child and family; respect the family's wisdom, priorities, and culture; and deliver services within the routines and activities that are a part of the family's daily life resulting in meaningful outcomes for both the child and family (Bernheimer & Weisner, 2007; Cambray-Engstrom & Salisbury, 2010; Dempsey & Keen, 2008). Although many professionals and program administrators believe that these characteristics describe their practice and their programs, closer examination suggests that this is generally not the case. Consider the story of Marta that describes service delivery in an approach that is not family centered.

 **Marta**

Marta is 28 months old. Her parents are very concerned because she seems to be regressing instead of progressing in the areas of socialization and communication. Until recently, Marta had seemed to be developing typically. She had said her first words at 12 months in both English and Spanish and had developed a vocabulary that allowed her to name her favorite objects and put two words together. Although she was never as cuddly as her older sister had been, she enjoyed being held and was socially engaging.

The family physician and a university clinic staff member assess Marta and tell her parents that they think that her increasing problems in social interactions and communication place her on the continuum of autism spectrum disorders. They suggest an early intervention program. Marta's mother contacts the program to express her concern and interest. Although the person who answers the telephone is friendly and sounds supportive, she makes it clear that they only accept referrals from other professionals. Marta's mother must ask the family physician or someone at the clinic to make the referral and send any reports that have been written so that program personnel can determine the appropriateness of the referral before they meet Marta or her parents.

Marta's mother agrees, requests the referral, and has the reports sent to the program. Program staff members decide that it is an appropriate referral but want to conduct their own assessment. In their assessment, various staff members administer various tests, play with Marta, and observe Marta's behavior. The only questions they ask Marta's parents have to do with birth history and developmental milestones. None of the staff members ask them any questions about their immediate concerns, what they have been told up to this point, their observations as parents, or what they need as a family to make this challenging time easier for them.

The program staff members meet and determine that Marta is eligible for services. They develop goals, objectives, and outcomes that they present in a finished-looking draft to Marta's parents at the IFSP meeting. Marta's mother and father were hoping that she could continue to attend the community toddler/preschool program that her sister attends, but the program administrator states that serving Marta in that setting would spread his staff too thin. They need to see Marta at their center 3 days a week. They also emphasize the importance of weekly home visits—something that is difficult for her parents to arrange because of their work schedules. The meeting ends with the staff's suggestions and draft accepted as is, and Marta begins to attend the program. During the subsequent home visits, a staff member demonstrates how to work with Marta. The staff member then leaves activities for Marta and her parents to do together and data collection forms for Marta's parents to complete before the next home visit.

Let us examine this vignette in relation to the principles of family-centered services. In this example, staff members did not recognize the parents or primary caregivers as experts on their child. They required a professional referral and professional reports before talking with the family about their concerns. In the assessment, program staff relied on the administration of various tests, observations, and play activities without soliciting or listening to the parents' concerns and asking about their observations. IFSPs and IEPs are to be jointly developed by parents and staff members. In this IFSP, no opportunity was given for the family's expertise to be incorporated. In fact, when they expressed their desire to keep their daughters together at the program Marta's older sister attends, they were simply told that it could not be done. Finally, the home visits were used only for instruction on the goals and objectives developed by the program. They were not related to any concerns expressed by the parents or integrated into the family's normal routines.

The professionals in this vignette did not acknowledge the family as the ultimate decision maker for their child and family. If families are the decision makers, their referral and concerns should be adequate for program staff to begin assessment for eligibility. Referral from another professional would not be required. Parental requests at the IFSP would have been heeded rather than ignored, and the need for, time, or place for home visits would have been discussed and negotiated.

When families are viewed as the constant in the child's life and the service providers and systems viewed as transitory, every effort is made to incorporate intervention into the daily life and routines of the family. Interventions that create additional burdens are less likely to be continued and less likely to be effective over the long term.

Viewing families and family members as the constant also leads to efforts to build capacity within the family and empower parents for a lifetime of negotiations and decision making related to their son or daughter.

In this vignette, Marta's parents' priorities, goals, and level of involvement were neither respected nor supported. Her parents were never really asked about their priorities and goals. The program staff developed the IFSP outcomes without consultation. The community toddler/preschool program that Marta's parents preferred was ruled out without investigation, and the home visits were conducted as a program requirement while ignoring the parents' concerns.

When programs value trusting, collaborative relationships between parents and professionals, the family-centered principles are not ignored. An ongoing attempt is made to examine practice, consider alternatives, and seek family input to determine ways to improve. Although these staff members may be competent in the technical skills of their professional disciplines, they have not shown that they value family–professional relationships.

To be family centered is to acknowledge, respect, and tailor programs and services to meet the cultural and sociocultural needs of families (i.e., to be culturally competent). In the case of Marta and her family, culture or preferred language was not considered. The service providers made the assumption that there was nothing salient about the family's cultural beliefs, values, or language that would affect intervention. When culture is not broached, it is never addressed, and services cannot be assumed to be culturally competent.

In this example, the program and professionals associated with it were not malevolent people. They did not deliberately bypass a family-centered approach. They were simply operating on a set of principles that are no longer acceptable in intervention, whether it takes place in health care, early intervention for children with disabilities, child care, or Head Start. Failing to provide family-centered services is a serious shortcoming of any program.

Myths and Misunderstandings in Family-Centered Practice

Although family-centered practice is the goal, all too often, programs and professionals have embraced the words without understanding the content. The subsequent sections illustrate some of the myths, misunderstandings, and mistakes that occur when service providers, programs, and policy makers do not fully understand family-centered practice.

Myth: The Role of Professionals Is Diminishing   Standards of practice in all fields change over time. They are influenced by research, philosophy, politics, economics, and policy decisions. It is not uncommon for the pendulum of practice to swing wildly from one approach to another in an attempt to align with the current trend. This often occurs before all of the data are in and is often based on a cursory reading and understanding of the underlying principles and goals of the trend. This certainly was and continues to be the case with family-centered practice. In a rush to become family centered, professionals and their skills were initially devalued and their roles disregarded. The children who had been the reason behind the families and professionals getting together in the first place were barely registering on the radar screen. Child-focused interventions were minimized in favor of a family focus. Professionals often misinterpreted critical research (e.g., Able-Boone et al., Summers et al., 1990) on family preferences and needs and asked new or recently referred parents what they wanted or needed without providing information to assist in decision making. In the absence of accurate information, it is impossible to make an informed decision.

Put yourself in the following situation. Imagine learning that you have a significant health problem. You find the specialists in this field, ask about their experiences with various treatment regimens, and request their recommendations for your particular situation. In this scenario, you would expect the specialists to listen to you, but you would also expect the professionals to share information freely and provide recommendations based on their knowledge of the possibilities, their experience with others with the same diagnosis, and your own unique circumstances. You would also assume that the professionals would use their skills in determining and carrying out your treatment. Few people would stay with a professional who assured them that they could treat themselves effectively but never taught them how.

The same can be said of working with families. By the time families seek professionals for assistance and support because of concerns about their children, they want more than a friendly face. They want knowledge and assistance in putting that knowledge into the family's context—their values, beliefs, strengths, and needs. Any interpretation of family-centered practice that excludes professional knowledge, experience, and expertise is faulty, as is any interpretation that leaves the child out of the picture. Trivette et al. clarified the perspectives on working with families consistent with family-centered practice:

> The model is implemented by practitioners by using capacity-building help-giving practices to have family members identify their needs, the supports and resources to meet those needs, the use of family members' existing capabilities (strengths), and the development of new abilities to obtain resources and supports to meet their needs. (2010, p. 3)

Professionals are vital to effective intervention. Their training, knowledge, skills, and experience complement the family's knowledge of their own child, their preferences and priorities as a family, and their commitment to care over a lifetime. Without equal respect for what each person brings to the relationship, there can be no partnership; this is one of the guiding principles of family-centered practice.

Myth: Only Family Concerns Are Important   An extension of the myth that professionals are devalued in a family-centered model of practice is the myth that service providers should address only those issues that the family identifies as important. Thus, if the family is only concerned that the child's behavior is a serious problem, the professional should not mention her concerns that the child may also have a hearing loss. This perspective, in fact, runs counter to family-centered practice. If families are to be the ultimate decision makers, they must be provided with the necessary information to make informed decisions (Able-Boone et al., 1990). If families and professionals are to develop real partnerships, professionals cannot withhold information that they consider to be important. They may consider the family's concerns first and work on one issue at a time, making the family's concerns the first priority; but they should also voice their own concerns and request the family's permission to proceed. Most important, information given to families should be given in capacity-building ways that support their self-confidence and ability to parent and facilitate their learning without threatening their knowledge and ability (Bruder, 2000; Trivette et al., 2010).

Myth: Formal Supports Are Bad   Another misunderstanding is that formal supports such as counseling, classes, or workshops on behavior support or agency-organized inclusive playgroups are inherently bad and should be avoided. Some people prefer formal supports to informal opportunities to learn, receive help, or socialize. One of the guiding principles of family-centered practice is the individualization of services to meet the preferences of diverse families. The definition of early intervention proposed by Dunst, Trivette, and Jodry (1997) included formal supports as part of the mix of supports that families may need.

Consider, again, the earlier example in which you learn that you have a significant health problem. In addition to seeking out the experts in the field, you may talk to friends and family members, attend a support group of individuals who have had the same problem, read articles about the problem (on the Internet, in medical journals, or in popular magazines), and investigate alternative treatments. Each person performing this exercise might do it differently. For example, one person might do one of these things, whereas another person might do them all. It is also likely that the value that each person places on each activity would vary, but all are strategies for learning about the problem and facing it emotionally.

This range of responses is no different for families with a child with disabilities, behavioral challenges, or health concerns. Considerable attention has been paid in recent years to informal support—the marshaling of resources that are part of a family's daily life, such as other family members, friends, neighbors, colleagues at work, and faith communities. These personal networks have been shown to be important resources for families and research has suggested that informal support through personal networks showed the strongest relationship to child and family outcomes (Dunst, 1999). Effective supports, however, may also be direct. They may include structured opportunities for families to participate in learning about resources, their child's disability, and strategies for working more effectively with the child, professionals, and agencies. Although informal supports are important and often make us feel good, they are seldom sufficient to address all of the issues surrounding a child with a disability or serious behavioral problems.

Myth: Only Professionals Must Change   A third myth is that for family-centered practice to be effective, only professionals have to change. Rather, for family-centered practice to be achieved, professionals, families, agencies, and policy makers may all have to change. Family-centered practice is not easy to develop or maintain (Bruder, 2000). At a time when an increasing number of families have more complex problems and children have more complicated needs, early interventionists are trying to provide comprehensive, coordinated, family-centered services (Krahn, Thom, Hale, & Williams, 1995). Professionals have had to engage in additional training, obtain new certifications in some instances, and spend increasing amounts of time collaborating with adults at other agencies when they entered the field to work with children. Sometimes all of the effort that professionals have put into retraining themselves has been negated by policy decisions at the state or agency level. The belief that well-trained professionals could singlehandedly make family-centered practice a reality *is* a myth.

Hence, other changes must occur for family-centered practice to be effective. Family members must have the resources and desire to participate in new ways. Participation may vary widely across families and within families over time, but each family must decide on what they want for their child and how they want to be involved in intervention. In family-centered practices, services vary. Service providers do not assume that a service that is helpful for one family is equally helpful for another. Customizing services requires that families put forth additional effort to make selections that they consider best for their child and family and that professionals work to ensure that customized services are integrated. Just as implementing a specific teaching strategy or behavior change technique takes learning and time, so do making decisions about priorities, formulating long- and short-term objectives, and monitoring outcomes.

Agencies and policy makers must also change if family-centered support is to become the norm. The current emphasis that some intervention programs place on offering a menu of services as opposed to integrated programs in early intervention has some serious, negative consequences. As McCollum articulated so well when discussing the fee-for-service approach to early intervention,

> The consequences have been a return to fragmented services at the level of the child and family and less opportunity for collaboration among professionals working with each child and family. It has become much more difficult for service providers of all disciplines to be "family-centered," to embed their interventions within the contexts of families' daily lives, and to integrate their interventions with those of other professionals in recognition of the integrated nature of early development. (2000, pp. 85–86)

Until the entire system can be designed to facilitate family-centered services, the burden will continue to fall on those closest to the issues—families and direct-service professionals.

Avoiding Myths and Misunderstandings   Each of these myths, misunderstandings, and mistakes can be overcome. At its simplest level, family-centered practice is providing supports and services that the family desires and values to enhance child and family outcomes within a respectful partnership between families and professionals. If practice is guided by this definition, myths and misunderstandings are likely to decrease.

FAMILY AND PROFESSIONAL ROLES AND RELATIONSHIPS

This section focuses on power, becoming empowered as a parent, and the variables that families and professionals identify as important to effective collaboration.

Power and Becoming Empowered

In most situations in which families and professionals interact, power is a factor—and professionals hold considerable power over information, possibilities, and outcomes of the interaction (Jenkins & Sullivan, 2011). Their power comes from real and attributed knowledge, the power of "the system," and long-held assumptions that the system cannot be critically questioned (Seligman & Darling, 2007). This has certainly been true in systems of care and education for children with disabilities and their families. Interventions in the not-so-distant past tended to focus on direct, hands-on, professional intervention with children. Parents were considered secondary in the treatment or intervention and were generally expected to follow directions dictated by professionals. Parents were provided with parent education opportunities typically designed and taught by professionals. Very often these opportunities focused on what professionals wanted parents to do rather than on what parents wanted to learn. As discussed in earlier sections of this chapter, this approach would not be considered to be family-centered.

From its inception, one of the guiding principles of a family-centered approach is empowerment (Dempsey & Keen, 2008; Dunst et al., 1988)—in other words, the skills needed to recognize family needs, find ways to get those needs met, and effectively plan and negotiate their implementation. Proactive empowerment through partnerships, described by Dunst (1985), included three tenets that emphasized 1) family strengths rather than deficits in early intervention practice; 2) family control over services rather than dependency-producing, disempowering practices; and 3) collaborative rather than professional-centered practice. These principles not only spawned considerable research but also became guiding principles in family-centered practice.

Empowerment in its most basic form is providing the tools that individuals need to gain access to services and make decisions about them. Empowerment enhances capability. To be empowered is to have the information and sense of personal competence necessary to advocate for oneself or someone else. Thus, for family–professional partnerships to flourish, balancing the power between families and professionals is critical to success. Being passionate about an issue does not necessarily empower individuals to do something about it. Empowerment often requires some coaching. Many families may need information and support to become empowered when it comes to issues involving their children. Part of the role of the professional in family-centered services is to help family members become empowered–to engage in capacity building–to ensure that families and professionals recognize that each comes to the relationship with different but equally valued knowledge and skills (Trivette et al., 2010).

Although providing the tools and support to assist family members to become empowered is a cornerstone of family-centered services, it is a concept that does not resonate equally with families across cultures. In a pilot study comparing African American and Latino mothers in Southern California with white, non-Latino parents of children with disabilities in Australia, issues of disempowerment and empowerment were clearest to the African American mothers (Hall, Lynch, Macvean, & Valverde, 2000). Many had had experience with the Civil Rights movement and were very aware of the parallels between the need to feel empowered as black women as well as mothers of children with disabilities. The Latino mothers interviewed had not had similar experiences, and empowerment and disempowerment were not terms that were familiar to them. Even when these terms were translated conceptually rather than literally, Latino mothers were less able to describe situations related to their child in which they felt a sense of competence and control rather than a sense that they had no control.

Because of the importance of issues of empowerment within a family-centered framework, cross-cultural work on empowerment needs to be pursued. Approaches to empowerment that conflict with cultural and sociocultural beliefs and approaches to interaction are, by definition, disempowering (Lynch, 2011).

Variables that Support or Interfere with Collaborative Partnerships

Professional and Family Variables In a large, national study of families and professionals, the variables that families and professionals bring to interactions were examined to determine which variables support and which hinder collaboration. Five categories and one subcategory of variables important to collaboration for both families and professionals emerged (Dinnebeil, Hale, & Rule, 1996). The categories included the following:

- Dispositions/personal and family characteristics
- Philosophical beliefs and attitudes

- Ways of working together
- Knowledge base
- Outside influences

The subcategory of putting beliefs into practice was an amalgamation of philosophical beliefs and values and ways of working together. Dispositions and characteristics were important to both family members and professionals. Being optimistic, friendly, open-minded, and caring were considered to be important traits. When the sociocultural and lifestyle match between professionals and families was missing, it was more difficult to collaborate. Philosophical beliefs and values contributed to or interfered with collaboration. Family-centered practices such as trusting, being nonjudgmental, respecting, and accepting differences contributed to effective collaboration, as did positive beliefs about disabilities. Some families thought that the professional's willingness to be involved as a friend was helpful; however, not all service coordinators felt that friendship enhanced the collaboration (in this study, the professionals were service coordinators). Ways of working together that supported collaboration included open communication, honesty, tact, establishing a positive atmosphere, and using expertise to share information and model ways of working more effectively with the child. Although the importance of the professional's knowledge base was mentioned fewer times than dispositions and philosophical beliefs, it was nonetheless considered important by family members.

Knowledge of disability, strategies, and resource information contributed to collaboration, as did cultural knowledge and the ability to communicate in the family's language. Outside influences, such as scheduling constraints, size of caseloads, limited options for service, and so forth were also identified as barriers or facilitators, when the constraints had been overcome, of collaboration. These influences were considered to

be very important to effective collaboration, but they were not considered to be under the control of families or professionals. Additional influences such as bad weather, distance from services, lack of resources, lack of transportation, and lack of opportunity for staff to be trained in collaboration were also identified. It is interesting to note that issues such as scheduling and availability of services were considered to be outside the control of professionals and parents alike. Given a model that supports empowerment, it would seem that professionals would begin by working to change the system to more satisfactorily accommodate family needs. The subcategory, putting beliefs into practice, showed that professionals "practiced what they preached." They scheduled appointments that were convenient for families, kept appointments, respected families as decision makers, and supported approaches to service that allowed families to live more normal lives.

A qualitative study by Brotherson et al. (2010) examined the extent to which parents' and professionals' emotional needs were met in an early intervention program using a home visiting model. They found that the emotional needs of both parents and professionals mutually influence the effectiveness of partnerships between parents and professionals. As in any relationship, when the emotional needs of both parties are congruent, there is greater satisfaction with the relationship. When they are not congruent, there is less satisfaction. This mismatch of emotional needs can play out in many ways when professionals and family members try to work together. In the study, researchers found that parents of children with disabilities often felt a sense of urgency and a sense of hope related to their child's disability. They urgently wanted to find answers and solutions to their child's problems, and they felt hopeful that this would occur. In most cases, these emotional needs were congruent with those of early intervention professionals. They, too, were eager to find the answers that parents wanted and felt that together they would succeed in finding answers and solutions. However, when professionals had a sense of urgency that parents did not share, professionals became frustrated because of what they perceived as parents' lack of follow-through (Brotherson et al.). As this study suggests, both professionals and parents are emotionally involved in providing services. Although professionals typically maintain some distance from the families that they serve and have boundaries that are part of their profession's code of conduct, there is always some degree of emotional involvement with each family and each family member.

A case study approach was used to determine the characteristics of professionals that lead to effective collaboration; five themes related to interpersonal interactions as well as two themes related to knowledge of children emerged (McWilliam, Tocci, & Harbin, 1998):

- Having a family orientation

- Being positive and viewing the family in a favorable light

- Sensitivity to the family

- Responsiveness or willingness to do what needs to be done

- Treating parents as friends

- Child and community skills, which included knowledge about disabilities and methods for interacting with and teaching children and integrating their work into the larger community

Although many would seek the majority of these characteristics in their search for a competent and understanding professional, the one area in which these descriptors and professional preferences may depart is in the area of friendship. Throughout a professional's career, many parents become friends, but a professional is neither trained nor encouraged in training to develop friendships with the families they serve. McWilliam et al. (1998, p. 215) acknowledged this difference in expectations and suggested that many professionals would "be more comfortable with the *friendly professional* stance than with a *professional friend*."

In a study of parents' and professionals' perspectives on services needed and services provided, professionals were enthusiastic about their family-centered practices but families reported that they were receiving less than a quarter of the services that they needed (Filer & Mahoney, 1996). Worth noting is that families rated child-level activities provided by early intervention programs as more important than family-level activities. Professionals reported substantially greater needs for service in four out of five categories than parents reported. Professionals felt that families needed 1) more information about their children and how to interpret test results, 2) additional support in preparing for the child's future and advocating for their son or daughter, 3) ways of coping with their child and getting support, and 4) assistance in finding resources or services. The findings of this study are particularly interesting because of families' emphasis on more direct assistance to the child. This certainly does not suggest that family support services are not critical to families. What it does indicate is that a truly family-centered model determines what families believe is most important and builds services on that basis. For these families, the most important support would have been more services for their children such as child care, therapies, and medical treatments.

In a small, qualitative study of the practices within home visits, Cambray-Engstrom and Salisbury (2010) found that joint interaction between the home visitor and mother led to greater participation among Latina mothers. In joint interaction, both the home visitor and mother worked with the child as partners, and the home visitor gave no explicit feedback. The researchers hypothesized that joint interaction may have provided a sense of equality in the interaction because the professional does not try to direct or influence the parent. As a result, parents may have felt comfortable participating more freely. Because the study included only 10 mothers and was limited to Latinas, the findings cannot be generalized. It may, however, provide a springboard for further research on specific practices that encourage family-centered interactions and perhaps an affirmation that the sense of parent–professional friendship is valued by some parents and families.

Program Variables   A study by Dinnebeil, Hale, and Rule (1999) that examined family and professional variables influencing collaboration also investigated program variables that support or interfere with collaboration. More collaborative programs had a philosophy and climate that supported collaboration, operated within a community context, used a team-based approach, implemented policies and procedures conducive to collaboration, and delivered services in ways that demonstrated that collaboration was valued. A subcategory was qualified personnel. Respondents frequently addressed the importance of having well-trained personnel with good communication skills. These findings suggest that program-level decisions, procedures, and processes influence the collaborative process and set the tone for developing partnerships.

The study of Latina mothers' participation during home visits suggested that joint interaction increased participation (Cambray-Engstrom & Salisbury, 2010). The researchers also suggest that the following program components were also critical to the collaboration between parents and professionals: administrative support, ongoing staff development and training, reflective practice, and an intraagency community of learning.

Synthesis   These studies provide an extensive list of professional, program, and family characteristics that support family–professional alliances. They also describe characteristics and behaviors that are not conducive to cooperation, collaboration, and partnership. It is clear that the ability to establish and participate in trusting relationships, communicate effectively, and respect families' roles and responsibilities as the ultimate decision makers for their child and family is critical. It is equally clear that possessing knowledge and skills related to children with disabilities, working within the context of the family and community, being positive and open-minded, and following through on promises contribute to effective collaboration with families. Professionals who are perceived to be dishonest with families, do not share information fully, do not respect family roles and responsibilities, display negative attitudes toward families or their job, and are not well trained for their jobs are not able to form collaborative partnerships. Though based on research, these findings are almost intuitive. In any relationship, respect, positive attitudes, and honesty are critical elements. In programs and services for families, they are essential.

Program variables also help or hinder collaboration. Even the most highly trained and experienced service provider can appear noncollaborative when working within agency policies and procedures that do not support collaboration. Putting all interactions "on the clock" in fee-for-service systems, working only during traditional hours, following required assessment protocols that minimize family input, or refusing needed services in order to underspend the budget in an effort to look good to superiors can make the most family-centered professional look bad. A family-centered professional would also use his or her skills and creativity to help change the system to make it more responsive to families and children rather than simply view the complaints as unsolvable problems, however.

In most of the literature about family–professional collaboration, the emphasis is on the characteristics of professionals and systems and how they can change to enhance family–professional collaboration. This is appropriate in that it is the job of the professional to be the collaborator, to meet families "where they are," and to support family goals and priorities—often not easy tasks. Parents and families sometimes have characteristics that interfere with collaboration and partnering. Dinnebeil et al. (1996) identified certain lifestyles, personality traits, attitudes, and a lack of communication skills as family characteristics that make collaboration extremely difficult. In a study of more than 350 families, Mahoney and Filer (1996) found that families with the most positive characteristics, such as enough time and resources, positive family functioning (cohesion, control, expressiveness), and the interpersonal skills to negotiate the system, received the most services. These findings, if they can be generalized, are not surprising, but they are troubling. They suggest that families with the greatest needs may be the least well served. Families that do not function well, those that lack the skills to navigate the system, and those that do not have the time to be involved may be in double jeopardy. They have more problems at the outset and are receiving less help in resolving them. Considering the numbers and range of families that this might include—teenage parents, families whose primary language is not English, those who are living in poverty, families with mental health problems, and families who have problems with substance abuse, addiction, and violence–the findings suggest that family–professional collaboration is far from reality in many situations.

Some data are promising, however. Unger, Jones, Park, and Tressell (2001) studied the involvement of low-income, single caregivers in an urban environment. Most of the 104 caregivers who participated were African American, lived alone, and were the biological mothers of the children being studied who were attending an early intervention program. In this study, caregivers who were stressed, had difficulties with family functioning, and were less knowledgeable about child development were more likely to become involved with the program. Their involvement was predicated on a welcoming climate and teachers' efforts to reach out to them.

No family will like every professional equally, nor will professionals resonate with each family in the same way. People respond to different characteristics in different ways. Individuals are inexplicably drawn to some people and not to others. It is the professional's responsibility to provide the same level of information, support, and energy to all families, however. For those who have worked with challenging families, the concern is usually that as professionals they have done everything they can do, but the family "continues to miss home visits," "doesn't follow through," "is so involved in their own issues that they have no time for the child," "doesn't have the skills/ability to parent effectively," "is unrealistic," or "wants everyone else to do the impossible but doesn't want to do anything themselves." All of these may be true, but it is the role of the professional to continue to meet the family "where they are" and to work to support the family and the child. When should a professional give up? The answer is never, where the child is concerned. When a professional feels that she or he may be endangered by continued interaction with the family, however, it is time for a change. Concerns about safety for the child, another family member, or oneself should be immediately reported to supervisors and any other authority or agency determined by state law and program policies.

In addition to families with limited resources, difficult circumstances, and inadequate interpersonal skills, there are families whose resources to challenge the system seem unlimited. They are often knowledgeable, articulate, and well defended (personally and with advocates and attorneys). They typically get what they ask for. For many of these families, the concerns are centered on the needs of the child and the families' willingness to go to any length to obtain what is necessary to improve functioning, opportunity, and daily life. For others, challenging systems has become a way of life. Being litigious in every interaction is one way of gaining power in a situation that one is powerless to change, such as having a child with a disability. As difficult as it is to work effectively with these families, it is essential to try and try again. If the energy that they spent fighting for their son's or daughter's needs could be used to effectively change the shortcomings of service delivery systems, they could be professionals' most important allies.

Research guides the thinking and practice of professionals. It provides data that define best and promising practices and evidence of approaches, models, and services that are effective and those that are not. It, along with professional ethics and codes of conduct, is foundational to working effectively with children and families. But there is something more. Every interaction with every family adds a little more knowledge to a professional's skills and understanding. When a professional is truly listening, families will tell you what they need and how they would like to join the partnership.

BUILDING FAMILY–PROFESSIONAL ALLIANCES

Considerable work remains in evaluating parent/caregiver involvement and family support in programs for young children who are at risk or who have special needs (Bailey, 2001). Although research continues to provide data that enables professionals to refine family-centered practices, until more comprehensive evaluation has been undertaken, professionals must rely on what is known about models and practices that support family-centered practices. Several of the studies discussed in this chapter suggest that family–professional collaboration requires more than a positive attitude or philosophy about the role of families in service delivery. Collaboration requires that these attitudes and philosophies be put into practice. This section describes promising and proven models and strategies for putting collaboration into practice.

Every interaction between a family member and a professional supports or interferes with collaboration. Whether the interaction is face to face, on the phone, in an e-mail or text, or through a form that has been mailed, it influences the likelihood of collaboration and alliance building. Therefore, interactions, procedures, and policies must be examined to determine the extent to which they facilitate collaboration or act as barriers. The systems-level issues are in some ways the easiest because they often do not require a change in personal behavior or a retooling of interpersonal skills.

Making Policies and Procedures More Family Centered

Almost all organizations have policies and procedures that are not customer friendly. Whether it is the registration process at a university, duplicate questions on health information forms, or the policies and procedures in an agency serving children and families, there is always room for improvement. One method of examining policies and procedures within programs and agencies is to invite a task force of parents to examine the policies and procedures to determine how they affect collaborative partnerships. The charge to the task force should be clear with timelines attached and should indicate that the program is committed to making its approach to services more family centered. It should also indicate that every concern identified will be considered and task force members will assist in sorting and prioritizing the concerns that they identify. In creating such a task force, it is important to remember that because it will take time and energy—time and energy that some parents may not have—there should be no pressure to accept the invitation. Developing multiple levels of involvement such as participating online, responding to a short survey, or reviewing the group's work during the process may make it easier for some parents to participate.

Staffing the task force with a professional who can act as an administrative assistant may be helpful, but it is important not to overload the group with professionals and administrators at the beginning. Those who have been involved in such groups know the temptation of administrators and program professionals to defend policies and procedures whenever they come under scrutiny. Although resolving issues jointly is a critical part of collaborating and developing alliances, identifying policies and procedures that inhibit collaboration may be something that should begin with families working together, apart from professionals, so that families will not have to work through their concerns *and* professional defensiveness.

In the second phase of the process, several professionals (including a program administrator) can join the task force. Family members should be in the majority, however. At this point, the initial charge should be restated and elaborated. The task of this expanded group is to sort and prioritize the concerns. Sorting may be done along a variety of dimensions. One approach is to sort by categories such as "can make changes internally," "requires external approval," and "cannot be changed because of regulation or law." The last category should have few, if any, items. Policies and procedures are often designed to enact law, but there are many ways to conform to law more creatively. Another approach to sorting is by the strength of families' concern. These categories might include "serious deterrent to collaboration, needs immediate attention," "needs to be changed but is not an immediate priority," and "room for improvement." Another approach to sorting and prioritizing concerns is to put issues into the component of the program that they involve. For example, problems might occur at intake, initial assessment, program planning (IFSP or IEP), intervention, progress monitoring, and transition. Although this categorization can be helpful, issues may overlap and it may place greater emphasis on child-level rather than family-level services. These approaches are simply illustrations. The group may have other ways of organizing and prioritizing concerns. The important piece is that the group develops priorities, action plans, and timelines.

In the third phase, those responsible for the action plan report periodically to the task force on their progress. Although it may ultimately be the administrator's responsibility to make changes, family members on the task force and others should be part of the process. For example, if the intake paperwork is determined to be unfriendly to families, task force members and other families should be involved in the revisions, assist in field tests of new forms, and give approval for the new and improved version.

Processes like the one described take time and energy. To be effective, the process must be authentic and result in change. Any process that is, or is perceived to be, a sham only makes matters worse. Nothing leads to the perception of deception more than filling a task force with the program's most supportive parents. Always include parents that the team would rather not include and listen carefully to what they say. Regardless of the time and energy involved, processes like this result in improved policies, procedures, and collaborative relationships. As family members gain ownership over program policies and procedures, the possibilities for partnerships and alliances increase.

Creating Parent-to-Parent Programs

Although this book focuses on professionals who work with children and families, professionals are not the only (or sometimes the best) people to work with a family. There are times when another parent with special training can provide the most support, assistance, and understanding: strategies for sharing information about your child's disabilities with neighbors, techniques for soothing a child in pain because of chronic health problems, how to have a successful trip to visit grandparents with a child with autism, or the best place to find reasonably priced clothes for a premature infant—many families face all of these issues and many more in daily life. Working on specific goals and objectives, teaching and learning from professionals, and having programs and services that provide help and support are important in the lives of most families of children with disabilities. There are, however, countless times when a conversation with another parent who has faced the same issues is more valuable than anything that professionals can offer. Other parents can often help bridge language and cultural differences in programs in which staff members are not as diverse as the communities being served. A Somalian parent, in some instances, may help another Somali family access and use services more effectively than any of the professionals on staff.

There are ways to create opportunities for parents to have access to other parents who have experienced similar joys and problems. One strategy that programs can use is to partner with community or state parent-to-parent organizations. These groups can link trained parents to novice parents face to face, on the phone, or online. Another way is to have one or more paid parents on staff. They can serve as the program's link to program and community resources. In some instances, they may even be the first point of contact with new families. In other instances, they would be available as requested or needed. Whatever strategy a program uses, having trained parents available to work with families and help professionals understand family concerns is one of the hallmarks of family-centered practice.

Encouraging Family-Centered Interactions

Changing the system is sometimes easier than changing individuals within it. Family-centered practice relies on the knowledge, interpersonal style, and commitment of the professionals who see families every day. Policies and procedures that are models of family-centered practice do not make up for the actions and interactions of a single individual who believes that families really do not know what is best for their children. Therefore, it is critical for new professionals to be well trained in family-centered principles and for veteran professionals to have opportunities to reevaluate their practices.

Focusing on What Services Families Want and Need

In 2006, a summit on the next steps in creating family-centered services was held at the Beach Center at the University of Kansas, Lawrence. The purpose of the summit was to create a vision for the future. Attendees agreed that the focus of family-centered practice had been on *how* to deliver family-centered services and not on *what* services should be available to children and families. In other words, there has been considerable attention given to the way in which professionals honor parent preferences, interact with families, establish partnerships, and so on. The emphasis has been on helping professionals develop interpersonal skills as opposed to developing the range and types of services that meet families' needs. The overriding theme of the summit was the need for the field to develop a conceptual framework of the types of services and supports that early childhood professionals should have the competence to provide and early childhood programs should have the resources to deliver (Turnbull et al., 2007). Although developing interpersonal skills should continue, the recommendation to attend to the development of needed services and the competence and resources to provide them is a critical next step in improving family-centered services.

Providing Preservice Training

Perhaps the greatest shortcoming in training programs for professionals entering family/child service fields is the lack of interaction with parents of children with disabilities. Although students typically take courses on working with families, are able to faultlessly recite the literature on family-centered practice, and have typically heard presentations by parents and other family members in their classes, few have been trained by parents or alongside parents in their classes. When such training opportunities do occur, they produce some remarkable benefits for students and parents alike (McBride, Sharp, Hains, & Whitehead, 1995; Murray & Mandell, 2006). The authors of this book have had multiple experiences that confirm the value of this model—having a parent as a facilitator in a class on working with families, having students in class who were also parents of children with disabilities, and requiring assignments that pair students with families in a nonprofessional, helping capacity. In each situation, the parent perspective increased dialogue and reflection and enhanced professional understanding. One of the most important and needed changes in preservice training is creating structures that enable faculty to align their instruction with the family-centered, interdisciplinary demands of early intervention (Stayton & Bruder, 1999).

Providing Ongoing Professional Development

Since the early 1990s, intervention programs across disciplines and throughout the country have put considerable emphasis on training staff members to be more family-centered and collaborative. Because of these efforts, changes have been made. In any profession, however, ongoing opportunities to learn, reflect on practice, develop new skills, and hone old ones are necessary. Knowledge about collaboration and alliance building is not new, and it is unlikely that anyone currently in a field that focuses on children and families has not been exposed to it. Each professional's skills in developing family–professional collaboration varies, however. Much of what is required is based on interpersonal skills, and the characteristics and behaviors that support collaborative partnerships are well documented in the research reported earlier in the chapter. Based on what is known, the following are important to effective collaborative partnerships: friendliness, optimism, patience, sincerity, open-mindedness, caring, trust, respect, commitment to the relationship, effective communication, responsiveness, willingness to share and disclose information, honesty, tact, a positive climate, flexibility, and knowledge (Dinnebeil, Hale, & Rule, 1996). Others also include empathy and an attitude of humility (Jones, Garlow, Turnbull, & Barber, 1996). The question is, can these skills and behaviors be taught? The answer is yes; these are behaviors that can be taught and learned, but what is equally important is that the underlying attitudes and beliefs exist within professionals who work with families. If that is not the case, the Japanese proverb will be affirmed: "Sooner or later you will act out what you really believe."

These characteristics and behaviors can be put into practice in every component of service delivery. They are part of getting acquainted with families and their children (intake), learning about the child as well as the family's values, strengths, and needs (assessment/diagnosis), jointly deciding on and planning services (IFSP/IEP/treatment), jointly reviewing progress and evaluating outcomes (monitoring progress), and assisting the family as they make plans for the future (transition). At every step in the intervention process, professionals have the opportunity to collaborate, form partnerships, and develop alliances with families.

PROGRAM EVALUATION AS A KEY TO FORMING FAMILY–PROFESSIONAL ALLIANCES[1]

The most thorough approach to determining the effectiveness of any program is to conduct a program evaluation. Comprehensive program evaluation involves periodic assessment preferably conducted by independent, external evaluators as well as ongoing

---

[1]The section on "Program Evaluation as a Key to Forming Family–Professional Alliances" is based on a chapter by Patrick Harrison (1995) and is used with the author's permission.

assessment by stakeholders (e.g., those who receive services, those who deliver services, agencies that work with the program, and the agency or organization that sponsors the program or services). In many settings, resources are not available for external evaluators, and the program administrator is tasked with evaluation. Perhaps the majority of evaluations conducted in settings that serve children and families focus on satisfaction: Are recipients satisfied with the services that they received? Although this is an extremely important component of evaluation, it is far from comprehensive evaluation. Comprehensive evaluation also asks questions related to implementation, resources, outcomes, philosophy and validity of practice, cost, and unplanned outcomes.

Implementation Questions

Implementation questions focus on how the program is being carried out. All programs begin with stated or unstated goals, objectives, and management plans. There is typically a target for the number of assessments that will occur, the number of children and families to be served, and the type and number of contacts such as home visits, consultations, or clinic visits. Implementation questions examine what is occurring compared to what was planned. If there are differences between the plan and reality, the evaluation seeks to determine what those differences are and why they have occurred. For example, a fully integrated, private preschool program opened 3 months ago in the community. Based on the projected need, classes should be full, but they are not. Surprised by this, the administrator decides to focus on implementation questions in her interim evaluation. In this she learns that far more families than expected have applied to send their children to the preschool. As a result, the entry assessments are behind schedule, creating a bottleneck in accepting and assigning children to classes. What appeared to be a situation in which the program was running seriously under capacity was in fact a miscalculation of the time and personnel that would be needed to make the program fully operational.

Resource Questions

Resource questions, as the name suggests, focus on the elements needed for the program or service to function effectively. Resources for programs and services for children and families typically include personnel, materials, space, equipment, supplies, transportation, insurance, and so forth. Having the necessary resources does not ensure that programs and services will be of high quality, but lacking significant resources can cause a program to be inadequate or fail. Consider a program in a remote, rural area developed to serve children with disabilities and their families. Many families live 60–80 miles from the program's center. Although home visits are the primary way in which services are delivered, the program also includes periodic center-based activities so that families can come together. The program provides a mileage stipend for families as well as breakfast and lunch. In the past, these events have been very well attended, but recently the attendance has dropped sharply. Concerned about this, the program administrator decides to conduct an evaluation of program resources to try to determine if their resource issues are part of the problem. The findings of the evaluation are clear. The attendance dropped off as the price of gas increased and the mileage stipends did not change. Many families felt that they could no longer afford the gas for the long drive. The administrator immediately increased the mileage stipend and at the next (well-attended) event asked participants if they would be interested in other ways of meeting with other families (e.g., video chats, creating a group on a social networking site). The families were not only happy about the increased stipend but several were very excited about the online opportunities.

Outcome Questions

Providing programs and services is, in itself, not enough. They must be effective, and outcome questions provide data on their effectiveness. In programs and services that are family centered, it is important to ask questions that focus on family outcomes as well as the outcomes of children being served. Are families given the opportunity to be full participants in the programs and services being offered? Are families meeting the goals that they set for themselves? In what ways are parents and families collaborative partners? These and similar questions would provide data on outcomes.

Imagine that a therapy service in the community believes that it has organized its services to be family centered, but they would like to learn how families experience their services. They conduct an evaluation of their outcomes. In addition to examining clients' progress on their speech and language, physical, and occupational therapy goals, they ask families to participate in a short interview or complete a written or online questionnaire about their perspectives on their involvement as partners in their child's therapy programs. The findings of the assessment are mixed. The majority of children seem to be making progress, but families report that they are involved in only limited ways. They are given handouts with directions for doing exercises at home and they can request therapy on a specific day of the week, although few report that their choice was honored. None reported that they had been asked what their therapy priority was. Finally, 97% of the families were satisfied with the services, but none reported that they felt an integral part of those services. The therapy program learned that their definition of family centered was far from that of the families that they served. They now have enough information to take the next step and learn what they might do to become more family centered. This is a good example of a common situation in intervention programs. Recipients of services, especially in programs for young children with disabilities, often report satisfaction with services they receive even when those services are not congruent with best practice.

Philosophy and Validity of Practice

Programs and services may satisfy families and the professionals who offer them, but they may not always reflect current knowledge, research, and best practice in the field. In ongoing programs that operate under numerous rules and regulations and many demands for service, there is seldom time to reflect on practice, review new research, and ensure that the program is doing a good job at the right thing. For programs and services to be good, they must be based on evidence that supports their validity. This is one of the most challenging forms of evaluation because it asks each person, team, and administrator to examine long-held beliefs and established practices. In essence, everything about the program or service must be open to minor or major revision.

Consider a program that has been in the community for many years. They have an excellent reputation and are very well schooled in their approach to serving children with reading problems. As part of their 25-year celebration of offering assessment and tutoring services in reading, they decide to conduct a comprehensive evaluation that includes all of the types of evaluation questions described in this section of the chapter. With one exception, the data that they collected were very positive. They learned from a review of literature on teaching reading to struggling readers that the method that they use does not result in the best outcomes. New studies of learning, the brain, and methods suggest that at least two other approaches have better results. Program staff and administrators are shocked; however, after careful scrutiny, it is clear that the evidence for the effectiveness of their approach is not there. It will be challenging in every respect, but they decide that they must retrain themselves and reorient their approach to one that is educationally valid.

Cost

Few programs and services are funded to the extent that they would like, but cost is a major consideration for administrators, legislators, and taxpayers. Evaluations of cost-effectiveness range from those that tally the expenditures for the program or various components of the program and divide by the number of individuals receiving services or the number of services provided. Cost-effectiveness and cost-benefit analyses are much more complex and have to be conducted by professionals with special expertise in that area of evaluation. At the most simplistic level, a program might want to determine the costs of providing bus transportation to its clients versus providing taxi vouchers. In determining the costs, the evaluator would need to determine the costs of purchasing or leasing buses, hiring drivers, maintaining buses, insurance, and so forth. The same kinds of calculations would be made for taxi vouchers. In addition to projected costs, the evaluation might also include other issues related to accessibility, client preference, safety, availability of taxis, and so forth. This combination of monetary and quality of service issues would help to make the decision about the kind of transportation that the program should use.

Unplanned Outcomes

One of the major questions that a program administrator, legislator, or community members may want to have answered is: What is happening as a result of this program? Although this question is less precise than those described earlier, it is an important question that may yield data about unplanned outcomes. Imagine a community that has successfully implemented a family-centered program for infants and toddlers with and without disabilities. The program has operated for over 10 years and has been so well received that the state would like to have it replicated in other communities. As part of a comprehensive evaluation that the state commissions, program description questions are included. The findings indicate that many unplanned outcomes have resulted from the integrated infant/toddler program. As a result of their experience in this program, parents have advocated for parks and recreation programs to be inclusive and serve children with and without disabilities together. A charter school has been developed that is also based on inclusive principles. Families of children with disabilities who attend the infant/toddler program and the charter school have not filed any complaints about their son or daughter's special education services whereas complaints from families in other programs have risen. Finally, in the charter school, general and special education teachers work as teams with each sharing loads and responsibilities. In other elementary schools, general and special education seem to be separate, unintegrated entities. This data suggests that the approach has resulted in many positive but unplanned outcomes.

Satisfaction

As mentioned initially, many programs and services assess the satisfaction of those that they serve. These data are valuable to both administrators and staff members and provide guidelines for improving services. As can be seen from the previous paragraphs, however, satisfaction data do not provide adequate information. In life, people often are satisfied with things that could and should be much better.

Evaluation is critical to all programs and services to ensure that they meet the standards that parents and children deserve and professionals want to provide. Evaluation data can also yield information about how family centered a program or service is. From this data, programs and services can be refined to optimize their effectiveness.

ETHICAL CONSIDERATIONS

Ethics are the principles that underpin our beliefs and behaviors. At the macro level, they help frame law and policy decisions. At the micro level, they guide daily interactions. Often referred to as moral principles, they may be grounded in religious, spiritual, legal, or utilitarian beliefs. One's personal beliefs are always consciously or unconsciously part of decision making; however, for professionals working with families, professional codes of conduct and legal requirements must supersede personal beliefs. For professionals, ethics may be thought of less as moral principles and more as core values, beliefs, and related legislation. Each professional discipline has its own ethical standards and code of conduct, but at the root of each is the phrase attributed to the Hippocratic Oath: First, do no harm. In all interactions with families, this phrase should be the starting point for assistance and intervention.

In professions that focus on working with children and families, codes of ethics often include principles such as respect for individuals, family units, and their diversity; evidence-based practice; acceptance of responsibility; advocacy; professional collaboration; family empowerment; confidentiality; and personal integrity. These, along with compliance with the law, legal mandates, and appropriate research protocols if research is being conducted, comprise the bulk of most codes for early childhood (National Association for the Education of Young Children, 2005, April), early childhood special education (Division of Early Childhood, 2009), social work (National Association of Social Workers, 2008), psychology (American Psychological Association, 2010), health and related health care professions (e.g., American Medical Association, n.d.; American Nurses Association, 2001; American Physical Therapy Association, 2011; American Speech-Language-Hearing Association, 2010; American Occupational Therapy Associations, 2010) . When professionals receive their certification, credential, or license, they agree to abide by the profession's code of ethics.

Although codes of ethics and conduct provide a framework and general guidelines, they do not always provide answers to questions that professionals may have about specific situations. The scenarios that follow illustrate some of the situations that may pose dilemmas for professionals in their work with children and families.

Bart's Family

Bart is 4 years old. He is able to read kindergarten books. He is also obsessed with spinning toys and has very limited interaction with other children and adults. Bart's parents believe that he is gifted. Bart's teacher has acknowledged his strength in reading but expressed concern about his difficulties with social interactions and his focus on spinning objects. On several occasions, she has talked with them about autism spectrum disorders and suggested that Bart be assessed to determine his needs. Bart's parents believe that his inattention at preschool, obsession with spinning toys, and limited social interactions are further evidence that he is highly gifted and bored by preschool children and class activities. Bart's preschool teacher is very fond of both Bart and his parents but feels that they are denying his problems and failing to get the kinds of services that Bart needs to make progress.

In the scenario presented in this section, Bart's teacher's ethical dilemma concerns balancing what she believes is best for Bart and her respect for the parents' perspective and opinions. She does not want to push Bart's parents, but she also wants to ensure that Bart is not being deprived of services that would be helpful to him. If you were Bart's teacher, what do you think you would do? Why?

Tyler's Colleague

Tyler's colleague, Josh, has been very late to several recent meetings at the clinic; over the past 6 weeks, he has said very little and seemed detached from clinic activities and his responsibilities. Much of the time, Josh just does not seem to be paying attention. Typically very neat and tailored, Josh has frequently appeared disheveled in recent weeks. Yesterday, Tyler had some private time with Josh. Over coffee, Tyler mentioned that lately Josh had seemed preoccupied and wondered whether there was anything that he could do. Josh became defensive and claimed to be fine.

Tyler's ethical dilemma is whether or not he should share his concerns about Josh with their supervisor. Although he does not want to cause any problems for Josh, he also does not want to ignore something that could be serious for Josh and the clinic. If you were Tyler, what would you do? Why?

Shanoor's Family

Shanoor Akwal is 6 months old, a premature infant who is slowly beginning to grow and thrive. She and her family participate in an early intervention program for children who are at risk or have disabilities. During home visits, Shanoor's father confers with his wife in Arabic about Shanoor's care and then relates her responses to the home visitor. Shanoor's mother understands and can speak English, but she does not comment during the visits. The home visitor can see Shanoor's mother's interest in everything that they discuss, and she feels that the program's parenting program would be a wonderful experience for both Shanoor and her mother. On the last home visit, she mentioned the program and suggested that they attend. Without conferring with his wife, Mr. Akwal said that she could not attend. The home visitor let it pass but came back to the program later in the visit. Again, Mr. Akwal said no. The home visitor thought that Mrs. Akwal seemed very interested in the idea but, as usual, she did not comment.

The home visitor's dilemma is related to cultural issues. The home visitor is aware that the Akwals are traditional Muslims and that Mr. Akwal's refusal to allow Mrs. Akwal and Shanoor to attend the parenting program is probably related to their beliefs. As an early interventionist and feminist, she really wants Mrs. Akwal to attend. On the other hand, she recognizes that it is not her place to interfere with the family's practices. What would you do if you were the home visitor? Why?

There are multiple approaches to resolving ethical dilemmas (Berkeley & Ludlow, 2008; Brophy-Herb, Kostelnik, & Stein, 2001; Sileo & Prater, 2012). Regardless of the approach selected, one must identify the ethical issue or concern, determine how the professional code of conduct relates to the issue, consider the perspectives of all of those involved, select a course of action, take action, and assume responsibility for actions taken. One of the most challenging aspects of ethical practice is separating one's own moral code from the code of ethics that applies to the workplace. As in the last scenario, a professional may take a very strong stand for women's rights in her or his personal and political life. That stand, however, may not be ethical when working with a family whose perspective on male and female roles differs from the interventionists.

In addition to ethics, there are laws that govern professional practice. States differ in their legislation and its interpretation, but it is critical for professionals to understand their professional obligations under the law. Reporting of child abuse is probably the most common law that affects many professionals. When child abuse or neglect is suspected, professionals are typically subject to mandatory reporting requirements. It is incumbent upon all professionals and the programs and agencies that employ them to have clear procedures for responding to legislated requirements.

Ethical practice is the right of every child, family, and individual that receives services and the obligation of those who provide those programs and services. Although resolving ethical dilemmas is not always as clear cut as other aspects of practice or problem solving, it can be and is done on a daily basis. Being aware of the parameters of ethical practice is the first step in achieving it.

SUMMARY

Family-centered services and creating family–professional alliances is one of the goals of programs that serve families and their children who are at risk for or have disabilities. Increasingly, it is also a goal of programs serving children and families in which disability is not an issue. Collaborative partnerships between families and professionals require mutual respect, trust, and the ability to agree on and pursue mutual goals. Family-centered services, a hallmark of quality services for children and their families, provide a first step toward family–professional collaboration and partnership. Its principles include the following:

1. Recognizing the parents or primary caregivers as experts on their child

2. Acknowledging the family as the ultimate decision maker for their child and themselves

3. Viewing the family as the constant in the child's life and the service providers and systems as transitory

4. Respecting and working toward supporting family priorities, goals for service, and their choice in involvement

5. Valuing trusting, collaborative relationships between parents and professionals

6. Working toward ensuring culturally competent services

Although considerable work has been done to realize the goal of family-centered practice, the goal has not been universally achieved. Making policies, procedures, and interactions more family friendly all contribute to more family-centered services. So, too, does a greater emphasis on family-centered approaches in preservice training and staff development. Program evaluation is a key tool in determining program effectiveness. In addition to assessing how family-centered a program or service is, comprehensive evaluations can provide data on all aspects of the program's functioning and performance. The information can then be used to highlight areas of strength and strengthen weaker components. A comprehensive program evaluation can provide information about services that need to be developed as well as about the unexpected outcomes of existing services. To be of high quality, programs and services must be grounded in ethical practice with guidelines provided by each discipline's code of conduct. Applying ethical principles as well as laws governing practice is the responsibility of every professional and every program and service.

ACTIVITIES TO EXTEND THE DISCUSSION

1. **Think about the last time that you visited a physician, registered for class, or applied for some service for yourself or a family member.** Write down a few words that describe the experience. Were there any aspects of the process that made it family centered (or perhaps consumer or client friendly)? What were they? What could have been done differently to make it easier for you as a client to use the service? Make a list of those things and share it with others in your group.

2. **Imagine that you were asked to give a presentation on family-centered practice.** How would you define it? What are some of its characteristics? Why would you say that it is important? Provide at least three illustrations of family-centered practices in an educational, social service, or medical/allied health setting.

3. **Think of a program or service that you are familiar with.** Develop an evaluation question for each of the components of a comprehensive evaluation.

4. **Find the code of ethics and/or the code of professional conduct for your profession or discipline or the one that you are studying for.** Review the code(s) and discuss them in relation to the code(s) of another professional discipline. What are the major differences? What are the major similarities?

TO LEARN MORE: SUGGESTED WEB SITES

The Beach Center on Families and Disability
http://www.beachcenter.org

Family Voices
http://www.familyvoices.org

The National Early Childhood Technical Assistance Center
http://www.nectac.org

National Parent Technical Assistance Center
http://www.parentcenternetwork.org

REFERENCES

Able-Boone, H., Sandall, S.R., & Frederick, L.L. (1990). An informed, family-centered approach to public law 99-457: Parental views. *Topics in Early Childhood Special Education, 10(1),* 100–111.

American Medical Association. (n.d.). *AMA's code of medical ethics.* Retrieved July 20, 2012, from http://www.ama-assn.org/ama/pub/physician-resources/medical-ethics/code-medical-ethics.page

American Nurses Association. (2001). *Code of ethics for nurses.* Retrieved July 20, 2012, from http://nursingworld.org/MainMenuCategories/ThePracticeofProfessionalNursing/EthicsStandards/CodeofEthics.aspx

American Physical Therapy Association. (2011). *Core ethics documents.* Retrieved July 20, 2012, from http://www.apta.org/Ethics/Core/

American Psychological Association. (2010). Ethical principles of psychologists and code of conduct: 2010 amendments. Retrieved July 20, 2012, from http://www.apa.org/ethics/code/index.aspx

American Speech-Language-Hearing Association. (2010). *Code of ethics.* Retrieved August 6, 2012, from http://www.asha.org/docs/html/ET2010-00309.html

Bailey, D.B. (2001). Evaluating parent involvement and family support in early intervention and preschool programs. *Journal of Early Intervention, 24,* 1–14.

Bailey, D.B., Raspa, M., & Fox, L.C. (2012). What is the future of family outcomes and family-centered services? *Topics in Early Childhood Special Education, 31*(4), 216-223.

Bailey, D.B., Simeonsson, R.J., Winton, P.J., Huntington, G.S., Comfort, M., Isbell, P., et al. (1986). Family focused early intervention: A functional model for planning, implementing, and evaluating individualized services in early intervention. *Journal of the Division for Early Childhood, 10*(2), 156–171.

Baird, S. (1997). Seeking a comfortable fit between family-centered philosophy and infant-parent interaction in early intervention: Time for a paradigm shift? *Topics in Early Childhood Special Education, 17,* 139–164.

Berkeley, T.R., & Ludlow, B.L. (2008). Ethical dilemmas in rural special education: A call for a conversation about the ethics of practice. *Rural Special Education Quarterly, 27*(1/2), 3–9.

Bernheimer, L., & Weisner, T. (2007). "Let me tell you what I do all day . . . : The family story at the center of intervention research and practice. *Infants & Young Children, 20,* 192–201.

Bronfenbrenner, U. (1975). Is early intervention effective? In B.Z. Friedlander, G.M. Sterritt, & G.E. Kirk (Eds.), *Exceptional infant: Vol. 3. Assessment and intervention* (pp. 449–475). New York, NY: Brunner/Mazel.

Brophy-Herb, H.E., Kostelnik, M.J., & Stein, L.C. (2001). A developmental approach to teaching about ethics. *Young Children, 56*(1), 80–84.

Brotherson, M.J., Summers, J.A., Naig, L.A., Kyzar, K., Friend, A., Epley, P., et al. (2010). Partnership patterns: Addressing emotional needs in early intervention. *Topics in Early Childhood Special Education, 30*(10) 32–45.

Bruder, M.B. (2000). Family-centered early intervention: Clarifying our values for the new millennium. *Topics in Early Childhood Special Education, 20,* 105–115.

Cambray-Engstrom, E., & Salisbury, C. (2010). An exploratory case study of providers' collaborative consultation practices with Latina mothers during home visits. *Infants & Young Children, 23,* 262–274.

Dempsey, I., & Keen, D. (2008). A review of processes and outcomes in family-centered services for children with a disability. *Topics in Early Childhood Special Education, 28*(1), 42–52.

Dinnebeil, L.A., Hale, L.M., & Rule, S. (1996). A qualitative analysis of parents' and service coordinators' descriptions of variables that influence collaborative relationships. *Topics in Early Childhood Special Education, 16,* 322–347.

Dinnebeil, L.A., Hale, L.M., & Rule, S. (1999). Early intervention program practices that support collaboration. *Topics in Early Childhood Special Education, 19,* 225–235.

Division of Early Childhood. (2009). *Code of ethics.* Retrieved July 20, 2012, from http://www.dec-sped.org/uploads/docs/about_dec/position_concept_papers/Code%20of%20Ethics_updated_Aug2009.pdf

Dunst, C.J. (1985). Rethinking early intervention. *Analysis and Intervention in Developmental Disabilities, 5,* 165–201.

Dunst, C.J. (1999). Placing parent education in conceptual and empirical context. *Topics in Early Childhood Special Education, 19,*141–147.

Dunst, C.J., Trivette, C., & Deal, A. (1988). *Enabling and empowering families: Principles and guidelines for practice.* Cambridge, MA: Brookline Books.

Dunst, C.J., Trivette, C.M., & Jodry, W. (1997). Influences of social support on children with disabilities and their families. In M.J. Guralnick (Ed.), *The effectiveness of early intervention* (pp. 499–522). Baltimore, MD: Paul H. Brookes Publishing Co.

Dunst, C.J., Trivette, C.M., Starnes, A.L., Hamby, D.W., & Gordon, N.J. (1993). *Building and evaluating family support initiatives: A national study of programs for persons with developmental disabilities.* Baltimore, MD: Paul H. Brookes Publishing Co.

Education of the Handicapped Act Amendments of 1986, PL 99-457, 20 U.S.C. §§ 1400 *et seq.*

Epley, P., Gotto IV, G.S., Summers, J.A., Brotherson, M.J., Turnbull, A.P., & Friend, A. (2010). Supporting families of young children with disabilities: Examining the role of administrative structures. *Topics in Early Childhood Special Education, 30*(1), 20–31.

Filer, J.D., & Mahoney, G.J. (1996). Collaboration between families and early intervention service providers. *Infants and Young Children, 9*(2), 22–30.

Hall, L.J., Lynch, E.W., Macvean, M.L., & Valverde, A. (2000, December). *Parent empowerment through early intervention and collaborative research.* Poster presented at the Division of Early Childhood's 15th Annual International Early Childhood Conference on Children with Special Needs, Albuquerque, NM.

Hanson, M.J. (1996). Early intervention: Models and practices. In M.J. Hanson (Ed.), *Typical and atypical development* (2nd ed., pp. 451–476). Austin, TX: PRO-ED.

Hanson, M.J., & Lynch, E.W. (1995). *Early intervention: Implementing child and family services for infants and toddlers who are at risk or disabled* (2nd ed.). Austin, TX: PRO-ED.

Harrison, P.J. (1995). Evaluating programs. In M.J. Hanson & E.W. Lynch (Eds.), *Early intervention: Implementing child and family services for infants and toddlers who are at risk or disabled* (2nd ed., pp. 288–322). Austin, TX: PRO-ED.

Harry, B. (2010). *Melanie, bird with a broken wing: A mother's story.* Baltimore, MD: Paul H. Brookes Publishing Co.

Hauser-Cram, P., Upshur, C.C., Krauss, M.W., & Shonkoff, J.P. (1988). Implications of Public Law 99-457 for early intervention services for infants and toddlers with disabilities. *Social Policy Report, 3*(3), 1–16.

Hobbs, N. (1975). *The future of children.* San Francisco, CA: Jossey-Bass.

Hobbs, N., Dokecki, P., Hoover-Dempsey, K., Moroney, R., Shayne, M., & Weeks, K. (1984). *Strengthening families.* San Francisco, CA: Jossey-Bass.

Individuals with Disabilities Education Act (IDEA) Amendments of 1997, PL 105-17, 20 U.S.C. §§ 1400 *et seq.*

Individuals with Disabilities Education Act (IDEA) 2004, PL 108-446, 20 U.S.C. §§ 1400 *et seq.*

Jenkins, L.A., & Sullivan, M.B. (2011). Professionals and families: Partners in care. In G.L. Ensher & D.A. Clark, *Relationship-centered practices in early childhood* (pp. 185–210). Baltimore, MD: Paul H. Brookes Publishing Co.

Jones, T.M., Garlow, J.A., Turnbull, H.R., & Barber, P.A. (1996). Family empowerment in a family support program. In G.H.S. Singer, L.E. Powers, & A.L. Olson (Eds.), *Redefining family support: Innovations in public-private partnerships* (pp. 87–112). Baltimore, MD: Paul H. Brookes Publishing Co.

Krahn, F.L., Thom, V.A., Hale, B.J., & Williams, K. (1995). Running on empty: A look at burnout in early intervention professionals. *Infants and Young Children, 7*(4), 1–11.

Lynch, E.W. (2011). Conceptual framework: From culture shock to cultural learning. In E.W. Lynch & M.J. Hanson (Eds.), *Developing cross-cultural competence: A guide for working with children and families* (4th ed., pp. 20–40). Baltimore, MD: Paul H. Brookes Publishing Co.

Lynch, E.W., & Hanson, M.J. (Eds.). (2011). *Developing cross-cultural competence: A guide for working with children and families* (4th ed.). Baltimore, MD: Paul H. Brookes Publishing Co.

Mahoney, G., & Filer, J. (1996). How responsive is early intervention to the priorities and needs of families? *Topics in Early Childhood Special Education, 16,* 437–457.

McBride, S.L., Sharp, L., Hains, A.H., & Whitehead, A. (1995). Parents as co-instructors in preservice training: A pathway to family-centered practice. *Journal of Early Intervention, 19,* 343–389.

McCollum, J.A. (2000). Taking the past along: Reflecting on our identity as a discipline. *Topics in Early Childhood Special Education, 20,* 79–86.

McDonald, G.S. (1978). Patents' home ground. In S.L. Brown & M.S. Moersch (Eds.), *Parents on the team* (pp. 123–127). Ann Arbor, MI: University of Michigan Press.

McWilliam, R.A., Tocci, L., & Harbin, G. (1998). Family-centered services: Service providers' discourse and behavior. *Topics in Early Childhood Special Education, 18,* 206–221.

Meyer, D.J. (1993). Lessons learned–cognitive coping strategies of overlooked family members. In A.P. Turnbull, J.M. Patterson, S.K. Behr, D.L. Murphy, J.G. Marquis, & M.J. Blue-Banning (Eds.), *Cognitive coping, families, and disability* (pp. 81–93). Baltimore, MD: Paul H. Brookes Publishing Co.

Murray, M.M., & Mandell, C.J. (2006). On-the-job practices of early childhood special education providers trained in family-centered practices. *Journal of Early Intervention, 28*(2), 125–138.

National Association for the Education of Young Children. (2005). *NAEYC Code of ethical conduct and statement of commitment.* Retrieved July 20, 2012, from http://www.naeyc.org/files/naeyc/file/positions/PSETH05.pdf

National Association of Social Workers. (2008). *Code of ethics of the national association of social workers.* Retrieved July 20, 2012, from http://www.socialworkers.org/pubs/code/code.asp

Sandall, S., Hemmeter, M.L., Smith, B.J., & McLean, M.E. (2005). *DEC recommended practices: A comprehensive guide for practical application* (2nd ed.). Longman, CO: Sopris West.

Santelli, B., Poyadue, F.S., & Young, J.L. (2001). *The parent to parent handbook: Connecting families of children with special needs.* Baltimore, MD: Paul H. Brookes Publishing Co.

Santelli, B., Turnbull, A.P., Lerner, E., & Marquis, J. (1993). Parent to parent programs–a unique form of mutual support for families of persons with disabilities. In G.H.S. Singer & L.E. Powers (Eds.), *Families, disability, and empowerment: Active coping skills and strategies for family interventions* (pp. 27–57). Baltimore, MD: Paul H. Brookes Publishing Co.

Santelli, B., Turnbull, A., Sergeant, J., Lerner, E.P., & Marquis, J.G. (1996). Parent to parent programs: Parent preferences for support. *Infants and Young Children, 9*(1), 53–62.

Seligman, M., & Darling, R.B. (2007). *Ordinary families, special children* (3rd ed.). New York, NY: Guilford Press.

Sileo, N.M., & Prater, M.A. (2012). *Working with families of children with special needs: Family and professional partnerships and roles.* Boston, MA: Pearson.

Simons, R. (1987). *After the tears: Parents talk about raising a child with a disability.* New York, NY: Harcourt Brace Jovanovich.

Singer, G.H.S., & Powers, L.E. (1993). Contributing to resilience in families. In G.H.S. Singer & L.E. Powers (Eds.), *Families, disability, and empowerment: Active coping strategies for family interventions* (pp. 1–25). Baltimore, MD: Paul H. Brookes Publishing Co.

Singer, G.H.S., Marquis, J., Powers, L.K., Blanchard, L., Divenere, N., Santelli, B., et al. (1999). A multi-site evaluation of parent to parent programs for parents of children with disabilities. *Journal of Early Intervention, 22,* 217–229.

Stayton, V., & Bruder, M.B. (1999). Early intervention personnel preparation for the new millennium: Early childhood special education. *Infants and Young Children, 12*(1), 59–69.

Summers, J.A., Dell'Oliver, C., Turnbull, A.P., Benson, H.A., Santelli, E., Campbell, M., et al. (1990). Examining the individualized family service plan process: What are family and practitioner preferences? *Topics in Early Childhood Special Education, 10*(1), 78–99.

The American Occupational Therapy Associations. (2010). *New occupational therapy code of ethics and ethics standards (2010).* Retrieved July 20, 2012, from http://www.aota.org/News/AOTANews/Code.aspx

Trivette, C.M., Dunst, C.J., & Hamby, D.W. (2010). Influences of family-systems intervention practices on parent-child interactions and child development. *Topics in Early Childhood Special Education, 30*(1), 3–19.

Turnbull, A.P., Patterson, J.M., Behr, S.K., Murphy, D.L., Marquis, J.G., & Blue-Banning, M.J. (Eds.). (1993). *Cognitive coping, families, and disability.* Baltimore, MD: Paul H. Brookes Publishing Co.

Turnbull, A.P., Summers, J.A., & Brotherson, M.J. (1984). *Working with families with disabled members: A family systems approach.* Lawrence, KS: University of Kansas.

Turnbull, A.P., Summers, J.A., Turnbull, R., Brotherson, M.J., Winton, P., Roberts, R., et al. (2007). Family supports and services in early intervention: A bold vision. *Journal of Early Intervention, 29*(3), 187–206.

Turnbull, A.P., & Turnbull, H.R. (1993). Participatory research on cognitive coping: From concepts to research planning. In A.P. Turnbull, J.M. Patterson, S.K. Behr, D.L. Murphy, J.G. Marquis, & M.J. Blue-Banning (Eds.), *Cognitive coping, families, and disability* (pp. 1–14). Baltimore, MD: Paul H. Brookes Publishing Co.

Turnbull, A.P., & Turnbull, R. (2001). *Families, professionals, and exceptionality* (4th ed.). New York, NY: Prentice Hall.

Turnbull, K. (2009). *Transcript of eulogy by Kate Turnbull.* Retrieved July 20, 2012, from http://www.beachcenter.org/in_memory _of_jay_turnbull/eulogy_by_kate_turnbull .aspx

Unger, D.G., Jones, W.C., Park, E., & Tressell, P.A. (2001). Promoting involvement between low-income single caregivers and urban early intervention programs. *Topics in Early Childhood Special Education, 21,*197–212.

Vacca, J., & Feinberg, E. (2000). Why can't families be more like us? Henry Higgins confronts Eliza Doolittle in the world of early intervention. *Infants and Young Children, 13*(1), 40–48.

Communicating and Collaborating with Families

Marci J. Hanson

"Seek first to understand, then to be understood."

—S.R. Covey (1989, p. 235)

"The biggest mistake is believing there is one right way to listen, to talk, to have a conversation . . . or a relationship."

—Deborah Tannen (1990, p. 297)

"When the trust account is high, communication is easy, instant, and effective."

—S.R. Covey (1989, p. 188)

"Clapping with the right hand only will not produce a noise."

—Malay proverb

Communication is an essential aspect of human existence. *Effective* communication is fundamental to building relationships with others and to advancing understanding among individuals. You are invited to pause for a moment to reflect on the role of communication in your daily interactions. Imagine your daily routines and consider the many interactions that occur with other human beings. Think back through the events of yesterday or those of today. In reviewing the day, certain interactions will come to the fore—usually those that were particularly gratifying or those that left feelings of anger or distress. Maybe you became agitated when your co-worker did not come to a meeting on time and expected you to take on the majority of the task at hand. Perhaps the grocery clerk was surly. Conversely, maybe a neighbor noticed that your dog had gotten loose and brought it back to you or someone paid you a compliment on your appearance. Each one of these daily, routine interactions and how you chose to respond had an impact on your feelings and behavior. Cumulatively, they added up and left you with a perception of having had a good day or a bad day. So many human interactions occur throughout the day that their impact may escape notice, but each

233

interaction is a transaction and has a ripple effect. Each interaction influences—and is influenced by—how you behave and feel.

Families of children with disabilities, chronic health disorders, social service needs, and other special needs are thrust into even more interactions than those encountered in most individuals' daily routines. The children's conditions and families' needs place these families in contact with a variety of support and service personnel, often from varying disciplines or agencies. The appointment calendars for these families often rival those of the busiest executives in large corporations. Many of these interactions may be emotionally draining due to the type and magnitude of the service needs.

The communications and the relationships that families and service providers have with one another often will dictate the effectiveness of the services. The process or way in which services are provided, in most cases, may be as important as the actual services provided. The roles and styles of service delivery are particularly compelling for those individuals who work in the helping professions. Professional approaches can determine if the service providers are part of the problem or part of the solution for families. To achieve the family-focused service approaches advocated in this book, each individual must make a commitment and concerted effort to develop effective working partnerships with families and engage in supportive interactions that are sensitive and respectful of the preferences and beliefs of the families being served. Although most professionals have the best intentions in their work with families, some strategies or processes are more promising than others in building true partnerships or alliances.

This chapter builds on the discussion of effective roles and relationships advanced in previous chapters. It describes strategies and applied practices that can lead to more satisfying and effective communication and relationships between professionals and families. All facets of service delivery necessitate effective working relationships or partnerships between professionals and family members built on effective communication and collaboration. From the first contact that a parent has with a care provider or a service agency to the actual implementation and evaluation of services and subsequent transition from that service environment, effective communications and relationships will be the key to positive outcomes. At every step along the service continuum, family–professional partnerships and effective communication will enhance the journey for both parents and professionals.

APPLYING PRINCIPLES OF FAMILY SUPPORT

Descriptions of family-focused services are not new, nor are recommendations for implementation. One primary model is the framework offered by Dunst, Trivette, and Deal (1994) that describes principles of family support. Based on a review of the literature and their own research, they identified six principles used to describe policies, practices, and personnel beliefs and behaviors that are conducive to family-centered service and support. These principles form the basis for structuring effective communication and collaboration.

First, service delivery approaches should *enhance a sense of community*. Such efforts support the interdependence and reciprocal exchanges among members of the community. This sense of community can serve to increase the range of supports and resources that are available to families within environments that are appropriate and meaningful to them. The notion of community is a personal one; thus, this approach increases the likelihood that the services and supports within the community will be better matched to the family's values, cultural background, and preferences.

Efforts should focus on *mobilizing resources and supports to build and activate informal social support* networks in ways that are responsive to the individual needs of families. This principle acknowledges that families bring a wealth of resources and personal support networks, such as other family members, friends, and neighbors. More optimal services systems recognize and capitalize on these meaningful and natural supports rather than create a system of dependency on more formalized services.

Third, *shared responsibility and collaboration* should characterize family support services. Roles and relationships that are mutually agreed on by the family members and professionals define collaborative partnerships. These relationships differ from the traditional roles of case manager and client that often have dominated in the field.

Fourth, supportive services should be concerned with *protecting family integrity*. On the one hand, the unique cultural and personal characteristics of the family must be preserved and respected. On the other hand, resources must be offered that serve to enhance healthy family relationships and family functioning.

Next, supportive services should be aimed at *strengthening family functioning by building on family strengths* and promoting practices that allow families to develop and demonstrate their own competencies and capabilities. This focus is in sharp contrast to the approach of prescribing services, correcting weaknesses, or attempting to "fix" child and family concerns. Emphasis is placed on the resources and capabilities that families have available to them even though they may be unconventional in some instances from the perspective of the service provider.

Finally, proactive human service practices should serve to *prevent risk conditions and promote healthy and positive family functioning*. Again, the central feature is emphasizing family strengths and supporting families to develop their capabilities.

Personal Actions that Promote Family-Centered Practices

What behaviors or personal actions can service providers take to enhance the likelihood that their services will be more family friendly and family centered? This section outlines nine family-friendly strategies that every family service provider can put into practice in every interaction with families.

Respect Family Values, Beliefs, and Practices   Each family has a unique set of routines and rituals that characterize their style of living. The family's culture, their history, their ancestry, the family's spiritual beliefs, their socioeconomic status, the opportunities they have, and their place of residence all reflect and influence family practices. In the course of service delivery, practitioners will encounter families whose values, practices, and styles differ—sometimes even radically—from their own. Despite the fact that some practices may feel strange or at odds with the belief of the professional, only when providers truly respect different families' perspectives can they effectively enter into a working relationship and overcome differences or conflicts.

Trust that the Family Knows Best   Service providers must trust that the family knows best about what is needed for their child and their family. Clearly, in the case of families in which neglectful or abusive practices occur, the practitioner must intervene on behalf of the safety of the child. In most cases, however, families are doing their best. Professionals are in their lives for what may seem only a flash in time, while the family must adjust and adapt to the many facets and circumstances encountered by all of the family members and across all the events of their lives over time.

Be Sensitive to Diverse Backgrounds   Be sensitive to and supportive of the needs of families from diverse cultural, linguistic, and socioeconomic backgrounds. Review your daily routine again as you did at the outset of this chapter. Only this time, pretend that you are transported to another country where you are less familiar with the customs, the services, and the regulations. In addition to this unfamiliarity, imagine that you do not speak the language fluently. Alternatively, in another scenario, imagine, as best you can, what it would be like to be homeless and not have access to even the most basic survival needs such as food and warm clothing. These are the situations in which many families find themselves as they try to thrive and procure services for their children and families. The jargon and policies associated with IEPs, IFSPs, and medical services are foreign to most individuals; these terms are likely to be even more perplexing to someone who is a recent immigrant to this country and speaks a language other than English or who has no concept of what these services entail. In some cases and for some families, the service options may even violate cultural preferences or practices, such as engaging in interactions with strangers in places outside of the home. Furthermore, families struggling to survive day to day may have more critical or urgent priorities than providing education or related services for their children.

Acknowledge Family Members as Decision Makers   Regardless of the situation and of professionals' judgments about what families need, family members are the ultimate decision makers regarding their priorities and life choices. Practitioners can support family members in this process by ensuring that they have access to resources and information, are full partners and participants in service decisions, and are provided the supports that they need to make informed choices. The acknowledgment of families as decision makers also means that one must respect the choices and decisions that they make even when these choices are difficult for providers to understand or accept.

Treat the Family Members as People First   Practitioners from the helping professions are trained to focus on a particular dimension of the individual or family. It may be the child's motor, speech, or cognitive development or the social support services needed by the family. Regardless, the child and family members are people first. They are not cases, nor are they defined by their service needs, their disabilities or health conditions, or their living circumstances. They are not problems waiting to be fixed.

Recognize that You Are a Guest in the Family's Home and Life   Family members are involved with each other for the long haul. Professionals participate for only a short time in their lives and they are guests for that period of time. It is a privilege not to be taken lightly. Whether the service is needed for an extended period or a short time, service providers often come into a family's home on a regular basis and are sometimes privy to individual family member's intimate feelings and routines. This invitation into families' lives carries heavy responsibility for maintaining confidentiality and a respectful presence.

Maintain Appropriate Boundaries   When building partnerships with families, most people would agree that a warm and positive relationship is valued. Professional boundaries must be maintained, however. A breach of conduct may interfere with the family's ability to develop a natural support system or make their own decisions. Reflective practice and consultation with other team members and supervisors can be useful in preventing blurred boundaries and difficult situations. A family, for example, may request or come to rely on the professional to find needed services such as housing, food stamps, or health care. Some families may even expect the helping professional to be on call to drive them to appointments or care for the children. Families may have crucial needs for these services. However, the professional will not always be available or able to obtain services, nor are these appropriate activities for the professional in some cases. Rather than fostering a long-term dependency, when the professional helps families acquire the strategies and supports that they can use to advocate for and obtain the services they need, it is likely that the family will use these skills at other times and in other places. Family members are more likely to feel competent about their own abilities and develop skills to effect change and advocate on behalf of the family.

Be Flexible   Given that families are characterized by a broad array of sizes, groupings, and dynamics and have a myriad of needs and goals, flexibility is a hallmark of the helping professions. As previously discussed, families are highly dynamic systems with their needs and perspectives constantly shifting. Service delivery structures and approaches must be able to adapt and adjust to these changing demands. For instance, during a crisis one family may prefer to have intensive supports, whereas another may prefer to be left alone to cope with the issue within the family. Some individuals may prefer frequent opportunities to speak with professionals supplemented by written materials as the optimal method for learning strategies and information about the child's needs. Other family members may prefer less frequent or less structured approaches or they may best acquire new strategies through listening to other parents or professionals tell stories or through observing others.

Enjoy the Children and Families   Service providers are indeed fortunate that they are welcomed into the lives of a variety of families. It is a privilege. At the least, it is a

wondrous education; at the most, it is an opportunity for personal growth in understanding, knowledge, and skills. For many family members, particularly when practitioners are involved in interventions in a child's early years, the service provider will
hold a special place of respect and honor in their hearts for years to come. Often the
professional will be in the position of offering special support or lending a helping hand
at a particularly emotional or difficult transition in the family's life. The opportunity to
engage at this level and in this type of relationship can bring joy and fulfillment to the
service providers as well as to the families.

ESTABLISHING RELATIONSHIPS

The relationship between the service provider and the family forms the foundation for
intervention practices (Dunst, Trivette, & Deal, 1994; McGonigel, 1991). It has been
argued that this relationship is fundamental to the outcome of intervention regardless
of the professional discipline: "The success of all interventions will rest on the quality of
the provider-family relationships, even when the relationship itself is not the focus of the
intervention" (Kalmanson & Seligman, 1992, p. 48).

There is no recipe or cookie-cutter approach to establishing relationships with others. In fact, one of the challenges that service providers face is tailoring their practices
to individualize services and relate to children and families in the moment. The family
is a dynamic system comprised of individuals with their needs and focus constantly
changing with every demand and across time. Each family will present different styles
and preferences for type of interaction and communication. The family's characteristics and life cycle also will influence the type of relationship and style of interaction
that develops.

Definition and Characteristics of Partnerships

Dunst and Paget (1991, p. 29) suggested an operational definition of a parent–professional
partnership—an association between families and professionals who "function collaboratively using agreed on roles in pursuit of a joint interest or common goal." Characteristics of partnerships include beliefs, attitudes, communicative style, and behavioral
actions (Dunst, Trivette, & Johanson, 1994). Beliefs are defined as the attributions about
how one should behave toward others, and attitudes are the emotional feeling states
about people, situations, or relationships. Communicative style refers to the methods
and modes of exchanging or sharing information among partners, in other words, how
information is given and received. Behavioral actions refer to the translation of attitudes
and beliefs into action.

Dunst, Trivette, and Johanson (1994) described optimal parent–professional partnerships as those that embrace effective helping through empowerment and enablement
of families so that families accomplish their own goals and demonstrate competence.
Professional beliefs that contribute to this approach are mutual respect, trust, honesty,
nonjudgmental and accepting perspectives, and the presumption of capabilities. Attitudes that are confident, warm and caring, understanding, and empathetic are more apt
to foster this approach. With respect to communicative styles, those that reflect openness, active listening, disclosure, and information sharing are most likely to contribute to
these partnerships. Finally, these beliefs and attitudes are manifest behaviorally through
services that are flexible, open, reciprocal, and respectful and those that are characterized by problem solving, humor, shared responsibility, and mutual support.

Stages or Phases of Partnerships

The dynamic qualities and the evolving nature of family–professional relationships have been noted in the clinical literature (Walker & Singer, 1993). The working relationship is not a fixed phenomenon that is established prior to the onset of services, but rather it is a changing and developing progression characterized by ups and downs as in any relationship. The process of establishing family–professional relationships has been described as occurring in stages or phases (Beckman, Newcomb, Frank, & Brown, 1996; Walker & Singer; Wasik, Bryant, & Lyons, 1990).

Phase 1: Getting Acquainted   In the initial phase, the foundations of trust and rapport are established. During this phase of getting acquainted, families and professionals exchange information. With some families, this phase will occur quickly; for others, it will develop over a prolonged period of time depending on the comfort of the family, characteristics of the service provider, match between the provider and family, issues of immediate concern to the family, and other external events. This exchange may occur in the formal setting of a service agency or it may involve a home visit. Families may invite the professional to share in a cup of tea or meal or even a walk around the garden as a means for getting to know one another and develop a level of comfort before exchanging information.

Phase 2: Exploration   The second phase, the exploration phase, typically continues the discussion of resources and services. The need to listen carefully to families is particularly crucial. Initial goals for intervention are explored and developed. The development of trust between the service provider and families is often a major focus at this stage.

Phase 3: Collaboration   During the collaboration phase, agreed-on intervention goals and procedures are implemented and continually monitored to meet child and family needs. As with all phases, the service provider must be attentive to the differences among family members in terms of their priorities and concerns and their preferences for types, frequency, or intensity of services.

Phase 4: Closure   The final phase, closure, is often overlooked. The end of the working relationship may occur for a variety of reasons—the child "graduates" to the next level of service or a new environment, the family relocates, the child or family no longer needs or desires services, and so forth. During this stage, the service provider and family end their working relationship. This can be difficult for both parties and may engender a sense of loss in anyone in the relationship. This phase should include a review or reflection on the experiences the parties in the relationship have undergone together. Future goals and needs should be addressed as well. Often, the professional is in an ideal position to help the child and family make the transition to a new service or place by transferring to the family the information and skills they need to best benefit from the demands of their new environment.

Creating Partnerships

Many issues can prevent effective family–professional partnerships. Salisbury (1992) described common barriers to such partnerships, including attitudes, perceptions, and values of service providers about the families with whom they work. Providers may not acknowledge the skills and knowledge that families bring to the working relationship, and/or a mismatch may occur between the goals and expectations of the professionals and the family members.

Communication issues can form major barriers to effective partnership and include concerns related to use of language, languages spoken, literacy levels, and affective components of communication. Lack of service provider knowledge or time and logistical issues, such as lack of child care or transportation, also function as barriers to the establishment of effective working partnerships between families and professionals.

Service providers can create more effective partnerships by using a variety of strategies, including identifying the families' concerns, priorities, and resources through holding discussions with them on their own terms and in their language of preference. Other suggestions center on asking family members about their preferred level and method of involvement, time schedules and constraints, preferred type of communication regarding their child's program, and the times and places in which they would like services to occur (Rosin, 1996). The potential for effective partnerships will be enhanced if families are provided a menu or range of service options so that they can choose those that best fit the needs, comfort levels, and preferences of the family.

Family service professionals and program resources must be committed to the process of developing partnerships because true partnerships develop over time and take time to establish. Partnerships must be based on flexible and creative models to meet the needs of individual children and families who come from such diverse backgrounds and perspectives.

EFFECTIVE COMMUNICATION

Effective communication is absolutely essential to establishing and maintaining relationships and partnerships with families. Treating others with dignity, respect, and honesty is the foundation of effective communication. From this foundation, trustful relationships can evolve.

Communication is pivotal to the social interactions that characterize human beings. Effective communication is likewise fundamental to productive and satisfying relationships between family members and professionals. Often, during periods of stress, these relationships are particularly challenged and even seemingly minor occurrences can exacerbate painful responses or create (or alleviate) distress and concern. Although all people have experienced stressful events and frustrating or negative communications, they usually are of somewhat short duration and most individuals have a chance to refuel at some point following the event. Families of children with disabilities or chronic health conditions or other special needs, however, may experience these challenges every day and have little time for that refueling process. Hardly a day passes without an interaction with some professional—a teacher, a health care provider, a therapist, a bookkeeper for an insurance agency, and so forth. In some of these interactions, effective communications occur and each individual is able to convey and receive information in a respectful and satisfying manner. In other interactions, the communication breaks down. Regardless, central to family-centered practice is the idea that every one of these interactions is a transaction and every one of them has an impact on that family.

Let us examine the influence of communicative events and reflect on the choices each practitioner brings to interactions. These choices involve both how the practitioner will respond to the communicative bids of others and also how he or she will choose to communicate to others. Recall a particularly stressful event in your own life that occurred in the last month. Maybe your car broke down as you were rushing down the freeway on your way to a meeting. Maybe your child fell down at school and was injured. Maybe your supervisor called you into the office and told you that the company was downsizing and that your job may be curtailed or cut altogether. Maybe a family member who lives in another state became seriously ill and you had to plan a trip to care for her. Try to picture the events that transpired as you tried to understand the stressful situation, adjust to the demands, and procure the services or supports that you needed. How did different styles and attempts at communication influence the outcomes and the subsequent interactions that you had with service professionals?

Using as an example one of these hypothetical events, one can examine the types of experiences and communicative episodes that the individuals involved may have encountered. Imagine that your elderly mother who lives 1,000 miles away had to have surgery suddenly, and you had to travel to be with her and also take care of her when she was released to her home. After making arrangements with those people in your immediate family and workplace (e.g., your home, your children, your pets, your job), which was no small matter, you booked a flight. Maybe you were unable to find an affordable flight through the airline's web site. You called the airline and explained the circumstances in an effort to locate a flight. You were put on hold for what seemed like an eternity. When you did talk to a ticket agent, you were told that the only flight that was available over the next 2 days left at 7 a.m. the next morning. You immediately booked the flight. The trip was a nightmare fraught with a delay and a nearly missed connection. When you arrived at your destination, you found your mother agitated and frightened. You met with the surgeon who allotted about 5 minutes to talk to you. He told you that he had explained everything to your mother already and that you could check with her and the nurse. You do not know how long the surgery will be, what all the risks are, when your mother could expect to come home if all goes well, or what all her care needs will be when she is released.

Now think about how each interaction and the communication involved in such a difficult scenario have either met your needs or added to your stress level. Consider how different your feelings might have been if communications were altered at various points. It is likely, for instance, that your anxiety would have been lessened if the surgeon and nurse had taken time to describe and outline the surgical procedures and care options for your mother and introduced you to other hospital personnel for follow through, rather than provide a perfunctory overview of your mother's prognosis and surgery. Everyone wants to be treated with dignity and sensitivity in all of their interactions. When embroiled in an emotional situation that causes stress, worry, or fear, these interactions assume even more importance and become even more compelling. Simple courtesies and effective positive communications can exert a major influence in our interactions. They allow an individual to review options and marshal resources, and they can "turn the tide" to help a person effectively cope with a changing situation.

What Service Providers Can Do to Improve Communication with Families

Effective communication requires careful attention and consideration for each partner. Service providers can hone their own listening skills and endeavor to communicate information clearly and respectfully to optimize the likelihood of achieving effective

working relationships or partnerships with families. The discussion that follows provides important strategies to enhance these listening skills

Listen Actively Active listening is foundational to the ability to understand others. Good communication cannot occur without the ability to understand the other person's point of view or perspective. Edelman, Greenland, and Mills (1992a) described the key elements to active listening: *be attentive, be impartial, reflect back, listen for feelings*, and *summarize*. Attention involves not only paying attention but also conveying attention through body language. Impartial listening requires that the listener just listen and does not give opinions or even agree or disagree. Reflecting back refers to paraphrasing or using similar words to capture what the speaker was attempting to say. This technique not only establishes clearer communications but also it helps to establish rapport and shows the listener's desire to listen.

Listening or acknowledging feelings is the fourth technique. Many interactions between family members and service providers will be about issues of tremendous concern to the families. Family members have feelings about these topics and these feelings should be acknowledged. For example, a professional may reflect, "It sounds like you are feeling frustrated with his progress." Finally, active listening involves summarizing. The listener should try to capture the speaker's intent and summarize the key points. This establishes whether the message has been both clearly communicated and received. It also serves to convey understanding. For instance, the professional may state, "Let me make sure that I understood. Dan is not responding when you do those exercises. You would like to adapt the procedure by using a new toy." These elements or components appear simple, but most people, particularly in the role of a professional, have a tendency to jump in too soon and provide an opinion or prescription for the family.

Communicate Clearly and Respectfully Other strategies for clear and respectful communication were offered by Edelman et al. (1992a, pp. 34–36):

- *Avoid making assumptions.* The service provider should not draw conclusions prior to meeting and discussing issues with the family. Informed opinions can only come from a period of data gathering.

- *Avoid jargon and explain technical terms.* Professional fields are fraught with technical jargon understood only by those people educated in the field. Terms such as NICU (neonatal intensive care unit), IEP (individualized education program), IFSP (individualized family service plan), OT (occupational therapy), and PT (physical therapy) typically make no sense to the layperson and should be avoided or explained to families.

- *Share complete, honest, and unbiased information.* Families can only make informed decisions if they have all of the information they need. For some, information may need to be provided in several modalities (e.g., written, oral) or in a different modality or form from the one being presented. Some families may prefer written materials (paper or e-mail) and others may be more comfortable with oral descriptions or simple graphics. The family members' preferred style of learning, language(s) spoken, and literacy level may influence the way that information is provided and received. In addition, a period of time may be needed for the family members to process the information and analyze their situation. Family members also must be given the opportunity to ask questions and express their concerns.

- *Offer opinions and specify that these are suggestions and they are not the only options.* Being family centered does not mean not offering professional opinion or expertise. Family members come to professionals to obtain a professional opinion and glean the expertise offered by the professional. Clinical advice, however, is one of many factors that the family must consider when making decisions. Professionals must respect their right to agree with the clinical opinion or follow another course of action.

- *Respond to questions directly and specify when the answer is not known.* If service providers do not know the answers to a query, they must be honest and tell the family that they do not know. They may offer to research the topic and get back to the family with information.

- *Avoid patronizing language and tone.* Using proper greeting titles, such as "Mr.," "Mrs.," or "Ms.," avoids demeaning or overly casual approaches until the service provider knows the parent's preference. Talking down to parents is inappropriate in all circumstances.

- *Recognize individuals' differing abilities to understand.* Given the range of experiences and backgrounds of family members, different means of conveying information must be used. Some people will prefer written information, whereas others will prefer verbal accounts. Literacy levels also vary greatly among individuals—some family members are strong readers and some do not read or they have limited reading abilities in English. Cultural backgrounds, too, will differ and influence the family members' levels of understanding, knowledge, and concerns. Ample time must be allowed for family members to process information and discuss issues of concern.

- *Clarify mutual expectations.* A shared vision of the roles and responsibilities of the family members and the professionals is essential to avoid misunderstandings. It may be useful to ask family members to relate what they heard and what they consider the expectations and roles to be. If each partner restates his or her expectations, mutual goals can be developed and achieved.

- *Identify next steps.* Specifically identifying the *who, what, when, where,* and *how* of the steps or procedures will prevent miscommunications. Often it is useful to write down next steps or diagram procedures.

- *Realign the power.* Traditionally, professionals have called the shots with respect to decisions about service delivery and service models. Partnerships will be enhanced when families are treated as equal partners and their suggestions and priorities are considered the driving force behind services.

- *Respect different cultural perspectives.* The power and influence of cultural issues must be understood as families express their preferences and concerns related to their child's services (Hanson, 2011). Learning about the family's culture and background and asking the family their preferences will help establish more culturally responsive services.

- *Respect constraints in families' time and resources.* Children's special needs and services are only two of the myriad factors with which the family must grapple each day. Although the services provided by professionals may appear crucial to them, the family members have to organize their time and resources to meet the needs of all family members. Again, asking families to describe the services they need and their preferences for service delivery will be useful.

- *Observe and respond to nonverbal cues.* With many people and in many cultures, what is *not* said is as or more important than what is said. Body language is often worth many words. Service providers are well advised to be aware of their own body language and the family's cultural interpretation of that language, as well as the family's nonverbal cues. For instance, a family member may nod his or her head up and down in response. The professional may interpret this signal as meaning that the family member is agreeing, when in fact the individual may be merely indicating that the information was heard. Another example relates to the use of eye contact. In some cultures, looking one directly in the eye is considered respectful, whereas in other cultures a direct gaze is considered disrespectful. One's gender, status, age, and other factors must be taken into account in judging the appropriateness of body contact (e.g., shaking hands, pat on the back), eye contact, order of speaking, and proper greeting.

- *Create opportunities for open communication.* Communicating with families in environments or spaces that are private, comfortable, and warm and inviting will do much to facilitate the interaction. These space considerations can help to overcome the natural distance and power issues between families and professionals.

Communication is an extremely complex process. It involves many components: the person or people chosen to address or engage, the things said or not said, the timing of expression, the place in which intent is expressed, and the ways in which the information is expressed. All aspects of communication—who, what, when, where, and how—play important roles in the ability to communicate effectively with family members.

What to Do When Communication Is Particularly Challenging

If it were easy to communicate clearly and effectively, there would not be shelves of self-help and psychology books devoted to this topic. Communication is crucial to all human interactions and it can be a difficult process. In the helping professions, most professionals will encounter situations that are particularly challenging, such as the need to deliver bad news or distressing information. At some time, most people will be embroiled in a conflict. In these circumstances, communicative attempts will require even more care and scrutiny.

Be Honest and Expect Conflict   No one wants to hear about distressing medical or health problems, limitations to one's abilities or options, or loss of services or supports. Yet at some time most professionals will be called on to deliver such information to families. A number of researchers and clinicians have examined family experiences when receiving diagnoses and/or distressing information. Most findings are in agreement that families want honest information that is presented in a direct and caring manner (Gowen, Christy, & Sparling, 1993; Turnbull & Turnbull, 1990). Time should be allowed for families to digest and process the information, discuss the issues, come to terms with the issues and their feelings, and ask any questions. As has been stated previously, providing information to families in their preferred language and in the modality of their choice is essential. Often, families will need to have the information presented multiple times or in chunks. The families' language fluency and literacy level must be considered also so that information is not provided at a technical level that is not understandable to the family.

Whenever two or more people interact, the possibility exists for conflict, misunderstanding, or disagreement. It would be an unusual professional indeed who never experienced conflict when working with families. Some methods of communication minimize misunderstandings and aid in achieving agreement when conflicts do occur, however.

Some Effective Techniques   Some of the techniques previously described may be particularly useful when communication breaks down. Listening actively (i.e., attentively, impartially, reflecting back, listening for feelings, summarizing) may prevent misunderstanding and help service providers and parents move toward understanding when difficulties arise (Edelman et al., 1992a). Other techniques include monitoring nonverbal and verbal cues used by both parties engaging in the communication. These cues must be analyzed in light of each person's background and preferences. In some cultures, for instance, it is acceptable to cross one's legs, touch or pat another person on the arm, or even kiss a stranger on the cheek or both cheeks, whereas in other cultures these actions would be deemed highly inappropriate, especially for a woman. These examples demonstrate how easy it is for misunderstandings to arise when we do not know one another well. Open and honest expressions are generally preferred. An individual can achieve clarity by offering illustrative examples or stories, speaking clearly, and choosing words carefully. At times, it is useful to check the listener's perception of what was said to avoid misunderstandings in meaning or terminology. Even if each person speaks the same language, words and phrases may hold different meanings for the speaker and the listener.

Edelman, Greenland, and Mills (1992b) offered strategies for moving toward agreement when conflicts occur. Their work is an adaptation of information presented by Fisher and Ury (1981, 1991). The first strategy as described by Edelman et al. (1992b) is to *separate the person from the problem.* This involves agreeing that there is a disagreement and trying to put oneself in the other person's shoes. It is important to avoid blaming the other person and reacting too emotionally. The second strategy is to *establish interests, goals, and priorities.* At this point, each person should articulate what they see as the problem and identify their goals and desired outcomes. Being flexible and creative helps to lead toward compromise and identification of mutual goals. The third strategy is to *generate options* that can achieve a win-win position. This is the brainstorming phase where all possible options are put on the table by all parties. If necessary, other people can be brought into the discussion to help identify and expand the range of options.

Finally, the fourth strategy is to *strive for agreement*. Everyone may need some time to weigh the information before making decisions. In this stage, taking a break can be useful to give all parties time to process the information. Ultimately, it is the family who must make the decision that best fits their needs. Striving for agreement also includes defining the next action steps for each party and what the follow-up will be. An example of one such conflict and its resolution is reflected in the following vignette.

The Davidsons

Mr. and Mrs. Davidson, the parents of Robert, a child with pervasive developmental disorder (PDD), were blazing mad when they came to the semiannual parent-teacher conference with Robert's classroom teacher. They had just spoken with another family, whose child was also diagnosed with PDD. This other couple had recently obtained a whole host of new services for their child from the school district, including a one-to-one paraprofessional who would help their child throughout the school day and increased speech therapy hours. The Davidsons believed that Robert deserved the same services and came to the school to demand that he receive them. The teacher, Kathy, listened patiently to the Davidsons' feelings and requests. She spent time endeavoring to understand their perspective and then she paraphrased their concerns and requests to ensure that she understood their concerns. At that point, she also suggested that she and the parents together re-examine Robert's educational goals and progress. When the teacher and parents looked at the observational data collected in the classroom and the outcome of recent assessments of his performance, they all agreed that Robert seemed to be making good progress and was benefiting from the curricular activities offered as part of the school program. His speech and language skills were advancing and he appeared to enjoy the classroom experience; he even had made several new friends. Kathy encouraged the parents to arrange play dates at home with these new friends.

Mr. and Mrs. Davidson were able to analyze the information Kathy had given them and look at the unique needs and goals for their son. They came to understand that what he needed may not have been identical to what another child might need. Kathy suggested that the classroom teachers and parents both make additional observations over the next month and revisit the goals and objectives at an appointed time the following month to consider if a shift in program or additional speech therapy was needed. The Davidsons went home reassured that their son was achieving his objectives and that his educational program would be reviewed for possible readjustment if necessary. Kathy was more aware of the parents' concerns and made a special effort to key into Robert's behavior and examine whether his current educational program was meeting his needs. Instead of an escalation in tensions that could have led to more meetings and even a fair hearing procedure, both parties were able to listen to one another, examine the options, and leave with a win-win understanding of one another's position and a plan for the future.

As this vignette illustrates, both professionals and parents must learn to engage in problem-solving collaboration to achieve optimal goals for children in need of services. It is a two-way street. Open and honest communication is the underpinning for these skills.

RELATIONSHIP BUILDING AND COMMUNICATION IN ALL PHASES OF SERVICE DELIVERY

Effective communication and collaborative relationships are essential to all phases of the intervention process. From gathering information and assessment to the analysis and planning of service options and objectives to the actual delivery of service, the relationship and communication between families and professionals will largely dictate whether these intervention activities will meet the needs of children and their families.

Service providers are challenged to be flexible and culturally responsive to meet the needs of the diverse range of families and children with whom they work. Families will differ along many dimensions: culture, spoken language, race and ethnicity, literacy skills, spiritual practices, socioeconomic status, education level and background, family structure, lifestyle, living arrangements, geographical location (e.g., area of country; rural, urban, or suburban), and the opportunities that they have. All these dimensions will influence methods of communication and relationship building.

Information Gathering and Assessment

Traditionally, professionals gathered information through interviews with families and by professional testing, often on a one-shot basis. A process of gathering information through extensive discussion with family members and using multiple observations and strategies has replaced the more traditional practices.

Appropriate practices now emphasize family involvement throughout the entire process (Greenspan & Meisels, 1996). Understanding children within the context of their most important environment, their families, is crucial to gleaning appropriate assessment information. Parents and other family members are the best and most knowledgeable informants regarding a child's needs, strengths, and developmental history. They also are best able to interact with the child and elicit the child's optimal performance. A collaborative alliance between professionals and families is essential to this process of information exchange.

This phase of assessment and data gathering requires professionals to individualize and make careful choices in the methods they employ to meet the needs of the vast range of children and families participating in services. Some common considerations are discussed in the areas of terminology, materials used, developmental values and expectations, type of needs assessment, and communication and interaction styles. Terminology must be carefully reviewed, particularly when interpretation or translation is involved. Some words do not readily translate or they may be misunderstood. Dale and Hoshino (1984) related one devastating and extreme example that demonstrates this point. They described a case in a neonatal intensive care unit involving a Hmong family in which the physicians recommended to the family that their child undergo a surgical procedure. When the word *surgery* was directly translated as "butchery" in the Hmong language, the family was understandably distraught and frightened.

Most examples are not so emotionally laden. Given the number of acronyms and technical jargon used in most helping professions and the many languages and cultural backgrounds of families served, however, the potential exists for grave misunderstandings. With respect to materials and symbols, professionals also are advised to choose carefully. Certainly it is crucial to choose materials that are nonbiased toward any race or gender. To ensure cultural sensitivity, one must also look to the ways that various cultures interpret symbols. Joe and Malach (1998) provided the example of an early interventionist who chose to meet an American Indian family at the Owl Café, not knowing that the owl was considered a bad omen in this family's culture.

Developmental values and behavioral expectations also will vary markedly from family to family. These values and expectations may differ from those of the professional as well, creating the potential for misunderstanding and miscommunication. For instance, families from various cultural and socioeconomic backgrounds may have quite different perspectives on the ages at which children are taught to use the toilet, sleep alone, and feed themselves (Spicer, 2010). Families differ with respect to views about children's schedules and the degree of dependence or independence in child behavior that should be fostered.

The manner in which information is gathered is crucial to building effective working relationships and successful communication. In the needs assessment phase, different strategies may be employed from interviewing families to using written checklists or questionnaires. Some families will welcome a direct face-to-face exchange and the opportunity to tell their story, whereas other families will experience being selected for an interview as shaming and not allowing them to save face. When written materials are used, the language and reading skills of the family members must be considered, particularly since most adults who are unable to understand written materials are reluctant to admit this.

Families' preferences for communication and interaction style also vary. Some families prefer open, direct communication and are comfortable with discussing their particular situation. For others, more indirect communication techniques are preferred and experienced as appropriate. Some families expect formal data gathering sessions and others prefer more informal situations and environments.

When working with families whose language is not spoken by the service provider, using interpreters or translators also requires planning and care. Guidelines for working with interpreters have been outlined in several publications (Chen, Chan, Brekken, & Valverde, 2000; Lynch, 2011; Ohtake, Fowler, & Santos, 2001). Major considerations when using interpreters include addressing remarks to the family members rather than the interpreter, avoiding culturally offensive language, learning some key words or phrases in the family's language if possible, speaking clearly and slowly as opposed to loudly, and allowing time for translation when presenting information (Lynch & Hanson, 2011).

Service providers must show sensitivity to families' socioeconomic and cultural backgrounds and to the meanings families ascribe to being interviewed or asked to divulge information. Guidelines for offering culturally competent services are provided in a number of publications (see Hanson, Lynch, & Wayman, 1990; Lynch & Hanson, 2011). The use of "cultural guides" or informants who are knowledgeable both about the family's cultural background and the service delivery system may be particularly beneficial to this process. Services can only be family centered if they are also culturally sensitive.

Collaborative Planning and Decision Making

The suggestions offered in the information gathering discussion apply to the planning and decision-making process as well. Families will differ—often markedly—in their styles and preferences with respect to planning and decision making. Many families desire to be treated as equal partners in the process. Other families expect the professional to take the most active role and make the initial determination or recommendation for goals and service objectives. Again the family's background and experiences in their culture and social strata will affect their expectations and preferences.

Several concerns apply to all families, however. One is the need to focus on the child and family's *strengths* rather than the problems. It is difficult for any person to hear that they or their family members have problems. Information needs to be presented sensitively, clearly, honestly, and in a caring manner. Time must be allowed for family members to digest the information and express themselves. A collaborative and trusting relationship established at the outset between the service provider and family will bolster the communication when these difficult conversations must occur. Another concern centers on the need to look for solutions, not the causes of difficulties. When both the family and the professional are focused on the problem-solving aspects of the interaction, they are likely to more effectively design appropriate service objectives and prevent blaming and misunderstandings.

Implementation and Monitoring

As services are delivered, monitoring and communication with families must be ongoing. The style and manner in which the information is exchanged should vary to ensure that families' preferences are honored. In addition, service providers must consider the many demands and challenges faced by families every day that go beyond the scope of services in which they are involved. Taking the family's perspective and imagining what it is like to live their lives can be an important professional tool. Families are challenged to meet the needs of all family members along many different dimensions. They may view the professional's involvement in their lives as taking up only a tiny fraction of their day or week, and the professional or the service may not be high on their list of priorities. Conversely, the professional might be of tremendous import to the family, and thus professionals should not play down their roles too much, either. Families may view professionals as lifesavers and sometimes the professionals themselves give the families the impression that the child is not a high priority for them. Thus, flexibility and understanding of the entire range of demands families face and the tasks they must achieve is essential to monitoring and attaining respectful partnering and communication.

PROFESSIONAL ISSUES

Collaboration is hard work. Because professionals are engaged with a range of families and their work often involves meeting families in their homes or preferred environment, professionals will be faced with many challenges and decisions that must be made with each family. Several considerations are highlighted. These include the need to examine and implement professional standards and attention to professional sustenance.

Professional Standards

The collaborative relationships and family-centered services advocated in this book demand that professionals develop professional standards to work closely and respectfully with families. Several key concerns are discussed: confidentiality, ethical dilemmas and standards, and communication among professionals.

    Confidentiality   Confidentiality is crucial. Professionals privileged to work closely with families will receive many intimate details regarding the family's life, especially when services are provided for young children and in families' homes. Professionals must adhere to strict standards of confidentiality in all phases of the intervention process to honor this partnership with families. This said, professionals should not discuss families' situations or divulge information to others about the family without the express permission of the family members.

    Ethical Dilemmas   Professionals will at times be faced with ethical dilemmas. Such dilemmas often center on the need to divulge information such as in the case of potential abuse or neglect, or they may center on whether it is right to become more actively involved in the family's life to guide them to a more productive or optimal outcome. Sometimes the decision is clear-cut, as in the case of abuse, but at other times it is in a very gray area. The development of a guiding framework is useful to address these potential dilemmas (Beckman et al., 1996; Wasik et al., 1990). It is recommended that intervention teams draw up a handbook of practices or operating principles that address such issues as child and family risk and health, confidentiality, and visitation practices. Many professional organizations, such as the Council for Exceptional Children, also provide professional standards and/or a code of ethics. Such standards should be readily available to and practiced by the professional. These professional guidelines also can inform the guiding framework developed by the intervention team. Wrestling with professional dilemmas can be difficult. Practicing self-reflection, consulting with other professionals and team members, and discussing the situation with a supervisor are valuable strategies for addressing the concerns. See also Chapter 9 for a further discussion regarding ethical dilemmas.

    Communication   Communication issues among and between various types of professional service providers present special challenges as well. Most families end up working with a myriad of professionals. Many of these professionals even visit the family on different times and days. Although the child and family may benefit enormously from the expertise of a range of disciplines and professionals, the type of information and the way in which it is delivered may be burdensome to families. Beckman and Kohl (1993) documented some of these difficulties, including professionals' contradictions of one another when making judgments or recommendations, as well as turf disputes. Multiple service providers making multiple visits may disrupt family privacy and schedules, too. Thus, it is incumbent on professionals to communicate with one another and to reflect on the effects of their choices and priorities on the family's routine and lifestyle. The identification of a key contact person for the family among a team of professionals may help to alleviate some of these concerns articulated by families.

Professional Sustenance

Developing and sustaining human relationships is hard work. Professionals today are provided the opportunity to work with the panoply of children and families. The work can be highly rewarding because of the opportunities to meet people, learn new practices and skills, and form bonds with other individuals. The work can be stressful, too. Relationship building does not always proceed as hoped or expected. Professionals, as well as families and children, have needs. They must turn to strategies that help prevent or alleviate burnout and provide them with the opportunity to refuel.

Certain techniques nurture and sustain professionals' ability to work closely with families. The first strategy is *reflective practice*, which includes a commitment of time and energy to consider one's work. Professionals may find it helpful to maintain a journal or a personal written log. They also may find it useful to engage in discussions with other professionals designed to reflect on the services provided. Strict confidentiality standards should be maintained in all such discussions and decisions should not be made about families without their participation; however, general discussions of strategies and concerns can be highly supportive to professionals and help them develop or hone their professional skills.

Second, *team support* is crucial to the helping professions. Even when professionals are assigned as home visitors and spend the majority of their time working independently, support from other professionals is essential. Often the team will have to be constructed. Activities for group discussion, team building, team recreation, and information exchange among team members must be carefully planned and a commitment must be made to this process.

Third, *supervision and mentoring by senior staff members and/or administrators* are essential components to effective service delivery. In a busy world, these components are often the first to go. Effectively supervising and mentoring professionals, particularly those new to or entering the field, is essential to the maintenance of high standards of quality service delivery.

Finally, *professionals must take care of themselves*. This need is reflected by an old expression, "If you don't take care of yourself, no one will." Self-care is a necessary and often overlooked component of effective service delivery, especially when services occur in high stress environments or situations. Different strategies of self-care will apply to different people, but they may include employing relaxation techniques such as yoga, meditation, participating in recreational activities, spending special time with family or friends, or pursuing an avocation, to name a few. Regardless, these activities can assist the service provider to avoid burnout and gain needed refueling time to accomplish the demands of their employment.

SUMMARY

According to Vohs (1998, ix), "The absolute bedrock for true partnerships and collaboration is trust. It will only arise from talking and listening." How simple and yet how complex this task is! Each professional and each family member brings so many personal characteristics and preferences to each interaction. Issues of culture, communication style, values, and beliefs all affect the interactions that occur.

Every single interaction that occurs is also a transaction. The interactions that take place will transform each participant and affect subsequent interactions. Developing collaborative partnerships and effective communication between families and professionals are the essential ingredients to positive outcomes for children and families served. These partnerships and collaborative relationships are forged over time and with commitment and effort on the part of both families and professionals. Given that all facets of intervention necessitate effective working relationships or partnerships between professionals and family members, the commitment to these collaborative and respectful practices is well worth the effort.

ACTIVITIES TO EXTEND THE DISCUSSION

1. **Map out or outline policies and practices in your agency or work site that form barriers to partnerships** (e.g., no transportation or child care; lack of interpreters or translators for presentations, home visits, meetings with families, discussions, materials [includes issues related to services for the hearing impaired]; staff members' attitudes; mismatch between services and family needs; modes of communication, such as written materials). For each barrier, develop an action plan to overcome that barrier.

2. **Try a role-playing activity with several colleagues.** Ask one person to describe an emotionally charged incident he or she experienced in working with a family. The second person, as a listener, can practice using active listening skills as the first person describes the incident. The third person can provide feedback on the listener's use of these skills. Everyone can take a turn as it is difficult and takes practice to hone these skills.

3. **Think back on a challenging interaction that you have had with a friend or with a family with whom you have worked over the past 2 weeks.** Did you adequately employ clear and respectful communication skills in your interaction? As you work with colleagues and/or families over the next week, stop after the interaction and perform a self-reflection and self-rating of your skills. Which skills did you employ effectively? Which skills do you need to practice in order to enhance your communication with family members in the future? Keeping a journal may be useful to enhance your self-reflection.

REFERENCES

Beckman, P.J., & Kohl, F.L. (1993). Working with multiple professionals. In P.J. Beckman & G.B. Boyes (Eds.), *Deciphering the system: A guide for families of young children with disabilities* (pp. 21–38). Cambridge, MA: Brookline Books.

Beckman, P.J., Newcomb, S., Frank, N., & Brown, L. (1996). Evolution of working relationships with families. In P.J. Beckman (Ed.), *Strategies for working with families of young children with disabilities* (pp. 17–30). Baltimore, MD: Paul H. Brookes Publishing Co.

Chen, D., Chan, S., Brekken, L., & Valverde, A. (Producers). (2000). *Conversations for three: Communicating through interpreters* [Videotape]. Baltimore, MD: Paul H. Brookes Publishing Co.

Covey, S.R. (1989). *The seven habits of highly effective people.* New York, NY: Simon & Schuster.

Dale, M.L., & Hoshino, L.B. (1984). Belief systems of Hispanic and pan-Asian populations in California: Implications for the delivery of care in the neonatal intensive care unit. *Journal of the California Perinatal Association, 4*(2), 21–25.

Dunst, C.J., & Paget, K.D. (1991). Parent-professional partnerships and family empowerment. In M. Fine (Ed.), *Collaborative involvement with parents of exceptional children* (pp. 25–44). Brandon, VT: Clinical Psychology Publishing Co.

Dunst, C.J., Trivette, C.M., & Deal, A.G. (1994). *Supporting and strengthening families: Vol. 1. Methods, strategies and practices.* Cambridge, MA: Brookline Books.

Dunst, C.J., Trivette, C.M., & Johanson, C. (1994). Parent-professional collaboration and partnerships. In C.J. Dunst, C.M. Trivette, & A.G. Deal (Eds.), *Supporting and strengthening families: Vol. 1. Methods, strategies and practices* (pp. 197–211). Cambridge, MA: Brookline Books.

Edelman, L., Greenland, B., & Mills, B.L. (1992a). *Building parent/professional collaboration: Facilitator's guide.* Baltimore, MD: Kennedy Krieger Institute.

Edelman, L., Greenland, B., & Mills, B.L. (1992b). *Family centered communication skills: Facilitator's guide.* Baltimore, MD: Kennedy Krieger Institute.

Fisher, R., & Ury, W. (1981). *Getting to yes: Negotiating agreement without giving in.* New York, NY: Penguin Books.

Fisher, R., Ury, W. (with Patton, B., Ed.) (1991). *Getting to yes: Negotiating agreement without giving in* (2nd ed.). New York, NY: Penguin Books.

Gowen, J.W., Christy, D.S., & Sparling, J. (1993). Informational needs of parents of young children with special needs. *Journal of Early Intervention, 17*(2), 194–210.

Greenspan, S.I., & Meisels, S.J. (1996). Toward a new vision for the developmental assessment of infants and young children. In S.J. Meisels & E. Fenichel (Eds.), *New visions for the developmental assessment of infants and young children* (pp. 11–26). Washington, DC: ZERO TO THREE: National Center for Infants, Toddlers, and Families.

Hanson, M.J. (2011). Ethic, cultural, and language diversity in intervention settings. In E.W. Lynch & M.J. Hanson (Eds.), *Developing cross-cultural competence: A guide for working with children and their families* (4th ed., pp. 2–19). Baltimore, MD: Paul H. Brookes Publishing Co.

Hanson, M.J., Lynch, E.W., & Wayman, K.I. (1990). Honoring the cultural diversity of families when gathering data. *Topics in Early Childhood Special Education, 10,* 112–131.

Joe, J., & Malach, R. (1998). Families with Native American roots. In E.W. Lynch & M.J. Hanson (Eds.), *Developing cross-cultural competence: A guide for working with children and their families* (2nd ed., pp. 127–162). Baltimore, MD: Paul H. Brookes Publishing Co.

Kalmanson, B., & Seligman, S. (1992). Family-provider relationships: The basis of all interventions. *Infants and Young Children, 4*(4), 46–52.

Lynch, E.W. (2011). Developing cross-cultural competence. In E.W. Lynch & M.J. Hanson (Eds.), *Developing cross-cultural competence: A guide for working with children and their families* (4th ed., pp. 41–77). Baltimore, MD: Paul H. Brookes Publishing Co.

Lynch, E.W., & Hanson, M.J. (2011). *Developing cross-cultural competence: A guide for working with children and their families* (4th ed.). Baltimore, MD: Paul H. Brookes Publishing Co.

McGonigel, M.J. (1991). Philosophy and conceptual framework. In M.J. McGonigel, R.K. Kaufmann, & B.H. Johnson (Eds.), *Guidelines and recommended practices for the Individualized Family Service Plan* (2nd ed., pp. 7–14). Bethesda, MD: Association for the Care of Children's Health.

Ohtake, Y., Fowler, S.A., & Santos, R.M. (2001). *Working with interpreters to plan early childhood services with limited-English proficient families.* Urbana-Champaign, IL: University of Illinois, Early Childhood Research Institute on Culturally and Linguistically Appropriate Services.

Rosin, P. (1996). Parent and service provider partnerships in early intervention. In P. Rosin, A. Whitehead, L. Tuchman, G. Jesien, A. Begun, & L. Irwin (Eds.), *Partnerships in family-centered care: A guide to collaborative early intervention* (pp. 65–79). Baltimore, MD: Paul H. Brookes Publishing Co.

Salisbury, C. (1992). Parents as team members: Inclusive teams, collaborative outcomes. In B. Rainforth, J. York, & C. Macdonald (Eds.), *Collaborative teams for students with severe disabilities: Integrating therapy and edu-cational services* (pp. 43–66). Baltimore, MD: Paul H. Brookes Publishing Co.

Spicer, P. (2010). Cultural influences on par-enting. *Zero to Three, 30*(4), 28–32.

Tannen, D. (1990.). *You just don't understand: Women and men in conversation.* New York, NY: Ballatine Books.

Turnbull, A.P., & Turnbull, H.R. (1990). *Fami-lies, professionals, and exceptionality: A special partnership* (2nd ed.). New York, NY: Merrill.

Walker, B., & Singer, G.H.S. (1993). Improv-ing collaborative communication between professionals and parents. In G.H.S. Singer & L.E. Powers (Eds.), *Families, disability, and empowerment: Active coping skills and strategies for family interventions* (pp. 285–316). Balti-more, MD: Paul H. Brookes Publishing Co.

Wasik, B.H., Bryant, D.M., & Lyons, C.M. (1990). *Home visiting: Procedures for help-ing families.* Beverly Hills, CA: Sage Publications.

Strategies for Supporting Families

Marci J. Hanson

"The family is our refuge and our springboard; nourished on it, we can advance to new horizons. In every conceivable manner, the family is link to our past, bridge to our future."

—Alex Haley (cited in Curran, 1984, p. 199)

"Act as if what you do makes a difference. It does."

—William James (n.d.)

"There are two ways of spreading light: to be the candle or the mirror that reflects it."

—Edith Wharton (1902)

The delivery of family services is a complex process. Families typically enter service systems because of a specific need, and they may require a wide variety of services. Their needs must be carefully matched to the array of services and professional practitioners in their communities. The service providers that families encounter must work with individual families to provide specialized interventions that support them to address their own goals and demands. Consider, for instance, the perspectives of a family and a professional (in this case, a nurse) as family needs arise and the family abruptly enters the realm of medical and early intervention services:

Emotionally, I was frustrated and sad that I didn't seem to know how best to care for him. My experience as the mother of two other children didn't much matter because I'd never cared for a premature baby before; my son's needs were clearly very different from our other children. My pragmatic side sought out the best resources we could find. Our developmental specialist was the key to helping us read his cues and nurture him in a way that was best for him.

—Parent (as cited in VandenBerg & Hanson, 2013, p. 39)

My goal as a neonatal nurse is to think of it as a journey. Every person I speak with, look at, walk with, is important. I try to realize that I am in a position of providing essential medical treatment. I have a tremendous responsibility to see that this baby not only survives but also receives the best that we (the health care system) have to offer. This may mean

255

heartbreak or miracles. I have to realize that everything I do leaves an impression. I need to remember compassion and care are essential.

—Nurse (as cited in VandenBerg & Hanson, 2013, p. 38)

These perspectives were offered by a parent of a child born prematurely and a nurse who works in a neonatal intensive care nursery; they capture many of the goals of service delivery both from the consumers' side (family) and from the angle of professional practitioners regardless of service delivery system. Family members may desire and need information about the family member's condition. They may seek resources for meeting the developmental and/or care needs, and they may need supports to help them cope and adapt to the altered circumstances. Service providers bring their knowledge, special training, and expertise to these interactions with families. They also convey their abilities to provide care and services in a sensitive and compassionate manner.

This book has focused on the context for providing services for families who are diverse in backgrounds, concerns, resources, and preferences for services and support. We have advocated family-centered or family-focused approaches to understanding and supporting families. At the heart of these approaches are the dispositions and behavior of professionals that are most likely to create effective partnerships or alliances with families. These dispositions and interpersonal characteristics include delivering services in a manner that is respectful, warm and friendly, compassionate and caring, responsive, and positive in its tone and view of family. These attributes are foundational for *how* family services are delivered by establishing collaborative relationships with families and effective communication. This chapter expands on the previous discussions as we consider family goals or outcomes of intervention and highlight the types of services that may lead to more successful outcomes. The focus here shifts to *what* is delivered across family settings and circumstances.

OUTCOMES OF FAMILY SERVICES

Most educational, health care, and social service systems are charged with providing a range of family services. A number of legislative statutes (see Chapter 5), maternal and child health, and mental health initiatives authorize supports and services specifically designed for families (Turnbull et al., 2007). These services and supports may range from community awareness and technical assistance to specialized instruction and family training. Some focus on counseling and/or psychological services. Many systems include case coordination of family services as well.

A family-centered approach to service delivery has been embraced as the philosophical approach used to define optimal service practices, particularly with respect to early intervention and pediatric services for young children and their families across professions. For example, see the recommended practices adopted by American Academy of Pediatrics (2003), early childhood special education (Sandall, Hemmeter, Smith, & McLean, 2005), and the American Speech-Language-Hearing Association (2008). As reviewed by Bailey, Raspa, and Fox (2012), some of the core components associated with these approaches include a focus on family strengths and a view of families as empowered decision makers. Other components include emphasis on models and services that are collaborative, flexible, show respect for family diversity and values, employ open communication with families, and recognize informal family support systems (Bailey, Raspa, Humphreys, & Sam, 2011; Brewer, McPherson, Magrab, & Hutchins, 1989; Dunst, 2000;

McWilliam, Tocci, & Harbin, 1995; Perrin et al., 2007; sources as cited in Bailey, Raspa, & Fox, 2012). Despite strong and broad support for such practices, these recommendations have not necessarily been translated into practice. Few efforts to examine implementation have been made and these principles remain an ideal rather than a set of defined practices.

The provision of these services for families is designed to address a broad range of family needs. Several national efforts have centered on defining the outcomes of these services and designing accountability systems to determine the degree to which the outcomes are being met. One such effort is the national Early Childhood Outcomes Center (2012). In 2003, the Office of Special Education Programs within the U.S. Department of Education funded the Early Childhood Outcomes (ECO) Center to promote the development and implementation of child and family outcome measures for infants, toddlers, and preschoolers with disabilities that could be used in local, state, and national accountability systems. These outcomes were designed to provide a framework for states and the federal government to document the extent to which the benefits of early intervention and preschool programs were providing benefits to families (Bailey et al., 2006). They were developed through an iterative process that included extensive input from stakeholders. An outcome was defined as the "benefit experienced by family as a result of services received" (Bailey et al., p. 228). The ECO process identified five family outcomes for use in accountability systems:

1. Families understand their children's strengths, abilities, and special needs.

2. Families know their rights and advocate effectively for their children.

3. Families help their children develop and learn.

4. Families have support systems.

5. Families are able to access desired services, program, and activities in their communities.

This process also developed three child outcomes to assess benefits to the young children served in programs funded through special education:

1. Positive socioemotional skills (including social relationships)

2. Acquisition and use of knowledge and skills (including early language/communication and early literacy)

3. Use of appropriate behavior to meet needs

This work was aimed at providing useful accountability indices for evaluating the effectiveness of education service programs for young children with special needs and their families. Although targeted for this specific group of young children and their families, these outcomes are instructive as the implications for a broader range of children and families are considered. In fact, these goals and outcomes are consistent with those of other national groups that address a full range of children and families, such as the national PTA (2012). The PTA's framework for family–school partnerships, for instance, includes the standards of welcoming all families into the school community, communicating effectively, supporting student success, speaking up for every child, sharing power, and collaborating with community.

The extent to which family outcomes, such as those identified by ECO, will be incorporated into program accountability systems remains to be seen (Bailey, Raspa, &

Fox, 2012). These outcomes, however, do help frame a discussion of the full range of services and supports that families may need. Above all, services should be meaningful to families. As highlighted by Turnbull et al. (2007), services should contribute to family quality of life. Each family will define quality and their own needs differently, but common concerns and service needs can be identified.

TYPES OF SERVICES AND SUPPORT FOR FAMILIES

Nearly everyone will need services from the educational, social service, and health care realms at some point in their lives. Service needs are varied and will change over the life cycle. Although professional disciplines differ in their approaches and service focus, there are some specific targets and strategies for supporting families that are congruent with the missions of most service systems for children and their families. These foundational types of service supports and principles of service are reviewed in this section. The examples and the research bases that are cited are primarily from the field of early intervention based upon the authors' backgrounds and experiences. However, we believe that they have application to a much broader array of families and concerns.

Providing Information to Families

Most families seek information services. They want to have questions answered, know about the services in their communities, understand what the services provide, and become aware of how to access these services. The need for information services is particularly relevant because most families enter a service system at a time of a concern or when a family member reaches a particular milestone, such as when the child goes to school. These points of contact also represent times of transition for the family as they adjust to a new life event or change in circumstances (e.g., giving birth to a child, becoming ill, going to school, losing a job). In many instances, these events are fraught with emotion and concern, such as in the case of the diagnosis of an illness or disability. It is at this time that the need for information becomes a priority.

Information can be provided through a variety of resources ranging from conversations with professionals who have special expertise and training to written materials to family groups led by professionals or other parents affiliated with an interest group (e.g., premature infants, autism, children's recreation, music). Most parents also find it helpful to glean information on typical developmental milestones and expectations, particularly when their children are young. Web sites, such as that provided by Centers for Disease Control and Prevention (2012), have been designed to supply these resources.

Providing information is not as straightforward a process as it may appear at first glance. Particularly with the marked cultural and linguistic diversity that characterizes the population today, individuals may differ considerably in their abilities to understand and access information. Options and variations will be needed in the types of materials and means or methods of providing information to ensure that families have equitable access. Professionals will want to consider a number of issues related to information services such as those that follow.

Provision of Information in Different Modalities   Optimally, information materials will be provided in a number of different modalities to accommodate family preferences—written, oral, web sites, or perhaps even as applications for a mobile device. Family members may differ markedly with respect to literacy levels and their opportunities, comfort, and access to written materials and/or technology. Thus, when multiple options are offered to families, the likelihood of their access to information will be increased.

Availability in Different Languages As service providers traverse the diverse landscape of families, they will meet families who are not proficient in English or who may require the use of manual or signed language. It will be important to work with interpreters and translators who are proficient in both the family's language (as well as dialect and cultural practices) and the interventionist's language (e.g., medical or educational practices and jargon). This process requires thoughtful preparation and considerable skill to ensure effective family–professional communication. The reader is directed to several resources for a discussion of strategies for working with interpreters and translators (Chen, Chan, Brekken, & Valverde, 2001; Chen, Haney, & Cox, 2012; Hanson & Lynch, 2013; Lynch, 2011; Ohtake, Fowler, & Santos, 2001).

Consideration of Families' Communication Styles and Preferences Families differ markedly in terms of their communication styles or patterns and preferences for receiving information. Some families will prefer direct and succinct information via conversation, written materials, or e-mail. Others will prefer an exchange of information only after they have established a relationship with the service provider that may have evolved over time. Information exchange may involve direct question-and-answer sessions or more indirect ways, such as family storytelling. For some families, their direct questions and requests will reflect what is important to them; for others, what is conveyed through silence or body language may hold more importance. The reader is referred to Barrera (2000), Lynch & Hanson (2010, 2011), and Chapter 10 of this text for further information.

Family Roles Information exchange also will be influenced by family roles. Service providers will need to determine which family members (e.g. father, mother) make the decisions in the family and to whom information should be targeted. Families may hold different beliefs in terms of who should represent them in speaking to outsiders.

Family Preferences Related to Information Sources Many families will hold service professionals in high esteem and deem formal service agencies as valued information providers. Other families may rely first on members of their cultural enclave or community such as community leaders, spiritual leaders, or elders as primary information resources; professionals will benefit from working with these meaningful supports for families.

PROVIDING EDUCATION AND TRAINING FOR PARENTS

In addition to providing information services for families, some families may benefit from parent education or training protocol designed to teach them specific strategies for how to support their children's development, adapt their home environments to meet child and family needs, or respond to developmental concerns, such behavior problems. Considerable empirical evidence establishes that teaching parents effective interaction strategies can enhance children's development. The model provided by Kaiser and Hancock (2003), for instance, provides the rationale for use of such strategies and describes procedures aimed at enhancing parents' communication strategies with their children in naturally occurring interactions. Other examples of parent education efforts include teaching families positive means of discipline and positive behavior support to address challenging child behaviors (Fox, 2010). Internet resources provide family tools and parent training modules to support families and service providers to enhance children's social and emotional learning; for example, see the Center on the Social and Emotional Foundations for Early Learning (2012). Tools and resources are available in many other learning areas as well. For instance, the Center for Early Literacy Learning (2012) offers tools and practice guides for parents to help them engage in fun early literacy activities with their young children using everyday activities in the home and communities.

Professionals may use a variety of strategies to assist or educate families, such as describing the technique, modeling the practice, coaching parents on how to implement a strategy, or using videos of others implementing the activities. The aim is to assist parents to foster their children's learning and meet their family needs in their living environment using techniques that honor family strengths and values about how best to achieve their own goals.

SUPPORTING PARENT–CHILD INTERACTIONS

The quality of parent-child relationships and the responsiveness of parents to their children are crucial determinants of children's developmental outcomes (Shonkoff & Phillips, 2000; Chapter 8 of this text). In his review of practice-based research syntheses in early intervention, Dunst (2007) emphasizes the benefits of parental contingent responsiveness to child behavior and parent sensitivity and responsiveness in the early years.

The underpinning of mutually satisfying parent–child relationships and interaction has its roots in infancy. A strong body of research literature has established that the behavior and characteristics of both the young infant and the parent exercise a powerful influence upon one another in this developing relationship. Goldberg (1977), for instance, observed that most parents routinely monitor their infant's behavior and

that their feelings of competency are undoubtedly linked to their infant's responsiveness to their own attempts to successfully interact with the child. Goldberg (pp. 171–172) noted that individual differences across infants can be considered in three different dimensions: their *readability*, or "the extent to which an infant's behaviors are clearly defined and provide distinctive signals and cues for adults"; *predictability* or "the extent to which an adult can reliably anticipate behavior from contextual events and/or immediately preceding behaviors"; and *responsiveness*, which is "the quality and extent of infant reactions to stimulation."

Professional practitioners can play an important role in so far as their interventions serve to foster these positive family relationships and parent responsiveness. In the early years, for instance, service providers may help parents get to know their child and understand their baby's cues. They may *alert parents to unique behavioral characteristics* of the child and ways of positively interacting with the baby. By *commenting or sharing observations*, either the parent or the professional may point out an area of need (e.g., "Marisela always arches when I pick her up"). Another effective method often used by professionals can be *serving as the child's interpreter* by speaking for the child; for example, the provider may say, "Oh, Eric, is that too much noise and excitement for you? Are you shutting down from too much stimulation?"

Professionals also may *guide or coach* parents on how best to interact with their child, particularly if the child has a disability or condition that necessitates some adaptations from typical parenting practices. Parents too should be encouraged to guide the professional by informing them about aspects of the child's development (e.g., "Maddy prefers bright and shiny objects such as pinwheels. I think she can detect some light and movement."). Another strategy that can be useful is *reframing a behavior* in a more positive manner. For example, in response to a parent's concern about the child's behavior and restlessness, an interventionist may comment, "Jamal really knows his mother. He starts to move whenever you come near. I don't think he's trying to kick you. I think he's just excited that you are holding him" or "Steven certainly does like to resist you when you help him with the spoon. I think he's trying to tell us he's becoming more grown-up and independent!" Another strategy is *commenting on the unique qualities of the parent or child*, such as "Kaitlin uses her hands and fingers to communicate with you since she can't see you" or "Anthony always uses that sound when he's hungry."

Professionals also may use *modeling* to demonstrate special techniques to help the parent interact with the child. For instance, a physical therapist may show a parent how to pick up a child with spasticity so that more normalized muscle tone can be achieved and maintained, thus supporting the parent in caring for their child. The professional also may demonstrate an effective way to calm or soothe a child who has difficulty in self-regulation. Service providers may find the technique of *highlighting* useful to help parents identify the benefits of their activities, such as "Sandra, what a great idea that you put her in the baby seat while you're eating dinner. That way she can see what is going on and you can be there to calm her when she needs you."

Often parents and professionals together will have to *experiment and evaluate* different strategies to determine how best to support the parent and the child. Through skillful interactions and by focusing on the strengths that parents bring to the relationship with their child, professionals can support parents to develop mutually satisfying relationships with their child and to respond appropriately to the child's needs. Across the age span, the overarching goal is to support parents in their roles as parents in order to help them become and feel competent and responsive to their children's needs.

GATHERING INFORMATION FROM
FAMILIES TO TAILOR INTERVENTIONS

This book has centered on the importance of sensitive and responsive services that are tailored to the diverse needs and perspectives of families. Identifying families' concerns and their values, beliefs, and preferences for services can be a complex process. It is predicated upon the use of effective communication strategies and the establishment of a working partnership or alliance between families and service providers. Practitioners may wish to consider a number of factors or questions as they endeavor to tailor their services and interventions to best address the needs of individual families. A guide for getting to know the family by becoming acquainted with the family's circumstances and preferences is provided in the appendix; this sampling of questions may help the service provider begin to understand different families' perspectives and the ways in which services may need to be tailored to be respectful of individual family needs and practices. In most cases, this information is best gleaned over time through conversation with families and through observations; paper-and-pencil questionnaires can be off-putting to families. This is a process of discovery that will be driven to a large degree by the relationship the professional is able to establish with the family. Several helpful resources include Barrera (2000); Barrera and Corso (2003); Hanson, Lynch, & Wayman, 1990; Harry, Kalyanpur, and Day (1999); Lynch and Hanson (2011); and Spicer (2010).

DESIGNING INTERVENTIONS IN MEANINGFUL CONTEXTS

Family members play many different roles and perform a variety of functions to meet the overall needs of the family. Every family has its own set of routines and tasks to address these needs. Many child and family services can be incorporated or provided within these everyday family routines and activities. This strategy may hold additional importance when a child or another family member develops a particular developmental or health concern, such as an injury or developmental delay; specialized services and interventions may be needed, such as physical therapy or special instruction, which require many adaptations and practice sessions. Family routines occur frequently, are meaningful to families, and are a part of daily living.

These everyday activities at home, in the community, and in settings such as child care also are sources of naturally occurring learning opportunities (Bernheimer & Weisner, 2007; Dunst, 2007). Part C of IDEA recognizes the importance of using natural environments as settings for early intervention services. Research attention also has been focused on the use of daily family routines and activities as learning and intervention settings; these studies lend support for this practice in early intervention/early childhood (Dunst, Bruder, Trivette, & Hamby, 2006; Dunst, Bruder, Trivette, Hamby, Raab, & McLean, 2006; Dunst, Raab, Trivette, & Swanson, 2010; Dunst, Trivette, Hamby, & Bruder, 2006).

Professionals may wish to work with families to identify and list or map family routines and everyday activities into which learning goals and other family objectives can be incorporated. McWilliam (1992) provides a comprehensive discussion of this approach, as well as sample interview suggestions for use in planning with families (McWilliam, 2005, 2010).

STRENGTHENING FAMILIES' CAPACITIES AND WELL-BEING

Core concepts of family-centered approaches to service are the focus on family strengths and use of support systems (Dunst, Trivette, & Deal, 1988, 1994). Help-giving practices are directed to building family capacities (Dunst, 2007; Trivette, Dunst, & Hamby, 2010). Dunst, Trivette, and Hamby (2006) investigated the effects of family-centered help-giving practices in early interventions designed to support parents' confidence, competence in fulfilling their parenting roles, and enjoyment of interaction with their children. They found participatory help-giving practices that promoted parental decision making and taking actions based on choices related to resources and goals were most associated with increased parental competence, confidence, and enjoyment.

The implications for practitioners are evident. This assets-based approach is in sharp contrast to service models aimed at fixing deficits or problems and that rely wholly on professional or expert skill. Rather, strength-based models of help-giving practices are construed as those that support families to develop and marshal their own supports; acquire knowledge, skills, and resources; and make decisions and advocate for themselves. Such approaches are more likely to lead to family members' feelings of self-efficacy and competence in meeting their own needs.

TIERS OF SUPPORT: LEVEL AND TYPES OF SERVICE SUPPORTS

All families will need services at various points of their lives. The need for information, for instance, is fairly universal for all families, although the type of information and how it is delivered will vary. Most families also will come to rely on both formal (e.g., professionals, service agencies) and informal supports (e.g., other family members, friends, spiritual leaders, interest groups) at different times for emotional support and assistance in finding resources to meet their goals. For some families, just as for some individuals, more intensive or targeted services and supports will be required to overcome a particularly problematic episode or circumstances faced by the family. These services may necessitate greater involvement of professionals; this involvement can occur for a short period or a prolonged period of time. Intensive plans and follow-up may be needed as well as collaboration with other professionals and agencies. The range of services thus can be viewed as somewhat fluid tiers of support that can be individualized and modified to accomplish the range of service goals presented by families.

CONCLUSION

Not all professionals and service providers will emphasize or implement the entire range of services types that have been outlined and described. However, they all will be required to tailor and individualize their service approaches as they encounter and strive to meet the needs of families whose values and beliefs, styles of interacting, and goals for their lives all vary. This work will demand collaborative working relationships with professional teams and community members to provide truly supportive care for families. Most of all, it will require special expertise and a commitment to support family functioning by helping families to mobilize meaningful resources and develop confidence and competency in achieving their own goals.

ACTIVITIES TO EXTEND THE DISCUSSION

1. **Identify the primary services that you provide in your work setting.** Determine with whom and in what ways you need to collaborate to effectively provide these services to families. Reflect on the breadth of these services and determine whether you would like to expand what you have to offer or whether you are overextended. It may be necessary to partner with a colleague or a supervisor to examine the service delivery system in which you work and the types of services that you deliver.

2. **Develop a set of guidelines or questions that you will consider as you get acquainted with families.** You may wish to use the questions provided in the appendix to get started. What information will you need to establish an effective working partnership with the family? How will you gather this information for this family? Discuss your observations with a colleague and determine what information you do and do not need to know about the family to effectively provide your services.

3. **Keep a personal reflection journal regarding your service practices**. After each interaction that you have with a family, take a moment to contemplate and reflect on the event. Did you communicate effectively? Did you use a family-centered approach? What would you do to improve your delivery of services? Do you need more information or support to become more effective?

4. **Outline a professional development plan for yourself for the next year**. Consider further training you may like to pursue, such as taking a course at a university or online, attending community events, or enrolling in continuing education or in-service training offered by the agency in which you are employed. You may wish to identify information resources that you would like in order to extend your knowledge (e.g., books, web sites, interviews with other professionals, applications for the iPad or your smartphone). An important component of such a plan can be identifying strategies for taking care of yourself to avoid burnout, such as building in time for regular exercise, yoga, or meditation/relaxation.

REFERENCES

American Academy of Pediatrics. (2003). Policy statement: Family-centered care and the pediatrician's role. *Pediatrics, 112,* 691-696.

American Speech-Language-Hearing Association. (2008). *Roles and responsibilities of speech-language pathologists in early intervention: Guidelines [Guidelines].* Available from http://www.asha.org/policy

Bailey, D.B., Bruder, M.B., Hebbeler, K., Carta, J., Defosset, M., Greenwood, C., et al. (2006). Recommended outcomes for families of young children with disabilities. *Journal of Early Intervention, 28*(4), 227–251.

Bailey, D.B., Raspa, M., & Fox, L.C. (2012). What is the future of family outcomes and family-centered services? *Topics in Early Childhood Special Education, 31*(4), 216–223.

Bailey, D.B., Raspa, M., Humphreys, B., & Sam, A. (2011). Promoting family outcomes in early intervention. In J.M. Kauffman & D.P. Hallahan (Eds.), *Handbook of special education* (pp. 668–684). New York, NY: Routledge.

Barrera, I. (2000). Honoring differences: Essential features of appropriate ECSE services for young children from diverse sociocultural environments. *Young Exceptional Children, 3,* 17–24.

Barrera, I., & Corso, R.M. (2003). *Skilled dialogue: Strategies for responding to cultural diversity in early childhood.* Baltimore, MD: Paul H. Brookes Publishing Co.

Bernheimer, L., & Weisner, T. (2007). "Let me tell you what I do all day . . .": The family story at the center of intervention research and practice. *Infants & Young Children, 20,* 192–201.

Brewer, E., McPherson, M., Magrab, P., & Hutchins, V. (1989). Family-centered, community-based coordinated care for children with special health care needs. *Pediatrics, 83,* 1055–1060.

Center for Early Literacy Learning (CELL). (2012). Retrieved from http://www.earlyliteracylearning.org/

Center on the Social and Emotional Foundations for Early Learning (CSEFEL). (2012). Retrieved from http://csefel.vanderbilt.edu/

Centers for Disease Control and Prevention. (2012). *Milestone moments.* Retrieved July 27, 2012, from http://www.cdc.gov/milestones

Chen, D., Chan, S., Brekken, L., & Valverde, A. (Producers). (2000). *Conversations for three: Communicating through interpreters* [Videotape]. Baltimore, MD: Paul H. Brookes Publishing Co.

Chen, D., Haney, M., & Cox, A. (2012). *Supporting cultural and linguistic diversity* [DVD]. Baltimore, MD: Paul H. Brookes Publishing Co.

Dunst, C.J. (2000). Revisiting "rethinking early intervention." *Topics in Early Childhood Special Education, 20,* 95–104.

Dunst, C.J. (2007). Early intervention for infants and toddlers with developmental disabilities. In S. Odom, R. Horner, M. Snell, & J. Blacher (Eds.), *Handbook of developmental disabilities* (pp. 161–180). New York, NY: Guilford Press.

Dunst, C.J., Bruder, M.J., Trivette, C.M., & Hamby, D. (2006) . Everyday activity settings, natural learning environments, and early intervention practices. *Journal of Policy and Practice in Intellectual Disabilities, 3,* 3–10.

Dunst, C.J., Bruder, M.J., Trivette, C.M., Hamby, D., Raab, M., & McLean, M. (2006). Characteristics and consequences of everyday natural learning opportunities. *Topics in Early Childhood Special Education, 21,* 68–92.

Dunst, C., Raab, M., Trivette, C., & Swanson, J. (2010). Community-based everyday child learning opportunities. In R.A. McWilliam (Ed.), *Working with families of young children with special needs* (pp. 60–92). New York, NY: Guilford Press.

Dunst, C.J., Trivette, C.M., & Deal, A.G. (1988). *Enabling and empowering families: Principles and guidelines for practice.* Cambridge, MA: Brookline Books.

Dunst, C.J., Trivette, C.M., & Deal, A.G. (1994). *Supporting and strengthening families: Methods, strategies and practices* (Vol. 1). Cambridge, MA: Brookline Books.

Dunst, C.J., Trivette, C.M., & Hamby, D. (2006). *Family support program quality and parent, family and child benefits.* Asheville, NC: Winterberry Press.

Dunst, C.J., Trivette, C.M., Hamby, D., & Bruder, M.B. (2006). Influences of contrasting national learning environment experiences on child, parent, and family well-being [Electronic version]. *Journal of Developmental and Physical Disabilities, 18*(2).

Early Childhood Outcomes Center. (2012). Retrieved from http://www.fpg.unc.edu/~eco/index.cfm

Fox, L. (2010). Helping families address challenging behavior and promote social development. In R.A. McWilliam (Ed.), *Working with families of young children with special needs* (pp. 237-259). New York, NY: Guilford Press.

Goldberg, S. (1977). Social competence in infancy: A model of parent-infant interaction. *Merrill-Palmer Quarterly, 23*, 163–177.

Haley, A. (1984). Cited in Curran, D., *Traits of a healthy family.* New York, NY: Ballantine Books

Hanson, M.J., & Lynch, E.W. (2010). Working with families from diverse backgrounds. In R.A. McWilliam (Ed.), *Working with families of young children with special needs* (pp. 147–174). New York, NY: Guilford Press.

Hanson, M.J., & Lynch, E.W. (2013). Diversity, cultural competence, and the assessment process. In M. McLean, M.L. Hemmeter, & M. Wolery (Eds.), *Essential elements for assessing infants and preschoolers with special needs* (4th ed.). Boston, MA: Pearson.

Hanson, M.J., Lynch, E.W., & Wayman, K.I. (1990). Honoring the cultural diversity of families when gathering data. *Topics in Early Childhood Special Education, 10* (1), 112–131.

Harry, B., Kalyanpur, M., & Day, M. (1999). *Building cultural reciprocity with families: Case studies in special education.* Baltimore, MD: Paul H. Brookes Publishing Co.

James, W. (n.d.). Retrieved August 13, 2012, from http://www.brainyquote.com/quotes/quotes/w/williamjam105643.html

Kaiser, A., & Hancock, T. (2003). Teaching parents new skills to support their young children's development. *Infants and Young Children, 16*, 9–21.

Lynch, E.W. (2011). Developing cross-cultural competence. In E.W. Lynch & M.J. Hanson (Eds.), *Developing cross-cultural competence: A guide for working with children and their families* (4th ed., pp. 41–77). Baltimore, MD: Paul H. Brookes Publishing Co

Lynch, E.W., & Hanson, M.J. (Eds.). (2011). *Developing cross-cultural competence: A guide for working with children and families* (4th ed.). Baltimore, MD: Paul H. Brookes Publishing Co.

McWilliam, R.A. (1992). *Family-centered intervention planning: A routines-based approach.* Tucson, AZ: Communication Skill Builders.

McWilliam, R.A. (2005). Assessing the resource needs of families in the context of early intervention. In M.J. Guralnick (Ed.), *The developmental systems approach to early intervention* (pp. 215–234). Baltimore, MD: Paul H. Brookes Publishing Co.

McWilliam, R.A. (2010). Assessing families' needs with the Routines-Based Interview. In R.A. McWilliam (Ed.), *Working with families of young children with special needs* (pp. 27–59). New York, NY: Guilford Press.

McWilliam, R.A., Tocci, L., & Harbin, G. (1995). Family-centered services: Service providers' discourse and behavior. *Topics in Early Childhood Special Education, 18*, 206–221.

Ohtake, Y., Fowler, S.A., & Santos, R.M. (2001). *Working with interpreters to plan early childhood services with limited-English-proficient families.* Champaign, IL: University of Illinois at Urbana-Champaign, Early Childhood Research Institute on Culturally and Linguistically Appropriate Services.

PTA. (2012). *PTA national standards for family-school partnerships: National standards implementation guide.* Retrieved July 27, 2012, from http://www.pta.org/Documents/BSP _Booklet.pdf

Perrin, J.M., Romm, D., Bloom, S., Homer, C. J., Kuhlthau, K.A., Cooley, C., et al. (2007). A family-centered, community-based system of services for children and youth with special health care needs. *Archives of Pediatrics and Adolescent Medicine, 161*, 933–936.

Sandall, S., Hemmeter, M.L., Smith, B. J., & McLean, M.E. (2005). *DEC recommended practices in early intervention/early childhood special education: A comprehensive guide.* Missoula, MT: Division for Early Childhood.

Shonkoff, J.P., & Phillips, D.A. (Eds.). (2000). *From neurons to neighborhoods: The science of early childhood development.* Washington, DC: National Academies Press.

Spicer, P. (2010). Cultural influences on parenting. *Zero to Three, 30*(4), 28–32.

Trivette, C.M., Dunst, C.J., & Hamby, D.W. (2010). Influences of family-systems intervention practices on parent-child interactions and child development. *Topics in Early Childhood Special Education, 30*(1), 3–19.

Turnbull, A.P., Summers, J.A., Turnbull, R., Brotherson, M.J., Winton, P., Roberts, R., et al. (2007). Family supports and services in early intervention: A bold vision. *Journal of Early Intervention, 29*(3), 187–206.

Wharton, E. (1902, November). "Vesalius in Zante (1564)," in *North American Review*, p. 631.

Appendix
11A

Getting to Know Each Family

FAMILY COMPOSITION

- Who is in the family? (Identify all the family members and their relationship to one another.)
- Where do the family members live?
- What are the major roles of each of the family members?
- Which family members are the primary caregivers for children?
- Who makes the decisions about child-rearing goals?
- Who makes decisions about disciplinary standards?
- Who makes the decision about health issues and treatments?
- Do family members make decisions together or does one member make the major decisions?
- What other family members or friends are included in the family's circle of support?
- How are these other individuals included?
- Are family members employed outside the home?

FAMILY CULTURE, ETHNICITY, AND LANGUAGE

- With which cultural, ethnic, and linguistic groups does the family identify?
- What languages do family members speak in the home?
- What is their language of preference in communication with professionals?
- Is an interpreter needed for communication?
- Do family members have a preference for written materials or information through another medium, such as oral discussion?
- Do written materials need to be translated into the family's preferred language?

FAMILY CUSTOMS AND PREFERENCES

- How would family members prefer to be greeted (e.g., by title, such as *Mr.* or *Mrs.;* by role, such as mother, father, grandmother, other)?

- Are service providers invited into the family's home?

- What are the family's customs in the home (e.g., removal of shoes when entering the home; shaking hands or not touching family members unless invited to do so)?

- Where and when would families prefer to meet or discuss issues?

- What are their hopes and dreams for the family and children?

CHILD-REARING PRACTICES

- What are family members' beliefs about child development? Children's goals? Children's developmental milestones (e.g., toileting, feeding, caring for self)?

- What are family mealtime practices? Are there dietary preferences or restrictions?

- Who is responsible for feeding the children? What practices are used?

- What are the children's sleeping arrangements and routines (e.g., does the baby sleep in the same room as the parents?)?

- What are the family's beliefs about standards of behavior and discipline?

- What disciplinary methods are used? When? How much? At what age?

EDUCATION, HEALTH CARE, AND HELP SEEKING

- What are the family members' beliefs and perceptions about the developmental or health condition of the family member/child?

- What are the family's beliefs and approach to health care or healing?

- On whom does the family rely for medical and health care treatment?

- What are the family members' beliefs about education of the children (e.g., readiness for school, goals of school)?

- What education and treatment approaches does the family use?

- Does the family seek help from other family members or individuals?

- Does the family seek help from any formal agencies, organizations, or community services? For what services?

- Do family members agree about the use of services/supports and the approaches that they use?

- What are the family members' feelings about seeking help and their degree of comfort in doing so?

For a more comprehensive list of questions and factors when serving young children and their families, readers are referred to Wayman, K.I., Lynch, E.W., & Hanson, M.J. (1991). Home-based early childhood services: Cultural sensitivity in a family systems approach. *Topics in Early Childhood Special Education, 10,* 56–75.

Conclusion

The Family as Possibility

Marci J. Hanson

I dwell in Possibility—
A fairer House than Prose—
More numerous of Windows—
Superior—for Doors—

—Emily Dickinson (from Poem #466 cited in Franklin, 1999)

Every individual begins life in a family, although the structures, inner workings, and continuity of those families are as varied as the individuals themselves. Families are diverse in structure, size, composition, and membership. Families also vary in terms of how they define themselves and what roles they ascribe to individual family members. Families vary in cultural beliefs and practices, ethnicity, primary language(s) spoken, place of origin, and geographical location. Families diverge according to the risks they may encounter—including poverty, violent acts, ill health, unemployment, and homelessness. They also vary in terms of their resources—economic, social, spiritual, and formal and informal supports.

Families vary along every conceivable dimension. What is consistent is the family context as a source of possibility. It is within the context of the family that individuals receive—at the most basic level—care and shelter as children, and it is within the family that individuals are socialized and supported as they grow. At times, that support must be bolstered or supplemented from outside or external structures when the family is unable to muster resources or fails to provide supports to its members. When professional services are needed or desired, practitioners are faced with decisions and challenges related to meeting family needs. The service delivery models advocated in this book recognize and respect the diverse characteristics and needs of families; they respectfully involve families as partners as family goals are identified and interventions are provided to facilitate family functioning.

THE INFLUENCE OF THE FAMILY CONTEXT: POSSIBILITIES FOR GROWTH AND DEVELOPMENT

Families typically function as a source of protection, nurturing, and support for all the members of the family. In some instances, however, families serve as a source of risk to one or all of the developing individuals within that family. Some aspect of family life or family relationships may constitute a risk at one point in development but a neutral or supportive force at another time.

This book has explored frameworks through which to view the development of the individual as well as through which to understand the family within the larger context of society. The transactional model has been advanced as one that fosters understanding of the effects of individuals' characteristics (e.g., personality, temperament, ability levels, health status, preferences, goals) as they interact with dimensions of the environment (e.g., quality of caregiving, educational opportunities, health and human service opportunities) in producing transactions or shifts in the individuals' development and behavior.

The ecological systems framework also was described to place individuals and families within the broader set of contexts in which they are nested and with which they continually interact. The framework depicts the interactions of individuals with their families and with other institutions such as education systems, health care facilities, child care, and community services. These interactions in turn are embedded within the larger web of structures and policies of the institutions and policies that affect these systems and services, as well as within the larger societal context. The influence on families of culture, geographical factors, and societal practices and philosophies, as well as the collective impact of families on those structures, are visible through this framework.

DYNAMIC NATURE OF FAMILIES: POSSIBILITIES FOR CHANGE

Families are dynamic and constantly changing. Throughout the life cycle of the family, significant changes occur in family composition and structure, in the relationships among family members, and in the function that the family may serve for a given member.

Such shifts in families underscore the dynamic nature of work with families. As professionals encounter families through their service environments, they must constantly be attentive to the changing needs and characteristics of the families with whom they work. Some events families encounter might disrupt their equilibrium or their abilities to perform their functions. In other instances, these events (even though traumatic) may enable positive shifts or adaptations. Professionals, hence, are presented with opportunities to support families in adjusting and adapting to changing circumstances.

FAMILY–PROFESSIONAL PARTNERSHIPS: POSSIBILITIES AND PATHWAYS FOR FAMILY SUPPORT

The service delivery approach advocated in this text emphasizes viewing the family as a system and recognizing that families must make decisions on their own behalf. Professionals are encouraged to bring their special knowledge and expertise to families through forming partnerships with families. The type of alliance will vary from family to family based on the families' preferences and belief systems, but effective alliances share a respect for family diversity and a commitment to assisting families to mobilize their resources and strengths. For some families who are faced with difficult circumstances, identifying and gaining access to resources may take longer or require more innovative and persistent measures. Regardless of the type or range of the family's need, the role of the professional is to support the family through a shared and collaborative service approach.

These collaborative partnerships can serve as a pathway through which families are helped to create new possibilities for resources and strategies to foster family competency and address the family's needs. They fashion more positive working conditions for professionals and produce learning opportunities for them as well. Rather than dwelling on the difficulties and problems faced by families, this orientation opens windows of opportunities. Indeed, both families and professionals are invited to dwell in the possibilities.

REFERENCE

Franklin, R.W. (Ed.) (1999). *The poems of Emily Dickinson* (Poem No. 466). Cambridge, MA: Belknap Press of Harvard University Press.

Index

Page numbers followed by *f* and t indicate figures and tables, respectively.